SAGE was founded in 1965 by Sara Miller McCune to support the dissemination of usable knowledge by publishing innovative and high-quality research and teaching content. Today, we publish over 900 journals, including those of more than 400 learned societies, more than 800 new books per year, and a growing range of library products including archives, data, case studies, reports, and video. SAGE remains majority-owned by our founder, and after Sara's lifetime will become owned by a charitable trust that secures our continued independence.

Los Angeles | London | New Delhi | Singapore | Washington DC | Melbourne

SOCIAL SECTOR DEVELOPMENT IN NORTH-EAST INDIA

SOCIAL SECTOR DEVELOPMENT IN NORTH-EAST INDIA

SAGE STUDIES ON INDIA'S NORTH EAST

Edited by
Ashok Pankaj, Atul Sarma
Antora Borah

Los Angeles I London I New Delhi
Singapore I Washington DC I Melbourne

First published in 2021 by

SAGE Publications India Pvt Ltd
B1/I-1 Mohan Cooperative Industrial Area
Mathura Road, New Delhi 110 044, India
www.sagepub.in

SAGE Publications Inc
2455 Teller Road
Thousand Oaks, California 91320, USA

SAGE Publications Ltd
1 Oliver's Yard, 55 City Road
London EC1Y 1SP, United Kingdom

SAGE Publications Asia-Pacific Pte Ltd
18 Cross Street #10-10/11/12
China Square Central
Singapore 048423

Published by Vivek Mehra for SAGE Publications India Pvt Ltd. Typeset in 10.5/13 pt Bembo by Zaza Eunice, Hosur, Tamil Nadu, India.

Library of Congress Control Number: 2020948405

ISBN: 978-93-5388-532-8 (HB)

SAGE Team: Rajesh Dey, Satvinder Kaur and Rajinder Kaur
Cover Photo Credit: Aniruddha Barua (top image); Prayash Sharma Tamuly (bottom image).

*Dedicated to the people of
North-east India*

Thank you for choosing a SAGE product!
If you have any comment, observation or feedback,
I would like to personally hear from you.

Please write to me at **contactceo@sagepub.in**

Vivek Mehra, Managing Director and CEO, SAGE India.

Contents

Section I: Introduction

Section II: Contexts

Section III: Education

Section VII: Challenges

List of Figures

List of Tables

List of Abbreviations

AAMR	Age-adjusted mortality rate
AAY	Antyodaya Anna Yojana
AIDS	Acquired immunodeficiency syndrome
AMC	Aizawl Municipal Corporation
AMD	Acid mine drainage
ANM	Auxiliary nurse midwife
APL	Above poverty line
ASER	Annual Status of Education Report
BADP	Border Area Development Programme
BPL	Below poverty line
BRGF	Backward Regions Grant Fund
BTAD	Bodoland Territorial Area District
BTC	Bodoland Territorial Council
CADC	Chakma Autonomous District Council
CBR	Crude birth rate
CD	Community development
CDR	Crude death rate
CHC	Community health centre
CNNS	Comprehensive National Nutrition Survey
CPR	Common property resources
DGHS	Directorate General of Health Services
DISE	District Information System for Education
DLHS	District-Level Household Survey
DML	Data manipulation language
DRDA	District Rural Development Agency
ECCE	Early childhood care and education
EWS	Economically Weaker Section
FCI	Food Corporation of India

FDI	Food diversity index
FPS	Fair price shop
FSU	Final stage unit
GATS	General Agreement on Trade in Services
GDP	Gross domestic product
GER	Gross enrolment ratio
GPSS	Gram Panchayat Samabaya Samiti
HDI	Human Development Index
HIV	Human immunodeficiency virus
HYV	High-yielding variety
ICMR	Indian Council of Medical Research
IFAD	International Fund for Agricultural Development
IFAS	Indian Frontier Administrative Service
IIPS	International Institute for Population Sciences
IMR	Infant mortality rate
IRRI	International Rice Research Institute
LADC	Lai Autonomous District Council
MADC	Mara Autonomous District Council
MDGs	Millennium Development Goals
MGNREGS	Mahatma Gandhi National Rural Employment Guarantee Scheme
MHRD	Ministry of Human Resource Development
MMASY	Mukhya Mantri Anna Suraksha Yojana
MNF	Mizo National Front
MPCE	Monthly per capita consumption expenditure
MPI	Multidimensional Poverty Index
NCD	Non-communicable disease
NE	North-east
NEC	North Eastern Council
NEDFI	North Eastern Development Finance Corporation Ltd.
NEET	National Eligibility cum Entrance Test
NEFA	North-East Frontier Agency
NEFT	North-East Frontier Tract

NEIGRIHMS	North East Indira Gandhi Regional Institute of Health and Medical Sciences
NEIP	National Entrepreneurship and Innovation Plan
NER	Net enrolment ratio
NERAMAC	North Eastern Regional Agricultural Marketing Corporation Ltd.
NES	North-eastern states
NFHS	National Family Health Survey
NFSA	National Food Security Act
NHP	National Health Policy
NNC	Naga National Council
NSS	National Service Scheme
NSSO	National Sample Survey Office
NTFP	Non-timber forest product
OBC	Other Backward Classes
OLS	Ordinary least squares
PBCR	Population-Based Cancer Registry
PDS	Public distribution system
PHC	Primary health centre
PLTU	Pawi-Lakher Tribal Union
PSU	Primary stage unit
RKVY	Rashtriya Krishi Vikas Yojana
SC	Scheduled Caste
SDGs	Sustainable Development Goals
SIP	State issue price
SSE	Social sector expenditure
SSU	Second stage unit
ST	Scheduled Tribe
TB	Tuberculosis
TFR	Total fertility rate
TMR	Truncated mortality rate
TTAADC	Tripura Tribal Areas Autonomous District Council
TUJS	Tripura Upajati Juba Samiti
U5MR	Under-five mortality rate
UGC	University Grants Commission

UNICEF	United Nations International Children's Emergency Fund
VDB	Village Development Board
WFP	World Food Programme
WHO	World Health Organization
WPR	Work participation rate

Preface

North-east (NE) India, consisting of eight states, namely, Assam, Arunachal Pradesh, Manipur, Meghalaya, Mizoram, Nagaland, Sikkim and Tripura, covers about 8 per cent of the total geographical area and holds about 4 per cent of the population of the country. The region, tucked away in the NE corner of India and known by the geographical nomenclature of the NE, shares 99.5 per cent of its boundary with foreign countries. It shares linguistic and cultural affinities with the people of Southeast Asia and has also been a route of trade and commerce with that region. The partition disrupted its traditional routes of trade and transport, apart from enhancing its geographical isolation and remoteness from the mainland. The region is strategically located for accessing Southeast Asia. It is envisaged as India's gateway to Southeast Asia.

NE India is rich in biodiversity, flora and fauna, and endowed with abundant natural resources, such as water, forest and mineral resources. It is known for ethnic diversities underlined by sociocultural pluralities of an incomparable scale within such a small geographical area. The diversities and pluralities of the region have been forged through a historical process of intermingling of people from different races, languages, religions and cultures. These diversities are often obfuscated by the stereotyping of the NE as a geographical entity. This has also affected India's policies towards the NE region, which have recently been heavily driven by strategic concerns and project of national integration.

The development of human resources of the NE has special significance for a number of reasons. For lack of any clearly formulated development framework, human development has not received as much importance as it deserves. Notwithstanding that, for a variety of historical and other reasons, NE India has better human development outcomes than many other states of India. Even this fact remains unnoticed.

This book is an attempt to underline the significance of human capital formation through social sector development in NE India. Social sector development is a strategic goal, as well as an objective of development per se. This book argues that while social sector development is both a condition for and a goal of development, its significant for NE India increases, as conditions of the NE are more conducive for the development of the service sector than the primary and secondary sectors. More importantly, investment in human capital formation through social sector development could be a strategic goal of the integration of NE India.

Social sector development of NE India presents a chequered picture. There are fabulous achievements, yet egregious/appalling deprivations. In the field of literacy, the region has performed outstandingly. Similarly, some of the health indicators of the region are better than those of many other states of India. Some of the states of NE India have achieved high social sector development with relatively lower levels of economic development, more precisely, per capita income. High social sector development has been achieved notwithstanding relatively poor levels of access to basic amenities, difficult geographical terrains and frequent natural calamities. There are some other interesting features of social sector development of the NE which have not been given attention and researched adequately.

This volume is a modest attempt to draw attention to some of the features of social sector development in NE India, including problems, issues and challenges. It also underlines the significance of social sector development for NE India. Some selected papers included in this volume were presented in a seminar on Social Development in North-east India: Problem, Issues and Challenges, organized by the Council for Social Development, New Delhi, on 15–16 July 2019, while others were commissioned afresh after the seminar, keeping in view the gaps in the broad theme of social development. The chapters in this volume cover education, health, poverty, unemployment, food security and governance. Some of them question conventional wisdom about the NE society and provide a different perspective for understanding NE India.

In the course of organizing the seminar, we received financial support from the India Council of Social Science Research (ICSSR) and National Institute of Educational Planning and Administration (NIEPA), which made it possible for us to invite scholars from NE India to participate and present their views. We are grateful to ICSSR and NIEPA for their financial support. We received extremely good responses from scholars working on NE India who presented their studies and shared their views and experiences. Although we included a select few papers for this volume because of the limitation of space and focused attention of the book, we would like to express our sincere thanks to all the paper presenters, chairs, panellists, discussants and participants. We benefitted from their ideas and views in various ways. We would like to record our special thanks to those who did not participate in the seminar, yet readily agreed to contribute papers on a very short notice. Without their contributions, the volume would have been incomplete. We received enthusiastic cooperation from our colleagues in the Council for Social Development, whose support was quite encouraging. We would appreciate and record our thanks to SAGE Publications, especially Rajesh Dey, who took keen interest in the volume from the very beginning of the proposal. Prabha Vati has done a wonderful job by meticulously typing and organizing the manuscript for publication. We would place on record our sincere thanks to all those from whose ideas we have benefitted in the preparation of this volume.

SECTION I

Introduction

Chapter 1

Social Sector Development in North-east India

Ashok Pankaj, Atul Sarma and Antora Borah

SIGNIFICANCE OF SOCIAL SECTOR DEVELOPMENT FOR NE

Social sector development is critical for human capital formation, an important objective by itself and a necessary condition for growth and development. While social sector development is important for all societies, it has added significance for North-east (NE) India for a variety of reasons. First, only three out of the eight states of NE India have plains, suitable for viable agriculture and industrial activities. The hills of NE India have some mineral resources, but their extraction is not without environmental hazards. There are administrative and political difficulties as well. The ownership of land, especially in the hills, belongs to tribal communities, though it varies across the various tribes. They have constitutional protection over their land and natural resources under the Sixth Schedule of the Indian Constitution. Land and other natural resources falling within the Sixth Schedule areas cannot be alienated. Since each community (tribe) has rights over a parcel of land and the number of such communities is large, it is difficult to procure land for big industries requiring large parcels of land. There are plenty of water and forest resources, but their commercial exploitation is ecologically unviable. Hydro power projects and timber industries have already done irreparable damage to the fragile ecology of NE India, so much so that the Supreme Court of India intervened to cease the commercial exploitation of timber in the region. Hydro projects in NE India have faced daunting protests from environmentalists and local people. Given its topography and ecology, and the limited scope of agricultural and industrial sector development, service sector development, which is contingent upon the development of the social sector, could be the most suitable strategy for the development of NE India.

Second, there have been intermittent inter-ethnic group conflicts in the NE whose roots lie in competitive claims over the limited natural resources and heavy dependence of the population on natural resource–based livelihoods in the region. Since natural resources cannot be created artificially and their exploitation has reached saturation points, only by investment in human capital can the dependency of the population on land-based livelihoods be removed. They can be provided gainful employment in service sectors. Moreover, the region has been characterized by a high population growth rate that has further increased the population pressure on natural resource–based livelihoods. Social sector development by pulling the population out from the traditional land-based livelihoods would also ease the element of inter-ethnic conflicts, which are largely due to competitive claims and excessive pressure over the limited natural resources.

Third, the prospect for a high level of social sector development in NE India is relatively greater, because of the high literacy rate. Except those of Assam and Arunachal Pradesh, the literacy rates of the other states are much higher than the national average. High literacy rate leads to better human development, as people take greater care of health, nutrition, education and other elements required for human capital formation (Schultz, 1961). With the greater prospect for high human development, NE India could be a hub of service sector development. Moreover, it has also been observed that NE people have great aptitude for work in service sector industries like hospitality, call centres, etc. In fact, it has been noticed that service sector industries like call centres, hotels, airlines, etc. have reportedly shown preference for candidates from the NE.

Fourth, NE India is yet to enter the phase of reaping demographic dividends. Compared to the rest of India, NE states have a much higher proportion of youth population. For example, the 0–25 age group constitutes 52 per cent of the total population at the all-India level, whereas it constitutes 62.35 per cent in Meghalaya, 58.76 in Arunachal Pradesh, 58.40 in Nagaland, 54.73 in Mizoram and 54.54 per cent in Assam. In terms of the 0–14 age group's population, against an all-India average of 30.75 per cent, it is 39.70 per cent in Meghalaya, 35.65 per cent in Arunachal Pradesh, 34.32 per cent in Nagaland, 32.43 per cent in Mizoram and 32.84 per cent in Assam. While many other states have a much higher percentage of elderly population, most of the NE states, as shown above, have a much higher proportion of youth population. Therefore, most of the NE states have a much wider window for demographic dividends, provided there is adequate investment in social sector development.

Fifth, the social sector development of the NE would also promote its greater integration with the rest of India. It is likely that highly educated and skilled manpower of NE India would move from the NE to different parts of the country, as there is much higher mobility among educated and skilled workers than among uneducated and unskilled workers. Contrarily, industries and service sectors might also move to the NE to tap its higher human capital resources at a cheaper rate at their place. It has been observed that in the era of globalization, capital has chased human resources at their place to obtain it at a cheaper rate, as the movement of capital has become easier than the movement of people. In both cases, there would be a much greater amount of interaction between the people of the NE and those of other parts of India, with considerable integration effects. One of the major difficulties in the integration of NE India lies, apart from geographical isolation, in the limited interaction of the NE people with the rest of India.

SOCIAL SECTOR DEVELOPMENT IN THE NE: PERFORMANCE AND CHARACTERISTICS

Social sector development is of utmost significance for NE India. However, experiences in social sector development have been mixed.

With respect to some indicators, primarily related to education and health, most of the NE states have not only achieved higher levels but also outperformed other states of India with a similar level of economic development, defined crudely in terms of per capita income. For example, the per capita income of only Sikkim and Mizoram (in 2015–2016) was higher than the national average, and the social development index (SDI) (2018) of all the states of the NE, except Assam, was higher than the national average. Three out of the eight states of NE India stand among the top 10: Sikkim at number 4, Mizoram at number 5 and Nagaland at number 9 (Deb, 2018, p. 310). In 2015–2016, the per capita annual income of Sikkim (₹1,95,066), Mizoram (₹91,845) and Arunachal Pradesh (₹85,356) was higher than the national average (₹81,874). The per capita annual income of Manipur (₹46,389), Assam (₹50,642), Meghalaya (₹56,039), Nagaland (₹60,663) and Tripura (₹64,173) was lower than the national average. Yet, social development indicators of most of the states were better.

High social development has been achieved amidst the persistence of a high level of poverty. For example, in 2011–2012, the head count poverty ratio in Assam (31), Arunachal Pradesh (34.90) and Meghalaya (36.90) was higher than the national average (21.90), whereas the social sector development index of all the states, except Assam, was higher than the national average.

There are historical and contemporary reasons for the paradoxical situation of low income, high poverty ratio, and yet a high level of social sector development indicators. The high level of literacy rate is an important driver of social sector development in NE India. But there are other factors as well, which vary from state to state.

In states like Mizoram, Nagaland and Meghalaya, the early penetration of Christian missionaries during the colonial period, and their involvement in the promotion of modern education since then, has played an important role (Chugh, 2009; Hluna, 1992; Syiemlieh, 2012). The British colonial rulers found it difficult to learn the various languages spoken by the different tribes and communities of the NE region. Thus, they promoted English education through Christian missionaries as a lingua franca for the administration of the region.

Moreover, some of the tribes were very good in guerrilla warfare, and therefore, they were recruited in the army. This was also one of the purposes of promoting English education among the tribal population of the NE region. The high literacy rate in Nagaland, Mizoram and Meghalaya has been historically driven by Christian missionaries. All the above three states, characterized by a sizeable Christian population, have some of the highest literacy rates in the country. As per Census 2011, Christians form 74.59 per cent of the total population in Meghalaya, 87.16 per cent in Mizoram and 87.93 per cent in Nagaland. The literacy rate is 74.4 per cent in Meghalaya, 91.3 per cent in Mizoram and 79.6 per cent in Nagaland.

Except Manipur, Sikkim and Tripura, other states were carved out of Assam, mostly to meet the ethnic and development aspirations of the people. Also, except Assam and Arunachal Pradesh, other states are small in geographical size. Arunachal Pradesh is large in geographical size but small in population. In terms of population, Assam and Tripura are the most populated states. Others have only a small size of population. Because of the small size of population and territory, in tandem with the formation of the new state, to meet the political and development aspirations of the local people, these states gave a great deal of attention to the development needs of the people. Moreover, governance was brought closer to the people, thereby making it more accountable and responsive.

The tribal population constitutes about one-third of the total population of the region but forms the majority in Nagaland, Mizoram, Meghalaya, Arunachal Pradesh, Manipur and Sikkim. In other words, except Assam and Tripura, the tribal population is in majority. The tribal society is generally egalitarian in structure, outlook and distribution of resources, partly because of the prevalence of community-based ownership of land in many of the tribes of the NE region. Although there are inter-tribe differentiations in terms of education and health indicators, education and health remain socially accessible to all. Much of the inter-tribe gaps in social sector development has emanated from the recent phenomenon of increasing inter-tribe inequality because of differential access to political, economic and government resources, which has emanated from political processes. With the formation of new states, as all NE states, except Sikkim and Tripura, have been carved out of Assam, politically dominant groups, which are invariably dominant in numbers, captured state resources and used them for the benefit of their own community. Sometimes, there were groups of people within the community who used political and administrative resources for their own advantage. In the process, both inter- and intra-community gaps increased.

Women in NE India have traditionally enjoyed a greater amount of freedom than their counterparts in other regions of the country. Because of the predominance of the tribal population in all states except Assam and Tripura and the tribal society being largely egalitarian, there is a much higher level of social and gender equality in the NE region. This also explains the incidence of high female literacy rate—higher than the national average in all states except Arunachal Pradesh.

Apart from high social sector development with relatively low per capita income, the social sector development experiences of NE India are characterized by pronounced inter- and intra-state variations. For example, in terms of overall social development indicators, as per SDI 2018, Sikkim stands at number 4, Mizoram at number 5, Nagaland at number 9 and Meghalaya at number 12, but Manipur at number 19, Tripura at 23 and Assam at 25 in the ranking of 31 states and union territories. This shows the level of inter-state variations among NE states.

The literacy rates of NE states, except that of Assam (72.2%) and Arunachal Pradesh (65.4%), are higher than the national average (74.04%). The literacy rate of Mizoram is as high as 91.3 per cent, Tripura's is 87.2 per cent, Sikkim's is 81.4 per cent, Nagaland's is 79.6 per cent and Manipur's is 79.2 per cent. The female literacy rate, except that of Arunachal Pradesh (57.7%), is higher than the national average (65.46%).

Similarly, there are inter-state variations with respect to health indicators. The overall health indicators of Sikkim and Mizoram are better than those of the other states of NE India. However, with respect to individual indicators of health, the position of different states varies. The infant mortality rate (IMR) of Assam (44), Meghalaya (39) and Arunachal Pradesh (39) is higher than the national average (34).

Institutional delivery in Arunachal Pradesh (52.3%) is lower than the national average (78.9%). The proportion of fully immunized children (12–23 months) is lower than the national average (62%) in Arunachal Pradesh (38.2%), Assam (47%), Mizoram (50.5%), Nagaland (35.7%) and Tripura (54.5%). The inter-state variations in health indicators are sharper than in the case of education. This is partly because of variations in health-related infrastructure and partly because of the different types of indigenous health-related practices adopted by different tribes and communities in the region. Further, health indicators vary across regions of a state, say across hills, plains and flood-affected areas of Assam, and across various tribes and communities.

Demographic indicators of NE India are also characterized by inter-state variations. The sex ratio is higher than the national average (943) in all other states except Sikkim (890), Nagaland (931) and Arunachal Pradesh (938). The total fertility rate is also higher than the national average (2.2) in Meghalaya (3.0), Nagaland (2.7), Manipur (2.6), Arunachal Pradesh (2.4), Assam (2.3) and Mizoram (2.3). The population growth rate varies across states and communities and within regions of a state.

Further, in terms of various components of social development indicators, the position of different states varies. The social component indicators (consisting of male–female literacy gap, inter-caste and inter-community literacy gap and child sex ratio) of all the eight states are higher than the national average. Similarly, in terms of education and health indicators, the positions of all the eight states of NE India are better than the national average. Assam, ranked 23rd in terms of health indicators, is at a relatively lower position. This is partly because a large part of it is exposed to floods every year, thereby creating health-related problems. Another sizeable part of Assam is the *char* area (riparian belt) with difficulty in accessing. Also, Assam has greater challenges in providing health infrastructure because of its geographical size and diversities. It has hills and riparian and forest areas. Moreover, it is much bigger in population size. It has a large number of immigrants from Bangladesh with an extremely low level of social development, and because of their surreptitious and illegal entry, they remain out of the purview of reach of social sector delivery programmes for years till they settle down to stable homes. The tea garden population also remains deprived of various social sector development benefits. Although there is a provision to provide education and health to the workers as per the Plantations Labour Act, it is not implemented effectively.

Compared to the education, health and social variables, the economic, basic amenities and demographic variables are not as good. In terms of demographic variables (life expectancy at birth, total fertility rate, infant mortality rate and old-age dependency), Assam stands at 26 and Tripura at 25, higher than the rank of the national average (23). Mizoram at 21 and Meghalaya at 20 are only slightly better. In terms of basic amenities (*pucca* house, electricity, drinking water, sanitation and clean fuel), against the national average rank of 22, Manipur stands at 30, Assam at 27 and Tripura at 23. Arunachal Pradesh at 20 and Meghalaya at 19 are slightly lower than the national average rank. Sikkim (3), Mizoram (4) and Nagaland (15) are, of course, better positioned. With respect to economic indicators (people below poverty line, unemployment rate, monthly per capita expenditure and population in the bottom 40% expenditure class), Assam at 29, Manipur at 28, Arunachal at 24 and Tripura at 23 are below the national average rank of 21. Sikkim at 7, Meghalaya at 13, Mizoram at 16 and Nagaland at 17 are better positioned (Deb, 2018, p. 315).

Inter-state variations are because of various reasons, but mainly due to socio-cultural diversities, different types of political and administrative structures and demographic factors—immigration from inside and outside India. The topography of the regions—riparian belt, hills and plains—are other important factors. Governance structure at local levels is not uniform in all the states. A large part of NE India comes under the purview of Sixth Schedule areas that have autonomous district councils (ADCs). These ADCs have different kinds of administrative and governance structures. Until recently, the ADCs under the Sixth Schedule areas had not been provided with development roles. The financial position of ADCs was weak and dependent on meagre allocations from the state government (Chapter 13 in this volume deals with the financial position of the ADCs).

Prolonged ethnic conflicts in most parts of NE India have also affected the course of social sector development. Mizoram made rapid progress after the end of violent conflicts in the mid-1980s. Tripura remained disturbed for quite a long period, and so was Assam. The latter continues to remain on the boil for one or the other reason. There have been violent conflicts in Nagaland and Manipur for quite a long period. Only Arunachal Pradesh, among all the NE states, has remained free from violence and ethnic conflicts to a great extent. Conflicts affect the delivery of social services. Schools often get closed, and hospitals become inaccessible and dysfunctional. The attention of the administration remains focused on maintaining law and order and peace.

Intra-state variations are equally sharp, especially in Assam, the largest state of NE India, with 68.37 per cent of the total population and 29.92 per cent of the total geographical area of the region. As per the Assam Human Development Report (2014), which divides the entire state into three regions, namely hills, *chars* (riparian alluvial areas) and plains (flood-affected areas), the headcount poverty ratio was 44.7 per cent in the hills, 42.6 per cent in the *chars* and 37.6 per cent in the flood-affected plains (Government of Assam et al., 2014, p. 206). Similarly, health deprivations are less in the hills and *chars* than in other areas. Educational inequality is the highest in regions with 'multiple diversities', followed by *char* areas. Inequality in terms of living standards is high in the hills (0.530), followed by flood-affected areas (0.474) and tea gardens (0.479) (Government of Assam et al., 2014, p. 196).

In other states, intra-state variations are exhibited through intra-community variations. For example, in Tripura, social development indicators vary across the tribal and non-tribal populations. In Meghalaya, there are variations across the three prominent tribes, namely Khasi, Jaintia and Garo. While Khasis are educationally more advanced, Garos are politically strong, as they are the largest numerical group, and Jaintias are rich in wealth because of their ownership of coal and limestone mines. Khasis who are settled in the Khasi hills, where Shillong (East Khasi Hills), the capital of Meghalaya and the erstwhile summer capital of Assam, is located, got early exposure to modern education. A number of them also converted to Christianity, influenced by the missionaries which had opened schools, colleges and hospitals in the area. Similarly, Nishis are a numerically dominant tribe in Arunachal Pradesh, but Adis are educationally more advanced because of their early exposure to education, as they were settled closer to Assam. The dominant tribes in these states have much greater access to economic and political resources and are better placed in terms of overall indicators of development. In states like Mizoram, minority tribes, namely Chakma, Mara and Lai, are much deprived in all respects. For example, since the formation of Mizoram in 1897, there has not been a single Chakma who has qualified for the state civil services.

PERSPECTIVES FOR THE SOCIAL SECTOR DEVELOPMENT OF NE INDIA

As shown earlier, the social sector development of NE India is characterized by pronounced variations across states, within states and between and within communities. One of the reasons for these variations is the heterogeneity and diversities of NE society, underlining which is not only important for understanding NE India but also for formulating policies and programmes for development, including that of the social sector. This, however, requires a proper understanding of the nature and dimensions of the diversities. The following section presents a brief account of the heterogeneity and diversities of NE India.

Heterogeneity and Diversities

NE India is characterized by incomparable racial, linguistic and religious diversities. At present, the NE consists of people of four races: Mongoloids, Indo-Aryans, Australoids and Dravidians. The Indo-Aryans and Dravidians had migrated from mainland India, and the Mongoloids from China and South-east Asia but much before the migration of the Aryans and Dravidians to the NE region. There are more than 200 languages that are spoken by the people in the region; a number of them are endangered (Deori, 2019), and the scripts of a few of them have already been lost. For example, Majhi in Sikkim, spoken by only four persons, and Dimasa in Assam are on the verge of extinction (Lalmalsawma, 2013). Although the Khasis in Meghalaya speak their language, they write it in the roman script. They have lost their own script. Out of the 22 languages in the Eighth Schedule of the Indian Constitution, six languages are spoken in the NE. Further, out of 99 non-scheduled languages, 69 are spoken in the NE. Assamese-, Bengali-, Hindi- and Nepali-speaking populations constitute about two-thirds of the linguistic population. The rest one-third speak their different indigenous languages. Hindus, Muslims, Christians and Buddhists are the main religions groups. Animists and followers of other indigenous religious groups, mostly in tribes, are other segments of religious groups.

There has been an intermixing of racial, linguistic and religious groups that has created trans-groups, which might belong to a particular race but might follow a different religion and speak a language other than the one the original racial group would have followed or spoken. This phenomenon is more pronounced in the case of plains tribes; some of them have become followers of Hinduism and speak a language other than their original language. They have also changed considerably in terms of cultural practices. They have become *sanskritized* to a great extent. The hill tribes, on the other hand, have remained largely unaffected, because of their limited interaction with the rest of the population and because of their isolation—geographical and cultural.

The NE is home to a large number of tribes. There are various estimates of the number of tribes.[1] This variation is because of the counting of sub-tribes who, importantly, constitute a sizeable proportion of the total population of the NE states. Whereas tribes constitute 8.63 per cent of the total population of India, they constitute 27.62 per cent of the total population of the NE. Their share varies across the NE states. They constitute 68.79 per cent of the total population in Arunachal Pradesh, 86.15 per cent in Meghalaya, 86.48 per cent in Nagaland and 94.43 per cent in Mizoram. In Manipur, they constitute 40.88 per cent, and in Tripura 31.76 per cent.

There are also variations in the population of different tribes in NE. Some of them are numerically dominant, but others have a population of less than even 5,000. Some of the numerically dominant tribes are spatially dispersed. Some of them are even transnational. Bodos, for example, are spread from lower to upper Assam. Nagas

---

[1] The estimate varies from 150 to 200, depending on the methodology, particularly the inclusion of sub-tribes in counting.

are transnational. They are also found in Myanmar. Misings are found in Arunachal Pradesh and Assam. Karbis are found in Karbi Anglong district of Assam, North-eastern Meghalaya and Western Nagaland. Although some of these tribes are trans-states and even transnational, a large number of them are identified with a particular region. Chang, Sema, Ao, Konyak, Lotha, Angami and Phom are found mainly in Nagaland, and each one has a population of not less than 1 lakh. Khasi, Jaintia and Garo tribes are found in Meghalaya; each one is identified with a hill range, that is, Khasis with Khasi hills, Jaintias with Jaintia hills and Garos with Garo hills. Mizos are found mainly in Mizo hills but also on the foothills of Cachar hills and Manipur. Tangkhul, Kabui, Thado and Hmar are the main tribes of Manipur, and Galong, Nishi, Wancho and Adi are the main tribes of Arunachal Pradesh.

In NE tribes, heterogeneity is seen along social, cultural and spatial patterns. While the Khasis, Jaintias and Garos of Meghalaya are matrilineal, other tribes are patrilineal, but most of them are patriarchal. In the matrilineal society of Khasis, the youngest daughter inherits property, and the surname of the mother is added to the child. However, the overall structure is patriarchal. In the Dimasa tribe, there is a system of bi-lineal descent. Immovable property is traced through the male line, but movable property is traced through the female line. There is a spatial variation in the characteristics of a tribe. For example, the clans of the Karbi tribe, namely Ingti, Terang, Inghi and Teron, are not only territorial groups, but each clan also has its own distinct sociocultural traits.

Many of the tribes have adopted sociocultural norms of other societies. Tribes living in the plains of Assam and Tripura have adopted the sociocultural norms of a Hindu society, whereas tribes on hills have adopted Christianity in great numbers. Consequently, many of the tribes have completely changed their original social character.

There is also administrative diversity in NE India. There is a provision for ADCs in the Sixth Schedule areas of Assam, Meghalaya, Tripura and Mizoram. These ADCs are part of constitutional arrangements under which people of the region have been given administrative autonomy to protect the identity and culture of their tribal society, to prevent the alienation of land and natural resources and to allow them to govern themselves. Apart from ADCs in the Sixth Schedule areas, there are statutory councils established by the state governments in Manipur and Assam. While there are no Panchayat Raj Institutions (PRIs) in the Sixth Schedule areas, there are PRIs under the statutory councils. Nagaland has a special right under Article 371(A) of the constitution, which provides that no act of Parliament shall apply to the religious and social practices of the Nagas, their customary laws and practices, administration of civil and criminal justice related to customary laws and ownership and transfer of land and other resources. There is a provision for village councils and village development boards for administering at the local level. Village councils have played a useful role in administering local areas. While the Sixth Schedule areas and statutory councils make different kinds of administrative arrangements, there is also a provision of inner line permit (ILP) for Arunachal Pradesh, Mizoram and Nagaland to prevent people from outside settling down in these states. There are a number of laws specific to regions which give distinct characteristics to the structure of governance of the region.

The NE is generally considered a gender-equal society, but there are noticeable gender inequalities. The matrilineal society of Khasis is romanticized for being female-headed. The high literacy rate including that of females in Mizoram is equated with greater empowerment of women. The truth is, however, different. In the matrilineal society of Khasis, the youngest daughter inherits ancestral property, yet the effective control remains with the brother—the male member of the family. There are a high number of incidences of divorce among Khasis that leaves a woman to take care of her children and household affairs on her own. Teenage pregnancy is at a high level in Meghalaya and Mizoram. In Mizoram, a divorced woman loses all rights over property. In Nagaland, a woman does not have any right over land. The point which is emphasized is that with respect to rights of women, there are variations. It would be misleading to treat all women of the NE on equal footing.

In terms of political representation, NE women are more deprived. In ADCs, women are not given assured representation of 33 per cent as they are given in PRIs and urban local bodies (ULBs). Only recently has the parliament made an amendment in the Sixth Schedule to ensure representation of women in the ADCs. In Nagaland, since the formation of the state, there has not been a single woman elected to the state legislature. The representation of women in other state legislatures is also small. Politics is largely male-dominated. In the matrilineal society of Khasis, women are not allowed to attend 'Darbar', the meeting of the village council.

Mrinal Miri (2019) has raised the issue of 'authenticity of understanding' of NE India and problematizes it at two levels. First, there has been a typical bureaucratic governance approach to understanding the cultural diversities of NE India. He argues that bureaucratic rules are largely insensitive to contextual differentiations and subtleties:

> Concepts such as equality, decency, civilized, free, ugly, welfare, promiscuity, justice, etc. are generally used in abstraction from the density of contexts and their variety and thus very often end up with only a surface and frequently distorted, therefore, dangerous assessment of a community's life and springs of action… This … has happened with communities, particularly, tribal communities in the north-east, and that substantial part of the anxiety of the people of the region arises from this fact. (Miri, 2019)

Second is 'the widely prevalent mainstream cultural baggage with which cultures on the peripheries of national life, such as tribal cultures, are sought to be understood' (Miri, 2019).

Miri explains further that the history of the NE region does not figure in discussions on the region. It is seen as it is, although its social, cultural and political history is vivid, diverse, and eventful. The incomparable cultural diversities, including the linguistic pluralities of the region, have a rich history. Disassociating them from their history and context, as is done often, is problematic. Miri further elaborates that respect for diversity, that is, for each other culture, is part of the NE's unique historical and cultural experiences, because of the long experiences of so many societies of living together and their interactions with one another. He also tries to put in perspective the issue of integration of NE India with the mainland. He argues that the economic dependence of NE on the mainland creates a profound sense of insecurity in the people of the region. This has to be handled carefully, as the region has a profound sense of autonomy of history. In the absence of economic self-reliance, this creates a sense of anxiety and unnerveness, including dissatisfaction. Thus, any project of economic integration of NE India must be calibrated with its sense of autonomy. Moreover, traditionally, NE societies have been interdependent on one another. Their economic interrelations—often ignored in policy discourse on NE India—must be nurtured to their full potentialities, which is also natural. As a point of caution, Miri suggests viewing 'Look East' policy not merely as the opening of border trade with neighbouring countries but also as an opportunity for the economic integration of the NE with the mainland, without jeopardizing or threatening their sense of history and autonomy.

DIVERSITY- AND PEOPLE-CENTRIC DEVELOPMENT OF THE NE

The profound ethnic, geographical and administrative diversities of the NE region necessitate an entirely different approach to dealing with them. There is an imperative to adopt a decentralized, people-centric development approach for NE India, against a one-size–fits–all policy, that too in a top-down approach. The latter has not only failed to uplift the people in proportion to the amount of resources spent there by the centre but has also created various kinds of distortions in development priorities. For example, too many dams and hydroelectric projects have displaced a huge number of people and disrupted their land- and natural resource–based livelihood, apart from creating environmental hazards. In the absence of creation of alternative livelihoods, they have been forced to the condition of destitution.

A particular policy might be useful for Arunachal Pradesh but might not be useful for the plains of Assam and Tripura. Similarly, a policy towards gender needs to factor in diversities in the gender experiences of different societies. There are dominant and small tribes with differential access to political and economic resources. Any policy or programme for the tribes of NE India as a whole might not be useful for the numerically small tribes which might need different kinds of treatment and approaches. The problems of tea tribes are different from those of other tribes. There are different geographical conditions warranting different kinds of approaches. Without taking into account these diversities of the region, any programme and policy imposed from the top is doomed to fail.

Investment in Governance and Local Institutions

Governance faces a huge deficit in NE India. There are historical reasons for this. The British colonial government did not take much interest in the development of the people of the region. Their main interest lay in exploiting tea, timber and oil, which were mostly found in Assam (Sharma, 2008, 2012). They were not much interested in the governance of inaccessible and hilly areas, which were further insulated by various acts, like the Bengal East Frontier Regulation Act, 1873, and provisions like ILP. They were largely left to their own, allowing their indigenous community–based governance system.

In the post-Independence period, the Government of India followed in the footsteps of the British and adopted a policy of non-interference in the affairs of the people of the NE. After the 1962 India–China war, there was an intervention for improving infrastructure but largely only from the viewpoint of security. Only after liberalization in the 1990s, and the emphasis on trade and export, was there a shift in approach. It was realized that the development of NE, a gateway to South-east Asia, would be crucial for the 'Look East' policy, now the 'Act East' policy. The point which is emphasized here is that governance of NE India has suffered from historical negligence.

It is emphasized here that governance should be given utmost priority to address social sector development issues, which, notwithstanding some good performance indicators, have serious gaps. The gaps are more in terms of inter- and intra-state variations and inter- and intra-community variations. Given the diversities of topography, society, polity and even governance structure, and given the local political economy, characterized by the dominance of some populations and some groups—some tribes—governance and service delivery issues can be better addressed only through the institutions of local governance. The NE has demonstrated the usefulness of community-centric local governance, and there are institutional arrangements as well to promote them. These institutional arrangements, however, are not uniform across the region. Even while maintaining the diversities of institutional arrangements, there is an urgent need to strengthen local institutions. For example, village councils should be established in ADC areas and PRIs should be strengthened in non-ADC areas. In the regions with a strong community-centric social and economic life having their own indigenous institutions, like Nagaland, institutions should not only be strengthened but also be given legal–constitutional status to empower them legally.

K. B. Saxena (2019) has underlined constraints and limitations of governance in the region. He argues that governance of the NE operates on a complex terrain in which it is a continuous process of negotiation and adjustment with multiple forces and different layers of the governance structure. The existing governance structure in NE has been inherited from the colonial government instead of evolving through a natural process in which traditional social structure, political organizations and processes played an important role. The NE has been characterized by ethnic conflicts. Saxena explains that many of these conflicts are externally generated, through misplaced and wrong policies adopted by the government. He further argues that the development needs of the region, including the population, have suffered because of excessive security concerns and the heavy deployment of security personnel disproportionate to the legitimate needs. The security concerns override decisions of the formal elected government through the instrument of the governor, who is a representative of the union government in state. Besides, there is also a disjunction between community processes and state processes in which political government is seen by communities as incapable of addressing their grievances, which has resulted in the formation of private militias of insurgent groups. In such a situation, effective governance becomes a challenge until the above issues are addressed.

DEVELOPMENT APPROACH FOR THE NE

The development approach for NE India has been marred by various kinds of policy weaknesses. Since the colonial time, there has been a cautious approach of 'not to interfere', including for development in the NE region. The British colonial government exploited the NE region for oil, timber, coal and tea but did not give attention to the development of the population of the region. The post-Independence Indian government followed the British policy of non-interference in the NE region. After the India–China war in 1962, security concerns dominated India's NE policy. Only in the post-liberalization phase did the development of NE get attention under the policy framework of 'Look East' and the recent policy of 'Act East' (Sarma, 2019). Both 'Look East' and 'Act East' are heavily infrastructure development–driven, with a view to increasing trade with the neighbouring countries. It is apprehended that in the absence of development of the people, the NE would become a transit point, merely a corridor for trade with South-east Asia, without much benefit to the people of the region. More importantly, the potentialities of the 'Look East', and now 'Act East', policy could not be realized without the internal integration of the NE market. Except Assam, the economies of the other states are too small in size to get the benefits of scale. Moreover, individually, except Assam, none of them is big enough to be competitive. However, integration of the NE economy with the mainland by allowing the free movement of goods, capital and human resources can enhance their prospects for reaping benefits from the Act East policy. The integration of the NE economy is much hampered by governance issues. A potent hurdle is the provision of ILP, which is applicable in four states, namely Mizoram, Arunachal Pradesh, Nagaland and Manipur. There is a demand for the introduction of ILP in Meghalaya and even in Assam. There are other governance issues as well.

This book argues that social sector development should be the strategic goal of the development of NE India, as the prospect for the development of service sector compared to that of the primary and secondary sectors is higher. The social sector development strategy of NE India should, however, be informed by pronounced ethnic diversities, cultural pluralism and regional variations. It should also take into account the plurality of institutional arrangements and recognize the significance of local bodies and decentralized development. The diversities and pluralities of the region can be addressed through local institutions in a decentralized manner. There is a need to shift from the top-down, physical infrastructure–based development approach to a people-centric, decentralized development approach. This can be done by mobilizing and investing in the capacity of local bodies, whose role and significance have never been appreciated in the NE region. They have been considered merely as institutions for accommodating political aspirations of the local people. This book further argues that the mainstream understanding of NE India has been problematic both at the conceptual and factual levels. At the conceptual level, heterogeneity and diversities of NE India has been overlooked. At the factual level, the interconnections between its low level of economic and relatively high level of social sector development have not been given adequate attention.

This book emphasizes the people-centric over the growth-centric development approach. The former is coterminous with 'human development', and the latter, as generally explained, in terms of GDP, per capita income and such other economic indicators which have a physical character. As per Human Development Report (HDR) 1990, there are three critical elements to achieving human development, which are: (a) 'to live a long, healthy and creative life; (b) to be knowledgeable; and (c) to have access to resources needed for decent standard of living' (United Nations Development Programme [UNDP] HDR, 1990, p. 1). They lead to 'expansion of opportunities and choices' (UNDP, 1990, p. 1); Sen (2000) has explained it as 'capabilities enhancement' and 'freedom of choices'.

Under a people-centric approach, welfare of the people would be the main goal of development. High growth rate is only a means to promoting high human development; the latter is a goal in itself. But there is a two-way relation between growth rate and human development. While growth rate creates conditions for achieving high human development, the latter, in turn, plays a critical role in achieving high growth rate in the economy (Becker, 1993; Schultz, 1961).

Social sector development is generally equated with human development. However, there are additional dimensions of equality, participation in political and social processes of decision-making and fairness of representation in institutions—social, economic and political. The concept of human development also emphasizes 'political choice, human rights and personal self-respect' (UNDP, 1990, p. 1). In the light of the above perspective, the book pleads for a people-centric development approach for NE India.

Understanding the NE Through the Lens of Diversities

Chapters 2 and 3 in Section II are an attempt to understand NE India through the perspective of diversities. It is argued in this section that the social sector development of NE India should be examined in its historical context, ethnic diversities, cultural pluralities and contemporary scenario. Chandan Sharma locates the historical, socio-cultural and contemporary contexts of social sector development of NE India. He explains that policies towards the NE, since colonial days, have played havoc with the unique sociocultural textures of this region. They have not only destroyed the natural salience of the society and ecology of the region but are also responsible for many of the contemporary issues and problems. The British colonial government, guided by a narrow vision of commercial exploitation of the tea, timber, coal and oil of the region, placed restrictions in the region through the Excluded Areas Act, Partially Excluded Areas Act, Inner Line Regulations, Outer Line Regulations, etc. which choked the natural flow of people and channels of economic activities from one to another region of the NE. It balkanized the region. Apart from stifling inter-community relations, including of trade and commerce, it created artificial communities that soon became antagonistic to one another. The colonial government opened the NE region to the mainland, but for the limited purpose of extraction of natural resources. While rail and road networks were laid down, inter-community relations were broken.

The partition of the sub-continent in 1947 created further havoc in the NE economy. It disrupted the road, rail and waterway links of the region with India and confined its connection to a narrow corridor, spread over 22 km. The NE region became landlocked as well.

Partly because of the policy of the British colonial government to bring tribes and other low-caste labourers from Eastern and Central India, mainly Jharkhand, Chhattisgarh, Bihar, Odisha and Uttar Pradesh (UP), to work on tea plantation and Muslim tenants (farmers) from present Bangladesh (East Bengal during the colonial period), and partly because of post-Independence illegal immigration from East Pakistan (now Bangladesh), the demographic composition of the plains, especially in Assam and Tripura, changed so much so that these two states have witnessed violent agitations against the Indian state for not checking illegal immigrations and allowing the demographic composition of the states to be changed. The original inhabitants of these two states are constantly agitated over this issue.

The above has also implications for the social sector development of the NE. For example, social sector development indicators of Assam are dragged by the low level of development of Adivasis and immigrant Muslims. In fact, as long as they remain at a low level of development—illiteracy, poverty, malnutrition, poor health indicators—the state would remain at a low level of development. A major challenge of the social sector development of Assam is to ensure the development of these immigrants, who now constitute a sizeable proportion of the total population of the state. Sharma has also raised the issue of a large number of youths migrating for education and employment and another large chunk of semi-literate youths migrating from outside the region in search of a job, who often get jobs in the informal sector. The local economy is not able to meet their needs and fulfil their aspirations.

SOCIAL SECTOR DEVELOPMENT EXPERIENCES[2]

Demographic

Inter-community population growth rates and demographic changes have been contentious issues in NE India. The changing religious and linguistic composition of the population has acquired so much attention that the other demographic aspects of the population of the NE have been obscured from attention, though they are significant for the economy and state for policymaking. For example, the proportion of working-age population is still high in the NE region. There have been two main issues related to the changing composition of the population.

---

[2] Some of the chapters have conducted analysis across all eight states, including Sikkim, but some of them have excluded Sikkim from analysis.

First, the proportion of Hindus vis-à-vis other religious groups, especially Muslims, has declined in Assam over a period of time. Second, the proportion of the Assamese-speaking vis-à-vis the Bengali-speaking population has also decreased. Both these issues have been highly emotive and sources of social and political tensions, including inter-ethnic conflicts in the region.

Bimal Kar and Suli Ayemi in their paper have examined both the changing composition of religious and linguistic groups and the demographic structure of the population across seven states of the NE. They have not included Sikkim in their analysis. They have analysed population growth over more than a century, from 1901 to 2011. Demographic and other changes have been analysed over the period between 1971 and 2011.

The population growth rate of NE India has been consistently higher than the national average in each decade between 1971 and 2011. In terms of pre- and post-Independence periods, the growth rate has been much higher in the post-Independence period, especially in the 1960s and the 1970s, largely due to the huge influx and immigration of population from Bangladesh. As a result of the consistently high population growth rate, the share of the NE in the total population of India has increased from 1.79 per cent in 1901 to 2.84 per cent in 1951 to 3.57 per cent in 1971 and, further, to 3.73 per cent in 2011.

Although birth and death rates of the NE region have been similar to those of the rest of India, different states have grown differently. Consequently, the shares of different states of the NE to the total population of the region have also changed. The share of Assam in the total population of NE India has decreased from 78.26 per cent in 1951 to 69.10 per cent in 2011. On the other hand, the shares of the other states have increased.

Other dimensions of population growth pertain to the changing composition of religious and linguistic groups. Hindus constituted 66.39 per cent of the total population of the region in 1971. Their share decreased to 53.97 per cent in 2011. As against this, the share of Muslims increased from 19.40 per cent in 1971 to 25.37 per cent in 2011, that of Christians from 9.12 per cent in 1971 to 17.34 per cent in 2011, and that of Buddhists from 0.77 per cent to 1.02 per cent during the same period. Similarly, the share of the Assamese-speaking population, the largest linguistic group of the region, declined from 45.71 per cent in 1971 to 33.68 per cent in 2011. On the other hand, the share of Bengali- and Hindi-speaking populations increased during the period. An important demographic feature of the NE is the high dependency ratio, especially of the 0–14 age group.

Education

Education is a crucial area of social sector development. Except Assam and Arunachal Pradesh, the literacy rates of the other states are higher than the national average. Even in Assam, the low level of literacy rate is because of the low level of literacy rate among the immigrant Muslim population and the tea garden tribes. But apart from literacy rates, there are other issues of educational development. Enrolment in secondary and higher education, male–female literacy gap, dropout rate at upper primary and secondary levels, school infrastructure, etc. are crucial for overall educational development, which need attention in the region.

Chapters 4–6 in Section III analyse three different aspects of education. Saket Kushwaha et al., Sushant Nayak and Jumi Kalita give an overview of the status of school education in NE India. Nirmali Goswami analyses the problem of gender gap, and Jayashree Doley, using the ethnographic method, explains the educational aspirations of the Mising tribespeople, who are found in Assam and Arunachal Pradesh.

Saket Kushwaha et al. analyse the status, access and outcome of school education in NE India. While all the states of NE India have made progress in the enrolment of children in primary, upper primary, secondary and higher secondary levels, there is a problem of enrolment of overage children at all levels. This is perhaps due to the late starting of schooling. Due to difficult geographical terrain, parents send their children late. Dropout rates at all the three levels, namely classes I–V, classes I–VIII and classes I–X are quite high, and higher than the national average except that of Sikkim for classes I–V and those of Mizoram for classes I–VIII and classes I–X. Gross enrolment ratio

(GER) at the higher education level increased in all the states except Nagaland between 2010–2011 and 2016–2017. Also, GER in higher education is higher than the national average in Sikkim, Manipur and Arunachal Pradesh. Perhaps, the opening of central universities in these states have increased the GER in higher education. Most of the NE states, despite the scattered population and difficult geographical terrain, have better school infrastructure, including the teacher–student ratio. Because of better provisioning, the learning outcome is also better, as this chapter shows.

Nirmali Goswami analyses social contexts of gender gap in educational attainment in Assam. She shows that from the beginning of modern education in the state, women lagged behind their male counterparts. Parents from upper classes showed interest in girls' education but mostly through tutors arranged at home, as patriarchal norms prevented them from sending their girls to schools. Although recently Assam and other NE states have achieved gender parity in enrolment, a new disparity in terms of government and private schools is emerging. The enrolment of girls is higher in government than in private schools. It is worrisome, as private schools are increasing in numbers.

Jayashree Doley shows how the Mising community, a scheduled tribe of Assam and Arunachal Pradesh, pursued modern education driven by aspiration for social and economic mobility. Their aspirational mobility supported by education facilitated their migration from rural to urban areas but not for all, as many of them decided to stay in rural areas and remain in agriculture. However, educational and economic mobility also produced a class–differentiated society in the traditionally egalitarian Mising community. How the Mising community would reconcile the increasing class cleavages and differentiated class structures with traditional bonds and social structures is yet to be seen.

Health

Like education, health indicators of most of the states of NE India are relatively better. This is despite the hills, sparse population, scattered habitations and regular floods in large parts of the plains. The health indicators of NE India are an outcome of a number of factors— consumption of protein-rich food, mainly meat and fish, longer duration of breastfeeding, access to potable water, clean air and other practices, including the use of herbs and medicinal plants. Of course, access to modern health facilities, which is uneven across the states, is also a factor.

Chapters 7 and 8 in Section IV deal with two different issues of health in NE India. Sushanta Nayak and Geling Modi have examined access to modern health facilities. Surajit Deb has looked into the prevalence of malnutrition among children of NE India.

Sushanta Nayak and Geling Modi have analysed the status of health facilities in different states of NE India. They show that providing health facilities is a challenge because of the scattered population, difficult geographical terrains and natural calamities like recurrent floods in the region. Except Nagaland, in all other states, the number of patients per doctor is higher than the national average. As against the national average of 1,411 patients per doctor, there are 5,157 patients per doctor in Assam, 3,100 in Meghalaya, 2,675 in Tripura and 2,597 in Mizoram. In terms of area per doctor, against the national average of 3.83 km per doctor, it is 113.16 km in Arunachal Pradesh, 50 km in Mizoram, 24 km in Manipur and 23 km in Meghalaya. The position of Tripura and Nagaland is better, with 7.64 km and 6.49 km per doctor, respectively.

Surajit Deb analyses the prevalence of child malnutrition in NE India across various age groups of children and states. The analysis has also been done across caste and gender. He shows that although most of the NE states have done better than the national average with respect to most of the indicators, the incidence of malnutrition increases after the breastfeeding age, that is, from 36 to 59 months. Also, while there was no gender differentiation with respect to malnutrition, it was visible across rural–urban and social classes. Another noteworthy point is the significant improvement in the indicators of nutrition between 2005–2006 and 2015–2016 in almost all the states of NE India.

Poverty, Unemployment and Food Security

Poverty, unemployment and food security are burning issues of NE India. They are also interconnected. Chapters 9–11 in Section V deal with poverty, unemployment and food security in NE India.

Joydeep Baruah examines the status of poverty in NE India and shows that the headcount poverty ratio in Arunachal Pradesh, Assam and Manipur is higher than the national average. In terms of rural and urban poverty, rural poverty in Arunachal Pradesh, Assam, Manipur and Mizoram is higher than the national average. Urban poverty in Arunachal, Manipur and Nagaland is higher than the national average. Like at the all-India level, poverty ratio in the NE has declined over the last two decades. However, the decline in poverty was sharp in Arunachal Pradesh, Assam, Manipur, Meghalaya and Nagaland between 1993–1994 and 2004–2005 and in Tripura and Sikkim between 2004–2005 and 2011–2012. During the period between 2004–2005 and 2011–2012, the overall poverty ratio increased in Arunachal, Mizoram and Nagaland. In Arunachal Pradesh, the poverty ratio increased mainly due to the increase in rural poverty. It decreased only marginally in Assam and Manipur.

In comparison to the first decade of liberalization, the decline in poverty was slower in the second decade (between 2004–2005 and 2011–2012) in NE India, although Tripura and Sikkim made substantial improvements in poverty reduction in the second decade, largely due to the better administration of centre-sponsored schemes and increase in social and welfare scheme expenditure. Agriculture is still the dominant source of livelihood for the people in the NE, and the decline in poverty has been mainly due to the decline in rural poverty. This decline in poverty has happened along with an increase in unemployment rate, especially in urban areas, where decline in poverty has been slower. Poverty also varies in severity across the states of NE India.

The poverty ratio varies across social classes as well. There is a clear trend of high incidence of poverty among the social groups that are in minority in a state. For example, the incidence of poverty is high among Muslims in Assam, Hindus in Mizoram and Buddhists in Arunachal

Pradesh. The incidence of poverty is higher among the casual labour in agriculture and non-agriculture in all the eight states. It is also higher among the self-employed in many states, especially in urban areas. It has further been found that states with increase or only marginal decline in poverty have witnessed increase in income inequality.

Kalyan Das examines the problem of unemployment, especially among the youth, outmigration of population in search of employment and the well-being of the migrant population. He argues that because of increasing population pressure and continued dependence on natural resource–based livelihoods, the NE region has reached a point beyond which it is no longer in a position to provide gainful employment to the increasing population in traditional sectors. For example, as per the periodic labour force survey, weighted with census data from 2011, youth unemployment rate is 56 per cent in Nagaland, 35 per cent in Manipur, 28.6 per cent in Mizoram, 27 per cent in Assam and 26 per cent in Arunachal Pradesh, against the all-India average of 17.8 per cent. Also, the overall unemployment rate of the NE region (8.3%) is higher than the all-India average of 6.1 per cent. Das also analyses the labour market trend and shows that employment possibility decreases with greater level of education. This is one of the reasons for the large-scale outmigration of educated youth from the region. He further examines various policies adopted for promoting industrialization in the region and analyses the failures of these policies due to various reasons. Consequently, people have started moving out from the NE region. As per the 2011 census, net immigration is negative in all the states except Arunachal Pradesh and Meghalaya. However, the migrants do not want to stay outside their native states for long. Their main aim is to earn and save some money for the future. This chapter indicates the urgency of creating employment opportunities, mostly in the secondary and tertiary sectors in the NE region.

Food security is always a challenge in the food-deficient NE region. In such a situation, the role of the public distribution system (PDS) becomes significant. Also, there is a high level of dependence of the population on the PDS in the NE region. Mahsina Rahman and Rajshree Bedamatta, through an empirical study of household food security and the role of PDS in the two riparian villages of Jorhat and Dhubri districts, show a high level of dependence of the population on the PDS for food security. There are, however, administration challenges in the implementation of the PDS, as Assam follows a different administrative procedure. It has adopted a policy of differential pricing for different geographical areas. Transportation costs are also fixed accordingly. In the process, beneficiaries are not fully informed of the issue price they have to pay for ration. The fair price shop (FPS) owners exploit this situation to the disadvantage of the beneficiaries. There is a need to review the administrative arrangement of the PDS in Assam. Similar problems could also be found in other states of the NE region, as most of them are hilly areas and transportation costs are generally higher in such areas.

Politics and Governance

Politics and governance of the NE have some distinct characteristics. Politics of the region has always centred around autonomy for protecting land and natural resources from alienation and preserving the culture and tradition of the myriad social groups. Governance of the region has been full of challenges, partly because of the nature of the autonomy-centred politics, inter-ethnic group conflicts, remoteness of the region from the national capital and, of course, topography and international borders. The colonial government was the first to tamper with their indigenous and community-based governance system. The post-Independence Indian state inherited the colonial legacy and, for quite a long period, followed in the shoes of the colonial government, except for some minor tinkering with the policy. From the mid-1960s onwards, the Government of India adopted a policy of accommodating political and cultural aspirations for autonomy through the formation of new states. Forming ADCs and allowing restrictions on the movement of people from outside the state have been other policy planks towards providing autonomy to the people of the region. Section VI of this volume deals with some of the issues related to politics and governance.

Bhupen Sarmah and Joseph Lalfakzuala trace the transition of the NE from colonial administrative units to political units of India's nation state in its historicity. They look into the formation of ADCs and their governance structure. They argue that while the ADCs have satisfied the urge of the local people for political and cultural autonomy, the local elite have captured ADCs and exploited them to grab common property resources. ADCs also suffer from democratic deficit through denying representation of women. Sarmah and Lalfakzuala are also critical of the developmental role of the ADCs, partly because they remain undemocratic and partly because they have been captured by the local tribal elite.

Vanlalchhawna and Haokip examine ADCs more closely. The former draws attention towards the fiscally weak position of ADCs, and the latter towards the formation of regional councils to meet the aspirations of minority tribes within the ADCs. Vanlachhawa analyses the flow of fund to the three District Councils of Mizoram and shows the heavy dependence of ADCs on fiscal transfer from the state government. Their own revenue mobilization is inadequate, and so is the transfer from the state government. Also, while PRIs are getting direct transfers from the union government through the 14th Finance Commission, ADCs have been left out. The low fiscal position of ADCs has implications for development work in the ADC areas. Vanlachhawa argues that to make ADCs meet the aspirations of the local people, their financial position needs to be strengthened. He suggests a set of measures for the administrative and fiscal strengthening of the ADCs to meet the development aspirations of the people living within ADC areas.

Thongkholal Haokip draws our attention towards a provision in the Sixth Schedule that is for the formation of regional councils for minority tribes within the Sixth Schedule areas. He shows that minority tribes within the ADCs are marginalized and discontented. Many of them have also become militants, which has disturbed peace in the area. Haokip argues that the provision for the formation of regional councils for such minority tribes should be activated to neutralize the sense of marginalization and discontent among the minority tribes within the Sixth Schedule areas. He suggests this as part of a conflict management mechanism.

Patricia Mukhim not only challenges the existing notions about the NE society but also raises important questions about social sector development in the NE. Her important concern is over the decreasing social bonding and weakening of the community-centric resource sharing arrangement among the tribal societies of the NE. The large amount of central funds meant for the development of the NE has been cornered by a group of tribal political, bureaucratic and business elite. This has not only created a schism in the society but also weakened the traditional bonding/cohesion of the tribal society. Informal institutions in the NE have a greater level of acceptance among the people. They are also closer to the people. However, these institutions too have been captured by the tribal elite, who have exploited them for their personal aggrandizement at the cost of the masses.

REFERENCES

Becker, G. S. (1993). *Human capital: A theoretical and empirical analysis, with special reference to education* (3rd ed.). The University of Chicago Press.

Chugh, S. (2009). Progress in literacy and elementary education: The study of Himachal Pradesh, Kerala and Mizoram. *Social Change, 39*(2), 216–238.

Deb, S. (2018). Social development index 2018. In T. Haque and D. Narsimha Reddy (Ed.), *India: Social development report 2018. Rising inequalities in India.* (pp. 285–325) Oxford University Press.

Deori, K. (2019). Northeast India: The Goldmine of languages. *The Northeast Today.* https://www.northeasttoday.in/northeast-india-the-goldmine-of-languages/

Government of Assam, Niti Ayog, and UNDP. (2014). *Assam human development report: Managing diversities, achieving human development.* Government of Assam.

Hluna, J. V. (1992). *Education and missionaries in Mizoram.* Spectrum Publication.

Lalmalsawma, D. (2013, September 7). *India speaks 780 languages, 220 lost in last 50 years—Survey. Rueters, US Edition.* http://blogs.reuters.com/india/2013/09/07/india-speaks-780-languages-220-lost-in-last-50-years-survey/

Miri, M. (2019). Inaugural Address in a Seminar on 'Social Development of Northeast India'. Council for Social Development, New Delhi, 15–16 July 2020.

Sarma, A. (2019). *Strings of thoughts on North East India: An economist's perspectives.* Aakar Books.

Saxena, K. B. (2019). *Structures undermined by policies and practices: Complexities of governance in North-East India.* Presented in a seminar on 'Social Development of North-east India' organized by the Council for Social Development, New Delhi on 15–16 July 2020.

Schultz, T. W. (1961). Investment in human capital. *The American Economic Review, 51*(1), 1–17.

Sen, A. (2000). *Development as freedom*. Oxford University Press.

Sharma, C. K. (2012). The immigration issue in Assam and conflicts around it. *Asian Ethnicity, 13*, 287–309.

Syiemlieh, D. R. (2012). Sectional president's address: Colonial encounter and Christian missions in North East India. *Proceedings of the Indian History Congress, 73*(2012), 509–527.

United Nations Development Programme (UNDP). (1990). *Human development report 1990*. Oxford University Press.

SECTION II

Contexts

Chapter 2

Contextualizing Social Development in North-east India

Chandan Kumar Sharma

INTRODUCING THE 'NORTH-EAST'

Introducing 'North-east (NE) India' is an onerous exercise. The heterogeneity within the region is one part of this difficulty. The other is that to make sense of 'NE India', one has to recognize the loaded nature of the term which goes beyond its mere geographical denotation. The discussion below unravels the nature of the heterogeneities as well as the nuances that the term entails and explicates why these need to be grappled with to understand the trajectories of social development[1] in the region.

As indicated, NE India, a region of remarkable natural and socio-cultural diversity, consists of eight states: Assam, Arunachal Pradesh, Manipur, Meghalaya, Mizoram, Nagaland, Tripura and Sikkim. Sikkim was made a part of 'NE India' in 2002 for administrative expediency, although historically the state has not been considered a part of the region. The region shares international borders more

---

[1] The term 'social development' is used here to refer to a process that promotes a sustainable and equitable society by allowing all its sections to meaningfully participate in that process (for details, see Midgley, 2014; Omer, 1979; Paiva, 1977).

than 5,000 km long with five foreign countries, namely Bangladesh, Bhutan, China, Myanmar and Nepal (after the inclusion of Sikkim). The region is today connected with the rest of India by a tenuous 22-km land corridor through Siliguri in the state of West Bengal—a link that has come to be referred to as the 'Chicken's Neck'. Comprising less than 8 per cent of India's geographical area, the NE is home to around 3.6 per cent of the total population of the country. Assam is the most populated state in the region, with a population of over 3.1 million, and Sikkim the least populated, with over 0.6 million people. The population density in Assam is the highest, with 398 people/km^2 and that of Arunachal Pradesh is the lowest with 17 people/km^2 (North Eastern Council Secretariat, 2015).

NE India can be geographically divided into two parts: the plains and the hills. The region is home to a large number of communities—both tribal and non-tribal. The tribal communities in the region are divided into the 'plains tribes', inhabiting the Brahmaputra and the Barak valleys, and the 'hills tribes'. However, there are many tribes which inhabit both the plains and the hills. Each tribe has its own distinct culture, which gives it a unique cultural identity. Quite a few of the tribal communities are transnational in nature, and members of such tribes regularly criss-cross the international border. The total number of languages, with their variations, spoken in the region is also incredibly large. Assamese is spoken by the majority of the population and was once considered the lingua franca of the region. Now, Hindi is gradually taking over it, on account of the proactive role of the union government in promoting Hindi. Other major languages spoken in the region include Bengali, Manipuri, Bodo, Nagamese, Khasi, Garo, Jaintia, Mizo, Mising, Kokborok, Nepali, etc.

Among the non-tribal population, while many are indigenous[2] to the region, many are immigrants from other states of India as well as from erstwhile East Pakistan (now Bangladesh) and Nepal. These

[2] Such non-tribal populations are mainly concentrated in Assam. Although the 'indigeneity' of a community is a much-contested issue in the state, here the term is being used to imply those non-tribal groups which were inhabitants of Assam before the advent of British colonialism in 1826 (see Sharma, 2012a, p. 288).

communities have been historically characterized by their own distinctive livelihoods, habitats, culture, religion, etc. The majority of those living in the plains of the region are Hindus and Muslims, while a majority of the hill tribes inhabiting the states of Meghalaya, Mizoram and Nagaland are Christians. In Arunachal Pradesh too, there has been a considerable increase in the number of Christians in recent times. Besides, there is a significant presence of Buddhist population in the region, especially in Arunachal Pradesh and Sikkim (Census of India, 2011). The most populous state of the region is Assam, which constitutes more than twice the combined total population of the region (Census of India, 2011).

There are stark differences among the eight states of NE India with respect to their resource endowments, sociocultural life and levels of socio-economic development. Besides the social characteristics mentioned above, it may be noted that most of the plains tribes, especially in the Brahmaputra Valley, to a greater or lesser degree, had historical interactions with the mainstream Hindu society and many of them got assimilated into it, laying the foundation of a liberal, syncretic society (Sharma, 2011). Such a process of *Hinduization* was also observed in the plains of Manipur (among the Meiteis), Cachar (among the Dimasa Kacharis) and Tripura. However, the hills tribes had remained mostly out of this (barring the Jaintias), mostly due to the remoteness of their habitats. However, this isolation of the hills tribes from the mainstream Hindu society made them early targets of the Christian missionaries during the colonial times. The missionaries also played a crucial role in the expansion of modern education among them. In the process, while an overwhelming majority of the hills tribes today are Christians, they are also ahead of most of the plains tribes in various parameters of social development.

The economies of all the north-eastern states remain underdeveloped and primarily agrarian. A large majority of the population of the region depends on natural resource-based livelihoods. Shifting cultivation (*jhum*) is a dominant traditional system of land use in the hill states and plays a critical role in maintaining agricultural biodiversity and providing food security. The Brahmaputra River system, which includes its tributaries, is the lifeline for the livelihoods, such as fishing and agriculture, of local communities living on its floodplains. The unique ecology of the river also determines the livelihood patterns, customs, food habits, religious beliefs, and so on of the indigenous communities of the region. Similarly, the Barak River system plays a critical role in sustaining the life and livelihood of the people in the Imphal Valley in Manipur, the Barak Valley districts in Assam and those living along its riparian areas in Bangladesh (Sharma, 2018, p. 317).

The industrial sector in the region is quite backward. It mainly developed around tea, oil and timber in Assam during the colonial period itself. In fact, when the Assam Company dealing with tea was formed in 1839, it happened to be the first joint stock company of India established under an Act of Parliament (Barpujari, 1963, p. 244) and was listed in the London Stock Exchange. Thus, through the tea industry, Assam was connected to the global capitalist market 180 years back. Similarly, the Digboi oil refinery, set up in 1901, was the first refinery in Asia. This way, Assam seemed to have been industrially more advanced than many parts of the country. However, the nature of these industries and their contribution to the development of the state has been much debated. The tea industry has been criticized as an 'enclave economy' (for detail see Guha, 1977). Misra, explaining the nature of resource exploitation from the state, describes it as a 'colonial hinterland' (Misra, 1980; also see Sharma, 1995).

In case of the other states of the region, the industrial sector revolves mostly around timber,[3] except Meghalaya, where the mining of coal and limestone also contributes significantly to the economy of the state. However, the nature of their extraction and the consequent social and environmental costs has raised serious questions in recent times.[4] Although with the region's rich natural splendour it could

---

[3] However, the Supreme Court of India's ban on timber trade in 1996 dealt a body blow to numerous poor forest dwellers and indigenous communities of NE India, though it came as a major victory for the environmentalists and wildlife lovers. See Nongbri (2001, pp. 1893–1900).

[4] http://theshillongtimes.com/2014/08/20/an-economic-perspective-on-coal-mining-in-meghalaya/; https://www.business-standard.com/article/current-affairs/illegal-coal-mines-in-meghalaya-how-miners-are-exploited-lives-threatened-118123000144_1.html; (accessed on 10 July 2019).

have been a great destination for nature tourism, various restrictive regulations[5] on the entry into several states of the region, coupled with poor infrastructure, have stood in the way of development of the tourism sector.

It is to be mentioned here that since the Independence of India, the north-eastern region has witnessed a series of ethnic insurgencies, beginning with the Naga insurgency and subsequently spreading to the Meiteis (Manipur), Mizos (Mizoram), Assamese and Bodos (Assam), Tripuri tribes (Tripura), and so on. These insurgencies have raised demands of the Indian state for various forms of self-determination. However, since the beginning, the response of the Indian state towards these insurgencies has been militarist. It was to counter the Naga insurgency that the draconian Armed Forces (Special Powers) Act was imposed in 1958. Subsequently, as the insurgencies spread to other areas of the region, the Act was clamped in those areas too. The atmosphere of violence and terror and the suffocation of the democratic polity that the insurgencies and the counter-insurgency operations have eventuated in the region are well recognized. Some of the worst outcomes of the insurgency in the region have been the inter-ethnic distrust and violent conflicts. While the state has blamed the insurgents for this situation, how the policies of the state have also been responsible for the rise of insurgency and the inter-ethnic conflicts has been brought out by many scholars (Fernandes, 2004; Kikon, 2005).

Further, insurgencies also witnessed a significant demolition of the traditional social structures, especially of the Naga and the Mizo societies. As an effective tool to counter armed struggle among them, the Indian state resorted to the grouping of the existing remote villages, which often involved their burning down and resettlement of the villagers in areas with easy access, mainly along the main roads, to the security forces. It is this repressive and disjunctive process which is behind Mizoram becoming the most urbanized state in India (Sundar, 2011, pp. 47–57).

---

[5] Protected Areas Permit, Restricted Areas Permit and Inner Line Permit are some such regulations which were either in force or are still in force in the region.

All these have a strong bearing on the social development of the communities in the region. Unless these specificities are recognized and addressed, an inclusive social development of the region will remain a distant dream.

TRANSITION FROM PRE-COLONIAL TO COLONIAL TIMES

Historically, NE India has been a continental crossroads, and groups from different sides have come and settled here. Identifying the routes of migration in Assam, historian David Ludden writes,

> (I)nland spaces of mobility historically important in Assam include (1) routes of Ancient Khasi Migration, which began in the Red River Basin of Vietnam and extended across Yunnan and Burma to the Gangetic basin as far west as Bihar; (2) Medieval Tai-Ahom migrations, which continued over centuries and built the most powerful premodern states in the Brahmaputra valley; (3) routes and heartlands of opium cultivation, consumption, and trade, with unknown origins, which extended in the 18th and 19th century from Bihar to China and today stop at the borders of India but extend south across the Golden Triangle of Southeast Asia; (4) the imperial expansion of Burma in the eighteenth and early nineteenth century; and (5) the military travels of armies of China, Japan, Britain and America along roads from Assam to Burma to Yunnan, during the 1940s – on roads that still exist today, though in a state of dilapidation. (Ludden, 2003)

Evidently, the region enjoyed its own centrality in historical times. The term 'Northeast' became a part of the geopolitical lexicon only after the region became a part of the colonial Indian subcontinent in the 19th century. Before that, the NE, more particularly Assam, had its own distinctive identity without being referred to as part of some larger landmass. Assam had a wide economic network that included Tibet, Bhutan, Nepal, Bengal and also China, to a limited extent. Assam also provided land routes for communities from Upper Burma to conduct trade with Tibet. It is worth noting that though Assam, more so its Brahmaputra Valley, had a long cultural engagement with the rest of India, it was never part of any political entity (barring a few partial and short-term occupations) from the Indian mainstream. The cultural linkage with the latter may be attributed more to the Aryan migration to the region from North India, which dates back to the early first millennium AD (Sharma, 2011).

Further, in the pre-colonial times, the inhabitants in the hills (tribes) and the plains (tribes, as well as non-tribes) in the region shared a relationship of mutual dependence. There were occasional conflicts, but such conflicts were addressed using traditional mechanisms. The foothills served as strategic passages for communities engaging in trade and commerce beyond their own habitats (Sharma, 2017, p. 1). During the Ahom period, Assam had links with the hill tribes bordering the plains, with whom commercial exchanges took place in the border *haats*.[6] It was the contact with the plains tribes of Assam that contributed to the development of the Nefamese (Arunachalese) and the Nagamese as lingua francas (Sharma, 2017, p. 4). The whole situation has been put in perspective by the historian H. K. Barpujari in the following words:

> (T)here had been regular traffic between the people of the plains and the hills. The hillmen had to depend by and large on the neighbouring plainsmen for their requirement of foodstuff and other necessaries. Every winter through the *duars* or the passes, the Bhutias and their neighbours in the east came down with mule-loads of rock-salt, gold-dust, musk, woollens, yak-tails, Chinese silk, etc. and carried up different kinds of cloth, raw-silk and thread, rice, dried fish and the like. The Mishmis, who served as the middlemen with the Kachins on the one hand and the Chinese on the other, bartered salt, woollens, ivory, copper, gold, amber, honey and Mishmi *teeta* (*Coptis teeta*). (Barpujari, 1993, p. 113)

Barpujari also mentions the various fairs that flourished at the foothills of Assam as they became centres of trade between the hills and the plains. This was especially true with Bhutan, which had strong trade relations with areas ranging from Central to Western Assam from ancient times (Bhuyan, 1949, p. 35).

However, all that changed with the annexation of Assam by the British in 1826, who, over a period spanning a few decades, annexed

---

[6] Periodic markets, usually once or twice a week.

the entire region into their territory. These annexations brought about drastic changes in the society, polity and economy of the region with the advent of new colonial institutions and capitalist enterprises (Guha, 1977, 1991). Writing on the consequence of this on the region, Sanjib Baruah writes,

> the region's difficulties as a result of the loss of connectivity and market access following the partition of 1947 are well known. But there is also an older story of colonial geopolitics that cut the region off from its neighbourhood across the eastern and northern borders. 19th century British colonial decisions to draw lines between the hills and the plains, to put barriers on trade between Bhutan and Assam, and to treat Burma as a buffer against French Indo-china and China severed the region from its traditional trade routes – the southern trails of the Silk Road. While colonial rulers built railways and roads mostly to take tea, coal, oil and other resources out of Assam, the disruption of old trade routes remained colonialism's most enduring negative legacy. (Baruah, 2005a)

It is to be noted that the colonial regime needed Assam's Brahmaputra Valley mainly for its tea, and later petroleum, and treated much of the north-eastern region as a buffer zone against Burma and China. The immediate objective of the colonialists was to establish effective military and political control over the Assam valley and then extend its control to the surrounding hills (Sharma, 2012b, p. 194). This resulted in the political reorganization of the region, with the Assam valley as its core. The new political units that came to be known as Assam incorporated the neighbouring hills with new concepts of boundary and territoriality, dismantling their traditional meanings (Sharma, 2017, p. 6). Since the early 1870s, the colonial regime introduced a plethora of restrictive regulations such as the Excluded Areas Act, Partially Excluded Areas Act, Inner Line Regulations, Outer Line Regulations, etc. which strictly prohibited the movement of people between the hills and the plains, stifling the traditional community relations, though, ostensibly, this was aimed at protecting the hill areas from the plainsmen. In fact, these legislations proved more enervating for the indomitable hill tribes, who now became fully dependent on the supplies facilitated by the British. Further, the British went on to categorize the tribes in the region based on their perceived habitats. Thus, these tribes were categorized either as the 'hills tribes' or as the 'plains tribes'. This was at variance with the reality, as members belonging to many tribes in the region lived in both the plains and the hills.[7] Baruah points out how the colonial writers (e.g., Reid, 1944, pp. 18–29) often used to describe the ethnic groups' spatial as well as civilizational location, such as the '"abode proper" and the "backward and degraded type" (that) point to the peculiar logic of colonial racial and ethnic classification: the fixing of "tribes" to their supposed natural habitats...' (Baruah, 2008, p. 15).

One awkward consequence of this colonial policy of fixating a tribe to a particular geographical habitat in the region is that today, many members of those tribes whose habits are incongruent with their supposed natural habitat are deprived of various benefits of the government. For example, even if the Scheduled Tribes from the autonomous hill districts of Assam reside permanently in the state's plains districts, they are not treated as Scheduled Tribes in the plains; they are called 'Hill Tribes in the Plains'. Similarly, Scheduled Tribes from plains districts, residing permanently in the hill districts, are called 'Plains Tribes in the Hills'. Such tribes do not enjoy the benefit of electoral reservation, though they are eligible for various economic, educational and employment benefits.[8] Persistence with such colonial notions have not only stood in the way of ensuring the desired social development of the tribal communities, they have significantly contributed to the contemporary space-centric consciousness in the region. Such notions are also behind the space-centric homeland policies pursued by the Indian state in the region (Baruah, 2008, p. 16; Prabhakar, 2005, p. 38; Sharma, 2012b, p. 195).

Colonialism also brought about a radical transformation in the demographic landscape in the plains of Assam, which was largely an unpopulated, land-abundant region when the British arrived (Butler, 1855, p. 23). The hill areas of the region, mostly coming under the Excluded areas, were spared from this. The expansion of the colonial

---

[7] Such tribes include the Mising, Karbi, Dimasa, etc. in the Brahmaputra valley and Hmar, Khasi, Kuki, Naga, Garo, etc. in the Barak valley.

[8] https://www.sentinelassam.com/guwahati-city/there-are-around-14-recognised-plain-tribe-communities-15-hills-tribe-communities-16-recognised-scheduled-caste-communities-in-assam-chandan-brahma/

dispensation in Assam created a demand for a significant number of trained manpower which was locally not available. Around the same time, large-scale commercial production of tea started. Some decades later, oil and coal were also discovered. Timber in the Assam forests was another economic resource that attracted the colonialists. In response to the above situation, since the 1830s, various groups of migrants either came or were brought to Assam as traders, as petty officials in the colonial administration, as labourers in the tea plantations, and so on (Sharma, 2012a).

With the introduction of the tea plantations in Upper and Central Assam in the mid-19th century began the process of transformation of the 'jungles' to (tea) 'gardens'. This resulted in the usurpation of a large number of village commons or community forest land during the period between the 1850s and the 1880s. With the introduction of the Bengal Forest Act, 1865, the common property resources such as forests, forest products and grazing lands were brought under the monopoly control of the colonial regime, depriving the common people access to them (Saikia, 2011 cited in Sharma & Sarma, 2014, p. 52). The new colonial forest conservation regime also posed a serious challenge to the future expansion of the Assamese peasant economy. Along with the expansion of tea cultivation, the colonial regime brought a large number of indentured labourers from tribal and marginal caste backgrounds from Central and Eastern India to work in the plantations. After the expiry of their contract, most of these labourers settled in Assam. Apart from them, there was a significant migration of Nepali population during the colonial period, who mostly settled in forest areas as grazers and cattle breeders (Sharma, 2012a).

Since the early 20th century, the colonial regime opened up the 'wastelands'[9] of Assam for jute cultivation for the peasants from East Bengal, as the local peasantry was not engaged in commercial cultivation of jute. The colonial regime also opened up additional wastelands

---

[9] Wasteland is a creation of the colonial state in Assam. It facilitated the use of the so-called unused land, including forests, grasslands, highlands, wetlands, etc. for the cultivation of commercial crops such as tea, sugarcane and (later) jute by the British planters and cultivators from outside Assam with the objective of collecting more revenue (Guha, 1991, pp. 149, 167–168).

for agricultural production, with the objective of producing more revenue, and therefore encouraged the migration of Muslim peasants from East Bengal. Under the Muslim League ministry in 'the late 1930s which had the tacit support of the colonial administration, this policy was carried out in an overzealous manner. Under such political patronage, immigration to Assam multiplied and vast areas of forest and wasteland of Assam became immigrant habitats' (Sharma, 2001, p. 4793). This immigration dramatically transformed the demographic and sociopolitical landscapes of the region within a matter of a few decades.

THE AFTERMATH OF THE PARTITION

After the Partition of India in 1947, immigration to Assam continued from the erstwhile East Pakistan and then (after 1971) Bangladesh, leading to acute anxiety among the smaller indigenous communities of Assam. This has assumed a much acute dimension, with the indigenous–immigrant debate reaching a climax in recent decades in the region, especially Assam, resulting in several bloody conflicts. The cry for the introduction of the Inner Line Permit, even from states like Manipur and Assam where it was not enforced by the colonial regime, testifies to the growing tension around the immigration issue.[10]

Another state in the region which underwent massive demographic transformation during the post-Independence period is Tripura. The uncontrolled Hindu Bengali migration from the erstwhile East Pakistan and then Bangladesh after 1971 not only reduced the indigenous tribal communities of the state into a minority, but their traditional land relations and livelihood systems were also pushed into a serious crisis (Bhaumik, 2005, pp. 144–174; Debburma, 2009, pp. 113–127). This gave rise to strong resentment among the tribal groups in the state, leading to years of insurgency. While Sikkim also has its own history of demographic change and the indigenous Lepcha community becoming a small minority in their own land due to the migration of the Nepalese

---

[10] https://www.indiatoday.in/who-is-what-is/story/what-is-inner-line-permit-people-manipur-are-demanding-260803-2015-09-02

and the Bhutias, this history, however, is somewhat old and different from that of Tripura.[11]

Thus, the restrictive forest conservation regime, the tea plantations and the large-scale immigration, among other things, seriously restricted the access of the local peasantry, both tribal and non-tribal, of Assam to the land resources as the once land-abundant state turned into a land-scarce one. Besides, the two great earthquakes of 1897 and 1950 had cataclysmic effects on the topography of the north-eastern region, especially Assam. The 1950 earthquake resulted in an alarming rise of the Brahmaputra River bed, which further aggravated the situation of flood and erosion, leading to land alienation among the indigenous peasantry. The post-1950 period witnessed large-scale migration of Upper Assam peasantry to the existing forest lands, grazing reserves, etc. in search of agricultural land, as the problem of landlessness got accentuated with various development projects (including the oil fields), military complexes, etc. coming up in Upper Assam. On the other hand, in Lower and Central Assam, besides the hazards of flood and erosion, the population of immigrant peasants has grown exponentially, creating a serious land crisis among the local peasantry (Sharma & Sarma, 2014, p. 53).

Further, simultaneous to its independence, as is well known, the partition of the Indian subcontinent considerably severed the road, water and railway connectivity that the north-eastern region had with other parts of India, and the region became landlocked. The narrow corridor through Siliguri in Northern Bengal, as mentioned earlier, remained the only physical connection of the region with the rest of India. Commenting on this, B. G. Verghese writes, '(I)f imperial politics distanced the North East from its trans-border neighbourhood further east, partition in 1947 all but physically separated the NE from the Indian heartland'(Verghese, 2004 [1996], p. 2). Besides, the other historical networks were also closed down, as the sensitivity of the region as a security frontier gained overarching importance. This had a stifling effect on the economy of the region.

---

[11] For details on the case of Sikkim, see Vandenhelsken (2009/2010, pp. 161–194).

PROBLEMATIZING THE 'NORTH-EAST'

For a section of observers of NE India, the nature of the problems in the region is inherent in its very nomenclature. Once the region had been attached to the British colonial India, it, for the first time, became a part and a frontier of India and lost its erstwhile geopolitical centrality. For example, Alexander Mackenzie used the term 'Northeast Frontier' to refer to the region in the title of his book in 1884 (Mackenzie, 2012). During the colonial period, the Assam province (consisting of the present-day north-eastern region, except Manipur, Tripura and Sikkim) was referred to as the 'Northeastern Frontier of Bengal'. In 1914, some areas of the present-day Arunachal Pradesh were carved out from the then Darrang and Lakhimpur districts of colonial Assam to form the North-East Frontier Tract (NEFT). After the independence of India in 1947, NEFT became part of Assam. In 1951, NEFT was reorganized into the North-East Frontier Agency (NEFA).

It is to be noted that at the time of India's independence, the nomenclature of 'Northeast' referred to undivided Assam and the princely states of Manipur and Tripura. Colonial Assam, however, went through a process of reorganization during 1963–1972, resulting in the formation of the new states of Nagaland, Mizoram and Meghalaya out of the erstwhile hill districts. Erstwhile NEFA was converted into a Union Territory with the new nomenclature of Arunachal Pradesh. However, the term 'Northeast' got a new lease of life with the constitution of the North Eastern Council (NEC) in 1972 with the declared objective of 'securing the balanced development' of the region.[12]

It is pointed out by observers that such endeavours with regard to the development of the region are informed by an understanding of the region as a homogenous entity. Mrinal Miri points out that to a vast majority of Indians from outside the NE, the latter evokes the image of a distant region that is more or less homogeneous in terms of culture, race and geography, grows tea, is infested with dense forests and is overwhelmingly dominated by 'primitive' tribes. He explains that this is an outcome of the dominant Indian tendency to understand

---

[12] NEC Act 1971.

the cultural scene in India by using the two supposedly dichotomous notions of 'mainstream' and 'marginality'. Miri argues that these 'concepts are natural allies of the view that if India is a nation, then it must be unicultural. And since India is a nation, then in some, as yet, invisible, but profound sense, it must also be unicultural' (Miri, 2005).

Contesting such an understanding, Udayan Misra calls India's NE 'an illusive construct' (Misra, 2000, p. 1). He argues that 'there is no denying the geographical reality' of the region and that the region's different states 'share a host of common problems ranging from communication bottlenecks to drug-trafficking, illegal infiltration and insurgency' (Misra, 2000, p. 1). However, there exist many other differences and idiosyncrasies among the various ethnic groups of the region which can hardly be included in one rubric. The similarities that exist between different states of the region should not overshadow their different stages of sociocultural and politico-economic development (Misra, 2000, p. 2). Misra further observes,

> The use of (this) illusive construct ... has not only led to discriminations in matters of financial allocation to resource rich and larger states like Assam, but more importantly, to serious administrative mishandling by the Centre of the complexities of the region. The tendency of the Indian State to treat this extremely diverse region as one unit has resulted in the growth of totally incomplete and often misconceived notions about the different states that make up the north-eastern part of the country. Such monolithic conceptions about a region, which stands out for its diversity of cultures and civilisations, would only help to nourish the biases and prejudices which have marked the Indian State's approach towards Assam and her neighbours since independence. (Misra, 2000, p. 3)

However, it does not seem that the Indian state is unaware of the ethnic and geographical diversity of the region. Evidently, this cognizance was behind the reorganization of the region during 1963–1972 despite the recommendation of the States Reorganisation Commission in 1955 to the contrary.[13] Yet, the 'monolithic conceptions' informing

---

[13] The report of the commission says, 'the hill districts, therefore, should continue to form part of Assam and no major changes should be made in their present

the state policies towards the region betray the dichotomous nature of state intervention in the region. This seems to have stemmed from the exigencies of the Indian nation state in the region that is treated as a security frontier.

SHIFTING SECURITY PARADIGM?

While the region has been a security frontier right since colonial rule, there seems to be a critical difference between the approaches of the colonial state and that of the Indian state towards the region. It is to be noted that the British had no necessity of nation (or state)-building in the region, which is why it could allow large tracts of the region to remain outside its direct administrative control as 'Excluded' or 'Un-administered' areas. However, despite the security-centric approach that the Indian state adopts toward the region, it being a nation state necessitates that it, unlike the colonial state, expands to every part of the region either by creating physical infrastructure or by pushing its political or cultural symbols, often at the expense of autonomy of the tribal communities. It is not that the Indian state has not made efforts to generate consensus for its role. Sometimes it has achieved some success, and sometimes it has failed miserably. Interestingly, while Baruah describes the expansion of the Indian state's presence in the region as a drive for 'nationalising space' (Baruah, 2005b, p. 53), Guyot-Réchard describes this process as an attempt at state-making rather than nation-building. According to her, the developmentalist policies of the Indian state in the region have often undermined the possibilities for nation-building (Guyot-Réchard, 2013, pp. 22–37).

In the post-Independence period, it is pointed out, the creation of (east) Pakistan (later Bangladesh) and then the Indo–China war of 1962 reinforced the extant security paradigm (Sharma, 2018, pp. 318). However, some observers of the region argue that since the 1980s, there has been some shift in the Indian state's approach towards the region from a 'security paradigm' to a 'development paradigm' which

constitutional pattern', p. 188.

is testified by a considerably increased amount of government expenditure in the infrastructure sector in the region (Ramesh, 2005, cited in Sharma, 2018, p. 318).

Here, some discussion on the establishment of the NEC and the role envisaged for it should provide a clearer perspective on the security-centric approach towards development in the region. It was indicated earlier that once the balkanization of the region (colonial Assam) was accomplished, the planning and development of the region was sought to be brought under a new entity, that is, the NEC. Although the latter was created as an advisory body, its mandate in formulating a regional plan is clear. Further, it wields significant influence in the respective state plans, especially those of the smaller states. Interestingly, while the NEC understandably was created to ensure all-round development of the region, till the early 2000s, it remained an agency of the Home Ministry of the Government of India, a ministry responsible for the law and order situation in the country.

The NEC Act was amended by the Parliament in 2002, which clearly enjoined the NEC to act as a 'regional planning body'. The council was subsequently brought under the Ministry of Development of North Eastern Region, Government of India, which was established in September 2001. However, in 2018, the council was again brought under the union Home Ministry,[14] clearly testifying to the dominance of the security perspective in matters of the development in the region. Illustrating this, Baruah writes how many of the governors in the region in the last couple of decades have been part of the country's security establishment (Baruah, 2001).

While earlier the Government of India was somewhat indifferent to making heavy investments in the NE, since the turn of the 2000s, it has adopted a policy of making heavy investments in infrastructure development in the region. This seems to have been influenced by several factors, including the growing recognition of the Indian state that it needs to assert its presence in the region, especially in Arunachal

---

[14] https://www.business-standard.com/article/current-affairs/north-eastern-council-to-come-under-direct-control-of-home-ministry-118061301003_1.html

Pradesh, which is claimed by China as its territory. The Indian state, as mentioned earlier, has already been able to make

> some penetration in Arunachal Pradesh (and other tribal-dominated parts of the region) in the political domain through various political institutions and agencies and in the cultural domain through expansion of education, Hinduism and Hindi… The recent big push for building infrastructure such as roads, bridges and hydel projects in the region is the manifestation of the Indian state's new developmentalism which seems to have been deeply informed by security concerns. (Sharma, 2018, p. 319)

It may be mentioned that one strong logic that the government uses to promote hydel projects on the perennial rivers in Arunachal Pradesh is what is called the 'first users' right' *vis-à-vis* China. It is argued that 'by building dams on the transnational rivers in Arunachal Pradesh before China does it in Tibet, India can legally deter China from building any major projects on the upstream of these rivers which might affect India's use of its water in future' (Sharma, 2018, p. 329). However, it is a flawed argument (Sharma, 2018, p. 329).

DIVERSITY AND DEVELOPMENT

The development agenda of the Indian state in the region, especially in the hills, hardly seems to have taken cognizance of the socio-economic, environmental and demographic specificities of the tribal communities living in these areas. The declared policy of the Nehruvian state that the tribal 'people should develop along the lines of their own genius'[15] has long been abandoned, with disastrous outcomes. The rapid transformation in the tribal societies of the region through the introduction of the cash economy, expansion of trade and commerce and various development activities has witnessed an array of damaging consequences.

---

[15] Jawaharlal Nehru's view on the nature of tribal development is enshrined in his 'Tribal Panchsheel' enunciated in his 'Foreword' to Verrier Elwin's *A Philosophy for NEFA* (1949).

In this context, it may be noted that one apparently strong logic put forth for building large dams in Arunachal Pradesh has been that because of the low density of population in the state, there will be a relatively 'small displacement' of people. However, if one considers other parameters of this sparsely populated landscape, this logic of 'small displacement' appears untenable. For example, *jhum* cultivation practiced by the tribal communities in the state covers a large tract of land, and usurpation of such land for dam-building and other allied activities will mount pressure on available land for *jhumming* and other livelihood practices. This will pose a serious threat to not only the livelihoods and food security of the *jhum*-dependent communities but also to the ecosystem as a whole. Further, the population of most of the tribes in the state is very small. For example, the total population of the Idu Mishmi tribe today would be barely around 10,000,[16] and at least 17 large hydel projects have been planned in their habitat, the Dibang Valley. As per the above argument of minimum displacement, there would be barely any social impact even if the entire Idu Mishmi tribe was displaced (Vagholikar & Das, 2010, p. 7). Further, the various development projects in Arunachal Pradesh have attracted large-scale influx of migrant labourers. These being long-term projects, the migrant labourers are likely to settle in the state for long periods, which poses a major threat to the existing demographic landscape in the state (Sharma, 2018, p. 324).

The region has witnessed such dam-related displacements throughout the post-Independence period. Kaptai Dam, for example, built in the Chittagong Hill Tracts of East Pakistan (now Bangladesh) in the 1960s, submerged the traditional homelands of the Hajong and Chakma communities and forced them to migrate into parts of NE India. This has led to conflicts over the years between the immigrant refugees and the smaller local communities in Arunachal Pradesh. In the 1970s, the Gumti dam in Tripura submerged large tracts of arable land in the Raima Valley and displaced the local tribal population (Bhaumik, 2003, pp. 84–89; Vagholikar & Das, 2010, p. 1). Projects such as the Loktak hydel project

---

[16] This figure is calculated on the basis of the statement of Dr Mite Lingi, Chairman of the Idu Indigenous Peoples Forum, quoted in Vagholikar & Das, 2010, p. 7.

commissioned in the 1980s have seriously impacted the wetland ecology of the Loktak lake in Manipur. In recent times, one witnesses anti-dam protests mounting in various parts of the region, including Sikkim (Bhaumik, 2003, pp. 84–89; Vagholikar & Das, 2010, p. 1).

Further, the traditional land ownership pattern in the tribal societies of the region has been undergoing a rapid transformation in the last couple of decades. Various development projects, urbanization and the expansion of cash crop plantation are contributing to this phenomenon, leading to the increasing privatization and commercialization of tribal community land. While the state has been the main perpetrator of this process, (Bhaumik, 2003, pp. 84–89; Sharma, 2001; Vagholikar & Das, 2010, p. 1) the emerging tribal elites, including politicians, bureaucrats, contractors, businessmen, etc., are also engaged in large-scale usurpation of the community land for various purposes, especially for cash crop plantations (Sharma & Borgohain, 2019, p. 17). As a result, in every tribal state in the region, one witnesses the accumulation of a large acreage of clan or community land in the hands of a few tribal elites, which is not permissible under the tribal customary law. The ordinary members of the community are becoming wage or even bonded labourers in these plantations. Elaborating on this in the context of the Khasi society of Meghalaya, Patricia Mukhim argues how the Khasi village chiefs, in collaboration with other members of the village councils, are involved in the surreptitious conversion of a large amount of community land (Mukhim, 2009 cited in Sharma & Borgohain, 2019, p. 18). This is true for most other tribal societies in the region, which threatens to destroy the very social foundation of these societies.

It needs to be noted here that the state and its various agencies are the main perpetrators in accentuating this crisis. Simultaneous to this, they are also engaged in a concerted campaign against *jhum* and have been in favour of cash crop cultivation for some time now. Although the government's argument has been that *jhum* is environmentally unsustainable, this campaign is aimed mainly at promoting individual ownership rights in the traditional tribal community land (Choudhury, 2012 cited in Sharma & Borgohain, 2019, p. 18). It is also interesting to note that even public sector financial institutions, including banks, offer loan to tribal entrepreneurs who are engaged in cash crop cultivation against mortgage of the community land. If such entrepreneurs fail to return the loan, the land is taken over by the bank. This is totally at variance with the constitutional mandate of protecting tribal land (Sharma & Borgohain, 2019, p. 18).

There is yet another process of land alienation among the tribal communities. In such cases, although the community land formally remains with the community, in practice, the control of such land has been transferred to non-tribal people. Sanjib Baruah makes a distinction between *de facto* and *de jure* property rights of such land (Baruah, 2005b, p. 194). Although there is no formal transfer of tribal land to non-tribal people, the cases of non-tribals using tribal land for agriculture or other purposes abound. This has happened extensively in the hills and in the tribal belts[17] in the plains of Assam and has been a major factor in some of the recent ethnic conflicts (Sharma, 2016, pp. 103–104). The recent land settlement act in Arunachal Pradesh, which seeks to enable the indigenous tribesmen of the state to lease out land to outsiders for up to 66 years, poses to accentuate the process of tribal land alienation in the sensitive hill state (Sharma & Borgohain, 2019).

There is no gainsaying that the ethnic diversity in the NE calls for such policies of social development which are sensitive to the specific socio-economic character of the communities and the geographies which they inhabit. However, since the colonial period, the policies formulated for the region have been mostly at variance with these specificities. In fact, the policies of the post-Independence Indian state have only perpetuated such policies.

While the consequences of the various development policies on the indigenous communities in the region since the colonial period have already been highlighted, the discussion cannot be complete without paying attention to the two immigrant communities of Assam which are considered to be the most marginalized, even though their specific roles in augmenting the colonial coffers are unparalleled. The first is the

---

[17] Tribal belts and blocks are certain areas in the plains of Assam which were created for the protection of the land rights of the tribal people. For details, Sharma (2001, pp. 4793–4794).

East-Bengal–origin Muslim peasantry, which has posed serious challenges to the indigenous communities in terms of access to resources on account of their sheer number and the pressure on land and forest resources that the community has created. This has found manifestation in several conflicts in recent times, especially in the tribal belts of Assam, between the immigrant Muslim peasantry, who are engaged in commercial agriculture, and the indigenous, especially the tribal, peasantry, engaged in subsistence agriculture. It is now a normal practice for the indigenous landowner, tribal or non-tribal, to lease out land to the immigrant Muslim peasantry, out of either compulsion or expediency, and eventually lose possession of his/her land (Sharma, 2016, p. 103). Such loss of land, however, has become a cause of resentment and conflict in recent times.

However, as indicated, the immigrant Muslim community is also one of the most backward in terms of various indices of social development. Although the community enjoys a strong political presence, it is characterized by various ills, such as illiteracy, poverty, high population growth, child marriage, polygyny, superstition, high maternal and infant mortality rates, and so on. They are also ghettoized for several reasons and often remain under the control of religious leaders (mullahs) and the local landed gentry class (*matbars*). A large section of them inhabit the riverine areas (known as *chars* and *chaparis*) which experience flood and erosion every year, resulting in their displacement. All these pose considerable challenges in bringing about social development among this community. While, of late, a section of the educated youth has emerged from among them and has begun newly articulating the importance of education and health facilities to bring about the desired social development among the community, the conservative forces still hold sway.

Another extremely backward community with a large population in Assam is the Adivasi[18] community. As mentioned earlier, their forefathers were brought to Assam from Central and Eastern India by the colonial regime to work in the tea plantations as indentured labour. They lived in sub-human conditions then, and still a large section of

---

[18] They are also known as the tea tribe.

them continues to be in that state of being. This is despite the Plantation Labour Act of 1951, which directs the tea garden management and the government to take various measures for the welfare of the tea garden workers. However, the plantation management, rather than paying due attention to the implementation of the welfare provisions of the act, has been involved in brazen violation of its provisions.[19] This has happened despite the fact that a significant number of political leaders in Assam hail from the community. As a result, most of the socio-economic malaises that characterize the immigrant Muslim community are also found among them. Further, the maladies of witch-hunting and alcoholism are also very prominently present among this community. On account of the prevailing illiteracy, an overwhelming section of the community has still been engaged in the tea plantations as permanent or temporary labourers.

It is striking that these two communities, which, unlike others, were either directly brought (the Adivasi community) or strongly prodded to come (the East Bengali Muslims) to Assam by the colonial regime, have been the 'beasts of burden' that have upheld its edifice of extractive capitalism. The underdevelopment of these two communities has a considerable bearing on the social development scenario of Assam, if not the entire region.

CONTESTING DEVELOPMENTALISM

The flawed development policy in the region has become all the more evident if one takes into account the considerable outmigration of the youth from all the states in pursuit of higher education and employment over the years. More importantly, in recent decades, the region has witnessed massive outmigration of the semi-literate rural youths to

---

[19] These are highlighted by many studies. Recently, a report titled 'Decent Work for Tea Plantation Workers in Assam: Constraints, Challenges and Prospects', funded by Oxfam Germany, brought out the poor conditions of work of the tea labourers: https://www.thehindu.com/news/national/assam-tea-estates-violating-labour-laws/article29649803.ece; https://economictimes.indiatimes.com/news/economy/agriculture/assam-tea-workers-get-only-7-per-cent-of-price-says-report/articleshow/71525197.cms; also, see Mishra et al. (2012).

the various metropolises and other developed states of India in search of jobs, mostly as casual workers in the informal sector, including in private security firms, cash crop plantations, hotels and restaurants, construction sites, etc (McDuie-Ra, 2012; Muktiar & Sharma, 2019). This outmigration has considerably transformed the rural landscape of the region, and the urban landscape as well in the case of some hill states. The remittances the out-migrants send to their homes have indeed been useful not only in meeting the household expenses but also in allowing a section of the rural households to invest some remittances in cash crop, especially small tea plantations. However, rural outmigration has left the agricultural fields fallow and the villages bereft of the youth, which have their own socio-economic implications. It is important to note here that the out-migrants hardly enjoy any job security, and many return to their villages with broken health or diseased after a few years (Muktiar & Sharma, 2019).

It may be mentioned that a significant segment of the out-migrants are from communities which are displaced from their traditional habitats on account of various development projects (Sharma, 2001). In recent times, such development projects, including the hydel projects, in the upper riparian areas of the Brahmaputra Valley, especially the hills of Arunachal Pradesh and Bhutan, have resulted in rapid deforestation, making the hills (made of highly fragile soil) dangerously exposed to landslides and soil erosion. While this has eventuated in multiple problems in the hills, the deposition of such soil carried by various rivers and streams has rendered vast swathes of crop land and wetland in the lower riparian areas of Assam unproductive, throwing the traditional livelihood of millions of people, tribal and non-tribal, out of gear. In the absence of a viable alternative livelihood, the rural youth have migrated to other, more prosperous Indian states in the last two decades, a totally new trend in Assam (Muktiar & Sharma, 2019).

In fact, the destruction caused by the hydel projects in the upstream is one important reason why people have been up in arms against their construction in the region in recent times. However, the government does not seem to have acknowledged the apprehension of the people. Instead, it has continued to chant the mantra of development, emphasizing that the hydel projects in the region will transform it into 'India's future powerhouse'. Yet, this developmentalist logic of the government has not convinced the people of the region. Indeed, the importance of development in the region can hardly be undermined. However, it is also required that such a vision of development is in tune with the social, cultural, economic and physical specificities of the region (Sharma, 2018, p. 331).

It may be noted here that the Government of India adopted its 'Look East' policy in the early 1990s, emphasizing greater engagement with the countries of Southeast Asia. Subsequently, in 2014, the policy was rechristened as 'Act East' policy. The NE, on account of its geographical proximity, as well as its close historical ties with Southeast Asia, was touted to take the centre stage in this new engagement.[20] There have been animated public debates and discussions in the region about the possibilities and pitfalls of the policy, whether it will transform the region into a hub of economic activities or a mere corridor for the flow of resources. Regardless of whether the arguments are for or against the policy, not much progress has been achieved till now in opening up the eastern border for trade and commerce with the Southeast Asian countries. However, the greater question remains: are the communities in the region ready to participate in the new economy that is envisaged for them, or are there any initiatives being undertaken by the government for empowering them to productively participate in it? The answer to this will determine the character of social development in the region and the direction it is going to take in the future.

REFERENCES

Barpujari, H. K. (1963). *Assam in the days of company, 1826–1858*. Lawyer's Book Stall.

Barpujari, H. K. (1993). *The comprehensive history of Assam* (p. 113). Publication Board Assam.

Baruah, S. (2001). Generals as governors: The parallel political systems in Northeast India. *Himal South Asian, 14*(6), 1–20.

---

[20] https://timesofindia.indiatimes.com/india/northeast-india-will-be-gateway-to-southeast-asia-says-pm-modi/articleshow/71869280.cms

Baruah, S. (2005a). *The problem*. Seminar, no. 550. https://www.india-seminar.com/2005/550/550%20problem.html

Baruah, S. (2005b). *Durable disorder: Understanding the politics of northeast India*. Oxford University Press.

Baruah, S. (2008). Territoriality, indigeneity and rights in the North-east India. *Economic and Political Weekly, 43*(12), 15–19.

Bhaumik, S. (2003). Tripura's Gumti dam must go. *Ecologist Asia, 11*(1), 84–89.

Bhaumik, S. (2005). India's northeast: Nobody's people in no man's land. In P. Banerjee, S. Basu Ray Chaudhury, & S. Das (Eds.), *Internal displacement in South Asia* (pp. 144–174). SAGE Publications.

Bhuyan, S. K. (1949). *Anglo-Assamese relations, 1771–1826: A history of the relations of Assam with the East India Company from 1771 to 1826, based on original English and Assamese sources*. Department of Historical and Antiquarian Studies in Assam.

Butler, J. (1855). *Travels and adventures in the province of Assam*. Smith, Elder, and Co.

Census of India. (2011). https://censusindia.gov.in/Tables_Published/D-Series/Tables_on_Migration_Census_of_India_2001.aspx/D-Series_link/D3_India.pdf

Choudhury, D. (2012). Why do Jhumias jhum? Managing changes in shifting cultivation areas in the uplands of northeastern India. In S. Krishna (Ed.), *Agriculture and a changing environment in Northeast India* (pp. 78–100). Routledge.

Debburma, S. (2009). Refugee rehabilitation and land Alienation Tripura. In W. Fernandes & S. Barbora (Eds.), *Land, people and politics: Contest over tribal land in Northeast India* (pp. 113–127). North Eastern Social Research Centre and International Workgroup for Indigenous Affairs.

Elwin, V. (1949). *A philosophy for NEFA*. Directorate of Research, Government of Arunachal Pradesh.

Fernandes, W. (2004). Limits of law and order: Approach to the North-East. *Economic and Political Weekly, 39*(42), 4909–4611.

Guha, A. (1977). 2006 *Planter Raj to Swaraj: Freedom struggle and electoral politics in Assam, 1826–1947*. Tulika Books.

Guha, A. (1991). *Medieval and early colonial Assam: Society, polity, economy*. Published for Centre for Studies in Social Sciences by K.P. Bagchi & Co.

Guyot-Réchard, B. (2013). Nation-building or state-making? India's North-East frontier and the ambiguities of Nehruvian developmentalism, 1950–1959. *Contemporary South Asia, 21*(1), 22–37.

Kikon, D. (2005). Engaging naga nationalism: Can democracy function in militerized societies? *Economic and Political Weekly, 40*(26), 2833–2837.

Ludden, D. (2003). *Where is Assam? Using geographical history to locate current social realities*. Centre for Northeast India, South and Southeast Asia Studies.

Mackenzie, A. (2012). *History of the relations of the government with the hill tribes of the North-East frontier of Bengal*. Cambridge University Press.

McDuie-Ra, D. (2012). *Northeast migrants in Delhi: Race, refuge and retail*. Amsterdam University Press.

Midgley, J. (2013). *Social development: Theory and practice.* SAGE Publications.

Miri, M. (2005). *Community, culture, nation.* Seminar No. 550. https://www.india-seminar.com/2005/550/550%20mrinal%20miri.htm

Mishra, D., Upadhyay, V., & Sarma, A. (2012). *Unfolding crisis in Assam's tea plantations: Employment and occupational mobility.* Routledge.

Misra, T. (1980). Assam: A colonial hinterland. *Economic and Political Weekly, 15*(32), 1357–1364.

Misra, U. (2000). *The periphery strikes back: Challenges to the nation-state in Assam and Nagaland.* Indian Institute of Advanced Study.

Mukhim, P. (2009). Land Ownership among the Khasis of Meghalaya: A Gender Perspective. In W. Fernandes and S. Barbora (Eds.), *Land, People and politics: Contest over tribal land in Northeast India* (pp. 38–52). North Eastern Social Research Centre and International Work Group for Indigenous Affairs.

Muktiar, P., & Sharma, C. K. (2019). In search of a better future: Nepali rural out-migration from Assam. *Sociological Bulletin, 68*(3), 307–324.

Nongbri, T. (2001). Timber ban in North-east India: Effects on livelihood and gender. *Economic and Political Weekly, 36*(21), 1893–1900.

North Eastern Council Secretariat (2015). *Basic statistics of North Eastern region 2015.* http://necouncil.gov.in/sites/default/files/uploadfiles/BasicStatistic2015-min.pdf

Omer, S. (1979). Social development. *International Social Work, 22*(3), 11–26.

Paiva, J. (1977). A conception of social development. *Social Service Review, 51*(2), 327–336.

Reid, R. (1944). The excluded areas of Assam. *The Geographical Journal, 103*(½), 18–29.

Prabhakar, M. S. (2005). In the name of tribal identities. *Frontline, 22*(24). https://frontline.thehindu.com/other/article30207429.ece

Ramesh, J. (2005). *Northeast India in a new Asia.* Seminar No. 550, pp. 17–21. https://www.india-seminar.com/2005/550/550%20jairam%20ramesh.htm

Sharma, C. K. (1995). Poverty and inequality: The case of Assam. *Economic and Political Weekly, 30*(7&8), 403–404.

Sharma, C. K. (2001). Tribal land alienation in Assam: Government's role. *Economic and Political Weekly, 36*(52), 4791–4795.

Sharma, C. K. (2011). Religion and social change: Neo-vaishnavism vis-à-vis the tribal groups in the Brahmaputra valley. In D. Nath (Ed.), *Religion and society in North East India* (pp. 111–142). DVS Publishers.

Sharma, C. K. (2012a). The immigration issue in Assam and conflicts around it. *The Asian Ethnicity, 13*(3), 287–309.

Sharma, C. K. (2012b). The state and the ethnicisation of space in Northeast India. In N. G. Mahanta & D. Gogoi (Eds.), *Shifting terrain: Conflict dynamics in North East India* (pp. 193–225). DVS Publishers.

Sharma, C. K. (2016). Immigration, indigeneity and identity: The Bangladeshi immigration tangle in Assam. In D. Gogoi (Ed.), *Unheeded hinterland: Identity and sovereignty in Northeast India* (pp. 89–113). Routledge.

Sharma, C. K. (2017). *Political economy of the conflicts along the Assam-Arunachal Pradesh foothill border.* Action Aid Association.

Sharma, C. K. (2018). Dams, 'development' and popular resistance in Northeast India. *Sociological Bulletin, 67*(3), 317–333.

Sharma, C. K., & Borgohain, B. (2019). The new land settlement act in Arunachal Pradesh: Road to empowerment or dispossession? *Economic and Political Weekly, 54*(23), 17–20.

Sharma, C. K., & Sarma, I. (2014). Issues of conservation and livelihood in a forest village of Assam. *International Journal of Rural Management, 10*(1), 47–68.

Sundar, N. (2011). Interning insurgent populations: The buried histories of Indian democracy. *Economic and Political Weekly, 46*(6), 47–57.

Vagholikar, N., & Das, P. J. (2010). *Damming northeast India.* Kalpavriksh, Aaranyak and Action Aid India.

Vandenhelsken, M. (2009/2010). Reification of ethnicity in Sikkim: 'Tribalism' in progress. *Bulletin of Tibetology, 45*(2) & 46(1), 161–194.

Verghese, B. G. (1996). *2004 India's northeast resurgent: Ethnicity, insurgency, governance, development.* Konark Publishers.

Chapter 3

Demographic Changes in North-east India

Inter-temporal Variations in Population Growth and Composition

**Bimal Kumar Kar and
Suli Vohana Ayemi**

INTRODUCTION

The north-eastern region of India comprising the states of Arunachal Pradesh, Assam, Manipur, Meghalaya, Mizoram, Nagaland and Tripura, characterized by a long history of human settlement, peopling, ethnic, religious and linguistic diversities and varied sociocultural practices, has witnessed a higher growth rate in population than the national average growth rate between 1901 and 2011. In 1901, the total population of the North-east (NE) region was 4.27 million and increased to 10.26 million in 1951 and then to 45.16 million in 2011. In terms of average annual exponential growth rate, it was 1.77 per cent during 1901–1951 and 2.50 per cent during 1951–2011 against the corresponding all-India average growth rates of 0.83 per cent and 2.04 per cent, respectively. The share of the NE region's population in India's total population increased from 1.79 per cent in 1901 to 2.84 per cent in 1951 and further to 3.73 per cent in 2011. The high growth rate of population in the region has been due to migration from within and outside India, as the birth and death rates of the NE have been similar to those at the all-India level (Kar, 2002; Sharma & Kar, 1997). Such a high growth in population has a number of demographic implications, including the changes in the ethno-religious and linguistic composition of the population in the region (Kar, 1995, 2007). This chapter attempts to analyse the pattern of population growth in different communities and across states and its implications, demographic and otherwise.

The NE region (seven states) has a total geographical area of 255,083 km², that is, 7.76 per cent of the total area of the country, with a population of 45,161,611, as per the 2011 census, accounting for 3.71 per cent of the country's total population (Figure 3.1). The NE region is surrounded from almost all sides, except the Assam–Bengal corridor of around 40 km width in the west, by foreign countries, namely Bhutan, China, Myanmar and Bangladesh. It thus occupies a strategic geopolitical position. Around three-fourths of the region's land area is covered by hilly and mountainous rugged terrains. The plain areas are largely confined to the states of Assam, Manipur and Tripura. The transport and communication system is poor, especially

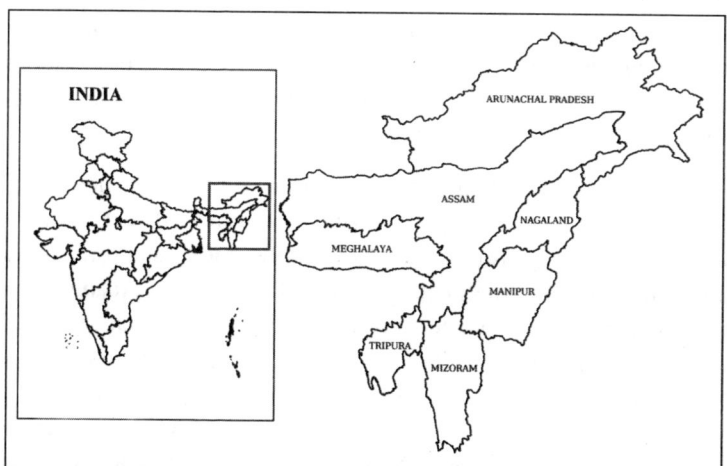

Figure 3.1 *Map of North-east India (Seven Sisters)*

Source: The authors.

Disclaimer: This figure has been redrawn and is not to scale. It does not represent any authentic national or international boundaries and is used for illustrative purposes only.

in the hilly areas. There is a lack of industrial development. Around two-thirds of the region's population are dependent on agriculture and allied activities. Hindus constitute 53.97 per cent of the total population of the NE region, Muslims 25.37 per cent and Christians 17.34 per cent. Scheduled Tribes (STs), on their part, account for 27.62 per cent. Assamese (33.68%) and Bengalis (26.54%) are the two dominant linguistic groups. Less than one-fifth (18.27%) of the total population of the region live in the urban areas.

The study is primarily based on Census of India data. It also uses special reports of B. C. Allen (1901), C. S. Mullan (1931) and R. P. Vaghaiwalla (1951) published by the Census of India. The data so gathered have been analysed through the use of statistical techniques, mainly ratios/percentages, average annual exponential/decennial growth rates, measures of central tendency and dispersion, exponential trend and correlation. Spatial variation in population growth rate and other associated characteristics has been analysed at the state level. For compatibility of the state-level temporal analysis of the population for both pre-Independence and post-Independence periods, unless otherwise mentioned, the adjusted population data as per the present administrative boundaries of the respective states have been considered. The findings have been supplemented through some field observations. The next part of this chapter shows trends in population growth and other associated characteristics of population.

Insofar as the peopling and composition of the population of the NE region are concerned, the region has witnessed several waves and streams of migration from all directions since prehistoric times. Ethno-linguistically, the people of the NE region are broadly composed of three groups: (a) Austro-Asiatic, (b) Tibeto-Chinese and (c) Indo-Aryan (Taher, 1997, 2012). The Austro-Asiatic group is formed by the Mon-Khmer-speaking Khasis and Pnars of Meghalaya and the Mundari-speaking Mundas, Hos, Santals, Oraons, Gonds, etc. constituting the tea tribes of Assam. Similarly, the Tibeto-Chinese group is broadly composed of Tibeto-Burmans comprising tribes like Monpa, Sherdukpen, Mising, Deori, Bodo, Garo, Naga tribes such as Angami, Ao, Lotha, Sumi, etc., Kuki-Chin comprising Lushai, Kuki, Vaishnavite Meitei, Reang, Chakma, etc., and Siamese-Chinese consisting of

Ahom, Khamti, Khamyang, Aiton, Phake, Turung, etc. The Indo-Aryan group, composed mostly of all the Hindus and Muslims, consists of non-tribal Assamese-, Bengali-, Hindi- and Nepali-speaking people. As per Census of India (2011b), the region is largely inhabited by religious groups like Hindus (53.97%), Muslims (25.37%) and Christians (17.34%), ethnic groups like STs (27.62%) and linguistic groups like Assamese (33.68%) and Bengalis (26.54%). Merely 18.27 per cent of the region's population lives in the urban areas. However, in view of the prevailing diversity in physical character and population composition, the north-eastern region may well be termed as a miniature India.

RESULTS AND DISCUSSIONS

Trend of Population Growth and Changing Population Composition

The north-eastern region of India has witnessed a high growth rate of population between 1901 and 2011. During the last 110 years (1901–2011), the region's total population increased from 4.27 million to 45.16 million (Table 3.1), a 10.6-fold increase compared to the 5.1-fold increase in the all-India population during the same period. The population growth rate of the region has always been higher than that of the all-India average throughout the period. However, it was not uniform throughout the century. The average annual growth rate of the region was 1.77 per cent mainly during the pre-Independence period (1901–1951) and 2.50 per cent during the post-Independence period (1951–2011). Of course, in recent times, especially between 2001 and 2011, as in other parts of the country, the growth rate of the population declined to 1.66 per cent against the all-India average of 1.64 per cent.

During 1901–1951, the NE region's total population increased by 140 per cent, as against the all-India average of 51 per cent. The decennial variation of population growth in this region ranged between 18.4 per cent and 20.2 per cent during 1901–1951, as against between −0.3 per cent and 14.2 per cent for the country as a whole (Table 3.1). Despite the low natural growth rate, the prevalence of the almost consistently higher growth rate of population in the region during this period as compared to the national average has been associated with the

Table 3.1 Trend of Population Growth in North-east India vis-à-vis India (1901–2011)

Year	Population	Annual Growth Rate (in %)		Percentage Share of NE Population to India's Total
		India	NE India	
1901	4,271,978	–	–	1.79
1911	5,058,699	0.56	1.70	2.00
1921	6,005,043	–0.03	1.73	2.39
1931	7,172,512	1.04	1.79	2.57
1941	8,618,116	1.33	1.85	2.70
1951	10,260,371	1.25	1.76	2.84
1961	14,500,572	1.96	3.52	3.30
1971	19,582,296	2.20	3.05	3.57
1981*	24,751,604	2.20	2.37	3.62
1991	31,547,314	2.14	2.46	3.73
2001	38,316,918	1.97	1.96	3.74
2011	45,161,611	1.64	1.66	3.73

Source: Census of India (1991a, 2001a, 2011a).

Note: *Assam's population for 1981 (18,041,248) is considered as per the estimation of the Census of India.

continued migration of people from other parts of the country and the erstwhile East Bengal to settle in the agriculturally productive vacant lands. In the case of Assam, although migration had begun since the British annexation of the state in 1826, it increased since the beginning of the 20th century (Kar & Das, 2012). The main streams of migrants during this period to the then–Assam were peasants from the erstwhile East Bengal (now Bangladesh), tea garden labourers from Central India and graziers from Nepal. Assam's immense economic potential, coupled with its huge forest resources and abundance of sparsely populated, cheap and virgin fertile lands, attracted migrants from both within and outside the country. Moreover, the Assam government, during the time of the Saadulla ministry in 1943, encouraged them by distributing wastelands and de-reserving grazing areas in order to accommodate the growing influx of immigrants (Guha, 1997). As mentioned in the census reports of India, the then state of Assam recorded an influx of 882,068 immigrants in 1911 (12.5% of the state's total population) and 1,408,763 immigrants in 1931 (15.2% of the state's total population), mostly from East Bengal. Besides, as the immigrant Muslim peasants occupied the vast areas of both the Brahmaputra and Barak valleys of Assam, in order to restrict their settlement in the areas largely occupied by the Hindus, Inner Line System was implemented in the state in 1938 (Datta, 2007). The early part of the 1941–1951 decade witnessed a considerable volume of immigration into some areas of Assam from the erstwhile Burma (presently Myanmar), as an after-effect of World War II in 1942, and from East Bengal, following the Bengal famine of 1943 (Dass, 1980). Further, during India's partition in 1947, a large number of Hindus from the erstwhile East Pakistan entered the region, a large proportion of which settled in the states of Assam and Tripura.

After Independence, the population of the NE region began to grow very fast, witnessing an increase of 340 per cent, as against the country's average of 235 per cent, during the period 1951–2011. This high growth of population in the region contributed to a net increase of 34.9 million people. The decennial growth rates during the period between 1951 and 2011, however, varied between 17.9 per cent and 41.3 per cent in the region, while varying between 17.7 per cent and 24.8 per cent for India as a whole (Table 3.1). Among all the states of the country, the population growth rate in NE India has been the highest during 1951–2011. The sharp fall in death rate compared to the slow decline in birth rate and migration have contributed to a phenomenal increase in population in the entire region. The gradual elimination of severe epidemics and famines, coupled with improvement in health and medical facilities, among others, has also contributed to the decline in the death rate. On the other hand, the measures to control the birth rate could not make any significant impact until recently. A host of interrelated socio-economic factors, such as the universalization of marriage, marriage at a lower age, religious belief of child being a gift of God, illiteracy, poverty, high infant mortality, etc., have also resulted in the high birth rate. While in the country the gradual expansion of the family planning programme and the increasing female literacy have contributed to a decline in birth rate (Gosal, 1993), this has also been the case in the state of Assam, which alone constitutes around 70 per cent of the north-eastern region's total population. There has been a marginal decline in the natural growth rate of population from 2.07 per cent to 1.48 per cent during the period. One of the main reasons for the decrease in the death as well as the birth rate in the region during the period is the decline in the infant mortality rate (IMR) of Assam from 139 in 1971 to 55 in 2011. However, there exists a significant spatial variation in birth and death rates across the region (Table 3.2).

Thus, the figures of birth and death rates show that migration played an important role in the high growth rate of the population during 1951–1991 (Table 3.2). Due to immigration, the annual population growth rate in the region shot up to 3.52 per cent and 3.05 per cent, respectively, during 1951–1961 and 1961–1971 (Table 3.1). The mass migration of Hindu refugees from East Pakistan to Assam and Tripura, which was a result of the 1947 partition, got further accentuated due to the loss of Sylhet district of Assam (Dass, 1980). This trend of migration from East Pakistan continued because of recurrent communal disturbances up till the formation of Bangladesh in 1971. The prevalence of a higher growth rate among the Muslims as compared to the Hindus in Assam, particularly during 1951–1961, was indicative of their immigration from East Pakistan. Even after 1971, migration from Bangladesh, mostly of Muslims, and Nepal has been continuing unabated, though it has declined in numbers. On the other hand, migration of people from other parts of India has not been so insignificant. After Independence, people, mainly from Bihar, West Bengal, Uttar Pradesh, Rajasthan, Odisha and Punjab, migrated in large numbers to Assam and other states of the NE region, mostly to urban areas, seeking economic opportunities in trade and commerce, industries, construction works and many other occupations. The migration of population has also affected the demographic characteristics of the region. For instance, the high fertility rate among immigrant Muslims has resulted in a high rate of population growth in the region. On the other hand, migration from the NE region to other parts of the country has been insignificant

Table 3.2 *State-Level CBR, CDR and IMR in North-east India (1971 and 2011)*

State	Crude Birth Rate (per 1,000)		Crude Death Rate (per 1,000)		Infant Mortality Rate (per 1,000)		Natural Annual Growth Rate (in %)	
	1971	2011	1971	2011	1971	2011	1971	2011
1. Arunachal Pradesh	36.8	19.8	19.8	5.8	–	32	1.7	1.4
2. Assam	38.5	22.8	17.8	8.0	139	55	2.07	1.48
3. Manipur	33.3	14.4	6.9	4.1	–	11	2.64	1.03
4. Meghalaya	–	24.1	–	7.8	–	52	–	1.63
5. Mizoram	–	16.6	–	4.4	–	34	–	1.22
6. Nagaland	–	16.1	–	3.3	–	21	–	1.28
7. Tripura	35.8	14.3	15.3	5.0	–	29	2.05	0.93
India	36.9	21.8	14.9	7.1	129	44	2.2	1.47

Source: Databook (2014).

until the recent past. Recent declines in birth rate and reductions in infiltration from Bangladesh brought down the overall annual growth rate of the population in the region, particularly during 1991–2011. If the population in the region continues to grow at the rate of that in the period 2001–2011, it is likely to reach 53.23 million by 2021. As per an exponential trend analysis of the period 1951–2011, the population of the region is expected to reach 62.82 million in 2021 (Figure 3.2 and Table 3.10).

Spatial Pattern in Population Growth

An analysis of state-level data for the period 1951–2011 reveals that there exist significant spatial variations in population growth rates across the states of the NE region, depending on the nature and volume of migration and a number of sociocultural factors influencing the natural population growth. The annual growth rate of population during 1951–1961 was quite high (above 3%) in all the states of the region barring Meghalaya (2.42%) (Table 3.3). However, the situation has improved considerably since 1991, with both Assam and Tripura able to check the natural growth rate and the volume of migration. The population growth rate, however, remained high in Nagaland during 1981–1991 (4.55%), in Mizoram (4.04%) during 1971–1981 and in Arunachal Pradesh (3.19%) during 1981–1991.

The population growth rate in most states of the NE region, except Nagaland, was significantly low during 1991–2001 (Table 3.3). As a matter of fact, the annual growth rate during this period has been as low as 1.5 per cent in Tripura and 1.75 per cent in Assam, as compared to the region and country's averages of 1.96 per cent and 1.97 per cent, respectively. On the other hand, owing to the considerably higher birth rates as compared to death rates and the rapidly declining IMR, the population growth rates have remained considerably higher in most of the tribal-dominated states of the region. This is, however, more striking in the state of Nagaland (5.11%), probably due to better coverage of enumeration unlike in the past. Due to the decline in the population growth rate in both Assam and Tripura during 2001–2011, the average growth rate of the region as a whole has come down to

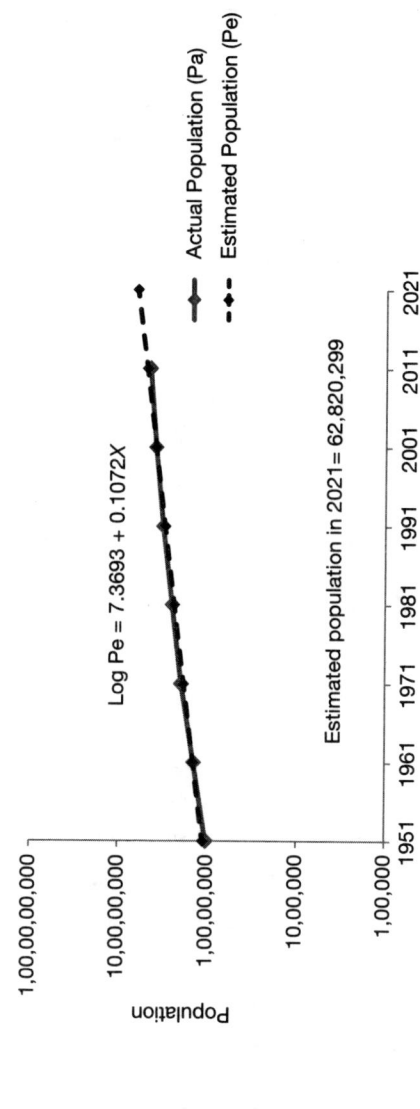

Figure 3.2 *Trend of Population Growth in North-east India (1951–2011)*

Source: Prepared by the authors based on analysis of the data from Census of India (1991a, 2001a and 2011a)

Table 3.3 Annual Growth Rates and Share of Population in the States of North-east India During 1951–2011

States	Annual Population Growth Rate (in %)						Percentage Share of Population to the Region's Total	
	1951–1961	1961–1971	1971–1981	1981–1991	1991–2001	2001–2011	1951	2011
1. Arunachal Pradesh	–	–	3.06	3.19	2.42	2.34	–	3.06
2. Assam*	3.04	3.04	2.12	2.19	1.75	1.59	78.26	69.10
3. Manipur	3.05	3.24	2.85	2.60	1.66	2.80	5.63	6.32
4. Meghalaya	2.42	2.78	2.82	2.88	2.71	2.50	5.90	6.57
5. Mizoram	3.09	2.25	4.04	3.40	2.57	2.13	1.91	2.43
6. Nagaland	5.66	3.41	4.14	4.55	5.11	-0.06	2.07	4.38
7. Tripura	5.98	3.14	2.81	2.99	1.50	1.39	6.23	8.14
NE India	**3.52**	**3.05**	**2.37**	**2.46**	**1.96**	**1.66**	**100**	**100**
India	**1.98**	**2.24**	**2.23**	**2.16**	**1.97**	**1.64**		

Source: Census of India (1991a, 2001a, 2011a).

Note: *Assam's population for 1981 (18,041,248) is considered as per the estimation of the Census of India.

1.66 per cent (Table 3.3). However, surprisingly, the state of Nagaland witnessed a negative growth rate (−0.06%) during the same period due to considerably exaggerated population enumeration during the previous 2001 census (PTI, 2011). While the share of Assam in the total population of the NE region has declined from 78.26 per cent in 1951 to 69.10 per cent in 2011, the respective shares of the other states have increased during the period. The increase has been the highest in the case of Nagaland, from 2.07 per cent in 1951 to 4.38 per cent in 2011 (Table 3.3). In any case, Assam, which constitutes about 70 per cent of the region's total population, greatly influences the overall pattern of population growth in the region.

Inter-community Variations in Population Growth

Depending on sociocultural factors and economic conditions, the growth rate of population varies from one community to another in the region. For example, during 1971–2011, the growth rate of Scheduled Caste (SC) population was 2.48 per cent and that of ST 2.65 per cent. At the all-India level, the growth rates of SC and ST populations were 2.29 per cent and 2.60 per cent, respectively, during the same period. Among the states, although the growth rate of population during 1971–2011 varied in respect of both SCs and STs, it was more striking in the case of SCs (from 2.26% in Assam to 6.98% in Mizoram). However, the growth rates among the ST population have been significantly higher than those of the SCs, both in the region and in the country. Moreover, among the states of the NE, Mizoram had the highest growth rate of the SC population, while Nagaland witnessed the highest growth rate of the ST population, during 1971–2011 (Table 3.4). It is further observed that due to the prevalence of considerably higher growth rates among the STs in most parts of the region, the proportion of the ST population increased differently during the same period in most states of the region except Arunachal Pradesh and Nagaland. Among the states of the NE, the highest increase in the proportion of STs to total population was recorded in Manipur (31.18% to 40.88%), and the highest decrease in Arunachal Pradesh (79.02% to 68.79%) (Table 3.4).

For the major religious groups, like the Hindus, Muslims, Christians and Buddhists, in the region, although there was a decline in the

Table 3.4 *Annual Growth Rates of the Scheduled Caste and Scheduled Tribe Population and the Changing Share Among Them in North-east India at the State Level (1971–2011)*

States	Scheduled Castes			Scheduled Tribes		
	Average Annual Growth Rate (1971–2011)	Proportion of SC Population out of Total Population (in %)		Average Annual Growth Rate (1971–2011)	Proportion of ST Population out of Total Population (in %)	
		1971	2011		1971	2011
1. Arunachal Pradesh	–	0.07	–	2.39	79.02	68.79
2. Assam	2.26	6.24	7.15	2.23	10.98	12.45
3. Manipur	4.55	1.53	3.41	2.88	31.18	40.88
4. Meghalaya	3.81	0.38	0.58	2.90	80.48	86.15
5. Mizoram	6.98	0.02	0.11	3.03	94.26	94.43
6. Nagaland	–	0.00	–	3.35	88.61	86.48
7. Tripura	3.10	12.39	17.83	2.41	28.95	31.76
North-east India	**2.48**	**5.75**	**6.65**	**2.65**	**18.17**	**27.62**
India	**2.29**	**14.82**	**16.63**	**2.60**	**6.82**	**8.63**

Source: Census of India (1971, 2011e).

average annual growth rate of population among all of them during 1971–1991, the growth rate was still higher among the Muslims (2.95%), Christians (4.49%) and Buddhists (4.45%) than among the Hindus (1.97%) during 1971–1991 (Table 3.5). While the growth rate among all the religious groups witnessed considerable decline during 1991–2011 compared to 1971–1991, it was as high as 2.67 per cent and 3.76 per cent among the Muslims and Christians, respectively, as compared to 1.31 per cent among the Hindus (Table 3.5). Again, among the states of the region, the annual growth rate during 1971–2011 varied between 0.88 per cent (Mizoram) and 3.46 per cent (Arunachal Pradesh) among the Hindus. For Muslims, it was 2.76 per cent in Assam and 9.06 per cent in Arunachal Pradesh, and for Christians, it was 2.83 per cent in Assam and 12.59 per cent in Arunachal Pradesh (Table 3.6). The high growth rate among the Muslims is attributed to their poverty and illiteracy, marriage at early age, continuous migration and influence of religion, including conversion. For instance, the literacy rate, as per the 2011 census, among the Muslims was as low as 62.58 per cent, as compared to 79.10 per cent among the Hindus and 77.09 per cent among the Christians. Contrarily, the prevalence of very high growth rates among the Christians in recent times in most parts of the region has been primarily associated with increasing conversion of Hindus and animists to Christianity and the slightly higher natural growth rates among the tribal Christians.

Thus, variations in population growth rates among different religious groups in the region contribute differently to the total growth of population in the region. For instance, the Hindus, who constituted 66.39 per cent of the total population in the NE region in 1971, have contributed to only 44.46 per cent of the total population increase during 1971–2011. On the other hand, the Muslims and Christians, with population shares of 19.40 per cent and 9.12 per cent in 1971, respectively, have contributed to 29.94 per cent and 23.64 per cent, respectively, of the population increase during 1971–2011. This has resulted in a marked change in the religious composition of the population in most parts of the region. Strikingly, while the growth rate of population during 1971–2011 among the Hindus was much lower in the region (1.58%) as compared to the national average (1.91%), among

Table 3.5 Population Growth Rate Among the Major Religious Groups During 1971–2011 and Percentage (Contribution of Each Group to the Total Population Increase in North-east India)

Religious Groups	Population Size		Average Annual Growth Rate (in %)			Percentage of Contribution of the Given Religion to the Total Population Increase in the Region (1971–2011)
	1971	2011	1971–1991	1991–2011	1971–2011	
1. Hindus	13,001,136 (66.39%)	24,373,682 (53.97%)	1.97	1.31	1.58	44.46
2. Muslims	3,799,092 (19.40%)	11,456,462 (25.37%)	2.95	2.67	2.80	29.94
3. Christians	1,785,820 (9.12%)	7,832,533 (17.34%)	4.49	3.76	3.76	23.64
4. Buddhists	151,449 (0.77%)	460,311 (1.02%)	4.45	0.26	2.82	1.21
5. Others	844,799 (4.31%)	1,038,623 (2.30%)	0.04	0.92	1.10	0.75
Total Population	19,582,296	45,161,611	2.41	1.96	2.11	100.00

Source: Census of India (2001d, 2011a).

the Muslims it was higher in the region (2.80%) than in the country as a whole (2.61%) (Table 3.6). The picture is also the same for the Christians and Buddhists in the region. It means that the population of Muslims, Christians and Buddhists has been increasing at higher rates in the NE region in recent times as compared to that of Hindus (Table 3.6 and Figures 3.3–3.7).

CHANGING POPULATION STRUCTURE

The variations in population growth rate and migration have also affected the demographic structure, including the age structure, and composition of scheduled and religious population groups in the region.

Age Structure

Due to the prevalence of a relatively high fertility rate, the age composition of the population in NE India remains similar to that of many less-developed countries of the world. The share of children in the total population is relatively high. Although the proportion of children's population (0–14 age group) in the region declined from 45.72 per cent to 32.88 per cent during 1971–2011, it was higher than the all-India average (Table 3.7). The scenario was somewhat encouraging in Tripura and Manipur and disappointing in Meghalaya and Arunachal Pradesh.

The prevalence of higher birth rates and lower life expectancy at birth in most parts of the NE region has kept the dependency ratio (proportion of children [0–14] and older people [60+] to adult [15–59] people) high in the region (Table 3.8). Although the dependency ratio in the region has witnessed a considerable decline from 102.8 per cent to 65.0 per cent during 1971–2011, as against the corresponding national averages of 92.3 per cent and 65.2 per cent, it was still high at 80.1 per cent in Meghalaya (Table 3.8). It is worth mentioning that while all the states of the NE region have witnessed a decline in the dependency ratio, the decline has been spectacular in Assam, Tripura and Manipur.

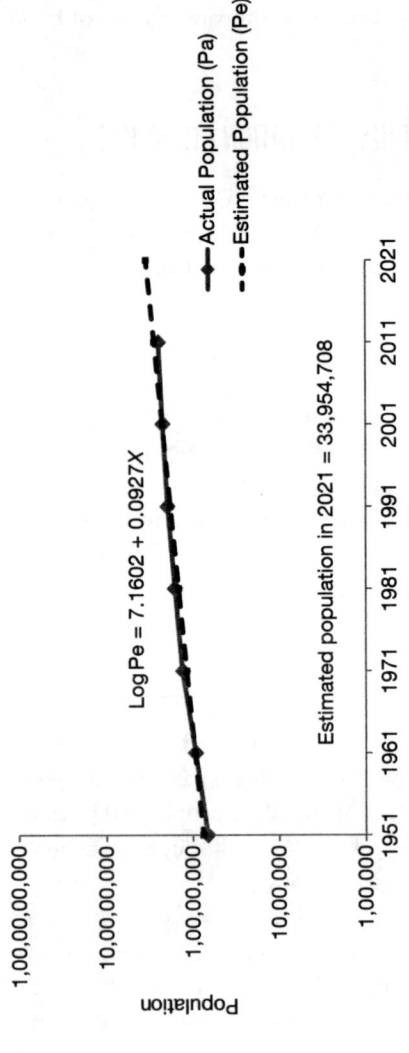

Figure 3.3 *Trend of Hindu Population Growth in North-east India (1951–2011)*

Source: Prepared by authors based on the analysis of following data: Census of India. (1991b [Religion (Table 9). Series IV, Part IV-B(ii). Assam], 2001g, 2011b).

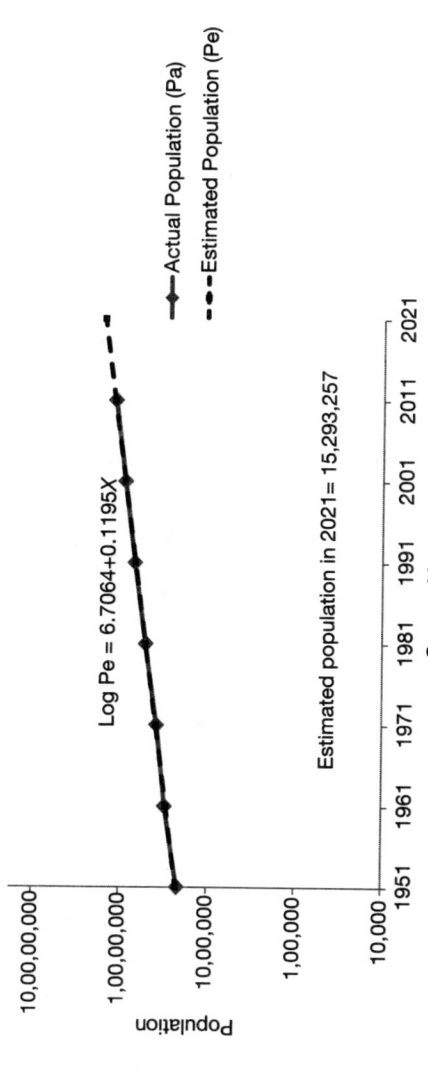

Figure 3.4 *Trend of Muslim Population Growth in North-east India (1951–2011)*

Source: Prepared by authors based on the analysis of following data: Census of India. (1991b [Religion (Table 9). Series IV, Part IV-B(ii). Assam], 2001g, 2011b).

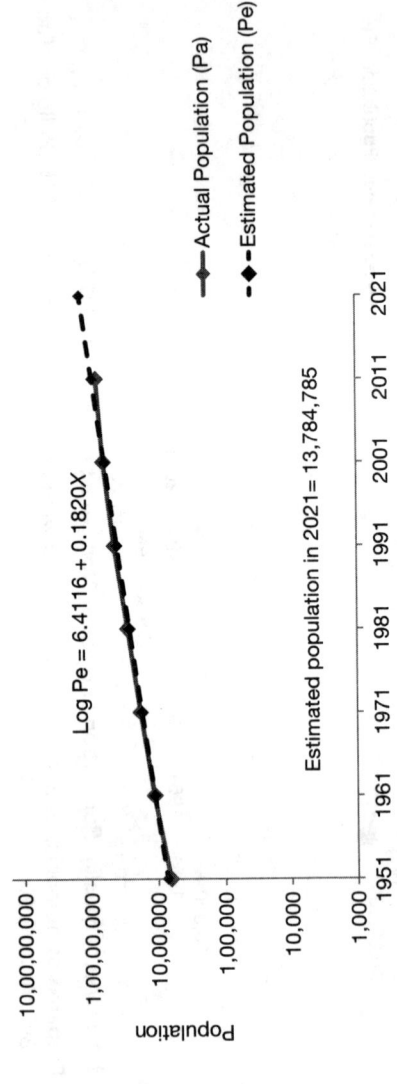

Figure 3.5 *Trend of Christian Population Growth in North-east India (1951–2011)*

Source: Prepared by authors based on the analysis of following data: Census of India. (1991b [Religion (Table 9). Series IV, Part IV-B(ii). Assam], 2001g, 2011b).

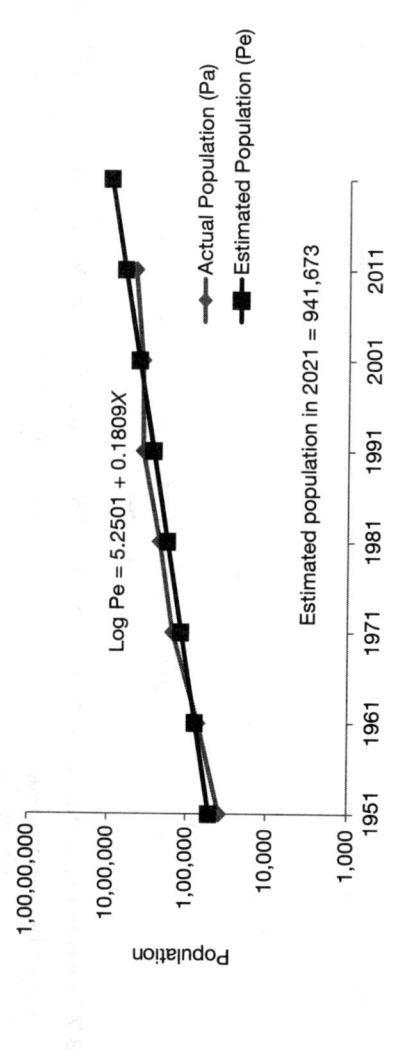

Figure 3.6 *Trend of Buddhist Population Growth in North-east India (1951–2011)*

Source: Prepared by authors based on the analysis of following data: Census of India. (1991b [Religion (Table 9). Series IV, Part IV-B(ii). Assam], 2001g, 2011b).

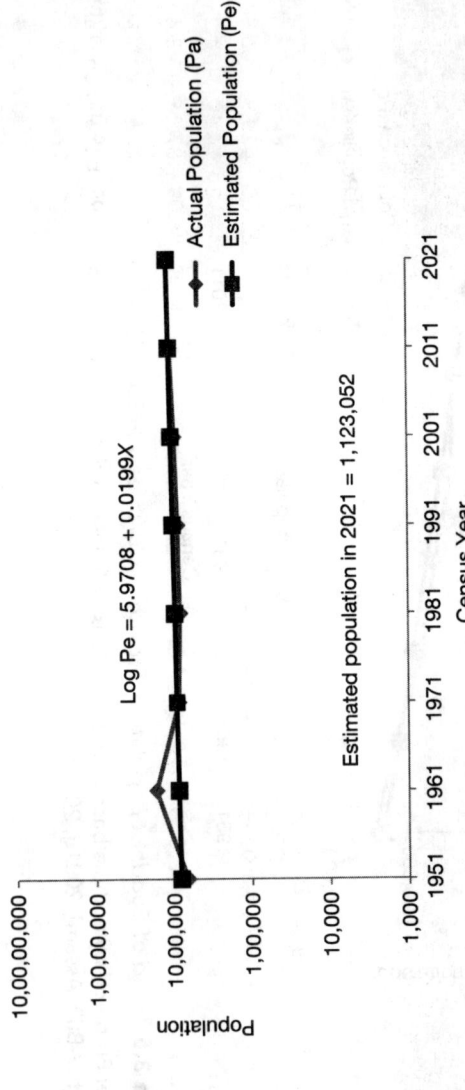

Figure 3.7 *Trend of Population Growth among Other* Religious Groups in North-east India (1951–2011)*

Source: Prepared by authors based on the analysis of following data: Census of India. (1991b [Religion (Table 9). Series IV, Part IV-B(ii). Assam], 2001g, 2011b).

*Other than Hindus, Muslims, Christians and Buddhists

Table 3.6 Growth Rates and Proportions of Population Among the Major Religious Groups in North-east India, 1971–2011

States	Hindus			Muslims			Christians			Buddhists		
	Average Annual Growth Rate (1971–2011)	Proportion of Population Out of Total Population (%)		Average Annual Growth Rate (1971–2011)	Proportion of Population Out of Total Population (%)		Average Annual Growth Rate (1971–2011)	Proportion of Population Out of Total Population (%)		Average Annual Growth Rate (1971–2011)	Proportion of Population Out of Total Population (%)	
	2011	1971	2011	2011	1971	2011	2011	1971	2011	2011	1971	2011
1. Arunachal Pradesh	3.46	22.00	29.04	9.06	0.18	1.95	12.59	0.78	30.26	2.47	13.13	11.17
2. Assam	1.49	72.51	61.47	2.76	24.56	34.22	2.83	2.61	3.74	2.25	0.15	0.18
3. Manipur	1.57	60.04	41.39	3.09	6.62	8.40	3.66	26.03	41.29	6.88	0.05	0.25
4. Meghalaya	1.52	18.50	11.53	4.08	2.60	4.40	3.92	46.98	74.59	4.23	0.19	0.33
5. Mizoram	0.88	6.39	2.75	5.30	0.57	1.35	3.06	86.09	87.16	3.60	6.81	8.51
6. Nagaland	2.72	11.43	8.75	7.26	0.57	2.47	4.13	66.76	87.93	9.50	0.03	0.34
7. Tripura	1.99	89.55	83.40	2.82	6.68	8.60	5.97	1.01	4.35	2.75	2.72	3.41
North-east India	1.58	66.39	53.97	2.80	19.40	25.37	3.76	9.12	17.34	2.82	0.77	1.02
India	1.91	82.72	79.80	2.61	11.20	14.23	1.69	2.60	2.30	1.96	0.71	0.70

Source: Census of India (1991b, 2011b).

Table 3.7 *Percentage Distribution of Population Across Different Age Groups in North-east India at the State Level, 1971 and 2011*

| States | Age Groups | | | | | |
| | 0–14 | | 15–59 | | 60+ | |
	1971	2011	1971	2011	1971	2011
1. Arunachal Pradesh	38.28	35.69	57.07	59.70	4.65	4.61
2. Assam	46.95	32.87	48.34	60,47	4.71	6.66
3. Manipur	42.50	30.25	51.41	62.73	6.09	7.02
4. Meghalaya	43.55	39.78	51.78	55.53	4.67	4.69
5. Mizoram	43.26	32.46	51.57	61.28	5.17	6.26
6. Nagaland	37.98	34.35	55.32	60.46	6.70	5.19
7. Tripura	44.19	27.72	49.77	64.40	6.04	7.88
North-east India	45.72	32.88	49.30	60.60	4.98	6.52
India	42.03	30.87	52.00	60.52	5.97	8.61

Source: Srivastava (1987) and Census of India (2011c).

Again, as the birth rate is still somewhat higher in the region, the increase in the ageing ratio (proportion of older people [60+] to children [0–14]) during 1971–2011 in the region (10.9% to 19.8%) has been considerably slower than that in the country's average ratio (14.2% to 27.9%) (Table 3.8). There is, however, significant spatial variation in this respect. Among the states of the region, ageing is found to be more in Tripura (28.4%) and Manipur (23.2%) and still quite low in Meghalaya (11.8%) and Arunachal Pradesh (12.9%) (Table 3.8). The tempo of ageing has been somewhat faster in the states of Tripura, Assam and Manipur. Unexpectedly, the state of Nagaland has witnessed a reverse trend in this respect. Thus, it indicates that most parts of the NE region are yet to attain the stage of demographic stability.

The proportion of the 0–6 age group children in the region has witnessed negligible decrease, from 19.5 per cent to 14.9 per cent during 1991–2011. What is more important here is the variation in the proportion of children in the age group of 0–6 among different

Table 3.8 *Dependency Ratio and Ageing Ratio in North-east India (1971 and 2011)*

States	Dependency Ratio (in %)		Ageing Ratio (in %)	
	1971	2011	1971	2011
1. Arunachal Pradesh	75.20	67.5	12.1	12.9
2. Assam	106.9	65.4	10.0	20.3
3. Manipur	94.5	59.4	14.3	23.2
4. Meghalaya	93.1	80.1	10.7	11.8
5. Mizoram	93.9	63.2	11.9	19.3
6. Nagaland	80.8	65.4	17.6	15.1
7. Tripura	100.9	55.3	13.7	28.4
North-east India	102.8	65.0	10.9	19.8
India	92.3	65.2	14.2	27.9

Source: Srivastava (1987) and Census of India (2011c).

population groups (Table 3.9). The proportion of children in the age group of 0–6 (as per the 2011 census) varies from 12.94 per cent in SCs, 15.64 per cent in STs and 14.86 per cent in the total population. There is also spatial variation, with the proportion being 9.93 per cent in Mizoram and 13.66 per cent in Meghalaya among the SCs and 13.21 per cent in Manipur and 19.86 per cent in Meghalaya among the STs. It is 12.47 per cent in Tripura and 19.16 per cent in Meghalaya among the total population. The variation in the proportion of children in the 0–6 age group is even more glaring among the religious groups. The proportion is 12.28 per cent in Hindus, 19.26 per cent in Muslims, 16.17 per cent in Christians and 16.63 per cent in Buddhists (Table 3.10). In the case of spatial variation, the proportion varies between 11.35 per cent in Mizoram and 13.67 per cent in Arunachal Pradesh among the Hindus, between 15.04 per cent in Arunachal Pradesh and 20.32 per cent in Meghalaya among the Muslims, between 13.22 per cent in Manipur and 19.81 per cent in Meghalaya among the Christians and between 11.53 per cent in Assam and 22.13 per cent in Meghalaya among the Buddhists in the region (Table 3.9). Thus, the population

Table 3.9 Percentage of 0–6 Age Group Population Among Different Communities in North-east India, 2011

States	Total Population	SC	ST	Hindus	Muslims	Christians	Buddhists	Others
1. Arunachal Pradesh	15.33	–	15.86	13.67	15.04	17.19	16.42	14.59
2. Assam	14.86	13.29	14.12	12.32	19.42	15.11	11.53	15.60
3. Manipur	13.14	12.92	13.21	12.24	17.36	13.22	14.31	12.99
4. Meghalaya	19.16	13.66	19.86	12.32	20.32	19.81	22.13	21.83
5. Mizoram	15.36	9.93	15.50	11.35	15.94	15.00	20.18	19.71
6. Nagaland	14.71	–	14.86	12.36	19.77	14.80	18.72	13.37
7. Tripura	12.47	11.77	15.03	11.87	15.59	14.67	16.09	17.15
North-east India	14.86	12.94	15.64	12.28	19.26	16.17	16.63	16.24
India	13.59	–	–	13.20	16.43	12.05	11.63	12.11

Source: Census of India (2011a, 2011e).

groups witnessing higher growth rates also have higher proportions of children's population.

Composition of Scheduled Castes and Scheduled Tribes

The variation in population and the changing growth rates among the SCs and STs have also resulted in the changing proportions of different groups in NE India during 1971–2011. It is found that due to the higher annual growth rate among the SCs during 1971–2011 (2.48%), the proportion of SCs in NE India's total population increased from 5.75 per cent in 1971 to 6.65 per cent in 2011 (Table 3.4). The proportion of STs, however, increased from 18.17 per cent in 1971 to 27.62 per cent in 2011, owing to a consistently high annual growth rate of 2.65 per cent among them during 1971–2011. The rise in the proportion of the SC population has been high in Tripura and Manipur during 1971–2011 (Table 3.4). However, in the case of STs, all the states except Arunachal Pradesh and Nagaland witnessed low-to-moderate increase in their proportion during the same period (Table 3.4). Arunachal Pradesh witnessed a substantial decrease in the proportion of the ST population, from 79.02 per cent to 68.79 per cent, during 1971–2011. This was due to the considerable decline in the birth rate among the STs, as compared to some non-tribal people, including Muslims, in the state and the outmigration of STs from the state.

Changing Composition of Religious Groups

With the considerably low and declining growth rate of population among the Hindus during 1971–2011, their share in the total population of the region decreased from 66.39 per cent in 1971 to 53.97 per cent in 2011. Although all the north-eastern states in the country, except Arunachal Pradesh, witnessed a decline in the share of the Hindu population, it was more than 10 per cent in the cases of Assam and Manipur (Table 3.6). On the other hand, with the considerably high growth rate of the Muslim population, their share in the total population increased from 19.40 per cent in 1971 to 25.37 per cent in 2011. In fact, the districts with a decline in the Hindu population during 1971–2011 experienced an increase in the Muslim population. In the process, the number of Muslim-dominated districts in the state of Assam increased from two (Dhubri and Hailakandi) in 1971 (Census of India, Assam-Religion, 1991b) to nine (Dhubri, Hailakandi, Goalpara, Bongaigaon, Barpeta, Darrang, Nagaon, Morigaon and Karimganj) in 2011 (Census of India, India-Religion, 2011b). Although a slight decline in the proportion of Hindus and a rise in the proportion of the Muslim population were also found at the all-India level, they were striking in the case of Assam and Manipur. Again, due to the prevalence of the considerably higher growth rate among the Christians, the proportion of the Christian population in the region has also increased from 9.12 per cent in 1971 to 17.34 per cent in 2011. An analysis of the trend of growth of the Hindu and Muslim populations in NE India reveals that by 2021, the proportion of Hindus would further decline to around 51 per cent, with a consequent rise in the proportion of Muslims to around 28 per cent (Table 3.10).

Table 3.10 *Estimation of Population Among the Major Religious Groups in North-east India and the Resultant Population Composition in 2021*

Religious Group	Estimated Population in 2021		Percentage Share of Population	
	As per Exponential Trend Method	As per Annual Growth Rate Method	As per Exponential Trend Method	As per Annual Growth Rate Method
Hindu	33,954,708	27,110,846	52.16	50.66
Muslim	15,293,257	14,823,385	23.49	27.70
Christian	13,784,785	9,851,617	21.18	18.41
Buddhist	941,673	570,539	1.45	1.07
Others	1,123,052	1,155,262	1.72	2.16
Total	65,097,475	53,511,649	100.00	100.00

Source: Calculations based on Census of India (2001a, 2011a).

Linguistic Composition

The variation in population growth rate among the diverse linguistic groups in NE India, due to both unequal fertility behaviour and migration, has also changed the linguistic composition of the population. The proportion of the Assamese-speaking population in the region, as against the increasing proportion of the Bengali- and Hindi-speaking populations, has declined during the period 1971–2011 (Table 3.11). The change was more striking in Assam, where the proportion of the Assamese-speaking population declined from 60.89 per cent in 1971 to 48.38 per cent in 2011. This phenomenon has also been associated with the switching of language among many tribal people, from Assamese to their respective tribal languages, due to the reassertion of tribalism.

CONCLUSION

The foregoing discussion reveals that the north-eastern region of India has experienced a very high growth rate of population due to both high fertility rates and migration from inside and outside India during the last century. Within the region, the population growth rates have been considerably higher in the states of Nagaland, Meghalaya, Mizoram and Arunachal Pradesh. Although the population growth rate in the states of Assam and Tripura has declined to a certain extent in recent years, largely due to a check on infiltration from across the border, the two states' share in the region's overall population growth is still very high, owing to their large population. The contribution of migrants from different parts of the country and across the border, until recent years, has also played an important role in keeping the population growth rate high in most parts of the NE region, especially in Assam and Tripura. As a consequence, the administrative efforts that have been made in the state of Assam in the post–1985 Assam Accord period have been instrumental in checking illegal migration to Assam from across the border.

The spatial variation in the population growth rate in the region shows a pattern across social groups like SCs and STs, major religious groups like Hindus, Muslims and Christians, and major linguistic groups

Table 3.11 Changing Linguistic Composition of the Population in North-east India (1971–2011)

States	Assamese			Bengali			Hindi			Nepali		
	1971	1991	2011	1971	1991	2011	1971	1991	2011	1971	1991	2011
1. Arunachal Pradesh	2.85	5.58	3.90	5.10	8.19	7.27	3.28	7.31	7.10	6.61	9.39	6.89
2. Assam	60.89	57.81	48.38	19.71	21.67	28.92	5.42	4.62	6.73	2.39	1.93	1.91
3. Manipur	0.16	0.09	0.09	1.40	1.06	1.07	1.08	1.31	1.11	2.46	2.53	2.23
4. Meghalaya	2.31	1.92	1.34	9.29	8.13	7.84	1.70	2.19	2.12	4.39	2.77	1.84
5. Mizoram	0.19	0.12	0.12	7.54	8.57	9.83	1.78	1.28	0.97	1.37	1.20	0.82
6. Nagaland	1.27	1.09	0.87	1.66	3.16	3.78	3.38	3.36	3.18	3.40	2.67	2.20
7. Tripura	0.01	0.04	0.06	68.79	68.88	65.73	1.48	1.66	2.11	0.14	0.11	0.08
North-east India	45.71	41.39	33.68	21.03	22.47	26.54	4.51	3.98	5.42	2.43	2.07	1.92
India	–	1.55	1.26	–	8.22	8.03	–	39.85	43.63	–	0.25	0.24

Source: Census of India (1991c, 2011d).

like Assamese-, Bengali-, Hindi- and Nepali-speaking populations over the period 1971–2001. Although the growth rate was quite high among both SCs and STs prior to 1971, it has come down significantly in recent times across the states of the NE region. In the case of religious groups, unlike Hindus, both Muslims and Christians have been experiencing significantly high growth rates of population throughout the region. Most districts of Assam have witnessed a change in the proportion of Hindu, Muslim and Christian populations, though at varying paces, during the last few decades. In the process, the number of Muslim-dominant districts in Assam has increased from two in 1971 to nine in 2011. On the other hand, owing to the declining growth rate among the Hindus, despite their still being the largest religious group, their share in the total population has declined. There has been a marked decline in the proportion of the Assamese-speaking population as against the rise in Bengali- and Hindi-speaking populations in the region. It has been more so in the state of Assam. The proportions of children in the age groups of 0–14 and 0–6 are high across the states of the region. The prevailing varying patterns of population growth among different population groups in NE India are likely to bring about further changes in the demographic structure of the population, with socio-economic and political implications. In view of such a situation, every effort needs to ensure equitable socio-economic development of all population groups for more balanced demographic changes. It is also important to check illegal immigration from outside, as it has various other implications, apart from demographic ones.

REFERENCES

Allen, B. C. (1901). *Census of India* (Vol. IV, Part I). Assam.

Census of India. (1971). *General population tables.* Series I, Paper I, India.

Census of India. (1991a). *Final population totals—Brief analysis of primary census abstract.* Series I, Paper 2.

Census of India. (1991b). *Religion* (Table 9). Series IV, Part IV-B(ii), Assam.

Census of India. (1991c). *Table C-7 Part A (i), distribution of the 18 scheduled languages—India, States and Union Territories.*

Census of India. (2001a). *Primary census abstract.* Total Population. India.

Census of India. (2001b). *Primary census abstract.* Scheduled Castes. India.

Census of India. (2001c). *Primary census abstract.* Scheduled Tribes. India.

Census of India. (2001d). *The first report on religion data.* India.

Census of India. (2011a). *Primary census abstract*. Series 1. India.

Census of India. (2011b). *Report on religion data*.

Census of India. (2011c). *Population in five year age-group by residence and sex (Table C-14)*. India.

Census of India. (2011d). *Distribution of the 22 Scheduled languages—India, States and Union Territories* (Part A).

Census of India. (2011e). *Table SC-08 and ST-08*.

Dass, S. K. (1980). Immigration and demographic transformation of Assam, 1891–1981. *Economic and Political Weekly, 15*(19), 850–859.

Databook. (2014). Basic Health Parameters (CBR, CDR and IMR)—State-wise Time Series Data. Data Tables: Planning Commission of India, Government of India. http://planningcommission.nic.in

Datta, L. (2007, July). Population pressure on agricultural land in Assam. *Journal of Geography, 5*, 34–50.

Gosal, G. S. (1993). India and the demographic transition model. In A. Ahmad (Ed.), *Social structure and regional development: A social geography perspective* (pp. 105–119). Rawat Publications.

Guha, A. (1997). *Planter-Raj to Swaraj: Freedom struggle and electoral politics in Assam, 1826–1947*. People's Publishing House.

Kar, B. K. (1995). Population growth trend in Assam and its socio-economic implications. *Geographical Review of India, 57*(4), 321–335.

Kar, B. K. (2002). Population. In A. K. Bhagabati, A. K. Bora, & B. K. Kar (Eds.), *Geography of Assam* (pp. 115–155). Rajesh Publications.

Kar, B. K. (2007). Population growth and changing demographic structure in Assam. *Journal of Geography, 5*, 1–20.

Kar, B. K., & Das, M. (2012). Population growth and changing demography in Northeast India. In S. Deka (Ed.), *Population development and conflicts in North East India* (pp. 54–74). EBH Publishers.

Mullan, C. S. (1931). *Census of India* (Vol. III, Part I). Assam.

PTI. (2011, April 1). *Nagaland records negative growth in decadal population*. The Hindu. https://www.thehindu.com/news/national/other-states/Nagaland-records-negative-growth-in-decadal-population/article14666718.ece

Sharma, H. N., & Kar, B. K. (1997). Pattern of population growth in North-East India. In A. Ahmad, D. Noin, & H. N. Sharma (Eds.), *Demographic transition: The third world scenario* (pp. 73–93). Rawat Publications.

Srivastava, S. C. (1987). *Demographic profile of North-East India*. Mittal Publications.

Taher, M. (1997). Ethnic situation in North-East India: A geographical perspective. *North Eastern Geographer, 28*, 1–15.

Taher, M. (2012). Mother tongues in North-East India. In S. Deka (Ed.) *Population, development and conflicts in North-East India* (pp. 21–32). EBH Publishers.

Vaghaiwalla, R. P. (1951). *Census of India* (Vol. XIII, Part I-A). Assam, Manipur and Tripura.

SECTION III

Education

Chapter 4

Status of School Education in North-east India

Saket Kushwaha, Sushanta Kumar Nayak and Jumi Kalita

INTRODUCTION

This chapter examines the status of school education in the states of North-east (NE) India, characterized by considerable variations in terms of status, access and outcome. For example, Ruma Dey (2016), in her study, examines the status of elementary education in NE India and finds pronounced inter-state and intra-state variations with regard to the implementation of the Right to Education (RTE) Act. The chapter also shows that while the NE states have made considerable progress in student enrolment and retention, the progress in learning outcomes has not been commensurate with the other achievements. This chapter argues that while there have been studies on the status of school education in NE India, there is a need to understand it in the socio-economic and even geographical contexts of NE India. This chapter, therefore, aims at examining the following:

1. Accessibility of education, through the analysis of variables like gross enrolment ratio (GER) and net enrolment ratio (NER), literacy rate, dropout rate, etc.;

2. Supply-side factors, like the availability of schools, pupil-to-teacher ratio, etc.; and
3. Variations in outcome variables across the states of NE India.

DATA SOURCE AND METHODOLOGY

The chapter is explorative in nature and based on secondary data. The data sources of this chapter are: various reports, such as Basic Statistics of North-Eastern Region, DISE Flash Statistics, Statistics of School Education, Ministry of Human Resources Development (MHRD) and All India Survey on Higher Education. Various indicators like GER, NER, dropout rate, literacy rate, etc. have been analysed in detail.

DEMOGRAPHIC AND GEOGRAPHICAL INDICATORS OF THE REGION

In simple terms, demography is the study of population, which includes various factors like age, sex density, etc. Table 4.1 shows the demographic indicators of north-eastern states in terms of population, area, population density, sex ratio and literacy rate. According to the 2011 census, the total population of north-eastern states is 45,587,982. Among them, the population of Assam is the highest and that of Sikkim is the lowest. Population density is also the highest in Assam and the lowest in Arunachal Pradesh. The literacy rate is highest in Mizoram, followed by Tripura, Sikkim, Nagaland, Manipur, Meghalaya, Assam and Arunachal Pradesh.

Geographical distribution of population is also a challenge in NE India, especially for providing basic services.

Table 4.2 shows the distribution of the population according to village size as per the 2011 census. It is observed that Arunachal Pradesh has 58.63 per cent villages with less than a population of 500, which is the highest among the north-eastern states. Around 0.58 per cent of villages in Arunachal Pradesh have a population of more than 5,000. Similarly, in Meghalaya, out of the total villages, 46.54 per cent have a population less than 500, 9.62 per cent come under the population group of 2,000–4,000, and 1.89 per cent villages have a population more than 5,000. In Assam, most villages have a population in the range

Table 4.1 *Demographic Indicators of the North-east States of India*

States	Population (in lakh) (2011)	Population Density (per km²)	Area (in km²)	Sex Ratio (2011)	Literacy Rate (in %) (2011)
Arunachal Pradesh	13.82	17	83,743	938	65.4
Assam	311.69	398	78,438	958	72.2
Manipur	27.21	128	22,327	992	79.2
Meghalaya	29.64	132	22,429	989	74.4
Mizoram	10.91	52	21,081	976	91.3
Nagaland	19.80	119	16,579	931	79.6
Sikkim	6.08	86	7,096	890	81.4
Tripura	36.71	350	10,486	960	87.2
Total NE states	**455.88**	**174**	**262,179**	**956**	**74.48**
India	**12,101.93**	**382**	**3,287,263**	**940**	**74.04**

Source: Government of India (2015, pp. 4–8).

Table 4.2 *Population of India According to Village Size (2011) (in %)*

States	Less than 500	500–999	1,000–1,999	2,000–4,999	5,000+	Total
Arunachal Pradesh	58.63	21.16	14.50	5.13	0.58	100
Assam	8.92	16.41	30.06	36.07	8.54	100
Manipur	16.97	14.61	17.86	33.17	16.85	100
Meghalaya	46.54	27.65	14.30	9.62	1.89	100
Mizoram	17.68	31.70	26.83	21.53	2.27	100
Nagaland	12.09	16.87	23.40	33.06	14.57	100
Sikkim	6.37	24.22	38.53	25.19	5.69	100
Tripura	0.74	2.23	10.93	44.80	41.30	100
India	5.10	11.01	21.05	30.77	32.06	100

Source: Government of India (2017, p. 10).

2,000–4,999, while only 8.92 per cent villages have a population less than 500. In Manipur and Nagaland, most of the villages come under the population group of 2,000–4,999. In Mizoram, 31.70 per cent villages are found with a population of 500–999, and in Sikkim, 38.53 per cent villages are found with a population of 1,000–1,999. Tripura has only 0.74 per cent villages with a population less than 500, while 41.30 per cent have a population more than 5,000. From the available data, we can say that except Tripura, all the states have a majority of villages with a small-sized population. Among the north-eastern states, the scattering of population is found to be the highest in Arunachal Pradesh and the lowest in Assam and Nagaland. In Tripura, the scattering of population is very less.

An encouraging aspect about NE Indian states is their increasing per capita expenditure on education. Table 4.3 shows the per capita expenditure on education, sports, art and culture. It shows that per capita expenditure on education has been increasing for all the north-eastern states. The per capita expenditure is the highest in Sikkim, followed by Arunachal Pradesh, Mizoram and Nagaland, for all the years.

Table 4.3 Per Capita Expenditure on Education, Sports, Art and Culture

States	2015–2016 (in ₹ crore)				2016–2017 (in ₹ crore)				2017–2018 (in ₹ crore)			
	Revenue Expenditure	Capital Expenditure	Total Expenditure	Per Capita Expenditure	Revenue Expenditure	Capital Expenditure	Total Expenditure	Per Capita Expenditure	Revenue Expenditure	Capital Expenditure	Total Expenditure	Per Capita Expenditure
Arunachal Pradesh	1276.26	118.91	1395.17	1009.530	1316.86	128.79	1445.65	1046.056	1731.91	117.27	1849.18	1338.046
Assam	10710.22	0	10710.22	343.618	16233.89	0	16233.89	520.834	14953.73	256.5	15210.23	487.992
Manipur	1062.52	73.3	1135.82	417.427	1400.82	61.23	1462.05	537.321	1476.23	14.65	1490.88	547.916
Meghalaya	1282.89	4.9	1287.79	434.477	1585.06	8.3	1593.36	537.571	2029.4	7.4	2036.8	687.179
Mizoram	1127.92	29.31	1157.23	1060.706	1262.41	26.03	1288.44	1180.972	1176.66	31.56	1208.22	1107.443
Nagaland	1229.17	48.78	1277.95	645.429	1621.14	33.58	1654.72	835.717	1722.48	26.34	1748.82	883.242
Sikkim	772.72	18.58	791.3	1303.624	920.11	72.34	992.45	1635.008	956.02	62.95	1018.97	1678.699
Tripura	1669.62	115.61	1785.23	486.306	2142.17	222.72	2364.89	644.209	2323.68	174.82	2498.5	680.605
NE States	19131.32	409.39	19540.71	428.63714	26482.46	552.99	27035.45	593.03874	2323.68	174.82	2498.5	680.605
All India	356819.5	11622.16	368441.66	304.44868	420139.41	17950.86	438090.27	362.00033	26370.71	691.49	27061.6	593.652

Source: https://www.rbi.org.in/Scripts/AnnualPublications.aspx?head=State%20Finances%20:%20A%20Study%20of%20Budgets

Thus, the higher the percentage of villages with less population, the higher is the per capita expenditure. Hence, the scattering of habitations is one of the main reasons for the higher per capita expenditure on education.

OUTCOME VARIABLES
Literacy Rate[1]

The literacy rates of the north-eastern states are presented in Table 4.4. The literacy rate of India, according to the 2011 census, is 74.04 per cent. Male literacy is 82.14 per cent, and female literacy is 65.46 per cent. Among the north-eastern states, the literacy rate is the highest in Mizoram (91.3%), with a 93.3 per cent male literacy rate and an 89.3 per cent female literacy rate. It is found to be the lowest in Arunachal Pradesh, at 65.4 per cent. The main reason for the low literacy rate

Table 4.4 *Literacy Rates of North-eastern States (2011) (in %)*

States	Total	Male	Female
Arunachal Pradesh	65.4	72.6	57.7
Assam	72.2	77.8	66.3
Manipur	79.2	86.1	72.4
Meghalaya	74.4	76.0	79.3
Mizoram	91.3	93.3	89.3
Nagaland	79.6	82.8	76.1
Sikkim	81.4	86.6	75.6
Tripura	87.2	91.5	82.7
NE States	**74.48**	**79.9**	**69.3**
All India	**74.04**	**82.14**	**65.46**

Source: Government of India (2015, pp. 7–8).

---

[1] Literacy rate is defined as the percentage of the total number of literate persons of the age group 7+ to the total number of population in that age group.

in Arunachal Pradesh is the remoteness of the state and it being a late starter in formal education. The female literacy rate of Meghalaya is higher than the male literacy rate.

Gross Enrolment Ratio

GER is defined as the ratio of the total number of children enrolled at a particular level of education, regardless of their age, to the total population of that particular official age group. Table 4.5 presents the GER of the north-eastern states. In 2010–2011, the primary level GER was more than 200 in the states of Arunachal Pradesh, Meghalaya and Mizoram. For all the states, it has been declining over time. This indicates that the number of overage children at the primary stage is declining over time. It is a good indicator of primary education. At the upper primary level, the GER is increasing across all the states. Perhaps, this is mainly because of the deterioration of the quality of education

Table 4.5 *Gross Enrolment Ratio (GER) of North-eastern States (Primary and Upper Primary Level of Education)*

States	Primary			Upper Primary		
	2010–2011	2013–2014	2015–2016	2010–2011	2013–2014	2015–2016
Arunachal Pradesh	246.01	128.46	126.76	115.18	113.94	130.13
Assam	136.14	113.43	106.11	90.01	93.13	93.05
Manipur	182.94	149.15	130.85	93.2	113.31	129.89
Meghalaya	238.66	135.35	140.90	94.77	110.97	135.89
Mizoram	213.37	125.96	122.99	99.62	118.72	134.78
Nagaland	157.52	118.78	99.50	89.73	102.68	102.28
Sikkim	180.97	124.42	102.87	98.0	138.84	150.61
Tripura	134.32	113.31	107.96	97.35	114.03	127.97
All India	118.62	101.36	99.21	81.15	89.33	92.81

Source: DISE Flash Statistics (2010–2016), http://schoolreportcards.in/SRC-New/Links/DISEPublication.aspx

at the upper primary level due to the introduction of the system of automatic promotion of students to a higher class at the primary and upper primary levels.

Scattered habitations and sparse population ostensibly affect the GER of the states. Since, scattering is found to be highest in Arunachal Pradesh and Meghalaya, GER is also found to be high as the children are admitted into school at a higher age because of non-availability of schooling facility in less populated villages located in the hilly regions. At both the primary and upper primary levels in 2015–2016, Nagaland and Assam had a GER of less than (or around) 100, which was mainly because of the low scattering of the population. There is no problem of overage enrolment in these states. Moreover, Assam is a plain region with the highest population, and therefore, accessibility of education is better in the state at the primary level compared to the other states.

Net Enrolment Ratio[2]

NER is not available for all the years. From the available data (Table 4.6), it is found that the national-level NER was 99.89 for the primary level in 2010–2011, which decreased to 87.30 in 2015–2016. With regard to the upper primary level, the NER was 61.82 in 2011–2012 for the whole of India, and it increased to 74.74 in 2015–2016. The all-India NER for the primary level has been decreasing; however, for the upper primary level, it has been increasing, which can be regarded as a good indicator.

At the primary level, barring in Nagaland and Sikkim, the NER is above 90 per cent in all the states. At the upper primary level, the NER is observed to be above 80 per cent in Arunachal Pradesh and Mizoram. Meghalaya and Assam occupy the bottom positions, with NERs of 72 and 77 per cent, respectively. Thus, the high GER and low NER indicate the problem of overage enrolment. They also show non-enrolment of children in schools at an appropriate age as a special attribute of the hilly terrain.

---

[2] Net enrolment ratio (NER) is defined as the ratio of the number of enrolled children of an official age group at a particular level of education to the total population of that age group.

Table 4.6 *Net Enrolment Ratio (NER) of North-east Indian States (Primary Level of Education)*

States	Primary			Upper Primary		
	2010–2011	2013–2014	2015–2016	2010–2011	2013–2014	2015–2016
Arunachal Pradesh	–	–	–	87.12	88.29	–
Assam	–	–	99.6	74.93	74.49	77.83
Manipur	–	–	–	84.44	–	–
Meghalaya	–	95.28	96.86	59.16	64.87	72.87
Mizoram	–	–	99	74.51	83.93	92.52
Nagaland	–	99.39	83.2	69.31	74.26	80.89
Sikkim	–	83.54	75.47	42.81	59.9	82.57
Tripura	–	–	97.99	83.51	–	–
All India	99.89	88.08	87.3	61.82	70.2	74.74

Source: DISE Flash Statistics (2010–2016), http://schoolreportcards.in/SRC-New/Links/DISEPublication.aspx

Gross Enrolment Ratio at the Secondary and Higher Secondary Levels

The GER at the secondary level of education for different states is presented in Table 4.7. Between 2010–2011 and 2015–2016, barring Assam, all the states had witnessed an increasing trend in GER at the primary level as well as at the higher secondary level. In 2015–2016, Assam and Nagaland had a GER below the national average at the secondary level, while Assam, Meghalaya, Nagaland and Tripura had a low GER at the higher secondary level. When a comparison is made in GER at lower level with the higher secondary level, in 2015–2016, Arunachal Pradesh, Manipur and Sikkim out-performed other States with higher ratio. This shows that the dropping out of children is more acute when they enter the higher secondary level in the states of Assam, Nagaland, Meghalaya and Tripura.

Table 4.7 *Gross Enrolment Ratio (GER) of North-eastern States of India (Secondary and Higher Secondary Level)*

States	Secondary			Higher Secondary		
	2010–2011	2013–2014	2015–2016	2010–2011	2013–2014	2015–2016
Arunachal Pradesh	74.61	86.65	89.63	42.2	65.27	61.81
Assam	92.11	71.21	77.59	18.84	32.94	38.81
Manipur	90.02	84.3	93.07	41.68	62.18	67.95
Meghalaya	80.22	72.8	87.27	11.65	22.94	43.35
Mizoram	98.93	106.62	109.02	35.49	59.88	55.68
Nagaland	51.74	68.24	71.62	19.77	32.98	36.43
Sikkim	71.18	98.37	119.78	26.52	62.62	68.23
Tripura	74.52	117.01	118.49	24.88	40.99	43.46
All India	81.94	76.64	80.01	31.06	52.21	56.16

Source: DISE Flash Statistics (2010–2016), http://schoolreportcards.in/SRC-New/Links/DISEPublication.aspx

Net Enrolment Ratio at the Secondary and Higher Secondary level

From the available data (Table 4.8), it is seen that the NER for all the states has been increasing over the years. In 2015–2016, five states, namely Arunachal Pradesh, Assam, Manipur, Mizoram and Tripura, had a higher NER as compared to the national average, while at the higher secondary level, only three had an NER above the national average. This trend further substantiates the high incidence of drop-outs in the states of Assam, Meghalaya, Nagaland and Tripura. The cases of Arunachal Pradesh, Manipur and Sikkim are different, as they have a low NER and a high GER both at the secondary and higher secondary levels. Thus, they have the problem of entry of children into the education system at a higher age level, and this happens to be a typical problem in access to education in the hilly region. The case of

Table 4.8 *Net Enrolment Ratio (NER) of North-eastern States of India (Secondary Level of Education)*

States	Secondary		Higher Secondary	
	2012–2013	2015–2016	2012–2013	2015–2016
Arunachal Pradesh	42.68	58.37	26.73	40.19
Assam	43.79	54.31	16.38	26.92
Manipur	59.29	79.44	45.95	53.04
Meghalaya	30.2	43.9	8.94	25.98
Mizoram	47.38	57.19	19.35	60.08
Nagaland	29.51	40.28	15.42	22.65
Sikkim	23.06	34.06	14.14	25.18
Tripura	67.04	88.55	23.9	31.77
All India	**41.9**	**48.46**	**23.73**	**32.3**

Source: DISE Flash Statistics (2010–2016), http://schoolreportcards.in/SRC-New/Links/DISEPublication.aspx

Mizoram is typical in the sense that the NER is higher than the GER at the higher secondary level, which is a statistical error.

Here, the scattering of habitations and population affects the GER and NER in different ways. Arunachal Pradesh, being highly scattered, has a better NER than moderately scattered states like Meghalaya, Nagaland and Sikkim and least scattered states like Assam and Tripura at the higher secondary level. Thus, the internal education policy of having a good number of residential schools might have manifested in the high NER of Arunachal Pradesh. In Mizoram too, there is a scattering of the population, but the state is not so highly scattered, and the driving force behind the high NER is the literacy rate. Moreover, in spite of the lower scattering in Assam and Tripura, the NER is found to be low, which is mainly because students are not interested in higher education and/or in their joining the labour force on completion of the secondary level of education.

Table 4.9 *Dropout Rates of Students of North-eastern States*

States	Classes I–V		Classes I–VIII		Classes I–X	
	2007–2008	2011–2012	2007–2008	2011–2012	2007–2008	2011–2012
Arunachal Pradesh	41.04	30.9	47.99	50.0	63.00	61.4
Assam	5.25	32.2	69.3	50.2	75.7	72.4
Manipur	37.5	44.8	41.9	53.7	44.6	71.1
Meghalaya	36.4	62.9	60.4	68.0	76.1	74.5
Mizoram	47.7	40.8	62.7	39.6	70.2	44.5
Nagaland	37.9	38.5	46.6	47.7	74.0	53.6
Sikkim	19.7	9.1	64.9	42.4	79.9	57.4
Tripura	22.6	26.8	54.8	42.4	73.4	49.6
All India	25.1	22.3	42.7	40.8	56.7	50.3

Source: DISE Flash Statistics (2010–2016), http://schoolreportcards.in/SRC-New/Links/DISEPublication.aspx

Dropout Rate[3]

Between 2007–2008 and 2011–2012, the dropout rate in the primary level increased in all the states except Arunachal Pradesh, Mizoram and Sikkim. Besides, the dropout rate was higher than the all-India rate in all the states except Sikkim. Paradoxically, all the states have reported a GER of more than 100 per cent consistently. In classes I–VIII and I–X, in 2011–12, all the states had a dropout rate above the national average, except Mizoram. The states reporting high dropout rates are: Meghalaya, Assam, Manipur, Arunachal Pradesh, Sikkim and Nagaland. The dropout rate of Tripura is almost equal to the national average.

Gross Enrolment Ratio at Higher Education

The GER for higher education is presented in Table 4.10. It is found to be increasing over the years for all the states of NE India. The GER was

---

[3] Dropout rate shows the percentage of students who were not able to complete their school education.

Box 4.1 *Dropout Rate and Wage Rate*

Since the dropout rate is substantially high in the north-eastern region compared to the national average, an attempt is made to relate it with the wage rate. Wage rate data are taken from Das (2018). A simple correlation between dropout rate (Class I–X) and regular wage rate was found to be –0.32 and that between dropout rate and casual wage rate was –0.5. The number of observations was seven, and the coefficients were not statistically significant. However, a testable hypothesis that can be derived is that the high dropout rate is because of the low wage rate, and it further pushes down the casual wage rate. Thus, the low wage rates of Assam, Manipur, Meghalaya, Nagaland and Tripura can explain the high dropout rate. In Mizoram, the casual wage rate is the highest and the dropout rate is also low. However, Arunachal Pradesh has a high dropout rate with a high casual wage rate. If we include the price index (as the general price level in Arunachal Pradesh is higher than that in Assam), the low real casual wage rate in Arunachal Pradesh might also explain, to some extent, the high dropout rate. Thus, we may conclude that the prevalence of a high dropout rate in the North-east region is mainly because of the low income of the family to which the child belongs.

Source: The author.

Table 4.10 *Gross Enrolment Ratio (GER) of North-east Indian States (Higher Level of Education)*

States	2010–2011	2013–2014	2016–2017
Arunachal Pradesh	26.9	26.1	28.9
Assam	13.4	15.8	17.2
Manipur	35.9	37.7	35.0
Meghalaya	17.5	19.3	23.5
Mizoram	21.6	23.2	24.5
Nagaland	21.5	15.4	16.6
Sikkim	24.2	27.8	37.3
Tripura	13.6	15.4	19.1
All India	**19.4**	**23.0**	**25.2**

Source: Government of India (2016–2017).

observed to be the highest in Manipur in 2010–2011 and 2013–2014. In 2016–2017, Sikkim occupied the top position. The GER was the lowest in Assam in 2010–2011 and 2013–2014. Assam improved its position and, in 2016–2017, Nagaland had the lowest GER.

The GER for higher education in Arunachal Pradesh, Manipur and Sikkim is found to be higher than the national average. This could be mainly because of the substantial presence of students of other states in central higher education institutes in these states who are counted in the numerator for computing GER. The lower GER in Assam, Nagaland and Tripura is mainly because of the dropping out of students after completion of school education.

PROCESS VARIABLES

The following section explains process variables that influence educational outcomes.

Schools at the Primary Level of Education

At the primary level of education, both lower primary (class I–V) and upper primary (class VI–VIII) schools are included. Table 4.11 presents the distribution of population and area per school for different years. The data reveal that in India, the population per school in 2005 was around 915, which decreased to 861 in 2015–2016, and the trend was the same for all the north-eastern states. Decrease in population per school is a good sign, as it indicates that the number of schools per unit of population is increasing. Similarly, in India, the number of schools per 1000 km^2 also decreased from 2.92 in 2005–2006 to 2.34 in 2015–2016.

Among the north-eastern states, the population per school in 2015–2016 was the highest in Tripura and the lowest in Meghalaya, Arunachal Pradesh and Mizoram. Similarly, the area covered per school in 2015–2016 was found to be the highest for Arunachal Pradesh and the lowest for Assam. Though Meghalaya is a hilly state with a high scattering of the villages, the area per school in the state is comparable with that in Assam. The remaining states have an area per school above the

Table 4.11 *Distribution of Population and Area per Primary School*

States	2005–2006		2012–2013		2015–2016	
	Population per School	Area (in km²) per School	Population per School	Area (in km²) per School	Population per School	Area (in km²) per School
Arunachal Pradesh	357.64	27.28	313.30	18.98	344.619	20.87
Assam	662.83	1.95	505.26	1.27	473.02	1.19
Manipur	595.97	5.80	584.70	4.80	559.46	4.59
Meghalaya	285.29	2.76	230.16	1.74	223.24	1.69
Mizoram	352.47	8.36	361.39	6.98	355.16	6.86
Nagaland	791.58	6.59	589.64	4.94	707.61	5.92
Sikkim	493.03	6.47	475.13	5.55	475.13	5.55
Tripura	901.18	2.95	773.66	2.21	757.85	2.16
NE States	**600.31**	**4.04**	**474.69**	**2.73**	**455.69**	**2.62**
All India	**915.22**	**2.92**	**845.28**	**2.30**	**837.04**	**2.27**

Source: Government of India (2015, p. 4), State Card Reports, DISE, as given in Table 4.5.

Note: Population and area were taken from Basic Statistics of NER, and the number of schools from http://schoolreport-cards.in/SRC-New/Links/DISEPublication.aspx

national average. Since the area per school is high in Arunachal Pradesh, the literacy rate is found to be low and the GER high. However, Assam is a plain area having the highest population with a relatively lower scattering. That is why the area per school is found to be low. Though Meghalaya is a hilly state comparable with Arunachal Pradesh, its performance is above the national average in terms of number of schools per unit of population and area covered by one school.

Teachers' Primary Level of Education

The population covered by one teacher and area per teacher for different years is presented in Table 4.12. For all the states, between 2005–2006 and 2015–2016, the population covered by one teacher has decreased over time. It is noticed that for all the states, over time, the population covered by one teacher has been declining, which is also below the national average for all the periods. This trend suggests that the north-eastern States are better off compared to the national average.

In 2005–2006, among the north-eastern states, Sikkim, Mizoram and Arunachal Pradesh were better off compared to the others. In Assam, the population served by one teacher was 103.21, which is also below the national average of 149.84. Thus, the availability of teachers per unit of population is satisfactory in all the states.

Similarly, the area served per teacher has also declined in all the states between 2005–2006 and 2015–2016. In the state of Arunachal Pradesh, which has a scattered population, one teacher serves $3.88\,km^2$, whereas in Meghalaya one teacher serves $0.51\,km^2$. The second disadvantaged state is Mizoram, where one teacher serves $1.14\,km^2$. Thus, only Assam and Tripura are positioned fairly well in terms of area served per teacher.

Number of Students per School (Primary)

The number of students per schools is an indicator of the availability of schooling facilities in the state. Table 4.13 shows the distribution of students per school. The indicator showed a declining trend during 2005–2006 and 2015–2016 across all the states. The number of students per school was the highest in Tripura in 2005–2006, followed

Table 4.12 *Distribution of Population and Area per Primary Teacher*

States	2005–2006		2012–2013		2015–2016	
	Population per Teacher	Area (in km²) per School	Population per Teacher	Area (in km²) per School	Population per Teacher	Area (in km²) per School
Arunachal Pradesh	102.32	7.80	67.50	4.09	64.06	3.88
Assam	166.71	0.49	112.31	0.28	103.21	0.26
Manipur	104.65	1.02	77.49	0.64	70.89	0.58
Meghalaya	91.13	0.88	72.21	0.55	67.14	0.51
Mizoram	67.15	1.59	57.10	1.10	59.03	1.14
Nagaland	102.71	0.86	79.78	0.67	65.32	0.55
Sikkim	68.39	0.90	82.61	0.96	40.31	0.47
Tripura	105.43	0.35	86.94	0.25	78.76	0.22
All India	**224.31**	**0.72**	**164.56**	**0.45**	**149.84**	**0.41**

Source: Government of India (2015, p. 4), and State Card Reports, DISE, as given in Table 4.5.

Note: Population and area were taken from Basic Statistics of NER, and the number of schools from http://schoolreport-cards.in/SRC-New/Links/DISEPublication.aspx

Table 4.13 *Distribution of Students per Primary School*

States	2005–2006			2012–2013			2015–2016		
	Total Students	Total Schools	Students per School	Total Students	Total Schools	Students per School	Total Students	Total Schools	Students per School
Arunachal Pradesh	252,302	3,070	82.18	333,415	4,413	75.55	322,458	4,012	80.37
Assam	3,952,262	40,215	98.28	5,704,044	61,689	92.46	5,432,053	65,894	82.44
Manipur	438,075	3,849	113.82	540,035	4,655	116.01	502,596	4,865	103.31
Meghalaya	433,524	8,128	53.34	712,715	12,878	55.34	775,613	13,277	58.42
Mizoram	220,086	2,521	87.30	254,713	3,019	84.37	214,317	3,072	69.76
Nagaland	421,879	2,514	167.81	417,791	3,359	124.38	349,696	2,799	124.94
Sikkim	117,759	1,097	107.35	125,330	1,279	97.99	105,297	1,279	82.33
Tripura	697,687	3,550	196.53	606,030	4,745	127.72	569,512	4,844	117.57
All India	163,671,994	1,124,033	145.61	199,711,243	1,431,702	139.49	187,625,797	1,405,027	133.54

Source: State Cards Reports DISE, http://schoolreportcards.in/SRC-New/Links/DISEPublication.aspx

by Nagaland, Manipur and Sikkim. It was the lowest in Meghalaya, Mizoram, Arunachal Pradesh and Assam. In 2015–2016, it was the highest in Nagaland, followed by Tripura and Manipur. In 2015–2016, it declined across all states except Meghalaya, and all the states had a less number of students served per school as compared to the national average. Since the number of students per school is not a perfect indicator of provision of primary education, it is important to examine another indicator, that is, the number of students per teacher.

Number of Students per Teacher (Primary)

Table 4.14 presents the distribution of students per teacher in different States of the NE. The number of students per teacher was the highest in Assam, Arunachal Pradesh and Tripura and the lowest in Sikkim, Meghalaya and Tripura in 2005–2006. In 2015–2016, it declined in all the states except Meghalaya, where it was stagnant. In India, the number of students per teacher decreased from 35.69 in 2005–2006 to 23.23 in 2015–2016. The performance of Sikkim in providing teachers to students in recent times has been far better than any other state of NE.

Table 4.14 *Distribution of Students per Primary Teacher*

States	2005–2006	2012–2013	2015–2016
Arunachal Pradesh	23.42	16.28	14.94
Assam	24.72	20.55	17.99
Manipur	19.99	15.38	13.09
Meghalaya	17.04	17.36	17.57
Mizoram	16.63	13.33	11.60
Nagaland	21.77	16.83	11.53
Sikkim	14.89	17.04	6.98
Tripura	22.99	14.35	12.22
NE States	**22.62**	**18.59**	**16.01**
All India	**35.69**	**27.16**	**23.23**

Source: State Card Reports DISE, http://schoolreportcards.in/SRC-New/Links/DISEPublication.aspx

This is an important reason for Sikkim performing better than other NE state in terms of outcome variables at primary and upper primary levels.

Other Indicators of School Infrastructure

Other indicators like single-classroom and single-teacher schools and student-to-classroom ratio are better indicators of schooling infrastructure. Data about these variables are given in Table 4.15. The percentage of single-classroom schools is found to be the highest in Assam (18.9%), followed by Meghalaya (15.0%). Barring these two states, the rest have better positions in terms of single-classroom schools. Moreover, the pupil-to-teacher ratio and student-to-classroom ratios are also found to be the highest in Assam and the lowest in Sikkim. However, the percentage of single-teacher schools is found to be the highest in Arunachal Pradesh, while the Assam, Mizoram, Nagaland, Sikkim and Tripura were performing better than the national average. The low levels of single-classroom and single-teacher schools and the low student-to-classroom ratio are the main reasons for the better

Table 4.15 *Infrastructural Indicators of Primary Education (2015–2016)*

States	Single-Classroom Schools (%)	Single-Teacher Schools (%)	Student-to-Classroom Ratio
Arunachal Pradesh	3.8	27.0	15
Assam	18.9	2	25
Manipur	0.7	6.8	19
Meghalaya	15.0	7.5	19
Mizoram	0.2	2.5	15
Nagaland	0.2	1.7	18
Sikkim	0.8	0.2	12
Tripura	3.1	0.2	23
All India	4.2	7.5	27

Source: State Card Report, DISE, 2015–2016, http://schoolreportcards.in/SRC-New/Links/DISEPublication.aspx

performance of Manipur, Meghalaya, Mizoram, Nagaland and Sikkim in primary education. Single-teacher schools in Arunachal Pradesh need more care, as they lag behind in primary education compared to the other states of the NE. In terms of student-to-classroom ratio, all the states are better-positioned than the national average.

Process Variable in Secondary Education

Table 4.16 depicts the population per school and area per school at the secondary level of education. It can be seen from the data that the population per school in 2010–2011 was the highest in Assam and the lowest in Mizoram. However, the area per school was the highest in Arunachal Pradesh in 2010–2011, with one secondary school serving 278.22 km². Nevertheless, in 2015–2016, population per school was found to be the highest in Tripura and the lowest in Mizoram. Area per school in 2015–2016 was the highest in Arunachal Pradesh and the lowest in Assam. Population per school and area per school for all the states have declined marginally.

The population covered per school was found to be the highest in Assam and Tripura because of their high population. Tripura has the highest NER and GER at the secondary level of education, and in Assam, the GER and NER are comparatively lower, despite the state having less single-teacher schools, which is mainly because of the high number of single-classroom schools. Population per school is found to be the lowest in Mizoram, which is reflected by its high GER and NER. The case of Nagaland is different, because despite having less population and area per school, it has a low GER and NER. Since the area covered per school is the highest in Arunachal Pradesh, and since the state has a highly scattered population, it has a low GER and NER at the secondary level.

The availability of teachers is another process variable in education. Table 4.17 provides data on population per teacher and area covered per teacher. In 2010–2011, population per teacher and area per teacher at secondary level were the highest in Arunachal Pradesh in 2010–2011 and 2015–2016. Both the variables have an increasing trend in Manipur, Nagaland, Sikkim and Tripura, which is a signal

Table 4.16 *Distribution of Population and Area per Secondary School*

States	2010–2011		2012–2013		2015–2016	
	Population per School	Area per School (km²)	Population per School	Area per School (km²)	Population per School	Area per School (km²)
Arunachal Pradesh	4,593.39	278.22	3,872.86	234.57	3,307.68	200.34
Assam	5,359.23	13.49	4,270.96	10.75	3,439.56	8.66
Manipur	3,327.33	27.29	2,584.76	21.20	2,454.24	20.13
Meghalaya	3,084.29	23.34	2,609.16	19.74	1,906.11	14.42
Mizoram	1,663.17	32.14	1,534.52	29.65	1,448.93	28.00
Nagaland	3,794.26	31.76	2,766.20	23.16	2,691.04	22.53
Sikkim	3,357.39	39.20	3,116.35	36.39	2,677.04	31.26
Tripura	4,391.19	12.54	3,892.93	11.12	3,620.35	10.34
All India	**5,862.97**	**15.93**	**5,286.56**	**14.36**	**4,749.00**	**13.04**

Source: Government of India (2015, p. 4), and State Card Reports, DISE, as given in Table 4.5.

Note: Population and area were taken from Basic Statistics of NER, and the number of schools from http://schoolreport-cards.in/SRC-New/Links/DISEPublication.aspx

Table 4.17 *Distribution of Population and Area per Secondary Teacher*

States	2010–2011		2015–2016	
	Population per Teacher	Area in km² per Teacher	Population per Teacher	Area in km² per Teacher
Arunachal Pradesh	428.58	25.96	412.72	25.00
Assam	423.46	1.07	339.09	0.85
Manipur	224.11	1.84	266.79	2.19
Meghalaya	333.03	2.52	265.95	2.01
Mizoram	348.91	6.74	183.99	3.55
Nagaland	277.24	2.32	355.84	2.98
Sikkim	216.18	2.52	221.22	2.58
Tripura	341.94	0.98	350.69	1.00
NE states	**374.61**	**2.15**	**322.57**	**1.86**
All India	627.37	1.70	915.97	2.49

Source: Government of India (2015, p. 4) and State Card Reports, DISE, as given in Table 4.5.

Note: Population and area were taken from Basic Statistics of NER, and the number of schools from http://schoolreportcards.in/SRC-New/Links/DISEPublication.aspx

of worry. At the national level also population per teacher increased from 627.37 in 2010–2011 to 915.97 in 2015–2016 and area served per teacher increased from 1.70 km² to 2.49 km². It implies that the number of teachers at the secondary level in many of the North-eastern states and India has decreased.

Population per teacher was the lowest in Mizoram. Because of its sufficient teachers, Mizoram has better educational indicators among the north-eastern states and also the highest NER at the higher secondary level. The case of Arunachal Pradesh is surprisingly different at the higher secondary level of education. Despite having disadvantages in terms of various school-related infrastructure, it has the highest GER at the higher secondary level.

The proportion of single-classroom schools ranges from 1 to 2 per cent for all the north-eastern states, while the percentage of single-teacher schools is 0 in all the states except Meghalaya (2%). The pupil-to-teacher ratio is found to be the highest in Arunachal Pradesh and the lowest in Mizoram. Further, the student-to-classroom ratio is found to be the highest in Tripura and the lowest in Mizoram (Table 4.18).

The infrastructural indicator shows that Mizoram is better off in terms of pupil-to-teacher ratio and student-to-classroom ratio. Perhaps, this is the reason why Mizoram has been performing better in terms of educational indicators.

The distribution of students per school at the secondary level is shown in Table 4.19. The number of students per school is decreasing across all the north-eastern states. In 2010–2011, the number of students per school was found to be the highest in Assam (251.34) and the lowest in Mizoram (105.41). In 2015–2016, it was the highest in

Table 4.18 *Infrastructural Indicators of Secondary Education (2014–2015)*

States	Single-Classroom Schools (%)	Single-Teacher Schools (%)	Pupil-to-Teacher Ratio	Student-to-Classroom Ratio
Arunachal Pradesh	2	0	26	49
Assam	1	0	15	45
Manipur	1	0	15	34
Meghalaya	2	2	14	37
Mizoram	0	0	11	32
Nagaland	1	0	18	33
Sikkim	2	0	19	34
Tripura	1	0	19	59
All India	1	2	31	47

Source: State Card Reports, DISE, http://schoolreportcards.in/SRC-New/Links/DISEPublication.aspx

Table 4.19 *Distribution of Students per Secondary School*

States	2010–2011	2012–2013	2015–2016	Change Between 2010–2011 and 2015–2016
Arunachal Pradesh	248.22	221.43	212.49	35.73
Assam	251.34	161.73	153.88	97.46
Manipur	187.59	125.00	131.53	56.06
Meghalaya	138.45	90.77	102.28	36.17
Mizoram	105.41	84.00	85.68	19.73
Nagaland	155.62	114.69	122.85	32.77
Sikkim	165.21	170.62	195.11	−29.9
Tripura	212.71	196.54	195.21	17.5
NE states	**216.15**	**149.45**	**146.92**	**69.23**
All India	265.01	238.35	253.32	11.69

Source: State Card Reports, DISE, http://schoolreportcards.in/SRC-New/Links/DISEPublication.aspx

Arunachal Pradesh and the lowest in Mizoram. The change in the number of students per school has been maximum in Assam, followed by Manipur. In Sikkim, the ratio has increased while in Tripura and Mizoram, the change has been the least. The national-level data show that the number of students per school decreased from 265.01 in 2010–2011 to 238.35 in 2012–2013. However, it again increased to 253.32 in 2015–2016. This was because, although the number of students and schools increased, the increase in the number of students was more than the increase in the number of schools.

The number of students served per teacher at the secondary level is shown in Table 4.20. It is observed that the ratio is increasing in Arunachal Pradesh, Manipur, Nagaland, Sikkim and Tripura. However, all the states have a consistently favourable ratio compared to the national average. In 2010–2011, the number of students per teacher was the highest in Arunachal Pradesh and the lowest in Sikkim. In

Table 4.20 *Distribution of Students per Teacher (Secondary)*

States	2010–2011	2012–2013	2015–2016
Arunachal Pradesh	23.16	34.95	26.51
Assam	19.86	16.65	15.17
Manipur	12.63	20.24	14.30
Meghalaya	14.95	14.90	14.27
Mizoram	22.11	10.39	10.88
Nagaland	11.37	35.53	16.24
Sikkim	10.64	20.03	16.12
Tripura	16.56	20.42	18.91
NE states	17.92	17.60	15.46
All India	28.36	30.87	NA

Source: State Card Reports, DISE, http://schoolreportcards.in/SRC-New/Links/DISEPublication.aspx

2015–2016, it was again the highest in Arunachal Pradesh and the lowest in Mizoram. In India, the number of students per teacher was 28.36 in 2010–2011, which increased to 30.87 in 2012–2013.

OUTCOME OF EDUCATION

There is no doubt that there has been substantial improvement in the education sector in the north-eastern states over time. The analysis above has brought out all the outcome and process variables. The 'Annual Status of Education Report (Rural), 2018' reveals quite a different situation regarding the outcome of education in the North-east region.

Table 4.21 shows the basic reading skills of Standard II–level text by children in different age groups. Across all age groups, only Manipur, Sikkim and Mizoram were performing above the national average (Table 4.22).

In the basic mathematical skill of doing subtraction, the performances of Arunachal Pradesh, Manipur, Mizoram, Nagaland and Sikkim were above the national average (Table 4.23).

Table 4.21 *Basic Reading Skills of Students by Age Group and Gender (2018) (Rural)*

States	Percentage of Children Who Can Read Standard II–Level Text								
	Age 8–10			Age 11–13			Age 14–16		
	Male	Female	All	Male	Female	All	Male	Female	All
Arunachal Pradesh	21.3	23.8	22.6	46.0	45.8	45.9	58.1	66.3	62.3
Assam	25.0	26.8	25.9	46.2	48.9	47.6	65.0	68.2	66.7
Manipur	39.6	41.4	40.5	71.5	70.3	70.9	82.7	89.1	86.1
Meghalaya	18.9	24.9	21.9	41.2	53.6	47.6	63.3	72.3	68.0
Mizoram	34.4	34.2	34.3	66.3	71.3	68.7	88.7	89.1	88.9
Nagaland	25.5	27.3	26.4	53.9	55.6	54.7	74.2	80.0	77.1
Sikkim	36.8	37.5	37.1	55.3	69.6	62.5	88.1	84.8	86.2
Tripura	23.9	27.0	25.5	54.4	56.7	55.5	66.4	81.4	74.1
All India	**33.2**	**36.8**	**35.0**	**61.2**	**64.1**	**62.7**	**76.9**	**76.9**	**76.9**

Source: Annual Status of Education Report (Rural) (2018).

Table 4.22 Basic Arithmetic Skills of Students by Age Group and Gender—I (2018) (Rural)

States	Age 8–10			Age 11–13			Age 14–16		
	Male	Female	All	Male	Female	All	Male	Female	All
Arunachal Pradesh	40.7	36.5	38.5	60.2	58.8	59.5	71.4	70.1	70.7
Assam	35.6	33.9	34.8	54.5	51.2	52.8	68.2	62.1	64.9
Manipur	57.4	56.2	56.8	81.0	76.6	78.8	83.4	85.6	84.6
Meghalaya	15.3	19.8	17.5	39.8	42.7	41.3	54.4	59.6	57.1
Mizoram	62.2	61.3	61.8	86.0	88.5	87.2	94.0	95.2	94.6
Nagaland	40.7	41.1	40.9	65.8	64.8	65.2	78.0	79.6	78.8
Tripura	33.2	33.0	33.1	51.7	50.6	51.2	59.3	67.0	63.2
Sikkim	49.8	49.0	49	74.5	76.9	75.7	86.7	81.1	83.5
All India	**36.4**	**35.7**	**36.1**	**61.1**	**58.4**	**59.7**	**69.6**	**64.4**	**66.8**

Source: Annual Status of Education Report (Rural) (2018).

In the basic skill of doing division, Manipur and Mizoram, in the age group of 8–10 years, and Manipur, Mizoram, Nagaland and Sikkim, in the age group of 14–16 years, are positioned above the national average. Thus, in terms of quality of education, the poor performers are Arunachal Pradesh, Assam, Meghalaya and Tripura. This calls for serious thinking about the education sector in the north-eastern states. Perhaps, the poor quality of education imparted at the school level is resulting in a high rate of dropouts after the higher secondary stage.

CONCLUSION

A good educational institution is one where every student feels welcomed and cared for, where a safe and stimulating learning environment exists, where a wide range of learning experiences are offered and where good physical infrastructure with appropriate resources are available. While attaining these qualities must be the goal of every individual educational institution, there must also be integration and coordination across institutions and across all stages of education. This is fundamentally different from the current structure where the early school years are completely separated from high school, which in turn is completely separated from higher education (GOI, 2019). Over 85 per cent of a child's cumulative brain development occurs prior to the age of 6, indicating the critical importance of appropriate care and stimulation of the brain in a child's early years for healthy brain development and growth. It is therefore of the utmost importance that every child has access to quality early childhood care and education (ECCE). Presently, quality ECCE is not available to most young children, particularly children from economically disadvantaged families. Investment in ECCE has the potential to give all young children such access, enabling all children to participate and flourish in the educational system throughout their lives. ECCE is perhaps the greatest and most powerful equalizer (GOI, 2019). The ability to read and write, and perform basic operations with numbers, is a necessary foundation and indispensable prerequisite for all future schooling and lifelong learning. However, various governmental, as well as non-governmental, surveys indicate that we are currently facing a severe learning crisis: a large proportion of students currently in elementary school—estimated to be over 5 crore in number—have

Table 4.23 Basic Arithmetic Skills of Students by Age Group and Gender—II (2018) (Rural)

| States | Percentage of Children Who Can Do Division | | | | | | | | |
| | Age 8–10 | | | Age 11–13 | | | Age 14–16 | | |
	Male	Female	All	Male	Female	All	Male	Female	All
Arunachal Pradesh	11.5	10.9	11.2	34.4	30.5	32.4	39.5	46.4	43.1
Assam	9.7	9.6	9.7	22.3	20.6	21.4	39.2	32.2	25.5
Manipur	29.1	27.1	28.1	57.6	54.2	55.9	67.6	69.1	68.4
Meghalaya	1.9	4.3	3.1	7.5	11.8	9.7	17.2	23.1	20.2
Mizoram	16.6	15.4	16.0	48.8	48.7	48.7	79.6	79.9	79.7
Nagaland	9.1	11.3	10.2	30.9	28.2	29.6	47.4	52.8	50.1
Tripura	9.4	8.6	9.0	22.0	19.4	20.7	31.1	36.4	33.8
Sikkim	11.9	11.5	11.7	28.6	34.5	31.6	56.9	53.4	54.9
All India	**15.7**	**14.4**	**15.0**	**38.0**	**35.0**	**36.4**	**50.1**	**44.1**	**46.9**

Source: Annual Status of Education Report (Rural) (2018).

not attained foundational literacy and numeracy, that is, the ability to read and comprehend basic text and the ability to carry out basic addition and subtraction with Indian numerals (GOI, 2019).

From the discussion in the chapter, we get an overall idea about the accessibility of education in the north-eastern states. The states are different in terms of their socio-demographic fabric, culture, geopolitical concerns and geographical positioning. However, they can be classified into two groups. The first group includes the states of Arunachal Pradesh, Meghalaya and Mizoram, where the scattering of villages is high, and the second includes Assam, Manipur, Nagaland and Sikkim, where the distribution is average. Tripura is a state where the scattering is very less, as 97.7 per cent of the villages have a population of more than 1,000. Thus, the scale effect is operative when a social good is provided to the population, and the outcome is more reflective in less scattered states as compared to others. The literacy rate in all the states is higher than the national average, barring in Arunachal Pradesh, which was a late starter in education. The GER at the primary and upper primary levels is more or less above the national average and is above 100 per cent. Similar is the case with the NER, which, for all the states, with the exception of Meghalaya, is above the national average. At the secondary level, the GER of all the states, except Assam and Nagaland, is above the national average, while the NER of Nagaland, Meghalaya and Sikkim is less.

At the higher secondary level, a substantial decline in the GER and NER has been noticed in the states of Assam, Meghalaya, Nagaland and Tripura. In Sikkim, though the GER is above the national average, the NER is much below the latter and is the same as that of Meghalaya. The dropout rate at the primary level (class I–V) in all the states is higher than the national average, except Sikkim. However, for class I–VIII and class I–IX, all the states except Mizoram, have a dropout rate above the national average. Thus, one may infer that starting from the primary level, the performance of Mizoram is better in terms of retaining students up to the secondary level. In terms of provision of school infrastructure, three states, namely Assam, Meghalaya and Tripura, perform better than the national average, whereas states like Arunachal Pradesh, Manipur, Mizoram, Nagaland and Sikkim are positioned below the latter. In terms of the population served per teacher and the number of students per school, all the states are better off except Assam (as the state is thickly populated). Thus, geographical factors act as a major constraint in the provision of school infrastructure in four states. The provision of school infrastructure is reflected in the performance of students at the different levels of education, as per the report prepared by Pratham,[4] with more than 70 per cent of the children from hilly states like Arunachal Pradesh, Meghalaya and Nagaland unable to read a standard textbook of class II. Though Assam and Tripura have a thick, concentrated population, the dismal performance is not related to the availability of school infrastructure but might be due to poverty. The latest report of NITI Aayog has put Sikkim, Meghalaya, Nagaland and Arunachal Pradesh among the bottom eight states in India in terms of students' performance.

Education must thus move less towards content and more towards learning about how to think critically and solve problems, how to be creative and multidisciplinary and how to innovate, adapt and absorb new material in novel and changing fields. While the gap between the current state of learning outcomes and what is truly needed is sizeable, closing the gap is most certainly achievable. Radical reforms are needed in order to bring the highest quality and integrity into the system, from early childhood education through higher education (GOI, 2019).

REFERENCES

Dey, R. (2016). Recent reforms in elementary education in north-east region states of India through RTE Act-Achievement and unfinished tasks. *International Journal of Applied Research, 2*(6), 887–892.

DISE Flash Statistics. (2010–2016). http://schoolreportcards.in/SRC-New/Links/DISEPublication.aspx

Government of India. (2015). *Basic statistics of North Eastern region.* North Eastern Council Secretariat.

Government of India. (2016–2017). *All India survey of higher education.* MHRD.

Government of India. (2017). *Selected socio-economic statistics.* Ministry of Statistics and Programme Implementation, Central Statistics Office.

---

[4] Annual Status of Education Report (ASER), India's largest Non-Governmental Organization (*NGO*)–run annual survey, has been conducted by *Pratham* since 2005.

Chapter 5

Contextualizing Educational Attainment in Assam
Reflecting on 'Gender Gap'

Nirmali Goswami

Pursuit of social development through education is not an easy task in a highly stratified society like India. The educational debates in India, for a long time, have centred on the question of how to maintain a balance between the seemingly divergent goals of universalizing the access to and maintaining the quality of education in ways that address issues of inequity pertaining to differences of class, caste, gender, language, religion, region and physical ability. Therefore, any analysis of the indicators of educational attainment has to necessarily rely on a methodology that can highlight the effect of the inequalities and their interaction with each other. The statements of the National Education Policy from time to time have reiterated its commitment towards the goals of access, quality and equity and suggested different ways of approaching these ideals. Meanwhile, international agencies have come up with declarations and policy statements, which have also shaped the government interventions in the field of education. In recent years, two divergent trends seem to have influenced the policy deliberations of the state in the Global South.

One is defined by gradual shifts in the nature of the state and its role in the sphere of education. It is reflected in an increasing reliance on the role of private players in the provisioning of education, who claim to provide a better quality of education to different segments of population. It calls for a critical interrogation of the institutional infrastructure of education from the perspective of the ideals of access, equity and quality. It becomes increasingly important at a time when educational policy discourse is guided by the notion of reforms through active promotion of private enterprise. The concerns about the quality of education that is offered in government schools in comparison to private schools usually are seen in isolation from concerns about access and equity. Second, global frameworks pertaining to gender equality have given a new impetus towards meeting goals, which are often defined in measurable terms through global declarations of Millennium Development Goals (MDGs) and Sustainable Development Goals (SDGs). A particularly useful goal in this regard is referred to as the notion of gender parity by bridging the gap between boys and girls. Gender gap is calculated by the ratio of the number of girls to that of boys at different levels of school education. The bridging of the same has been celebrated in the recent announcement of the SDGs. These goals have, in a way, shaped government effort in a particular direction. These trends have brought the focus back on questions of gender inequality but in ways that are different from the language adopted by the feminist movements focused on these issues. Amidst these conflicting visions of educational goals of equality and quality, what sense do we make of flash educational statistics which aim at capturing a complex social reality through summative representations like the notion of gender gap?

This chapter is concerned with the question of how to make sense of figures of literacy and of the enrolment ratio of boys and girls with respect to schooling at a time which is marked by a specific kind of relation between the state and the market with respect to educational provisioning. It seeks to engage with the question of gender inequality in India's context, with an understanding that there are multiple dimensions of inequality and that gender intersects with the categories of race, caste and class at any given moment. Such an understanding is needed particularly in the north-eastern region, where the indicators of educational development often present a conflicting picture.

For example, according to the latest District Information System for Education (DISE) figures of 2015–2016, Assam lags behind states like Mizoram and Sikkim in terms of enrolment in schools. However, if seen through the tool of gender parity, the state seems to be doing well. Here, government schools are over-represented by girl students in comparison to boys. What does it tell us about the social landscape of the state of Assam? This chapter makes a case for a context-sensitive understanding of educational attainments in Assam. In particular, it advocates the need to look beyond numbers when it comes to indicators of girls' primary education in the state. At a time when educational policies are highly influenced by outcomes of policy in measurable terms, the chapter seeks to raise issues concerning equity, which is a much larger goal than the immediate and attainable goal of closing the gender gap.

GENDER GAP IN SCHOOL EDUCATION

The idea of gender-based inequality in education is a much broader concept which, because of the global frameworks discussed earlier, is often viewed through the notion of a gap between the achievements of men and women on specified measures such as literacy, enrolment rate, income level, etc. If the ratio equals one, it is believed to be a situation of gender parity. Achieving gender parity has been referred to as one of the most important MDGs. It is within such a framing that the bridging of the gap comes to be celebrated. For example, it has been highlighted that the 1990s were the period when for the first time significant improvements were seen, as the gap between the male and female literacy rates showed some decline. Another gap that seems to have been almost bridged is the gap between the enrolment rates of boys and girls at the primary levels of schooling. The latest educational statistics released by different agencies often point to a situation in which the number of girls has almost equalled that of the boys in primary schools. All these achievements are significant and are being celebrated as a move in the right direction. Much of the impetus towards such a celebration of the increase in the number of women in schools is derived from global institutions setting the development agenda for the Global South. For example, the MDG 3 aims to promote gender equality and empower women, with an associated target of 'eliminating gender disparity at all levels of education'. The indicator which is to be used to measure the same is the ratio of girls to boys in primary, secondary and tertiary education. Similarly, the Dakar Framework for Action (UNESCO, 2000), while providing for the somewhat broader goals of gender equity in education, also focused on closing the gender gap. It may be noted that it did identify a range of sites of gender inequality, from the lack of provision of early childhood education to low levels of adult literacy to the nature of learning. However, one also feels that it contributes to the overall push towards attaining these measurable goals as an end in itself. Thereby, non-state actors in various capacities have added to the tendency to refer to measurable goals like closing the gap between men and women. While closing the gap is important in itself, in most cases, it appears to be the most convenient and an easy goal. The real battles of inequalities are more difficult but are worth fighting.

Such framing of concerns of gender equity has also been questioned from various quarters. The criticisms range from problems pertaining to the reliability of available data in a regime of assessment framework, where schools tend to over-report, to the problem of equating gender parity with equality in education. Many of the latter form of criticisms are based on the idea that equality would mean deeper engagement with issues of rights in and through education than the mere fulfilment of gaps (Unterhalter & North, 2011). This is not to deny that in the political and economic context of global recession and the rise of neoconservative politics the world over, such a framework, which at least makes a formal commitment towards the expansion of school infrastructure towards a goal of getting more women to attend school, is in itself important, but it is not enough when viewed from the perspective of the ideals of gender equity and gender justice. As Connel has pointed it out, this is only one of the approaches, and an inadequate one at that. In a policy discourse focused on the notion of gap, the binaries of girls and boys are sharpened to an extent that a consideration of how gender intersects with class, caste and other social indicators gets minimal attention in policy formulations (Connel, 2010, p. 604). Also, it is often seen that a misplaced emphasis in getting girls to school shifts the attention away from issues pertaining to curriculum and pedagogy inside the schools and patriarchal norms and values outside the school which limit the conditions under which women gain entry into schools. In the Indian context, Vimala Ramachandran identifies the shortcomings of a policy which focuses only on issues of access and ignores the significance of 'backward and forward linkages' to school in the lives of students from marginalized groups, which affect whether these children actually benefit from the system or not. She has also discussed 'hierarchies of access' which continue to affect the educational experiences of girl students in spite of their entry into the formal system in large numbers. (Ramachandran, 2002). In other words, reducing the goals of education to the mere fulfilment of gaps without complementing it with a nuanced analysis of how gender interacts with vectors of class, caste, religion, region and location at macro and micro levels will not help in assessing the educational advancement. The need for a more nuanced analysis acquires greater urgency at a time when the meaning of education as a 'public good' and the role of the state and the market towards the attainment of educational parameters are being shaped in novel ways. The role of the state is being redefined from that of the major provider of education to that of a regulator in the context of expansion of the school market in India (Winch, 2018). It is also important to note that in such times, the Indian school-going population is divided not just in terms of unequal access to civic resources but also in terms of provisioning of services through the private sector. School education emerges as one of the chief sites of conflicting claims over resources valued in the job market. The private school market has considerably expanded in India and continues to grow in the remotest corners, with enormous implications for issues of class-, gender- and caste-based inequality.

While a number of studies and reports have demonstrated that private schools have made significant inroads in the urban, as well as the rural, population (Tooley, 2009; Kingdon, 2017), others have pointed out the unequal access to these schools on the basis of class, caste, gender and a number of context-specific factors. The imagery of a market in the field of education is problematic for many reasons. It necessarily constructs education as a commodity which can be consumed privately and de-contextualizes the parents from their real social settings and views them as mere consumers. In a different context, Bowe et al. have argued that rather than talking about an abstract individual unit of a consumer parent who is believed to be making the choice of a particular type of school over others, we need to engage in a more context-specific understanding of the *social landscape* within which these actors articulate some actions as choice (Bowe et al., 1994). Winch and Sarangapani (2010), in their critique of a de-contextualized understanding of the phenomenon of the expansion of private schools in Hyderabad, argue for an understanding of the regional, religious and linguistic factors that constitute a social context.

The entry and greater role of private capital in the field of school education has also affected the popular perception of what is meant by quality of education. The government schools are being derided for their 'cost-inefficiency' and for delivering 'poor quality of education' to parents often viewed as consumers of educational goods. In fact, much of the literature on parental choice of school is based on such a vision of an abstract individual consumer who makes an informed rational choice in the school market.

This moment of conflicting pulls and pressure on the state, of commitment towards the attainment of gender parity in schools, on the one hand, and the imperative to make education free from the inefficient handling of the government, on the other, is an opportune one to re-examine the goals of education from the perspective of gender equality. Such a re-envisioning of the goals of women's education is needed in an analysis of the achievements pertaining to the levelling of the gender gap at the level of primary schooling. To illustrate the point, classrooms of government schools at the primary and upper primary levels seem to be increasingly filled by girl students, thereby filling the gender gap in the field of primary schooling (according to the latest figures of DISE and confirmed by reports like Public Report on Basic Education and Annual Status of Education report [ASER]). However, such gaps remain in private schools. For example, in the latest data available through DISE for the year 2014–2015, it is reported that for all the three categories of primary schools run by the government, the

Table 5.1 *Percentage of Boys and Girls' Enrolment at the Primary Level in Government- and Private-Managed Schools*

	I–V		VI–VIII		I–VIII	
	Boys	Girls	Boys	Girls	Boys	Girls
All India (Govt)	49.62	50.38	48.62	51.38	49.31	50.69
All India (Pvt)	55.56	44.44	55.42	44.58	55.51	44.49

Source: DISE (2014–2015).

proportion of girl students was above 50 per cent, but in the case of private schools, it remained less than 45 per cent (Table 5.1).

In such a scenario, the gender gap seems to have been bridged only in government schools. A closer analysis of the studies investigating family strategies pertaining to school choice suggest that such a scenario emerges when families are not as keen on investing in girls' education and make a gendered decision of sending boys to the private and more expensive schools and girls to the government schools that are cheaper (De et al., 2011). It indicates that a wider tendency to invest less in girls' schooling at the family level can coexist with an increase in women's enrolment in schools.

This paradox may be explained only by a close analysis of the context of family in the Indian setting, where decisions regarding the future roles of children are deeply influenced by hierarchies of sex and age, and ideologies of conduct, which shape gendered identities of young men and women. These identities are played out differently in a plural society where different communities have their own ways of preparing their young generations for adult roles (Goswami, 2015). In South Asian societies, the upbringing of children is marked by gender ideologies of seclusion and segregation, which influence decisions about girls' schooling among Hindu and Muslim families (Dube, 1997; Hasan & Menon, 2005). In India, the linkages between family structures, gendered norms of marriage and girls' schooling have been reported in several studies (Chanana, 1993; Seymour, 1999; Hasan & Menon, 2005). However, the implications of the linkages between ideologies of sexual segregation and educational choices have not been examined in the context of expansion of the school market in recent years. Among more recent studies in post-Independence India, Radhika Chopra (2005) presents the linkages of educational choices with particular acts of feminine identity constructions to gain access to a globalized marriage market among landowning caste families in agrarian Punjab. She argues for a view to understand differential choices within a family not just on the basis of gender but also in terms of age and the sexualized identity of a marriageable woman. One can argue, therefore, that schooling decisions continue to be guided by considerations of gendered norms of families, which put a premium on girls' safety and marriageability across the spectrum of class. Such a reading indicates that amidst promising indicators of bridging the gap, an ideology of segregation continues. It is ironic how some things remain unchanged after so many years of change, because it was the ideology of segregation that defined girls' schooling in the late 19th and early 20th centuries. The ideology of segregation was then institutionalized in the form of the *zenana* system of education (Chanana, 2001; Karlekar, 1986).

GIRLS' SCHOOLING IN COLONIAL ASSAM

An analysis of the material conditions of expansion of educational infrastructure in the colonial period is crucial for a measure of the educational developments in contemporary times. It is noteworthy that educational infrastructure development, particularly for women, largely relied on community-based initiatives through a system of *grants in aid,* which were insufficient to cater to the needs of marginalized groups from different castes and communities and of women in general. The poor attainment of literacy levels, particularly among women and lower-caste groups, is glaring in the census reports on literacy rates (Chaudhary, 2007, 2009).

The investments in girls' education was among the lowest in the province of Assam in absolute terms as well as in terms of percent of total government share till late nineteenth century (Medhi, 2013). As it turned out, literacy figures for women continued to remain poor in the census reports of the early decades of the 20th century. It was also the time when an intense debate on the need to invest in women's education had gained sufficient ground in Bengal and Assam (Karlekar, 1986; Mahanta, 2008). The government machinery also made a note of the need for women's education but did little at the ground level in terms of actual investments. Moreover, the terms of debate which defined the vision of education for women also affected the nature of investments in Assam. In this context, it is important to revisit the reformist and nationalist discourses on women's education which were gaining ground in the late 19th and early 20th century in Assam.

The colonial rule of Assam ushered in the process of bureaucratization and formalization of the educational space, leading to the setting up of new institutions through government and private initiatives. These institutions were believed to have been instrumental in the creation of an educated class which would serve the administrative machinery at lower levels. Before that, a number of indigenous institutions of learning are known to have existed in Assam, but these schools were not uniform in nature and did not have the kind of link with modern occupation that the colonial education system promised. The bureaucratic system of education relied on a standard form of education which imparted skills of literacy and numeracy in a form that would be useful in carrying out the new administrative tasks. For example, with the introduction of the new land revenue system in 1835, the need for locally trained personnel with basic literacy in the official language emerged. Educational policies of the state were, therefore, connected to the political economy of the colonial rule but that is not to suggest that it was meant to serve, merely a technical requirement of providing cheap labour for lower administrative positions. They also meant to serve a wider 'civilising purpose' among the native population. Within colonial discourse, Assam was seen as an area with the problem of 'deficit labour', and the native population was construed as 'lazy' and lacking in the 'industrious' attributes needed for the flourishing of the plantation economy (Sharma, 2009). The initial investment in the field of school education in Assam, particularly in the field of secondary education, was meant to serve the need of moral refinement of the Assamese people (Sengupta, 2012).

The initial advances towards the spread of formal education in the region came in the form of the opening up of elementary schools through the personal initiatives of the missionaries and the Company officials. Contributions of the American Baptists, in the Brahmaputra Valley and in Nagaland, and of the Welsh missionaries, in the Khasi and Jaintia Hills, are noteworthy in this regard. In later years, particularly after Wood's despatch in 1854, which laid down a standard form of school system ranging from primary to secondary to high school level, the *grants in aid* system was proposed for the financing of school education. In this system, educational goals were to be achieved by encouraging private enterprise and supporting them through grants from the government. This led to an expansion of the private school market in the colonial period, and by the end of the 19th century, the expenditure on education by the provincial and local bodies was equal to that by the private enterprises. While this policy was a direct result of the fiscal constraints of the government, it was also advocated in the name of promoting 'self-reliance' and sensitivity to the local needs and encouraging 'civic spirit' and participation among the natives (Jain, 2018). However, such encouragements could not result in the education of the masses in the absence of proper government support for the same. It is argued that the system of grants in aid, though applicable to all the provinces of India, was particularly unfavourable for the province of Assam, because of the paucity of funds with the local bodies that were expected to maintain the schools. Moreover, the grants were to be given only on the basis of the school results. In such a scenario, many of the earlier existing indigenous schools closed down, and a new category of aided and unaided schools following the colonial model of education emerged on the basis of private entrepreneurial pursuits of the emerging middle class. Additionally, the local bodies which were entrusted with the task of maintaining the schools had fewer representatives from among the local population, but upper caste elites had a considerable presence among the non-official board members, and they had power to influence the decisions (Chaudhary, 2007). Overall, government expenditure on public education was very limited in this period. According to the comparative estimates brought out by historians and economists of education, it was lower than that of any other British colony and was even lower than the expenditure incurred by the princely states (Chaudhary, 2007). It is a historic fact that by the time mass education was becoming a reality in colonial Europe, and in Britain, in India, the Company and the Crown were not keen in the complete public provisioning of education and kept delaying the matter till education became a matter of provincial governments in 1919 (Jain, 2018). With such an understanding of the social context, it becomes easier to grasp why the literacy levels remained at abysmally low levels in this period and figures for women and for marginalized groups were even worse. In the decennial census of 1911, the average literacy was only at 9 per cent, and according to new estimates of these figures, the percentage of literate women was below 1 (Table 5.2; Chaudhary, 2007). The limited achievement in terms of literacy, as reflected in the census of 1911, can be attributed to smaller expenditure on educational provisions, leading to a skewed development of educational infrastructure in the province, and the hierarchic social relations, which might have affected the abysmally low levels of literacy among women in general and among men of lower caste groups, Muslims and aboriginal tribes, in comparison to men from upper caste groups from among the Hindus, Jains and Christians. However, an understanding of lower educational attainment would have to rely on the understanding of the public perception of 'women's education' which shaped the already meagre contribution of the colonial state in particular ways.

In the late 19th century, the colonial government relied more on community-based initiatives. However, these initiatives could not take care of the deep-rooted structural inequalities based on caste, class and gender, as is reflected in the census result. The much-lauded ideal of 'civic spirit', which the colonial policies sought to invoke among the middle class, does find an echo in the debates surrounding women's education in the form of publication of articles in Assamese magazines, and in memorandums submitted to educational commissions. Education of the masses, particularly of women, assumed 'national' importance in the late 19th century, which is extensively documented in studies examining the gendered nature of nationalist consciousness in this period (Chatterjee, 1989). In these studies, it is found that the awakening of national consciousness among the native population necessarily involved defining the role of women. The nationalist leaders had to address the question of the right kind of education for women in a way that would counter the colonial representation of Indians as a backward race in texts like 'Mother India' (Sinha, 2006).

As one of the first educated women of Assam, Nalini Bala Devi notes in her autobiography that her father, though supportive of women's education, did not want her to visit the school in town, because it was a Bengali-medium school and was located in a bazaar area, and arranged for a private tutor at home (Nath, 2011). The practice of arranging for a private tutor for girls' education was common among the upper classes in this period. The concerns of community honour defined the norms of education for women. An examination of the debate in Assamese literary magazines of the late 19th century and the early 20th century reveals that women's education in schools was either ridiculed or seen as desirable only when leading to the fulfilment of household duties and contributing in the service of the emergent nation (Mahanta, 2008). Most advocates of education for women adhered to these lines. In the early decades of the 20th century, women's associations emerged in Assam, which contributed significantly to these debates. One of the few exceptional voices come from the leader of Assam Mahila Samiti (AMS), Chandraprabha Saikiani, who not only advocated women's education but also urged women to come out of their segregated dwellings and participate in public life (Mahanta, 2008). It is important to note that in her first address as the president of the AMS, she argued for the proactive involvement of the local board members entrusted with secondary education in Assam towards girls' schooling. In her estimation, the expenditure on girls' education constituted less than 10 per cent of the total expenditure (Mahanta, 2008). Recognizing the social barriers in girls' education, she makes an appeal to women in their capacity as mothers and educational administrators to ensure that girls are sent to schools (Mahanta, 2008). However, such voices remain muted for a long time, and women's education is mostly seen as a means to a greater end like nation-building, which begins from ordering the domestic life.

Women's education had turned into a contested arena and a litmus test of the progress of a community. In Assam, the terms of the debate oscillated between positions about whether women should receive any school education to one that insisted on a form of education which was suitable to a woman's role in the family and in the nation. The varied representations and submissions made to the Sadler Commission which visited the state in 1917 reflected these views (Sadler, 1919; Karlekar, 1986). The commission did not succeed in bringing significant changes in the expansion of educational infrastructure for women at higher levels. As a result, investing in the higher education of girls was confined to selected families who could afford to send their daughters to Calcutta. The costs were high not just in monetary terms. There was also a social sanction against the higher education of women. Segregation of the sexes and strict control over women's sexuality were the dominant features of the caste Hindu society, and they were extended to the sphere of education and continued to influence and shape the practice of education (Dube, 1997; Chanana, 2001). The *zenana* form of education was an institutionalization of this practice of segregation of space for women in the field of education, which is frequently reported in colonialist accounts of Indian women and government reports, and also in the memoirs, autobiographies and other such first-hand accounts of educated women from that period (Karlekar, 1986; Nair, 1990). The Sadler Commission report also mentions that a separate *zenana* system must be introduced by the government to respect the sentiment of the community if it wanted to make any progress in the field of women's education (Calcutta University Report, 1917–1919).

The site of education remains an important battleground to resolve questions of community and gender in post-Independence India, in which women continue to be seen as citizens and as emblems of culture. The state policy, in its approach towards the north-eastern states, has oscillated between creating the narrative of a resource-rich and economically backward region to creating one which represents a homogenized picture of the region where tribal communities live in an egalitarian society.

In Assam, many identity-based movements have raised educational issues from the colonial period onwards, foregrounding the questions of community. For example, the modern Assamese gets constructed and shaped by challenging Bengali as an official language and as a medium of instruction in schools. In the post-Independence period, similar conflicts pitched Bodo and other tribal languages like Mishing and Karbi against the Assamese language (Baruah, 2001). There was also an important gender dimension to these demands when each of these mobilizations tended to create a separate women's organization while failing to ensure their rightful political representation in important bodies of decision-making. The demands in the field of education were also gendered in subtle ways that argued for not just selection of the appropriate language of education for school and higher education but also that of the appropriate dress for girl students at the secondary level, such as *sadormekhela* for Assamese, *saree* for Bengali and *dokhona* for Bodo women.

CONCLUSION: PROCESS THAT CAN EXPLAIN THE GENDER GAP IN SCHOOLS

The chapter is aimed at a critical interrogation of the idea of educational attainment focused on the bridging of the gender gap. It is argued that gender-based inequality cannot be explained through a reliance on summative figures of enrolment and literacy alone. We need a more nuanced and context-sensitive understanding of the social processes which determine how women's experiences of education are being shaped. The need for such an understanding is more at a time when the relations of the state and the market are being framed anew in matters related to the provisioning of education. In a rather paradoxical development, while a larger number of girls are being sent to schools than ever before, their numbers and proportion vary significantly between government and private schools. The trend holds true at an all-India level as well as for the state of Assam (Tables 5.1 and 5.2).

Part of the answer lies in the finding that community-specific norms on education might affect the schooling of girls by pushing girls towards schools that are cheaper, which is widely reported in studies conducted in different settings (De et al., 2011; Ramachandra, 2002). In the specific context of Assam, a similar study on school choices in a multi-ethnic village was conducted by the author during 2012–2014 as part of a University Grants Commission (UGC)–sponsored project. Among other things, it attempted to examine the process of school choice among a set of working-class families from ethnically diverse communities in a village in Assam. It suggested that in such settings, a deeply gendered choice is exercised by parents, having implications on who gets to attend which kind of school and for how long

Table 5.2 *Percentage of Boys and Girls' Enrolment at the Primary Level in Government- and Private-Managed Schools in Assam*

	I–V		VI–VIII		I–VIII	
	Boys	Girls	Boys	Girls	Boys	Girls
Assam (Govt)	49.47	50.53	47.88	52.12	49.03	50.97
Assam (Private)	56.43	43.57	49.08	50.92	52.43	47.57

Source: DISE (2014–2015).

(Goswami, 2015). While overarching concerns about the costs of schooling were articulated by everyone, the meaning of cost varied within and between families. For example, total cost was often measured along with the notion of distance from the place of dwelling. Moreover, it was not just cost in monetary terms. More pressing concerns about the security of the girl child were mentioned, which shaped their preferences for specific kinds of schools which, in their estimation, maximized the security needs. For example, for working-class women, in the absence of extended family support, sending the daughter away to a nearby school was preferable to keeping her alone at home. In some cases, therefore, girls were even sent to a private school nearer home which was perceived to be safe for her. The perception of a school among parents improved if it was seen as a school that instilled strict discipline among students. One can argue, therefore, that the process of choice-making by parents remains highly gendered according to the prevalent norms of conduct expected of women. It was clearly reflected in the centrality of discourse of control and segregation through which school preferences were expressed, particularly for daughters (Goswami, 2015).

Statistics alone is, therefore, misleading in giving a clear sense of the social processes of exclusion. Statistics, particularly summative data, provides only a flash vision of the social reality. It illuminates a certain aspect of social life and leaves out the details of the complexity of exclusionary processes from that. There is a need to look at the figures of literacy and enrolment more carefully. One has to look for aggregated and disaggregated data pertaining to education for a clearer understanding of how gender inequality continues to operate when seen through the interaction of class, caste and community in the Indian context. However, such analyses also need to be matched by the examination of social processes like discrimination, exclusion and segregation, which can then provide a better grasp of the social reality of the differential educational attainment of different groups. To conclude, unless our understanding of 'gender parity' is matched with an understanding that the social processes through which decisions of sending children to schools are made are gendered and are affected by considerations of costs, we cannot have a fuller picture of the complex reality. Such a multi-pronged approach towards the analysis of educational indicators is all the more needed at a very critical moment of education when the goals of education are being redefined under the pulls and pressures of various agencies and interest groups. There is an increasing trend of normalizing the belief that market-based mechanisms are the most effective ways of realizing the ideals of quality access and even affordability. Our readings of educational indicators need to be more critical and context-specific now than ever before.

REFERENCES

Baruah, S. (2001). *India against itself: Assam and the politics of nationality*. Oxford University Press.

Bowe, R., Gewirtz, S., & Ball, S. J. (1994). Captured by the discourse? Issues and concerns in researching 'parental choice'. *British Journal of Sociology of Education, 15*, 63–78.

Chanana, K. (24 April 1993). Partition and family strategies: Gender-education linkages among Punjabi women in Delhi. *Economic and Political Weekly, 28*(17), WS25–WS34.

Chanana, K. (2001). Hinduism and female sexuality: Social control and education of girls in India. *Sociological Bulletin, 50*(1), 37–63.

Chatterjee, P. (1989). Colonialism, nationalism, and colonised women: The contesting India. *American Ethnologist, 16*(4), 622–633.

Chaudhary, L. (2007). Essays on education and social division in Colonial India. *The Journal of Economic History, 67*(2), 500–503.

Chaudhary, L. (2009). Determinants of primary education. *The Journal of Economic History, 69*(1), 269–302.

Chopra, R. (2005). Sisters and brothers: Schooling, family and migration. In R. Chopra and P. Jaffrey (Eds.), *Educational regimes in contemporary India* (pp. 299–315). SAGE Publications.

Connel, R. (2010). Kartini's children: On the need for thinking gender and education. *Gender and Education, 22*(6), 603–615.

DISE. (2014–2015). *School report card.* http://schoolreportcards.in/SRC-New/Links/DISEPublication.aspx

De, A., Khera, R., Samson, M. & Kumar, A. (2011). *Public report on basic education revisited.* Oxford University Press.

Dube, L. (1997). *Women and kinship.* United Nations University.

Goswami, N. (2015). Costs, security and discipline. *Indian Journal of Gender Studies, 22*(2), 243–264.

Hasan, Z. & Menon, R. (2005). *Educating Muslim girls.* Women Unlimited.

Jain, M. (2018). Public, private and education in India: A historic overview. In M. E. Jain (Ed.), *School education in India: Market, state and quality* (pp. 31–66). Routledge.

Karlekar, M. (1986). Kadambini and the Bhadralok: Early debates over women's education in Bengal. *Economic and Political Weekly, 21*(17), WS25–WS31.

Kingdon, G. G. (2017, February). *The private schooling phenomenon in India* (Working Paper). CSAE.

Mahanta, A. (2008). *Journey of Assamese women 1836–1937.* Publication Board Assam.

Medhi, H. (2013). A Herculean task: Womens education and Christian missionary intervention in colonial Assam. *Man and Society: A Journal of Northeast Studies, 10*(Summer), 77–91.

Nair, J. (1990). Uncovering the Zenana: Visions of womanhood in the Englishwomen's writing. *Journal of Women's History, 2*(1), 8–34.

Nath, J. G. (2011). Autobiography as history: Understanding society and patriarchy in colonial Assam. *Proceedings of the Indian History Congress, 72*(Part I), 814–827.

Ramachandran, V. (2002). The new segregation. *Economic and Political Weekly, 37,* 1600–1613.

Sadler, M. 1919. Recommendations of the Commission. Chapters XXX–XXXIX. In *Calcutta University Commission 1917–1919.* Superintendent Government Printing.

Sarangapani, P., & Winch, C. (2010). Tooley, Dixon and Gomathi on private education in Hyderabad: A reply. *Oxford Review of Education, 36*(4), 499–515.

Sengupta, M. (2012). Orienting progress. *Economic and Political Weekly, 47*(29), 53–60.

Seymour, S.C. (1999). *Women, family and child care in India.* Cambridge University Press.

Sharma, J. (2009). Lazy natives, coolie labour and the Assam tea industry. *Modern Asian Studies, 43*(6), 1287–1324.

Sinha, M. (2006). *The spectre of mother India*. Duke University Press.

Tooley, J. (2009). *The beautiful tree*. Penguin.

UNESCO (2000), *Dakar framework for action*. https://www.right-to-education.org/resource/dakar-framework-action

Unterhalter, E., & North, A. (2011). Girls' schooling, gender equity, and the global education and development agenda: Conceptual disconnections, political struggles, and the difficulties of practice. *Feminist Formations, 23*(3), 1–22.

Winch, C. (2018). Markets, state and quality in education: Reflections on genuine educational markets. In M. Jain, A. Mehendale, R. Mukhopadhyay, & P. Sarangapani, *School education in India* (pp. 67–81). Routledge.

Chapter 6

Education, Modernity and Tribal Identities
Narratives of Schooling from Mising
Youths of Assam

Jayashree Doley

In the era of neo-liberalism, the concept of education as a means of empowerment is increasingly getting pushed to the background. At the same time, with Universal Elementary Education, formal schooling has become accessible more and more people from marginalized communities. This chapter examines the case of the Mising community of Assam, a Scheduled Tribe (ST) traditionally residing in the riverine belt of Assam. People from this community face devastating floods almost every year that adversely affects schooling. Yet, education has been able to make significant inroads into the Mising community. It is against this backdrop that this chapter seeks to explore how the community has negotiated modern education as part of their sociocultural life.

Narratives were collected from college-going students belonging to the community regarding the different aspects of their educational journeys—their relationship with teachers and peers, their construction of aspirations, identity negotiations, perceptions about the role of education and the culture around schooling. Even though on one hand, there is hope associated with education as a means for entry into good jobs, there is at the same time other wage-earning opportunities opening up that do not require formal schooling. There were also considerable differences in social background (both class and caste) between teachers and students. As a result, it reinforced students' perception of their own community as 'backward', and there was nothing in the schooling process that helped them cope with these differences in social background. However, there was a thread of love, care and generosity in the teacher–student relationship that provided hope while being a source of inspiration to the students who perceived their teachers as role models. It was also found that higher educational institutions provided an enabling space for their political expression.

When rural development activist Sanjoy Ghose was working in the river island of Majuli during the late 1990s, he came across several families who had either mortgaged their land or given away parts of it for share-cropping arrangements, so that their children could go to school and not have to work in the fields (Ghose, 1998, p. 107). Such is the power that education wields over people. It is a different issue, however, if education is able to fulfil the aspirations of the people, especially of the most marginalized or oppressed sections (STs, Scheduled Castes [SCs], Other Backward Classes [OBCs] and Economically Weaker Sections [EWS]). Xaxa (2008) shows their under-representation in jobs and education and Wankhede (2013) attributes it to caste discrimination and systemic exclusion at every stage of the educational process.

The Misings are a ST residing in the Indian states of Assam and Arunachal Pradesh. In most historical accounts, and even in the Constitution, they are referred to by their exonym 'Miri'. They have a population of about 6.8 lakh in Assam and 57,000 in Arunachal Pradesh. They are primarily a riparian tribe, settled along the riverine districts and predominantly engaged in agricultural work. Staying near rivers, they are affected almost every year by floods that damage their houses and fields and impinge on their livelihood.

Amidst all the difficulties, modernity and modern education have been able to make significant inroads into the lives of the Mising tribespeople and their villages. *Pucca* roads, which were *kachcha* once, have increased their mobility, including to cities. There is a demand for bridges, roads, hospitals and education among the people. Some of them have moved to towns and cities and are taking up new occupations that are different from the traditional ones.

Tribal communities have a history of complex negotiations with the Indian state. Since they were located mostly outside the social structure of Indian society, their tryst with modernity and modern institutions occurred a little later compared to the rest of Indian society. While schooling or education is regarded as an agent of modernization, tribal communities were excluded from its purview. Even prior to modern education, they remained outside the education system. While indigenous education was available for other communities, especially the caste Hindus and certain other communities, in the form of *pathsalas* or *tols*, it was not available for the tribes, at least not in the same form.

In Assam, particularly, tribal representatives, since the 1930s, have been demanding education for their people (Pathak, 2010). Education had become one of the important demands during the Independence struggle, when people from the marginalized and oppressed sections of Indian society were demanding distributive justice in matters relating to educational opportunities (Kumar, 1991, pp. 16–17). The educated among the tribes consistently pushed for the agenda of education and mobilized their communities towards the same, which explains why one has large numbers of tribal student organizations in post-Independence Assam. They played a key role in articulating the grievances of the tribal communities, especially issues of land alienation and cultural protection. Even today, student organizations and student politics remain an important part in the lives of the Mising youth. Educational institutions, especially colleges, are not just places for passive reception of knowledge but also spaces that enable students to engage with different societal issues and get involved in student politics.

For the purposes of this study, interviews were conducted with Mising youths from both rural and urban regions regarding various aspects of their education. Only those students who were pursuing undergraduate studies were selected. They were asked to narrate their schooling journeys, which involved their experiences with the schooling process, relationship with teachers, expectations from education and their future career plans. The data, thus gathered from these interviews, were then analysed, keeping in view each individual respondent's context, which implied their family occupational and educational histories. Before the findings of the interviews are presented, it would be helpful to understand the historical contexts of the relationship between Misings and modern education in contemporary times.

MISINGS AND EDUCATION: A HISTORICAL BACKGROUND

Since the time of the Ahom dynasty in Assam, the Misings were involved in shifting cultivation and remained mostly outside the social structure of Ahom society. They were, in fact, depicted in the Ahom chronicles as rebellious troublemakers, raiding the plains' villages, thus indicating that they were very resistant to the political authority of the Ahom state (Nath, 2019, pp. 77–78). In contrast, the rest of medieval Assamese society, according to Guha (1966), was stratified and characterized by distinct classes. The topmost strata consisted of both the administrative aristocracy composed of the leading Ahom clans and the spiritual aristocracy. The Misings neither formed any such kingdom or state nor did they want to integrate themselves with the existing Ahom state in the region.

With regard to the formal educational system, there already existed some form of schooling for certain sections of the society in medieval Assam. There were *pathsalas* for Hindus, *tols* for Brahmins/upper-caste Hindus, *madrasas* for Muslims and *satras* for Vaishnavites (Debi, 1987, p. 1). Such an indigenous institutionalized system of education was, however, absent for tribes like the Misings, evident from the lack of any written records, as is mentioned by Phukon (2007, p. 196).

Even if some people from among the Misings did manage to gain entry into these indigenous schools, the impact on the larger Mising community was negligible or, at the most, limited. As there were many *satras* present in regions where the Misings lived, in Majuli island of Assam for instance, their influence was, therefore, inevitable. Apparently, many people from the Mising community had also become agents of these *satras*. But later, the exploitative tendencies of the *satras* resulted in a sense of resentment among them (Sharma,

2011). They realized that these institutions did not have their best interests in mind.

For quite some time, officials from the days of the former Ahom rule, educated in indigenous schools, were recruited in the judicial and revenue departments of the British state (Debi, 1987). However, as administrative work started getting more and more sophisticated, it was beginning to dawn on the British that these indigenous schools were not useful for them, especially in training people in matters of record-keeping and documentation. Therefore, a need was felt for bringing in English-educated officials from other parts of India to Assam. This paved the way for a new system of governance where a middle layer, comprising the newly brought in Bengali clerks, was created between the government and the governed. They were called *amolahs* and soon started occupying important positions in the administration (pp. 2–3).

These developments took place much to the chagrin of certain sections of the ex-nobility and the upper classes. This was noticed by some of the British officials too, who, therefore, felt the need to establish English-medium schools for the locals of Assam and began planning for setting them up. Meanwhile, Bengali dislodged Assamese as the court language and the medium of instruction in schools. Government posts were increasingly getting monopolized by Bengalis, leading to growing resentment among the local elites. All these factors prompted the British to start the first English-medium school at Gauhati (now Guwahati) in 1835 (p. 4).

Even though only the privileged caste Hindus and members of former aristocracies were benefitted the most from such schools, some members of the tribal communities also managed to get education in these formal schools, which socialized them with the institutions of the colonial state.

However, wide gaps were seen to be developing between the English-educated people and the general masses. The neglect of mass education had led to widespread illiteracy. Attention was, therefore, once again on indigenous schools. The colonial government started giving grants-in-aid to such local institutions. This led to a fall in government school numbers but stimulated the growth of indigenous *pathsalas* (p. 11). In addition, Christian missionaries were invited to start schools in places which were inaccessible to the government, especially for the hill tribes. Missionary activities in education had certain features that are worth mentioning here. Missionaries emphasized education through the mother tongue, developed Roman scripts for tribal dialects, published Anglo–Assamese dictionaries and Assamese magazines and were the first to start schools exclusively for women (p. 13).

According to Chakravarty (1989), at the administrative level, the main motive of the British for encouraging Christian education was to encourage what they called civilized habits among the hill tribes, who were perceived as a threat to their possessions, to establish a link with them and to completely establish their dominion over the whole of Assam (p. 124).

Christian missionaries were one of the pioneers in language-related development activities in Assam. Along with Assamese dictionaries and magazines, they also published Mising and other tribal-language dictionaries. *A Dictionary of the Abor-Miri Language* was written by J. Herbert Lorrain in 1910, and *Outline Grammar of the Shaiyâng Miri Language* by J. F. Needham in 1913.

English education, even if it was helping the Assamese locals get recruited into government services, also encouraged them to fight against the British. According to Pathak (2010), growing political consciousness in the 1920s and 1930s was leading to the emergence of many tribal associations in Assam like those of the Sutiyas, the Morans, the Rabhas and the Deoris, which were mostly inspired by Congress mobilization and the emergence of caste associations in the 1920s. The unfair policies adopted by the British, especially those related to land, compounded the problems of the tribes, who were having a hard time adjusting to colonial modernity. These problems, therefore, gave further impetus to the formation of tribal associations, which were led by the educated middle class from the said communities and which eventually united to form the Tribal League in 1933.

One of the demands of the representatives of the various tribes in the state legislature was that of education. These demands, however, were articulated in a language that was imported from the Western view of tribes as backward and uncivilized beings. They referred to their fellow community members as poor, ignorant and weak, and this also formed the rationale behind their demand for special protection and education of the tribes. They felt that pushing for education and employment was the only way they could empower themselves. They demanded schools and scholarships for tribal students. Moreover, local tribal people too started opening schools called 'venture schools', with the hope that these schools would be taken up by the board and they would be permanently employed (Pathak, 2010). These venture schools still continue to run and are a unique feature of Assam's educational scenario. In fact, Sanjoy Ghose (1998) had once said the following about the venture schools of Assam:

> The other mystery about schooling in Majuli (and I suppose all over the State) is this profusion of 'venture' schools. Started by a couple of enterprising graduates from the village, the way the programme works in theory is very different from the way that it finally plays itself out in the field. A concerned village group gets together, and donates land for the setting up of a school. The entire community contributes the labour to build the school, and the teachers are employed for free, as volunteers. (p. 108)

Even after Independence, identity politics remained an integral part of the sociopolitical life of tribal people. Phukon (2007) argued that education was giving rise to a new class of people—the educated elites, who felt the need to distinguish themselves from the caste Hindus and to protect their own culture. He surmised that since the Misings did not have any occupational background or history in industry-related work, the emerging elites mostly preferred administrative services and could not occupy any space in industrial and commercial activities (p. 190). They were, thus, brought into direct competition with the privileged caste Hindus and the Bengalis who were able to take utmost advantage of whatever educational opportunities were provided under the imperialist government. This might have nudged them to turn their gaze upon their own community and make them realize how deprived they were of these opportunities. They also realized that the only way they could fight for their rights was through proper organization, and identity provided the basis for uniting and organizing their community (p. 197).

Meanwhile, the problem of land alienation continued. Encroachment and the consequent loss of land were turning a previously independent, rice-cultivating people into daily wage labourers. The government too failed to actively resolve their issues. Permanent land settlement had still not been carried out. Residents did not have land *pattas*. Floods and erosion continued to wreak havoc on their villages. Educationally too, they were disproportionately disadvantaged compared to the rest of the Assamese population (p. 196). The 1971 census showed the dismal educational scenario of the Misings, compared to even that of the other tribal groups (p. 196). Their literacy rate stood at 18.20 per cent, with glaring gaps between that of male and female populations (28.54% for males, 7.54% for females). Compared to that, the literacy rates of the other tribes were 20.51 per cent for the Bodo Kacharis, 22.24 per cent for the Rabhas, 27.72 per cent for the Deoris, etc.

All these factors pushed the Misings to organize themselves with even more vigour. The first Mising student association was formed in 1933, even before Independence, at about the same time when the Tribal League was formed. It was called the *Asom Miri Chatro Sonmilon* (Pegu, 2013, 2019). After Independence too, many such separate Mising student associations sprang up, which all later united into the Assam-NEFA Miri Chatro Sonmilon in 1971. In 1974, it was renamed as Assam–Arunachal Mising Students' Union. The change in their nomenclature from Miri to Mising shows that it was during this time that they decided to forego a name which was given to them by others and adopt a name that they could call their own. The union was finally and permanently renamed as Takam Mising Porin Kebang (TMPK) in a 1985 session at Jengraimukh, Majuli. This association, later, played a leading role in the autonomy movement of the Misings of Assam.

Left out and excluded from both traditional and modern state structures, education has, in fact, helped the Misings fight for their rights, as seen from the role played by the educated in articulating the grievances of their community. But today, with people getting educated and moving away to distant cities, are their Mising identities fading away? With traditional occupations on the decline and modernity making a grand entry into their lives, as is the case with thousands of other communities in India, how is education being perceived today? Can the Misings still be called a community or are there other types of solidarities getting formed?

OCCUPATIONS AND EDUCATIONAL MOBILITY: RURAL TO URBAN MIGRATION

Even though the Misings have traditionally been farmers and still maintain linkages with agriculture, as was seen from the occupations of the respondents' family members, farming no longer remains a lucrative option for them, and they would rather encourage their children to switch to other occupations. For instance, in the case of Binod (name changed for privacy), an Economics undergraduate student studying in a college in Majuli, government jobs are what most people aspire for in his village. Even the fact of his running a vegetable farm with his brother, apart from pursuing higher education, is not well received by his family members, as they had hoped that he would be well-settled with a secure government job after getting educated. It is probably the security associated with a government job that make it such a lucrative option for them. As it happens, agriculture, as a livelihood, has definitely failed to provide that security. Education, therefore, becomes an important means for realizing these new aspirations. Teaching and contract work seem to be the most popular and prestigious of the emerging professions among the Misings, as has also emerged from other studies in Mising villages like that of Nath (2009). In his study on the socio-economic and cultural life of people in Majuli island, which has a significant Mising population, he notes:

> There are three categories of people in the society of this island who possess monetary strength – school and college teachers, service holders and contractors.... Most of the service holders are from among the Kalitas, Brahmins and the Koches. A good part of them are also from among the educated Mishings. (p. 145)

While, on the one hand, education seems to have given some hope to the people as a path to secure government jobs, on the other hand, rising unemployment among the Mising youth of the village is slowly beginning to crush these hopes associated with education. The youth migrate to the cities, especially to the metro cities outside the state, and work temporarily as labourers or security guards. This has definitely brought about certain changes in the outlook of the local people towards education–livelihood linkages. In Binod's own words, when they (migrating labourers) come back, they bring back all these modern gadgets and bikes with them, which he then says 'tempt the children of the village and distract them from their studies'.

The entry of a vast number of Mising youth into the labour force seems to have taken Nath (2009) too by surprise. Even though he talks specifically in the context of the labour situation within Majuli island, the trend he mentions is definitely worth noting. He says:

> ...and till a few decades ago, physical labour was done in Majuli for wage by the labourers from Bihar or immigrants from East Bengal... In this connection a new trend has arisen recently in Majuli. In our investigation it was found that almost the entire labour force in the island – truck and taxi drivers, wage earners, and the like, is now supplied by the Mishings. A good number of the rickshaw pullers in nearby Jorhat town also belong to this community, and are from Majuli. (p. 143)

While one type of migration relates to the search for work opportunities in the labour market, another type of migration was seen among the more affluent families within the community. As seen in a few of the respondents' families, their migration from villages to towns was motivated by the desire to provide their children better educational opportunities, which, in practice, meant an English education. Admission to an English-medium school was considered necessary for a better career, even though a sudden shift from a vernacular-medium school to an English one entailed tremendous hardships and extra tuitions for the child. One of the respondents, Ripun, who is currently studying Zoology in Delhi University, recalls this phase of his life when he had to repeat a grade after changing to an English-medium school. He talks about how it had been one of the most difficult phases of his life because, in comparison to his classmates, he had the additional task of coping with a completely foreign language and, therefore, had no time even to play. Yet, he was ready to face these hardships, as it promised better opportunities for him in the future. Incorporating the English language into one's life happened not just at the level of the institution but also at the personal level. Binod talks about how he encourages the younger children in his family to speak in English even at home, which shows how institutional values spill over to home environments as well.

However, English education also became a gendered issue in the case of one of the respondents whose parents could not afford English education for both their children and, therefore, preferred to let the boy have that opportunity instead of the girl. It was, nonetheless, vehemently opposed by the mother, who wanted her daughter also to have this chance.

One interesting observation was that whenever the occupational status of women members of the respondents' families was asked about, the reply would almost always allude to the marital status of the woman. Further, any career-related advice was usually taken from an elder brother, but never from the elder sister. In fact, even female respondents looked to their brothers for advice, although they did have elder sisters who were educated.

It also seemed like male respondents were more inclined to rebel against their parents when it came to career choices, compared to female ones. As a case in point, Binod and Silpi, two respondents from a Mising village, had different attitudes towards their career or livelihood choices. While there was a conflict seen in Binod's case regarding his career choice, where he went against his family's wishes, in Silpi's case, it appeared as if there was perfect harmony between what she wanted and what her parents hoped for. She had always wanted to become a teacher, and that was always encouraged and supported by her family. But since the college nearby did not have any education department, she had to settle for Sociology, which was also approved by her family. Even though she emphasized her agency while talking about why she made those choices, there was an underlying concern for the financial status of her family and the distance of her college from home. Thus, family concerns did play a decisive role in many of her career/educational choices. Binod, on the other hand, went against the wishes of his family to join his brother in their newly opened vegetable farm.

An overarching concern for family issues in relation to educational choices was also seen in the case of another respondent, Nancy. When asked about what she wanted to do after completing her undergraduate studies, she said,

> I think that after completing my degree, I will prepare for competitive exams. My mother wants me to go for M.A (Masters programme) after this. But I have a feeling I won't get the required percentage. The financial condition of our house is also not that great. So I need a job to help my parents out. My parents had high hopes on my brother. They had spent a lot on my brother's education and medical coaching. But he couldn't succeed. But he will apply for NEET (medical entrance test) again. Actually he did qualify once but because of money problems he couldn't go. So he is now compelled to study in Dhemaji. Actually my brother is very bright even if he studies a little. So I feel that if I get a job, I will be able to help both my parents and my brother.

SCHOOLING, ETHNIC IDENTITIES AND PERCEPTIONS ABOUT COMMUNITY

The formal educational space seems to have had very diverse impacts on how the respondents identified themselves with the Mising community at large, depending on factors like where they grew up, the ethnic backgrounds of their neighbours or the teachers they idolized in school.

At one level, the values of modern schooling play a disabling role by alienating children from their traditional values. I would like to point towards two studies in this regard, conducted by Krishna Kumar (1989) and Dolly Kikon (2003). Different aspects of the school curriculum were studied to examine the question of voice and representation. They looked at the question of how marginalized communities were represented in school textbooks. Even though Kumar wrote in relation to a tribal boy in central India and Kikon in relation to the Naga tribe of NE India, the findings were similar. Through critical analyses of texts and teacher–student interactions in classrooms, it was found that there were glaring problems in the way tribal communities were depicted in school textbooks. They perpetuated stereotypes about who was a tribal or who was a Naga. In the name of representation, certain cultural artefacts like images of a tribal dance were shown. In the case of the tribal boy in Kumar's study, teachers mostly hailed from upper-caste backgrounds and were not equipped to handle diversity—neither were they sensitized to the cultural milieu of their students nor were they empowered to negotiate the differences in social backgrounds. Kikon used the phrase 'recolonization of the Naga mind' to depict the situation where the oppressed start internalizing their backwardness. The result, she stated, is an educated community trying to imitate the mainstream and rendering themselves unable to articulate a sense of self. Once that happens, they then themselves become unwitting accomplices in perpetuating the stereotypes of backwardness.

In this study, however, varying responses were obtained when respondents were asked to articulate their feelings about the Mising community. Although all the respondents felt that they did belong to a 'backward' community, the reasons they gave were very different. Both Binod and Madhab talked about the backwardness of Mising villages and how children do not get a good environment for studying at home. They pointed to the noisiness of the village atmosphere where people frequently visited each other's houses, in contrast to urban families which are more individualistic and, therefore, educationally more conducive. Binod, in fact, went one step further and talked disapprovingly about many of his community practices, right from the 'unhygienic and unscientific rearing of pigs' and the disproportionately high costs of observing certain Mising traditional rituals like *dodgang* and *uromapin*, which result in huge debts, to the drinking habits of some of the elderly community members.

Discourses of 'scientific practices' and a 'quiet environment for studying' had, in fact, become core values around which their perception of their own community was getting built. All these discourses reinforced the image of the 'backward' tribal person. Assertive identity politics, which is so integral to these communities, has failed to shake off the image of the 'backward' tribal person, and the discourses generated by the education system only go on to reinforce it. This also happens through college programmes like the NSS (National Service Scheme), where problems of the community are framed in a language that berates them and focuses on the negatives alone. Education has failed to provide them with a reassuring alternative image they could take pride in or work towards.

Furthermore, the fact that most of the teachers in the schools hailed from non–ST and non–Mising backgrounds compounded the respondents' perception of their communities. When asked about the teachers who had made the most impact in their lives, most of the respondents mentioned teachers who were not from their community, were non–ST and came from privileged classes. They were role models for them, especially in the case of respondents who were from villages. The difference in their backgrounds was, however, sharply felt by the respondents when they were younger, and it seems like these differences hardly got addressed. Here's an excerpt from Binod's narrative:

> When they (teachers) came to school smartly dressed, in expensive cars, I too felt like emulating them. And then I go home and tend cows... and then I realize that their lifestyle is different. Mine is different. I wonder if we too had a life like that...'.

There was a yearning for the lifestyle of the teachers, which, on the one hand, inspired them to study harder, but also, on the other hand, intensified their sense of backwardness.

When it came to respondents from the city, back home in Assam, their upbringing happened in towns that had an apparently cosmopolitan character, and they, therefore, ended up speaking the regional language, Assamese, rather than Mising as their home language. While they felt that the Misings, an ethnicity which they definitely identified with, were backward, they talked about it in terms of representation. They said that if they looked at the number of Misings in jobs or higher education, they felt they were grossly under-represented.

Even if the idea of 'backwardness' is central to their perception of Misings and even if those settled in the urban areas do not speak their mother tongue any more, there is good reason to believe that the Mising identity is not something that is going to die anytime soon. At the regional (Assam) level, in both the rural and urban areas, there is continuous mobilization happening in the form of Mising student politics or Mising festivals being organized. In the case of even the respondents living in cities outside Assam, although they grew up speaking Assamese or formed new solidarities with other North-easterners, they continue to identify themselves as Mising. One of the respondents, Tulika, who lives in the city, grew up among non-Mising neighbours and hardly has any Mising friends, aspires to be a writer and has written poems with conspicuously Mising protagonists. Mising student organizations have spread their branches in cities outside Assam as well, helping aspiring students from back home get settled in an alien place. Looking at these developments, it, therefore, does not feel like this is an identity that is going to fade away anytime soon.

GROWING DIFFERENTIATION WITHIN THE MISINGS

When it comes to the heterogeneity within tribal societies, Virginius Xaxa (2008) says:

> Tribal society has never been static, but change has never been as unprecedented and dramatic as in the last fifty years. As a result, tribal society has moved from homogeneity, the hallmark of tribal society, to considerable heterogeneity. (p. 24)

He adds that this heterogeneity can take various forms, from occupational differentiation to class-based social stratification. Even though increasing changes can be seen within tribal communities, he cautions against depending too much on this framework of differentiation to study tribes, as it leads us to conclude, incorrectly though, that such communities are becoming like any other part of Indian society and, therefore, cannot be characterized as tribes anymore.

Conflict theories in education talk about how education actually reinforces existing societal inequalities. Education has the unintended effect of exacerbating societal inequalities. In India, one of the processes through which this happens is school differentiation, where the moneyed send their children to English-medium private schools and the poor remain in vernacular government schools (Vasavi, 2003). For instance, when we compare Ripun, a student of a central university in Delhi, with Madhab, who studies in a small town in Assam, and consider their family backgrounds, it can be seen that Ripun already had the upper hand in terms of, what Max Weber would say, his life chances. Most of Madhab's relatives are farmers, and he is the first one among them to pursue any sort of education after completing his 12th standard. Ripun, on the other hand, had doctors, teachers and professors in his family, who could, therefore, help him plan out a more robust career strategy. He too, like Madhab, was born in a village, but his parents moved to town and could afford to provide him with better schooling opportunities. Applying Bourdieu's terminology, Ripun had more social capital than Madhab, which was why more opportunities opened up for him.

In this study, the selected respondents were well placed in the education system. They were all pursuing their undergraduate studies. They were also among the privileged few. When questions were asked about where their school friends were now, it became clear that most of them had left schooling and migrated to other cities to do menial labour. This was especially the case with the respondents from villages.

The differentiation happening within these Mising villages has resulted in an interesting dichotomy. While there is a section of people who still pin their hopes on education as an agent of change and a pathway to secure jobs, another section has been disenchanted with the whole educational process.

CONCLUSION

A section of the Misings has integrated themselves into modern society, mainly through education and mobility from rural to urban areas. The development of class cleavages and the struggle for constructing a positive image of the tribe are some of the issues that the community will have to deal with in the coming years. Also, while education is seen as a facilitator of occupational mobility, the Mising society is becoming more heterogeneous, largely due to differential educational and the gradual shift from traditional to modern occupations.

ACKNOWLEDGEMENT

This study was conducted as part of my MPhil programme in Department of Education, Delhi University. I am grateful to Dr Radhika Menon for her guidance in conducting this study.

REFERENCES

Chakravarty, A. (1989). *History of education in Assam: 1826–1919*. Mittal Publications.

Debi, R. (1987). *Progress of education in Assam*. Omsons Publications.

Ghose, S. (Ed.). (1998). *Sanjoy's Assam: Diaries and writings of Sanjoy Ghose*. Penguin Books.

Guha, A. (1966). Land rights and social classes in Medieval Assam. *The Indian Economic & Social History Review, 3*(3), 217–239.

Kikon, D. (2003). Destroying differences, schooling consent: A critical analysis of education policy in Indian-administered Nagaland. *Inter-Asia Cultural Studies, 4*(2), 232–248.

Kumar, K. (1989). Learning to be backward. *Social character of learning*. SAGE Publications.

Kumar, K. (1991). *Political agenda of education: A study of colonialist and nationalist ideas*. SAGE Publications.

Nath, D. (2009). *The Majuli island: Society, economy, and culture*. Anshah Publishing House.

Nath, D. (2019). The Misings in the social system of Assam in the middle ages. In J. J. Kuli (Ed.), *The Misings: Their history and culture* (pp. 257–264). Kaustubh Prakashan.

Pathak, S. (2010). Tribal politics in the Assam: 1933–1947. *Economic and Political Weekly, 45*(10), 61–69.

Pegu, M. (2013). On questions of identity and the Mising autonomous movement. *Journal of Tribal Intellectual Collective India, 1*(1), 15–26.

Pegu, R. (2019). Autonomy movement of the Mising people. In J. J. Kuli (Ed.), *The Misings: Their history and culture* (pp. 147–158). Kaustubh Prakashan.

Phukon, G. (2007). Ethnic assertion in Assam: Understanding the political economy of Mising identity. In R. K. Bhadra & MitaBhadra (Eds.), *Ethnicity, movement and social structure: Contested cultural identity* (pp. 188–201). Rawat Publications.

Sharma, C. K. (2011). Religion and social change: Neo-Vaishnavism vis-a-vis the Tribal groups in the Assam Valley. In D. Nath (Ed.), *Religion and society in North East India*. DVS Publishers.

Vasavi, A. R. (2003). Schooling for a new society? The social and political bases of education deprivation in India. *IDS Bulletin, 34*(1), 72–80.

Wankhede, G. G. (2013). Caste and social discrimination: Nature, forms, and consequences in education. In G. B. Nambissan & S. Srinivasa Rao (Eds.), *Sociology of education in India: Changing contours and emerging concerns* (pp. 182–198). Oxford University Press.

Xaxa, V. (2008). *State, society and tribes: Issues in post-colonial India*. Pearson.

SECTION IV

Health

Chapter 7

Accessibility to Health Services in North-east India

Sushanta Kumar Nayak and Geling Modi

INTRODUCTION

The North-eastern region of India is one of the backward regions in the country owing to its harsh climate and poor infrastructure. Though backward, the North-east (NE) states have a better life expectancy at birth and better child mortality rate compared to the rest of India (Ghatak & Narayan, 2015). During the pre- and post-Independence periods, the region was plagued by diseases like diarrhoea, malaria, tuberculosis, etc., which took a heavy toll on lives. No effective medical facilities were available at that time.

The significance of the health services lies in the fact that they cover physical, social and mental health and quality of life. More access to healthcare services leads to better health outcomes. In NE Indian states, some of the regional issues like insurgency, communal violence, land ownership and disputed international borders lead to the hindrances of development (Prakash, 2016). This leads to poor health services in the region.

INSIGHTS FROM THE EXISTING LITERATURE

Accessibility of health services refers to the ability to access and derive the benefits from the use of available medical facilities. Accessibility of health services is important for better performance of health parameters. It is important for maintaining and promoting health, preventing and managing disease, reducing unnecessary disability and premature deaths and achieving health equity for all people (healthypeople.gov, 2020). Many policies are formulated for achieving health equity, but the policy processes are scantly fulfilled (Gopalan et al., 2011) The health of a person is very crucial for productivity. In a developing country where most of the work is manual and agrarian in nature, poor health leads to decrease in productivity (Ghatak & Madheswaram, 2011).

Every country has a different healthcare and service system. Peters et al. (2008) pointed out that a naturopathic system prevails in developing countries, with developed countries having a conventional medical system. Within developing countries, the poor have less access to healthcare. The study shows not only a correlation between poverty and accessible healthcare but also causation. Lack of knowledge, lack of medical practitioners and lack of resource are the factors that lead to diminishing access to healthcare in developing countries (orbisbio. com). Donnel (2007) has found that people in developing countries forego medical facilities from which they could benefit greatly and that the poor make the least use of effective medical services and facilities. Even if there are skilled medical practitioners in developing countries, the phenomenon of 'Brain Drain' takes place (Peters et al., 2008). According to World Population Review 2019, Finland has the best healthcare system (based on the quality-of-life index), followed by Norway and Sweden. Canada, Qatar, France and Norway were found to have the best healthcare services based on the prosperity index. According to the annual Global Retirement Index 2019, Malaysia has the best healthcare system in the world, followed by France, Thailand, Ecuador and Costa Rica. In developed countries, most of the literature is based on computerization and digitalization of the healthcare system, which helps in greater health equity and inclusion. Some studies have found that differences in health services and outcomes are the result of societal disparities (Veinot et al., 2019). Health informatics is necessary to reduce these disparities. Social determinants of health data are not systematically and adequately added in health research. It is necessary to transform the systematic and standard data into electronic health records for better access in health equity and to reduce barriers to mental healthcare (Deferio et al., 2019).

Mihaylova et al. (2018) highlight the importance of human resource planning for healthcare services. The study concludes that human resource planning in the health sector is very vital for the effective management of human resources. This further leads to a better performance of any healthcare centre. Liver-related mortality has been increasing in the world (Perazzo et al., 2017). Most of the deaths are related to hepatitis C, and most of them are of males aged between 55 and 60 years. *The New York Times,* on 1 June 2016, reported that there was a rise in deaths in the United States in 2015. This increase in the death toll was due to drug overdose, suicide and Alzheimer's.

In India, as per National Health Policy 2018, the birth rate, death rate and natural growth rate are showing a consistently decreasing trend. Maternal mortality rate has been recorded to be the highest in Assam and the lowest in Kerala. The healthcare sector in India is unevenly distributed. It is because of the different geographical, socio-economic and political conditions of the regions. Communicable and chronic non-communicable diseases lead to a double health burden in India (Ghatak & Narayan, 2015). Health inequalities are largely found in India. Some studies are of the view that extreme economic inequalities (the result of the new liberal economic policies since the mid-1980s) adversely affect the disadvantaged groups. This further leads to inequalities in health in the country (Ravindram et al., 2018). Some studies further analysed that social class categorizations and social groupings also attribute to the health status of a society apart from health parameters. Lack of nutrition, poor health behaviour and an increasing number of mortality cases have been found among lower-caste people (Coelho & Beldon, 2016).

The healthcare facilities in the NE states of India are much weaker in comparison with those in India as a whole (Mal et al., 2013). NE states have the least knowledge regarding the Ayurvedic system. The maternal mortality rate, under-five mortality rate and infant mortality rate (IMR) are decreasing, but the rate of decrease is much lower than the expected outcome. Also, the North-eastern region of India has a better life expectancy at birth and IMR (Ghatak & Narayan, 2015). Health burden can have a direct and indirect bearing on economic performance. Morbidity is higher in women than in men in India. There is a high dependency of people on the government healthcare system. The study also shows that health is a prerequisite for success in poverty eradication. Prakash (2016) shows that there is a high incidence of human immunodeficiency virus/ acquired immunodeficiency syndrome (HIV/AIDS) and high level of tobacco consumption in the states of Nagaland, Manipur, Mizoram and Meghalaya. There is a high prevalence of hypertension among children. There is a high inflow of drugs in NE states because of their sharing international borders with other Asian countries. This results in high consumption of drugs among the youth in the NE region. Keeping these insights in view, this chapter attempts to give an overview of the availability of healthcare services in NE Indian states. It focuses on the inter-temporal changes and the variations of process variables and their impact on the health parameters. It also attempts to analyse the reasons behind the poor performance, with regard to health parameters, of the NE Indian states. This chapter is exploratory in nature. The source of the data is mainly secondary. The specific objectives of the chapter are:

1. to examine the outcome variables of health parameters like crude birth rate (CBR), crude death rate (CDR), IMR and children immunization; and
2. to analyse the inter-temporal changes and the variations of process variables like the number of doctors, beds and hospitals to examine the relationship between the process variables and the outcome variables.

HEALTH STATUS OF NORTH-EAST INDIA

For proper appreciation of the health outcomes of the region, it will be useful to note the following demographic and physical features of the region. The NE states constitute 3.77 per cent of India's population. They cover an area of 262,179 km². Mizoram has the highest literacy rate of 91.33 per cent, with a female literacy rate of 91.58

Table 7.1 *Demographic Indicators of the North-east States of India*

States	Population (in lakhs) (2011)	Population Density (per km²)	Area (in km²)	Sex Ratio (2011)	Literacy Rate (in %) (2011)
Arunachal Pradesh	13.82	17	83,743	938	65.4
Assam	311.69	398	78,438	958	72.2
Manipur	27.21	128	22,327	992	79.2
Meghalaya	29.64	132	22,429	989	74.4
Mizoram	10.91	52	21,081	976	91.3
Nagaland	19.8	119	16,579	931	79.6
Sikkim	6.08	86	7,096	890	81.4
Tripura	36.71	350	10,486	960	87.2
Total NE states	458.88	174	262,179	956	74.48
India	12,101.9	382	3,287,263	940	74.04

Source: Basic Statistics of North-eastern Region (2015, pp. 4–8).

per cent. Arunachal Pradesh has the lowest population density, that is, 17 persons/km². Arunachal Pradesh is the largest state among the north-eastern states in terms of area, followed by Assam. Assam has the highest population among the North-eastern region states (Table 7.1).

Table 7.2 shows the population distribution of North-eastern region according to village size. In Arunachal Pradesh and Meghalaya, around 58 per cent and 46 per cent of the villages, respectively, have a population size less than 500. Only around 1 per cent of the villages in Tripura have a population size less than 500. In Mizoram, 31 per cent of the villages have a population size of 500–999. Only Tripura has around 44 per cent and 41 per cent of villages having population sizes of 2,000–4,999 and 5,000+, respectively. This shows that apart from Tripura, all other North-eastern region states have small-sized villages, to varying proportions. This means that there are scattered and sparse settlements in the North-eastern region states.

Table 7.2 Population Distribution of States According to Village Size (2011) (in %)

State	Less than 500	500–999	1,000–1,999	2,000–4,999	5,000+	Total
Arunachal Pradesh	58.63	21.16	14.50	5.13	0.58	100
Assam	8.92	16.41	30.06	36.07	8.54	100
Manipur	16.97	14.61	17.86	33.71	16.85	100
Meghalaya	46.54	27.65	14.30	9.62	1.89	100
Mizoram	17.68	31.70	26.83	21.53	2.27	100
Nagaland	12.09	16.87	23.40	33.06	14.57	100
Sikkim	6.37	24.22	38.53	25.19	5.69	100
Tripura	0.74	2.23	10.93	44.80	41.30	100

Source: Selected Socio-economic Statistics India (2017); Central Statistics Office, New Delhi; Ministry of Statistics and Programme Implementation.

HEALTHCARE STATUS IN NE STATES

It is in this background that an attempt is made to understand different health parameters like IMR, CBR, CDR and total fertility rate (TFR), institutional delivery, child immunization, number of healthcare centres and number of doctors.

INFANT MORTALITY RATE

IMR is the number of deaths of children under 1 year of age per 1,000 live births. IMR is an indicator of standard of living and social inequality, which comprises the dimensions of human development. IMR is one of the most important outcome variables under the healthcare system. Table 7.3 shows the trend of the IMR of NE Indian states from 1997 to 2017. In the year 1997, Assam's death toll was the highest, accounting for 76 deaths per 1,000 live births. The overall Indian IMR was 71 deaths per 1,000 live births. There was a decline in the IMR in all the states of the NE until 2012, except Mizoram, where

Table 7.3 *Infant Mortality Rate in North-east Indian States (1997–2017)*

States	1997	1998	2007	2012	2017
Arunachal Pradesh	47	44	37	33	42
Assam	76	76	66	55	44
Manipur	30	25	12	10	12
Meghalaya	54	52	56	49	39
Mizoram	19	23	23	35	15
Nagaland	NA	NA	21	18	7
Sikkim	51	52	34	24	12
Tripura	51	49	39	28	29
India	71	72	55	42	33

Source: Sample Registration Survey, 2013, 2014, 2015, 2016, 2017.

Note: NA=Not available.

the number of deaths increased from 19 per 1,000 live births in 1997 to 35 per 1,000 live births in 2012. In 2015, the death toll decreased across all the NE states. Assam recorded the highest IMR, with 44 deaths per 1,000 live births, which was higher than the all-India death rate, (33 deaths per 1,000 live births) in the year 2017.

Examining side by side Tables 7.2 and 7.3, it can be observed that the more the number of villages with a population size less than 500 (the more the scattering), the higher is the IMR (Arunachal Pradesh and Meghalaya). The high IMR of Assam and Tripura can be attributed to a high incidence of poverty (Govt. of Tripura, 2007 and Government of Assam, 2014). Some of the hilly states like Manipur, Mizoram, Nagaland and Sikkim have a low IMR, mainly because of high female literacy and better health infrastructures.

CRUDE BIRTH RATE AND CRUDE DEATH RATE

CBR represents the number of live births during the year per 1,000 population, estimated mid-year. CDR is the number of deaths occurring during a year per 1,000 population, and it is also estimated

Table 7.4 Demographic Indicators: Health (Crude Birth Rate and Crude Death Rate from 2009 to 2012)

States	Crude Birth Rate				Crude Death Rate			
	2009	2010	2011	2012	2009	2010	2011	2012
Arunachal Pradesh	21.1	20.5	19.8	19.4	6.1	5.9	5.8	5.8
Assam	23.6	23.2	22.8	22.5	8.4	8.2	8.0	7.9
Manipur	15.4	14.9	14.4	14.6	4.7	4.2	4.1	4.0
Meghalaya	24.4	24.5	24.1	24.1	8.1	7.9	7.8	7.6
Mizoram	17.6	17.1	16.6	16.3	4.5	4.5	4.4	4.4
Nagaland	17.2	16.8	16.1	15.6	3.6	3.6	3.3	3.2
Sikkim	18.1	17.8	17.6	17.2	5.7	5.6	5.6	5.4
Tripura	14.8	14.9	14.3	13.9	5.1	5.0	5.0	4.8
India	22.5	22.1	21.8	21.6	7.3	7.2	7.1	7.0

Source: Census 2011; Data Book for Planning Commission, SRS September 2013; Data Book for Planning Commission, 22 December 2014, p. 174.

mid-year. These two parameters are used to measure the increase or decrease in the population of a state. The CBR was 24 per 1,000 mid-year population in Meghalaya, the highest among the NE states and even higher than the all-India rate (22.5) (refer to Table 7.4). Meghalaya's birth rate remained constant at 24 per 1,000 mid-year population from 2009 to 2012. The CBR shows a declining trend in the remaining states. Assam has the highest CDR of around 8 per 1,000 mid-year population, which is higher than the all-India rate of 7 per 1,000. The CDR shows a declining trend over the years in all the NE states of India. It is much lower than the CBR, because people enjoy a longer lifespan brought by higher accessibility of health facilities like better medical care, such as immunization and antibiotics, better food, clean drinking water, etc. However, the low reported CDR could be because of non-reporting of deaths in the tribal societies.

Scattering of the population plays an important role in determining the increase or decrease of the population. By and large, the CDR is high in states where the village size is less than 500. Table 7.2 shows that Arunachal Pradesh and Meghalaya, where 60 per cent of villages have a population size less than 500, have a high CBR and CDR (Table 7.4). However, the case of Assam is different, where both the CBR and CDR are high even though the percentage of smaller villages is less. This is mainly because of a high incidence of poverty, which is one of the major determinants of high numbers of deaths and births.

TOTAL FERTILITY RATE

TFR is used to estimate the average number of children a woman can have during her childbearing years, that is, from age 15 to 49. Developed countries have comparatively lower TFRs than developing countries, because of greater wealth, education and other factors, such as higher accessibility of contraceptives (Wikipedia.org). In underdeveloped countries, there is a 'Demographic-Economic Paradox', which results in high fertility rates. Table 7.5 shows the trend of TFR in the north-eastern states of India. At the all-India level, the TFR was three

Table 7.5 *Total Fertility Rate (2000–2015)*

States	2000	2003	2006	2009	2012	2015–2016*
Arunachal Pradesh	–	–	–	2.7	–	2.4*
Assam	3.1	2.9	2.7	2.6	2.4	2.3*
Manipur	2.1	1.7	1.5	1.7	1.5	2.6*
Meghalaya	3.7	3.1	3.2	3.0	2.7	3.0*
Mizoram	1.7	1.6	1.9	1.8	1.5	2.3*
Nagaland	1.3	1.2	2.1	1.8	1.6	2.7*
Sikkim	2.4	2.3	2.0	1.8	1.5	1.2*
Tripura	1.8	1.5	1.7	1.5	1.3	1.7*
India	3.2	3.0	2.8	2.6	2.4	2.2*

Source: Data Book for Planning Commission.

Note: *National Family Health Survey 4 (NFHS-4) (2015–2016), accessed from http://rchiips.org/nfhs/factsheet_nfhs-4.shtml on 15 October 2019; www.Niti.gov.in, SRS.

children per woman during the year 2000. Since then, it started declining, and in year 2016, the TFR was 2.3 children per woman. Among the NE states, Meghalaya had the highest TFR, 3.7 per woman, followed by Assam, in the year 2000. Over the years, the TFR declined up to the year 2012, as per NITI Aayog data. However, the National Family Health Survey (NFHS) data paint a different picture. Barring Sikkim and Tripura, all the NE states have a TFR higher than the national average (Table 7.5). The high TFR indicates the preference of the tribal societies for more children.

INSTITUTIONAL DELIVERIES

Institutional deliveries simply mean that birth takes place in a hospital with skilled attendants so as to avoid any complications during delivery. Institutional delivery is an important indicator for improved and better health services for women in the pre- and post-delivery phases. Using the NFHS and District Level Household Survey (DLHS), the extent of institutional deliveries in different states is discussed (Table 7.6). According to NFHS-3, only 38.7 per cent of the total childbirths in the country as a whole took place in hospitals in 2005–2006. Mizoram recorded the highest percentage of institutional deliveries, 60 per cent, much higher than the national-level percentage, during 2005–2006. Besides Tripura and Sikkim, in addition to Mizoram, the other NE states had less than 40 per cent institutional deliveries out of the total deliveries. Following the adoption of several health policies and programmes, the number of institutional deliveries has been soaring. By 2015–2016, all-India institutional deliveries went up to 79 per cent, and Sikkim's institutional deliveries were even higher than that, at 94.7 per cent. This shows that women's access to medical facilities has increased and that there has been an increasing use of medical services.

In view of the scattered settlements in most of the NE Indian states, it is difficult to create a healthcare centre in every village. This is the reason why a significant percentage of women still do not go for institutional deliveries. States with more small-sized settlements, such as Arunachal Pradesh, Manipur, Meghalaya and Nagaland, have less

Table 7.6 *Institutional Deliveries (as a Percentage of Total Deliveries)*

States	NFHS-3 2005–2006	DLHS-3 2007–2008	DLHS-4 2012–2013	NFHS-4 2015–2016
Arunachal Pradesh	28.5	47.6	49.5	52.3
Assam	22.4	35.1	65.9	70.6
Manipur	45.9	41.0	61.2	69.1
Meghalaya	29.0	24.5	47.3	51.4
Mizoram	60.0	55.7	72.4	80.1
Nagaland	11.6	.-.	30.1	32.8
Sikkim	47.2	49.2	82.7	94.7
Tripura	46.9	46.2	72.7	79.9
India	38.7	46.9	NA	78.9

Source: Health and Family Welfare Statistics in India, NFHS-3 (2005–2006), DLHS-3 (2007–2008), DLHS-4 (2012–2013) and NFHS-4 (2015–2016).

Note: .-. Survey not conducted; NA=not available.

institutional deliveries as compared to Tripura, Mizoram and Sikkim having more larger villages (population more than 2,000). Thus, the scattered population is the main reason for the low incidence of institutional deliveries in north-eastern states.

IMMUNIZATION

Immunization is a process of making a person more immune and resistant to any infectious disease by the use of vaccines. Immunization has been in operation since India's Independence. Many programmes like congenital rubella syndrome, MR vaccine, Many vaccination programmes are under implementation in India, but it has a long way to go to achieve its target. In India, 35 per cent of the children were fully immunized during the first round of the NFHS in 1992–1993. In the NE states, around 60 per cent of the children were not fully immunized in 2010–2011 (Table 7.7). After NFHS-4, it was found that most NE states have achieved 50 per cent full immunization of children.

Table 7.7 *Percentage of Children Fully Immunized (Age: 12–23 Months)*

States	NFHS-1 1992–1993	NFHS-2 1998–1999	NFHS-3 2005–2006	NFHS-4 2015–2016
Arunachal Pradesh	22.5	20.5	28.4	38.2
Assam	19.4	17.0	31.4	47.1
Manipur	29.1	42.3	46.8	65.9
Meghalaya	9.7	14.3	32.9	61.5
Mizoram	56.4	59.6	46.5	50.5
Nagaland	3.8	14.1	21.0	35.7
Sikkim	NA	47.4	69.6	83
Tripura	19.0	NA	49.7	54.5
India	**35.4**	**42.0**	**43.5**	**62.0**

Source: Health and Family Welfare Statistics in India, NFHS-1 (1992–1993), NFHS-2 (1998–1999), NFHS-3 (2005–2006), DLHS-3 (2007–2008), CES (2009), DLHS-4 (2012–2013) and NFHS-4 (2015–2016).

Note: NA=Not available.

Sikkim recorded the highest (83%) immunization percentage, which was higher than that of India as a whole (62%). Most of Sikkim's villages have a population size above 2,000. Arunachal Pradesh and Nagaland are at the bottom among the NE states, with only around 35 per cent of the children (12–23 months old) fully immunized, and most villages of these states have a population size less than 500. This shows that accessibility of immunization is determined by the size and scattering of villages.

HEALTHCARE CENTRE

Healthcare centre, also known as community health centre, is a network of clinics with a group of medical practitioners and nurses who provide healthcare to people in a particular area. A healthcare centre plays a vital role as a health service provider. Table 7.8 shows the number of healthcare centres in the NE states of India. During the year

Table 7.8 *Health Infrastructure (Healthcare Centers) in the North-east States of India*

State	2005				2015				
	No. of Rural Healthcare Centres	No. of AYUSH Hospitals	Total No. of Healthcare Centres	Population per Healthcare Centre	No. of Rural Healthcare Centres	No. of Urban Healthcare Centres	No. of AYUSH Hospitals	Total No. of Healthcare Centres	Population per Healthcare Centre
Arunachal Pradesh	495	2	497	2,209.1	455	212	10	677	2,042.2
Assam	5,819	4	5,823	4,577.6	5,786	1,137	4	6,927	4,499.6
Manipur	508	3	511	4,489.0	523	30	22	575	4,733.4
Meghalaya	526	1	527	4,400.0	563	40	10	613	4,835.2
Mizoram	432	1	433	2,052.1	436	36	8	480	2,272.9
Nagaland	502	0	502	3,964.2	545	36	2	583	3,397.2
Sikkim	175	1	176	3,073.0	173	33	1	207	2,935.6
Tripura	622	2	624	5,126.9	1,128	118	4	1,250	2,936.8
All India	**172,608**	**1,354**	**173,962**	**5,914**	**184,354**	**38,747**	**3,632**	**226,733**	**5,337.5**

Source: Ministry of Statistics and Programme Implementation; Health and Family Welfare, as on 1 April 2016.

2005, the number of healthcare centres (government institutes) in India was 173,962. Among the NE states, Assam had the highest number of health centre facilities during 2005. The lowest number of healthcare centres were in Sikkim (175), and the number of AYUSH (Ayurveda, Yoga & Naturopathy, Unani, Siddha and Homeopathy) hospitals was zero during 2005. Allopathic hospitals (urban health centres) were not included in the total health centres in 2005. The number of rural healthcare centres was greater than that of urban health centres in the year 2015. The numbers of rural health centres in Arunachal Pradesh, Assam and Tripura show a declining trend. The increase in the number of rural health centres was the highest in Tripura, from 622 in 2005 to 1,128 in 2015. The number of AYUSH hospitals in all the states shows an increasing trend, except for Assam. Being the largest state, Assam had the highest number of health centres in 2015 among the NE states, followed by Tripura. However, the number of population served per health centre in Assam in 2015 was the third-highest, followed by Manipur and Meghalaya, while it was the least in Arunachal Pradesh (Table 7.8).

The smaller the population covered by a health centre, the better would be the quality and quantity of health services and facilities expected from it. Mizoram and Arunachal Pradesh are the states that have smaller numbers of population covered per healthcare centre, but these two states have opposite health outcome effects in terms of institutional deliveries, percentage of fully immunized children, fertility rate and IMR. Despite the low population coverage per health centre, Arunachal Pradesh has performed rather poorly, while Mizoram has done quite well. Meghalaya is a state where, on average, a healthcare centre covers a population of 4,835.2, the highest among the NE states. Arunachal Pradesh's performance in most of the health outcome variables is far from satisfactory. This could be because of the low access of the widely scattered small settlements to health service institutions, which is not really captured by the average number. Healthcare centres are constructed in few villages, and this makes it difficult for people from other villages to access the healthcare facilities. On the other hand, in Assam, Manipur and Meghalaya, the population covered per healthcare centre is very large, because of which the quality and efficiency of the health services suffer hugely.

DOCTORS

A doctor is one of the human capitals that determine the quality of health service. Table 7.9 shows the population served and area covered per doctor in the NE states. It can be seen that in 2009, in all the states, the population served per doctor was less than the national average. In 2015, it went down in all the states except Sikkim. The decline was substantial in Nagaland, because of the massive recruitment of AYUSH doctors.

Further, the area served per doctor has also declined in all the states except Sikkim, with the decline being substantial in Nagaland. Thus, the best performers in the provision of healthcare (area served per doctor in km²) are Nagaland, Tripura and Assam, while the average performers are Manipur, Meghalaya and Sikkim. The states lagging behind are Arunachal Pradesh and Mizoram. In terms of population served per doctor, Arunachal Pradesh, Nagaland and Sikkim are better off as compared to the others. In the case of Assam, the population served per doctor is the highest because of its large population size.

CONCLUSION

The analysis above has demonstrated the behaviour of various input and outcome variables in health sectors in the north-eastern states. Thus, it becomes important to examine the heterogeneity in outcome variables like IMR *vis-à-vis* the input variables for explaining the patterns.

The highly scattered NE states are Arunachal Pradesh and Meghalaya, and they have a high IMR and CDR. The area served per doctor in Arunachal Pradesh is huge (113.16 km²/doctor), whereas in Meghalaya it is less (23.46 km²/doctor). Also, the population served per doctor is low in Arunachal Pradesh but high in Meghalaya. These average figures camouflage the feature of widely scattered human settlements in Arunachal Pradesh. This feature stands as a major impediment to the service delivery of doctors, resulting in a high IMR and CDR. On the other hand, shortage of doctors is responsible for the poor health outcomes in Meghalaya.

Table 7.9 Accessibility of Health Infrastructure: Population and Area per Doctor

States	2009		2013		2015*	
	No. of Population per Doctor	Area (in km²) Covered per Doctor	No. of Population per Doctor	Area (in km²) Covered Per Doctor	No. of Population per Doctor	Area (in km²) Covered per Doctor
Arunachal Pradesh	2,263.85	172.66	3,331.59	201.79	1,868.39	113.16
Assam	6,777.40	19.94	6,422.68	16.16	5,157.06	12.97
Manipur	3,705.80	36.06	3,389.48	27.80	3,041.06	24.94
Meghalaya	4,170.54	40.33	4,457.15	33.72	3,100.42	23.46
Mizoram	6,104.40	64.66	4,584.09	88.57	2,597.65	50.19
Nagaland	1,527.82	46.83	5,594.92	46.88	775.49	6.49
Sikkim	1,325.61	17.39	1,960.28	22.89	1,960.28	22.8
Tripura	3,813.11	12.49	4,166.89	11.90	2,675.67	7.64
India	7,515.67	24.01	6,737.52	18.30	1,411.13	3.83

Source: Medical Council of India and Dental Council of India as on 31 December 2016; Ministry of AYUSH.

Note: *Doctors under the AYUSH system are also included.

The moderately scattered NE states are Manipur, Mizoram, Nagaland, Assam and Sikkim. When a comparison is made in terms of outcome variables, Manipur, Mizoram, Nagaland and Sikkim are seen to have a low IMR. The low IMR of Nagaland and Sikkim can also be attributed to the lower population served by a doctor. The case of Nagaland is somewhat different, as the incidence of institutional deliveries is comparatively less. It is the high female literacy coupled with the high number of doctors which probably explains the low IMR in Nagaland despite its lower percentage of institutional deliveries. In the case of Assam, the settlements are moderately scattered and doctors cover a smaller area. Given these facts, better health outcomes could be expected. However, that is not the case. In reality, the state's IMR is the highest among the NE states and also above the national average. Assam Human Development Report, 2014, attributes the high IMR to high risk associated in post-neonatal childcare practices.

The cases of Mizoram and Manipur are comparable in terms of the dispersion of population settlements (moderately scattered) and also the performance of outcome variables like the percentage of institutional deliveries and IMR. However, in terms of the area served per doctor, the figure for Manipur is much lower than that for Mizoram. Thus, the better health outcomes of these states can be attributed to the high literacy and moderately better presence of doctors per unit area.

Tripura is a state wherein the population is highly concentrated in the plain areas, and this helps in providing scale economies in service delivery. Though a doctor, on average, has to serve a large population, the area to be served per doctor is low. In both these aspects, Tripura is comparable to Nagaland. Even with these favourable factors, Tripura's IMR is 29, accounting for the state's fourth rank among the NE states. Since Tripura's child immunization rate is comparable to that of Assam, its moderate IMR, as compared to Assam, could perhaps be attributed to lower post-natal risk factors in comparison with Assam.

The North-eastern region is one of the backward regions in the country, owing to its harsh climate and poor infrastructure. During the pre- and post-Independence periods, the region has been plagued by diseases like diarrhoea, malaria, tuberculosis, etc. which have led to high death tolls. NFHS-4 (2015–2016) found that most of the states of the NE have achieved a 50 per cent immunization rate of children. Improved sanitation, immunization against infectious diseases, increase in number of doctors and hospitals, education and other public health measures, especially institutional deliveries, have improved the healthcare services. However, the geographically disadvantaged population, particularly in the hilly regions of Arunachal Pradesh, Meghalaya and other parts, are still not able to access healthcare services. Many micro-level studies have substantiated these facts.

The performance of outcome variables is good, but the process variables are not adequate to provide efficient and effective health services in the North-eastern region of India. People living in remote areas have to travel long distances to consult a doctor. There are many villages with a small population size in the North-eastern region of India. Healthcare centres have been created only in a few villages. Remoteness and bad infrastructure make it difficult for many small settlements to access their facilities. As a result, they forego healthcare from which they could benefit greatly (Donnel, 2007). Finally, the issue of governance in the region cannot be ignored for proper delivery of healthcare services, as 'good governance is imperative as much for growth and development as for human development' (Sarma, 2018).

REFERENCES

Coelho, K. R., & Beldon, C. (2016). A systematic review of the literature on the relationship between caste membership and health related risk factors in India. *International Journal of Medicine and Public Health, 6*(2), 61–68.

Deferio, J. J., Breitinger, S., Khullar, D., Seth, A., & Pathak, J. (2019). Social determinants in mental health care and research: A case study for gender inclusion. *Journal of American Medical Informatics Association, 26*(8–9), 895–899.

Ghatak, A., & Narayan, L. (2015). *Health in North East States of India: An analysis of economic vulnerabilities.* Conference paper. Paper for oral presentation at the national seminar on health and poverty with special emphasis on north-east India. NEHU and ISI Kolkata in Shillong from 8 to 10 October.

Ghatak, A., & Madheswaram, S. (2011). *Burden of income loss due to ailments in India: Evidence from NSS Data* (Working Paper No. 269). Institute of Social and Economic Change, Bangalore.

Gopalan, S. S., Mohanty, S., & Das, A. (2011). Challenges and opportunities for policy decisions to address health equity in developing health system: A case study of the policy process in the Indian State of Orissa. *International Journal for Equity in Health, 10.* https://doi.org/10.1186/1475-9276-10-55.

Mal, S., Bhattacharya, P., & Ghosh, B. (2013). Consequence of health infrastructure of North East India in comparison with India. *Radix International Journal of Research in Social Science, 2*(7), 1–14.

Mihaylova, T., Dimitrov, T., Gradinarova, N., & Todorova, D. (2018). Characteristics of human resource planning in healthcare. *Journal of IMAB, 24*(1), 1953–1956.

Donnel, O. (2007). Access to health care in developing countries: Breaking down demand side barriers. *Rio DE Janeiro, 23*(12), 2820–2834.

Perazzo, H., Pacheo, A. G., Luz, P. M., Castro, R., Hide, C., Fittipaldi, J., Rigolon, C., Carsoda, S. W., Grinsztejn, B., & Veloso, V. G. (2017). Age-standardised mortality rates related to viral hepatitis in Brazil. *BMC Infectious Disease.* 10.1186/s12879-017-2619-y.

Peters, D. H., Garg, A., Bloom, G., Walker, D. G., Brieger, W. R., & Rahman, M. H. (2008). *Poverty and access to health care in developing countries.* The New York Academy of Science: 1136.

Prakash, A. (2016). Health in North East region of India—The new focus of attention. *Indian Journal of Medical Specialities, 8*(3), 93–94.

Ravindram, T., Sundari, K., & Gaitonde, R. (2018). *Health infrastructure in India.* Springer Singapore. 10.007/978-981-10-5089-3.

Sarma, A. (2018). *String of thoughts on North East India: An economic perspectives.* Aakar Book.

Veinot, T. C., Ancker, J. S., & Bakken, S. (2019). Health informatics and health equity improving our reach and impact. *Journal of American Medical Informatics Association, 26*(8–9), 689–695.

Chapter 8

Child Malnutrition in North-east India

Surajit Deb

INTRODUCTION

The prevalence of under-nutrition remains a major public health issue that creates chances of increasing childhood morbidities or premature mortality. It has been generally observed that under-nutrition intensifies with increasing birth order in many developing countries. Therefore, families with more children remain vulnerable, since children born after a short birth interval are more likely than other children to be stunted or underweight. Similarly, inadequate diet or chronic illnesses are commonly found to be associated with poor nutrition among children. On the other hand, deficiencies in some vital micronutrients also bear some disabling effect on children's health. It is often argued that the burden of malnutrition in India remains unacceptably high, and the progress unacceptably slow. According to the National Family Health Survey (NFHS-4) 2015–2016 data, nearly every third child in India is undernourished, that is, underweight (35.7%) or stunted (38.4%), and 21 per cent of the children under 5 years of age are wasted. Moreover, the NFHS-4 data also indicate that every second child within age 6–59 months is anaemic (58.4%). A comparison of NFHS-4 (2015–2016) data with those of NFHS-3 (2005–2006) indicates that there has been a decline of around 7 per cent in underweight prevalence and about 10 per cent in the prevalence of stunted children below 5 years of age. However, it also reveals that the proportion of wasted children in the same age group has gone up from 19.8 to 21 per cent between the two NFHS rounds in the country. A recent study conducted by the Indian Council of Medical Research (ICMR), Public Health Foundation of India and Institute for Health Metrics and Evaluation, and supported by the Ministry of Health and Family Welfare, examined the malnutrition burden and its trends in key indicators for all the major Indian states during the period from 1990 to 2017. According to the report's estimate of disease burden, malnutrition remains the leading risk factor for children in every state of India, as about two-thirds of the 1.04 million deaths in children below 5 years of age in India were attributable to malnutrition in 2017 (India State-Level Disease Burden Initiative Malnutrition Collaborators, 2019).

India has been trying to address child malnutrition for many decades through various policy initiatives. While different regions or states have progressed at varying degrees in certain malnutrition indicators, the north-eastern region provides an interesting case study for child nutrition. The eight states in this region are characterized by a diverse population with indigenous tribal groups and the practice of fermented foods in the diet. These states are also found to be backward with food and nutritional insecurities and are therefore included under the category of 'special category' states. The regional literature has revealed specific nutritional features across states in the region, namely, Ao and Lhungdim (2014), Mondal and Terangpi (2014), Rengma et al. (2016), Das and Guha (2017) and Chyne et al. (2017). Further, the state-level disease burden that is attributed to malnutrition in children can be observed to vary widely across the north-eastern states. According to India State-Level Disease Burden Initiative (2019), it remained high in Assam, Nagaland and Tripura in the North-east (NE) region, besides in states from other regions, namely, Rajasthan, Uttar Pradesh, Bihar, Madhya Pradesh, Chhattisgarh and Odisha. On the other hand, the Comprehensive National Nutrition Survey (CNNS), conducted by the Population Council in collaboration with the United Nations International Children's Fund (UNICEF) and the Ministry of Health and Family Welfare, found that many states in the north-eastern region, such as Mizoram, Sikkim, Manipur, Arunachal Pradesh and Nagaland, had the lowest prevalence of underweight children in India (Government of India [GOI], 2019). Against this background, this chapter explores the malnutrition challenges for children in NE India. For this, we first examine the extent to which the malnutrition burden diverges across the various states of the region and subsequently attempt to determine the intensity at definite age-groups among children below 5 years. We have mostly used recent data gathered from the state volumes of the National Family Health Survey (NFHS-4), 2015–2016. Our succeeding analysis proceeds in the following sequence. The second section provides an account of the important issues relevant to the malnutrition burden in the NE region. The next section deals with the malnutrition trends of individual states in the NE region, including age classifications of the malnutrition burden. The final section provides a summary and conclusion.

ISSUES IN NORTH-EAST INDIA

The north-eastern states of India, consisting of Arunachal Pradesh, Assam, Manipur, Meghalaya, Mizoram, Nagaland and Tripura, are usually known as the 'seven sister states'. The state of Sikkim has recently been added to this regional group due to its proximity to the region and identical features of development. The characteristic of these eight states are similar in terms of climate, ethnicity, culture, land system and food habits. The physical divisions of this region include active flood plains, flood-free plains and valleys, low hill areas and high hill areas. The region remains home to over 200 tribes, and the eight states fall under the category of 'special category' states, given the low development indicators. Agriculture remains the main occupation of the tribes, which practice *jhum,* or shifting cultivation, in which they grow cereals, vegetables and fruits. Indigenous and fermented foods have remained an inherent part of the diet for the ethnic tribes of the north-eastern states in India. Fermented products in the north-eastern states are region-specific and have their own preparation methods from various sources like cereals, milk, fruits and vegetables, leaves, bamboo shoots or fish and meat products. While different tribes prepare and consume many diverse types of fermented foods and alcoholic beverages, certain ethnic groups in NE India may consume them as part of their daily diet.

There are several papers that discuss issues pertaining to the health and nutrition aspects in NE India (Ao & Lhungdim, 2014; Das & Guha, 2017; Mondal & Terangpi, 2014; Rengma et al., 2016). Some of the papers also highlight the child under-nutrition and micronutrient deficiencies in particular states or regions (Chyne et al., 2017).

The recent round of the NFHS-4 has revealed wide variations in child health and under-nutrition outcomes across the eight north-eastern states. It may be mentioned that the infant mortality rate, as well as the under-five mortality rate, in Assam remains higher than the Indian average. However, the average birthweight of children across all the north-eastern states is found to be higher than the national average. According to the recent CNNS, states in NE India, such as Mizoram, Sikkim, Manipur, Arunachal Pradesh and Nagaland, have the lowest prevalence (16%) of underweight children, as against 33 per cent in India for the age group 0–4 years.

TRENDS IN UNDER-NUTRITION

The anthropometric indices of stunting, wasting, underweight and overweight provide information about the growth and body composition for evaluating the nutritional status of children. In this section, we examine the standard anthropometric indicators of malnourishment, namely, underweight, stunting, wasting and anaemic, for the states of NE India. The underweight or low weight-for-age is a composite index that takes into account both acute and chronic under-nutrition. Children are defined as underweight if their weight-for-age is more than two standard deviations below the World Health Organization's (WHO) Child Growth Standards median (World Health Organization [WHO], 2006, 2009). Figure 8.1 provides information on the percentage of malnourished children (below 5 years of age) in the north-eastern states. It can be seen that all the north-eastern states have done better than the all-India level in respect of underweight prevalence in the fourth round of NFHS (2015–2016). It may further be noted that within the north-eastern states, the prevalence of underweight children

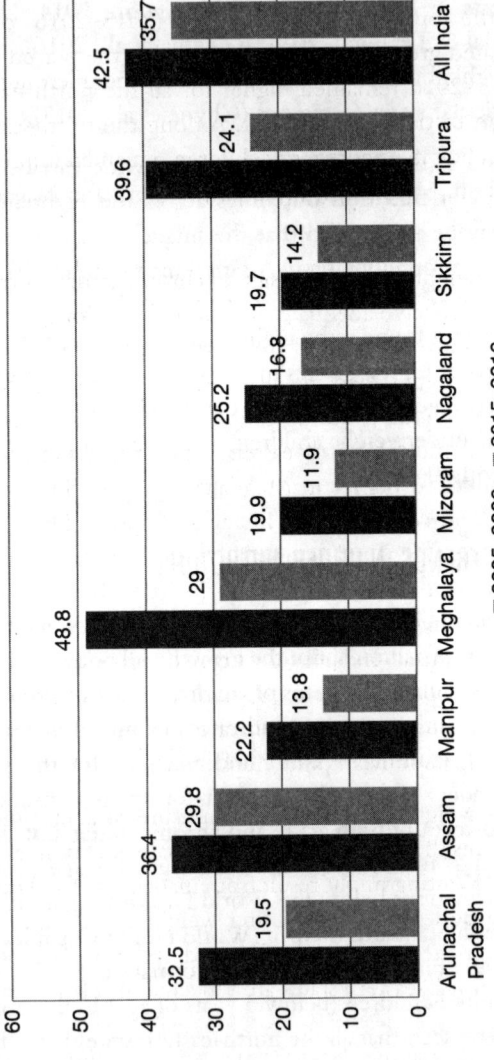

Figure 8.1 *Percentage of Underweight Children (below 5 years of age)*

Source: State Fact Sheets of NFHS-3 and NFHS-4 from IIPS (2007 and 2017).

Note: Underweight children are defined according to weight-for-age (% below −3 standard deviation).

remained higher in Assam, Meghalaya and Tripura and comparatively lower in Mizoram, Manipur and Sikkim. Figure 8.1 also reveals that the prevalence of underweight children declined across all the north-eastern states, as well as in India, between the third-round survey year (2005–2006) and the fourth-round survey year (2015–2016) of the NFHS. The calculated growth rate of decline during the period from 2005–2006 to 2015–2016 remained higher for all the north-eastern states in comparison to the all-India level. Among the north-eastern states, the rate of decline in underweight children remained impressive for Arunachal Pradesh, Meghalaya, Mizoram, Tripura and Nagaland, and poor in Assam.

Stunting, or low height-for-age, is a sign of chronic under-nutrition that reflects failure to receive adequate nutrition over a long period.[1] It is evident from Figure 8.2 that all the north-eastern states except Meghalaya have done better than the all-India level in respect of the prevalence of stunted children during the year 2015–2016. Further, it can be seen that within the north-eastern states, the prevalence of stunted children remained higher in Meghalaya, Assam, Sikkim and Arunachal Pradesh, and comparatively lower in Tripura. The prevalence of stunted children declined across all the north-eastern states, as well as in India, between 2005–2006 and 2015–2016. The calculated growth rate of decline in the time period from 2005–2006 to 2015–2016 in comparison to the all-India level remained higher across all the north-eastern states except Manipur and Assam. The rate of decline in stunted children remained better in Arunachal Pradesh, Tripura and Mizoram, and inadequate in Manipur, Meghalaya and Sikkim.

Wasting, or low weight-for-height, is a measure of acute under-nutrition and represents the failure to receive adequate nutrition leading to rapid weight loss. Wasting might result from inadequate food intake or from a recent episode of illness causing weight loss.[2] Figure 8.3 provides evidence on the percentage of wasted children, and better standards for all the north-eastern states are reflected in relation to the

---

[1] Children are defined as stunted if their height-for-age is more than two standard deviations below the WHO Child Growth Standards median (WHO, 2006).

[2] Children are defined as wasted if their weight-for-height is more than two standard deviations below the WHO Child Growth Standards median.

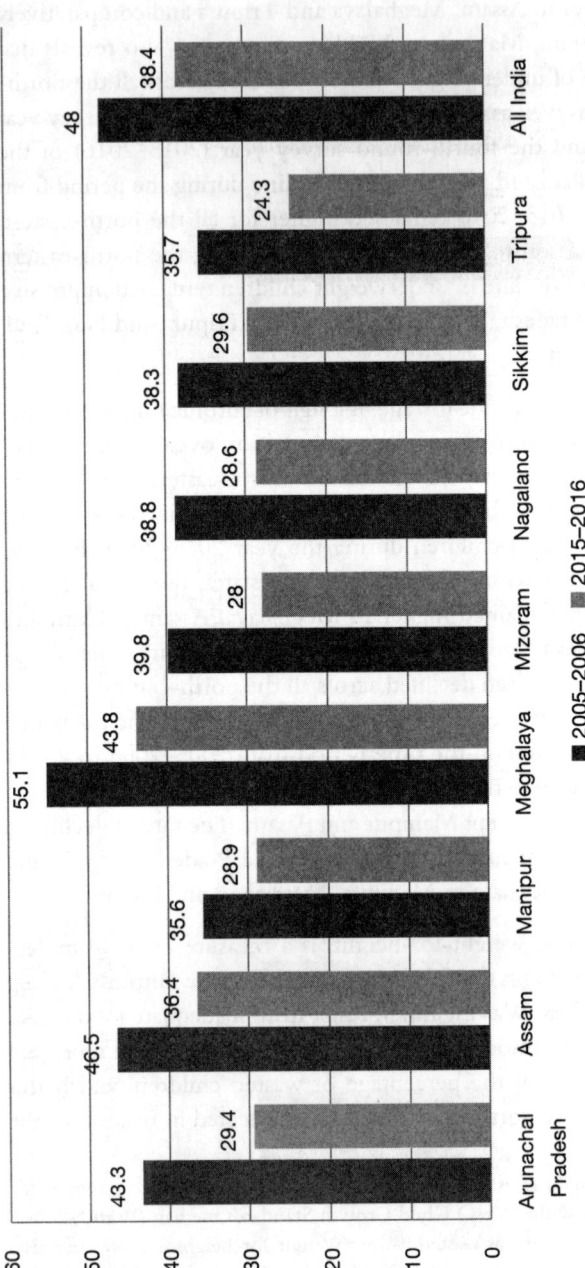

Figure 8.2 *Percentage of Stunted Children (below 5 years of age)*

Source: State Fact Sheets of NFHS-3 and NFHS-4 from IIPS (2007 and 2017).

Note: Stunted children are defined according to height-for-age (% below −2 standard deviation).

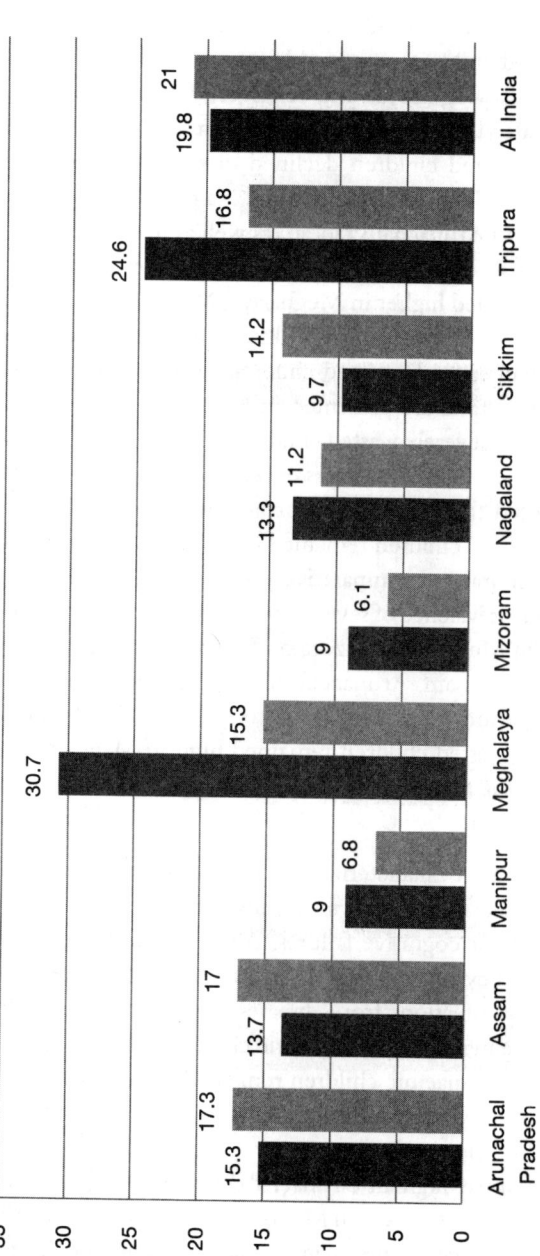

Figure 8.3 *Percentage of Wasted Children (below 5 years of age)*

Source: State Fact Sheets of NFHS-3 and NFHS-4 from IIPS (2007 and 2017).

Note: Wasted children are defined according to weight-for-height (% below –2 standard deviation).

all-India level for the year 2015–2016. It can also be observed that the prevalence of wasted children remained higher in Arunachal Pradesh, Assam, Tripura and Meghalaya, and relatively lower in Mizoram, Manipur and Nagaland within the north-eastern region. Interestingly, the prevalence of wasted children declined in some states (namely, Meghalaya, Mizoram, Tripura, Manipur and Nagaland) but increased in Sikkim, Assam and Arunachal Pradesh, as well as in India, between 2005–2006 and 2015–2016. The rate of decline in the prevalence of wasted children remained higher in Meghalaya, Mizoram and Tripura, but the rate of growth intensified for Sikkim and Assam. The figures on the percentage of severely wasted children (below 5 years of age) in the north-eastern states are presented in Figure 8.4. It is observed that the prevalence of severely wasted children in 2015–2016 remained lower across all the north-eastern states except for Arunachal Pradesh. It may also be noted that within the north-eastern states, the prevalence of severely wasted children remained high in Arunachal Pradesh, Meghalaya and Tripura, and comparatively low in Manipur, Mizoram and Nagaland. The prevalence of severely wasted children can be found to have declined in Meghalaya, Mizoram, Tripura and Nagaland, and increased in Sikkim, Assam, Arunachal Pradesh, Manipur and also in India during the period from 2005–2006 to 2015–2016. The rate of decline in severely wasted children remained high in Meghalaya and Mizoram, whereas the rate of growth remained high in Sikkim, Assam and Arunachal Pradesh.

Anaemic children are characterized by the lack of haemoglobin in blood that could result in increased morbidity from infectious diseases, several impairments or cognitive failures. Anaemia can be caused by a nutritional deficiency of iron and other essential minerals and vitamins, as well as by infections from diseases like malaria. Figure 8.5 arranges data on the percentage of anaemic children, and it is revealed that the prevalence of anaemic children remained lower across all the north-eastern states in comparison with the all-India level in the year 2015–2016. Within the north-eastern states, the prevalence of anaemic children remained high in Arunachal Pradesh, Meghalaya and Tripura, and comparatively lower in Manipur, Mizoram and Nagaland. Figure 8.5 also reveals that the prevalence of anaemic children declined across all the north-eastern states, as well as in India, during the period

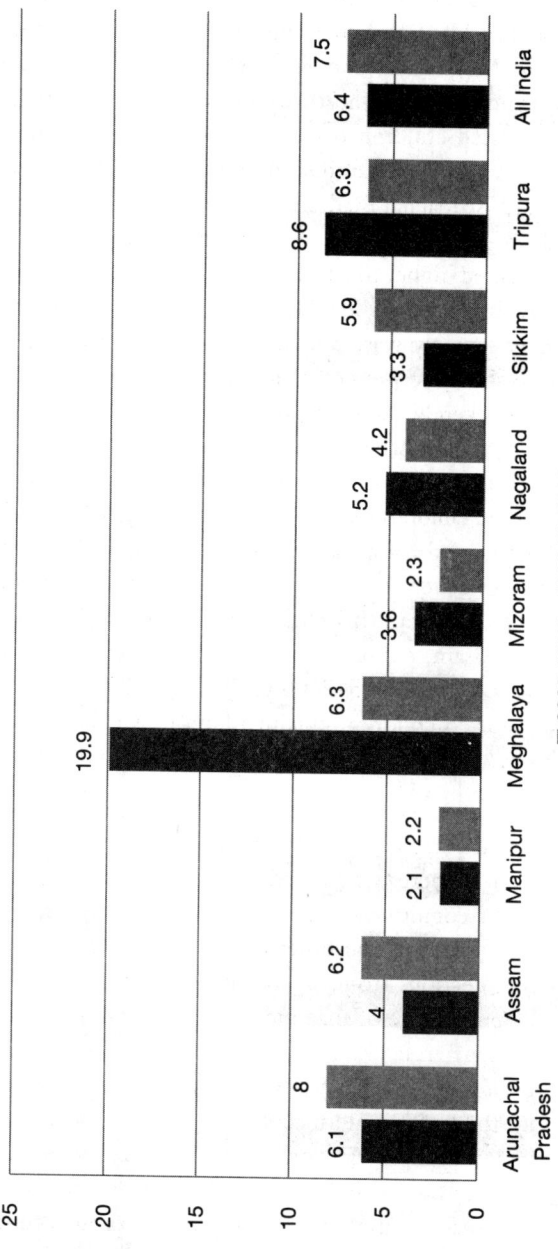

Figure 8.4 *Percentage of Severely Wasted Children (below 5 years of age)*

Source: State Fact Sheets of NFHS-3 and NFHS-4 from IIPS (2007 and 2017).

Note: Severely wasted children are defined according to weight-for-height (% below −3 standard deviation).

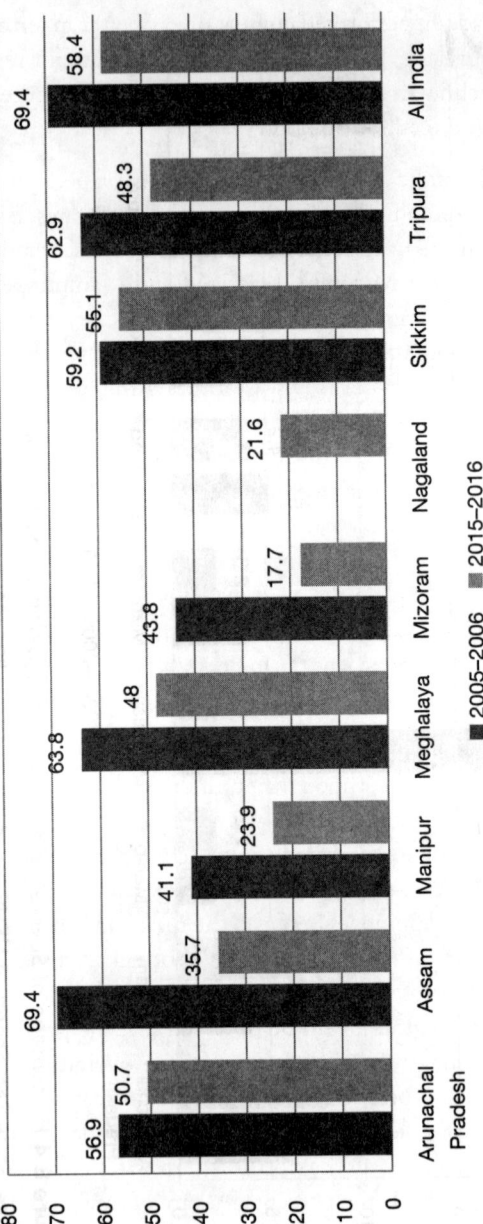

Figure 8.5 *Percentage of Anaemic Children (below 5 years of age)*

Source: State Fact Sheets of NFHS-3 and NFHS-4 from IIPS (2007 and 2017).

Note: Includes any anaemia (less than 11 g/dL).

from 2005–2006 to 2015–2016. In fact, all the states, excepting Sikkim and Arunachal Pradesh, performed comparatively better in terms of the rate of decline. The states of Mizoram, Assam and Manipur registered better rates of decline among the north-eastern states, whereas poor performances are noticed for Sikkim.

Figures 8.1–8.5 indicates the varying degrees of performance in different malnutrition indicators for the north-eastern states. Although no clear pattern on the nutritional indicators can be discerned for the region, we observe that Mizoram, Nagaland and Manipur remained better off in the maximum numbers of indicators, whereas Assam, Arunachal Pradesh and Tripura performed poorly on the same criteria. The report by India State-Level Disease Burden Initiative (2019) has provided detailed estimates of the annualized percentage change in various malnutrition indicators during the period from 2010 to 2017. Table 8.1 highlights the severity of malnutrition in individual indicators for the north-eastern states while revealing the variations across the states in the region. It can be noticed that most of the states in the region have done better than the all-India level in respect of progress regarding birthweight, stunting, wasting and anaemia but not in the context of underweight prevalence. On the other hand, the prevalence of overweight children seems to have gone up for all the states in the region as well as in India as a whole.

It is often argued that childhood malnutrition is typically a less severe problem in urban than in rural areas (Ruel et al., 1999; von Braun et al., 1993). The rural–urban divide in the child nutritional status is evident form the NFHS-4 survey data for a large number of states. In view of the observed differences between the rural and urban nutrition levels across states of different regions, we also make a basic inquiry into the child under-nutrition levels separately for areas of residence in the north-eastern region. It can be observed that the prevalence of under-nutrition in children below 5 years of age (weight-for-age) in rural areas remains far worse than that in the urban areas of all the NE Indian states (Figure 8.10). It is also important to note that the majority of the population in almost all the north-eastern states remained rural. According to Census 2011, the percentage share of rural population in all the states, excepting Mizoram, remained at more than 70 per cent.

Table 8.1 *Annualized Percentage Change of Malnutrition Indicators in North-east India (2010–2017)*

States	Low Birthweight	Child Stunting	Child Wasting	Underweight Children	Child Anaemia	Overweight Children
Arunachal Pradesh	–0.64	–2.98	–0.75	–1.96	–1.53	4.06
Assam	–1.27	–2.73	–1.06	–2.61	–7.27	4.94
Manipur	–1.84	–2.29	–1.93	–2.88	–5.52	5.66
Meghalaya	–1.23	–1.22	–4.04	–5.37	–4.04	2.63
Mizoram	–0.87	–2.88	–1.18	–2.38	–8.35	2.49
Nagaland	–1.17	–2.68	–1.34	–2.99	–6.17	2.87
Sikkim	–3.76	–3.15	–2.35	–3.41	–1.79	2.86
Tripura	–1.37	–2.89	–1.94	–2.73	–3.06	4.29
All India	**–1.12**	**–2.63**	**–1.23**	**–3.22**	**–1.81**	**4.98**

Source: The India State-Level Disease Burden Initiative (2019).

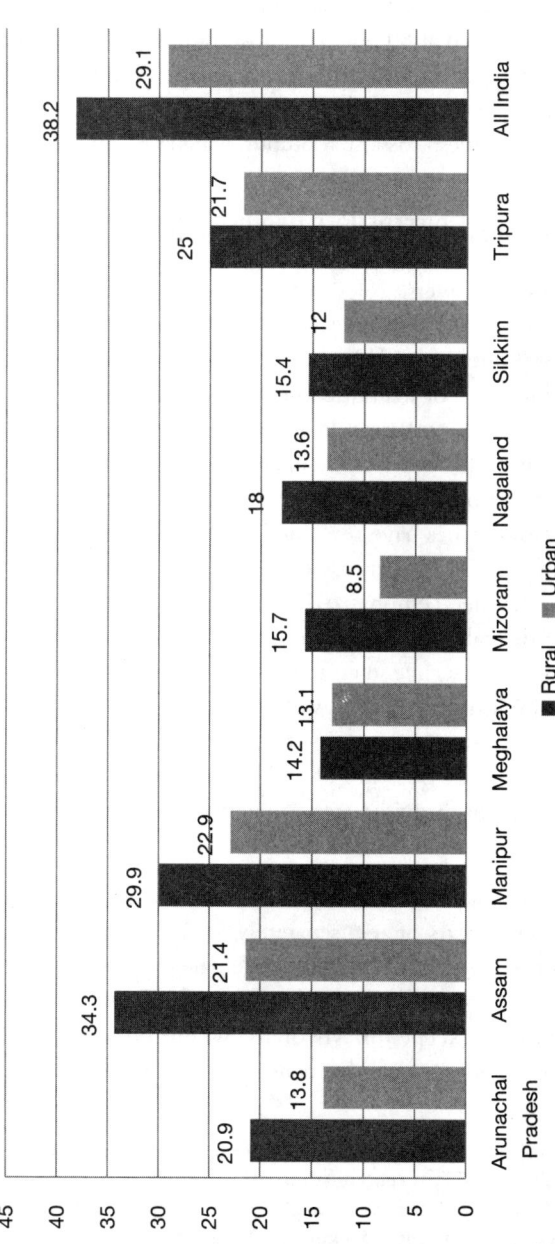

Figure 8.6 *Percentage of Underweight Children, Rural and Urban, 2015–2016*

Source: State Fact Sheets of NFHS-4 from IIPS (2017).

Note: Malnutrition is defined according to weight-for-age (% below −2 standard deviation).

While the rural population constituted about half of the total population in Mizoram, it remained at 80 per cent or more in the states of Assam and Arunachal Pradesh.[3] The nutrition level of children in the urban areas was noticeably better than the level in rural areas for certain states, namely, Arunachal Pradesh, Assam, Manipur, Meghalaya and Nagaland.

GENDER AND CASTE DIFFERENCES IN CHILD UNDER-NUTRITION

Gender relations play diverse roles in the families and societies of the north-eastern states, as determined by the cultural norms across the region. It is very often found that the women in different parts of India are at greater risk of malnutrition than men in households that are vulnerable to food insecurity. It is necessary that the principle of improvements in child under-nutrition ensure that there is gender equality in the nutrition levels among children. This is because gender and under-nutrition issues have remained as integral parts of the poverty trap and cycles. This is because the issue of gender inequality in India has sometimes been emphasized by an examination of the differences between the male and female hunger and under-nutrition levels. Country-level evidences have so far indicated that female children with access to nutrition learn better and well-nourished girls with access to education are able to earn more during their lifespan. Since bringing up the gender aspect on the question of child under-nutrition challenges is essential, this section provides some disaggregated analysis on male and female children for the NE Indian states.

Figure 8.7 provides information on the underweight prevalence of children below 5 years of age, separately for boys and girls, in the north-eastern states. It can be inferred that female children have better nutrition levels, according to the weight-for-age criterion, in all the north-eastern states, except for Mizoram, where boys are marginally better. The gaps between the male and female nutrition levels

---

[3] The individual percentage shares of rural population in these states as per Census 2011 ranges from 77 per cent in Arunachal Pradesh, 86 per cent in Assam, 70 per cent in Manipur, 80 per cent in Meghalaya, 49 per cent in Mizoram, 71 per cent in Nagaland, 75 per cent in Sikkim and 74 per cent in Tripura, as against 69 per cent at the all-India level.

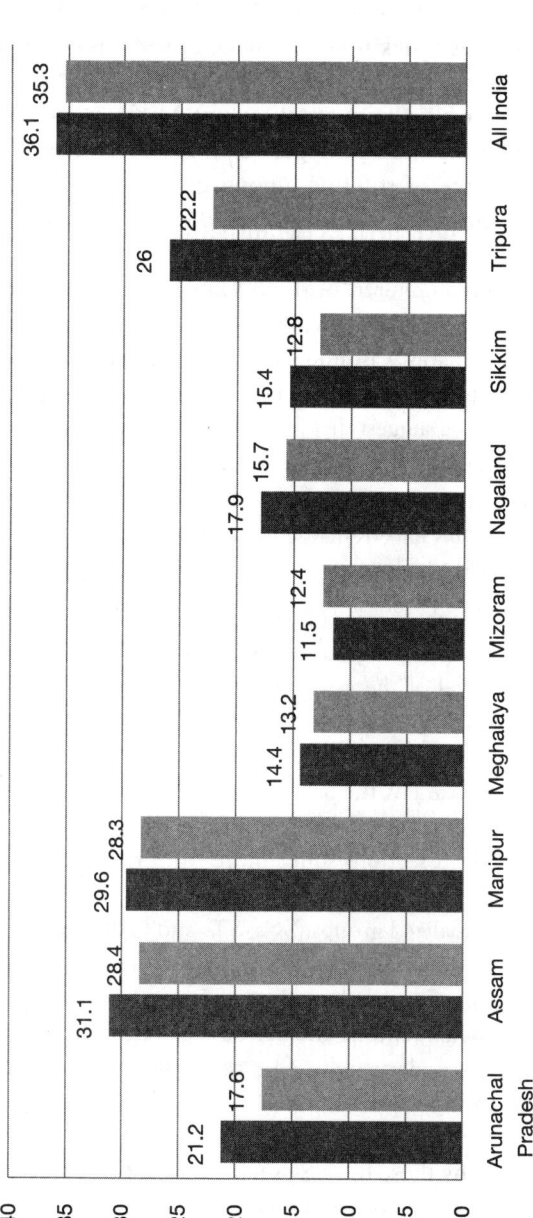

Figure 8.7 *Percentage of Underweight Children, Male and Female, 2015–2016*

Source: State Fact Sheets of NFHS-4 from IIPS (2017).

Note: Underweight children are defined according to weight-for-age (% below −2 standard deviation).

are, however, only moderate (Arunachal Pradesh and Assam) or low (Meghalaya, Nagaland and Sikkim). The disaggregated representation of the prevalence of stunting for male vis-à-vis female children also indicates that all the north-eastern states, except Mizoram, achieved better standards for female children (Figure 8.8). However, the extent to which the prevalence of stunting among girls outperforms the same among boys varies from state to state in the region. Figure 8.9 further suggests that female children made better progress in terms of the prevalence of wasted children below 5 years of age in almost all the north-eastern states. However, while the gap between male and female nutrition benchmarks was moderate in Arunachal Pradesh and Tripura, it remained insignificant in other states. Finally, the data on the prevalence of anaemia suggest that female children have done only marginally better in most of the north-eastern states (Figure 8.10). It may be noted that the phenomenon of girl children performing better in terms of the prevalence of underweight, stunting and wasting also remains valid at the all-India level.

The prevalence of high degrees of malnutrition among the poor, particularly among specific social groups, has always remained a concern at the policymaking level of the government. In recent times, it has been argued that although the malnutrition level in India is declining at the overall level, it has remained at relatively higher levels among marginalized social groups, namely, the Scheduled Castes (SCs), Scheduled Tribes (STs) and Other Backward Classes (OBC). This part examines whether the marginalized sections suffer more from the malnourishment and are therefore deprived of a healthy children's life. Table 8.2 indicates that the marginalized groups (SCs, STs and OBCs) suffer the most from nutritional deficiencies at the all-India level. In fact, the children (under 5 years of age) belonging to STs are found to be the most nutritionally deficient among the various social groups. Among them, 45.3 per cent are underweight, 43.8 per cent are stunted, 27.4 per cent are wasted and 63.1 per cent are anaemic. Consequently, the underweight prevalence is found to be the highest among children from STs (45.3%), followed by those from SCs (39.1%) and OBCs (35.5%), as against 28.8 per cent among those in the general population. Among the social groups, stunting is found to be the highest among children from STs (43.8%), followed by those from SCs (42.8%) and OBCs

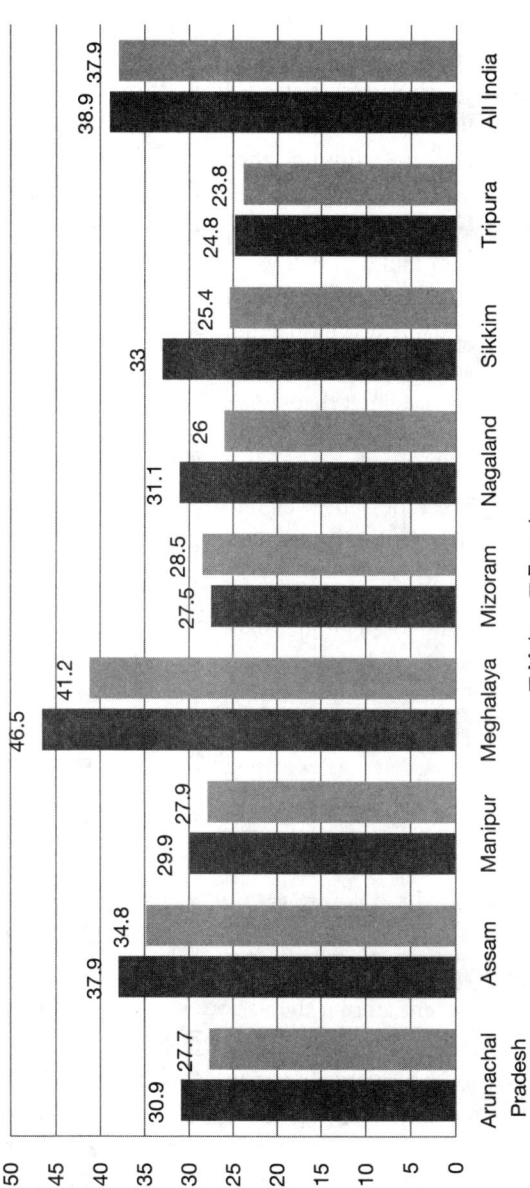

Figure 8.8 *Percentage of Stunted Children, Male and Female, 2015–2016*

Source: State Fact Sheets of NFHS-4 from IIPS (2017).

Note: Stunted children are defined according to height-for-age (% below −2 standard deviation).

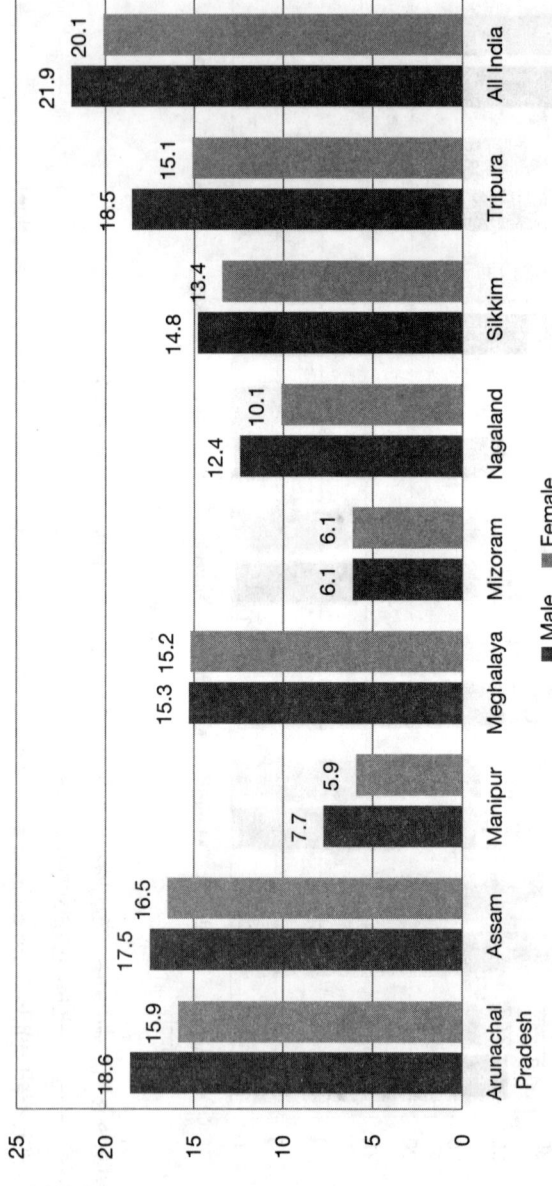

Figure 8.9 *Percentage of Wasted Children, Male and Female, 2015–2016*

Source: State Fact Sheets of NFHS-4 from IIPS (2017).

Note: Wasted children are defined according to weight-for-height (% below −2 standard deviation).

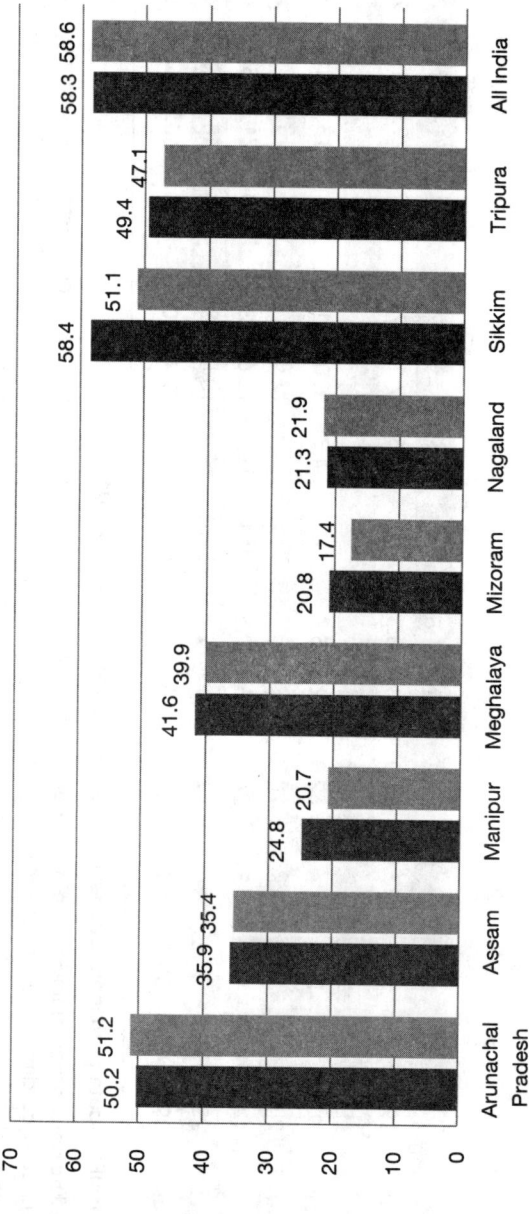

Figure 8.10 *Percentage of Anaemic Children, Male and Female, 2015–2016*

Source: State Fact Sheets of NFHS-4 from IIPS (2017).

Note: Includes any anaemia (less than 11 g/dL).

Table 8.2 Child Under-nutrition Indicators Disaggregated over Social Classes, 2015–2016

States	% of Underweight Children (weight for age)				% of Stunted Children (height for age)				% of Wasted Children (weight for height)				% of Anaemic Children (any anaemia)			
	SC	ST	OBC	General	SC	ST	OBC	General	SC	ST	OBC	General	SC	ST	OBC	General
Arunachal Pradesh	13.1	18.1	23.5	27.1	21.6	30.5	25.1	29.1	21.0	16.4	21.9	18.5	57.3	45.5	51.1	63.1
Assam	27.8	18.5	26.8	34.0	36.6	28.2	31.6	40.2	16.2	10.5	17.9	18.4	31.5	37.4	37.3	35.4
Manipur	19.8	12.6	16.8	12.9	32.0	34.3	28.3	24.3	7.6	7.1	7.3	6.5	29.0	19.8	23.4	24.3
Meghalaya	16.0	28.6	–	36.8	38.6	44.3	–	39.5	2.9	14.9	–	23.6	27.5	40.1	–	51.2
Mizoram	9.5	11.6	27.7	–	62.0	27.2	45.4	–	4.3	6.0	11.7	–	13.7	18.6	37.3	–
Nagaland	24.7	16.3	18.9	17.1	28.2	28.9	25.9	30.6	15.9	11.0	11.0	10.9	18.7	21.8	21.8	17.8
Sikkim	14.8	14.2	15.1	13.4	26.9	29.6	30.5	28.4	13.0	16.6	13.8	12.0	71.2	58.3	48.0	56.3
Tripura	28.8	20.9	20.9	26.6	27.5	24.9	17.8	25.4	17.7	18.5	15.0	15.5	48.6	54.8	45.2	42.0
All-India	39.1	45.3	35.5	28.8	42.8	43.8	38.7	31.2	21.2	27.4	20.5	19.0	60.5	63.1	58.6	53.9

Source: NFHS data from International Institute of Population Sciences (2017).

Notes: The percentage of underweight children is defined according to weight-for-age (% below −2 standard deviation), stunted children are defined according to height-for-age (% below −2 standard deviation), wasted children are defined according to weight-for-height (% below −2 standard deviation) and anaemia includes any anaemia (less than 11 g/dL).

(38.7%), in comparison to those in the general population (31.2%). The highest prevalence of child wasting is found among those from STs (27.4%), followed by those from SCs (21.2%) and OBCs (20.5%), as against 19 per cent among those in the general population. ST children also performed the worst in terms of anaemia prevalence, namely, 63.1 per cent, as against 60.5, 58.6 and 53.9 per cent for ST, OBC and general population children, respectively.

It may be noted that the share of ST population remained very high in the states of Arunachal Pradesh, Meghalaya, Nagaland and Mizoram, ranging between 69 and 94 per cent of the total population according to Census 2011 data. In the states of Manipur, Sikkim and Tripura, the share of ST population was around one-third of the respective state population. It was only in the state of Assam in this region that the share of ST population remained at par with the all-India benchmark of 17 per cent. On the other hand, the share of SC population remained much lower in each north-eastern state, excepting Tripura, in comparison to the all-India average of 17 per cent. Table 8.2 also reveals that the nutritional deprivation of SC and ST children vis-à-vis that of children in the general population is not evident in the NE Indian states. In fact, the SC and ST children in the states of Arunachal Pradesh, Assam and Meghalaya presented a superior state of affairs in many child nutrition indicators in relation to those in the general population. On the other hand, the SC and ST classes lagged behind the general population in a majority of the child nutrition indicators for the states of Manipur, Nagaland, Sikkim and Tripura. Furthermore, while the SCs seem to have done relatively better than the STs in preventing child malnutrition in the states of Arunachal Pradesh, Meghalaya and Mizoram, the opposite phenomenon appears to be prominent in the states of Assam, Manipur, Nagaland and Tripura. Our empirical evidences do infer some social class inequalities, which calls for some specific policies and measures to bring children from the marginalized sections of the society out of the malnutrition trap.

AGE CLASSIFICATION OF UNDER-NUTRITION

In this section, we attempt to distinguish the concentration of under-nutrition in the north-eastern states among children of different age groups below 5 years of age. For this, we perform re-classifications of the malnutrition prevalence and define four relevant age groups, namely, children less than 8 months, 9–17 months, 18–35 months and 36–59 months. The data provided in Figure 8.11 reveal that malnutrition sets in during the exclusive breastfeeding period and increases immediately after the early breastfeeding age, namely, from the ninth month, in all the five NE states besides Arunachal Pradesh, Mizoram and Tripura. The rise in malnutrition catches up slower than the other states and actually declines in the final age groups only for Arunachal Pradesh and Mizoram. The malnutrition prevalence for the five states, viz., Assam, Manipur, Meghalaya, Nagaland and Sikkim can be seen to be increasing steadily in each of the successive age groups. On the contrary, Tripura happens to be the only state in this region where malnutrition declines in the second age group (9–17 months). The growing under-nutrition along with age continues till the 17th month and subsequently to the next age group (18–35 months) in all the five states. It may be perceived that the age group of 18–35 months and the following age group of 36–59 months are marked with the highest concentration of malnutrition in almost all the states. Overall, the results on the prevalence of under-nutrition along with age in the sample of the north-eastern states indicate that malnutrition sets in during the breastfeeding age of the children and rises rather sharply as the weaning period is approached. The remaining part of this section uses the results of the changing prevalence of under-nutrition along with age to throw light on the role of breastfeeding in the child nutritional aspects of the north-eastern region.

It is often argued in the context of child under-nutrition that the feeding practices for infants and young children shape the nutritional status of children under 2 years of age. According to the Government of India (GoI) (2019), optimal feeding practices during infancy and early childhood, comprising early initiation of breastfeeding, exclusive breastfeeding in the first 6 months of life, continued breastfeeding till age 1 year, timely introduction of complementary foods, diversity of diet and frequency of diet are critical for the survival, healthy growth and development of children under 2 years of age. Improper feeding practices and diarrhoeal diseases are frequently held responsible for causing under-nutrition and therefore controlling child survival. The Government of India recommends that children be exclusively

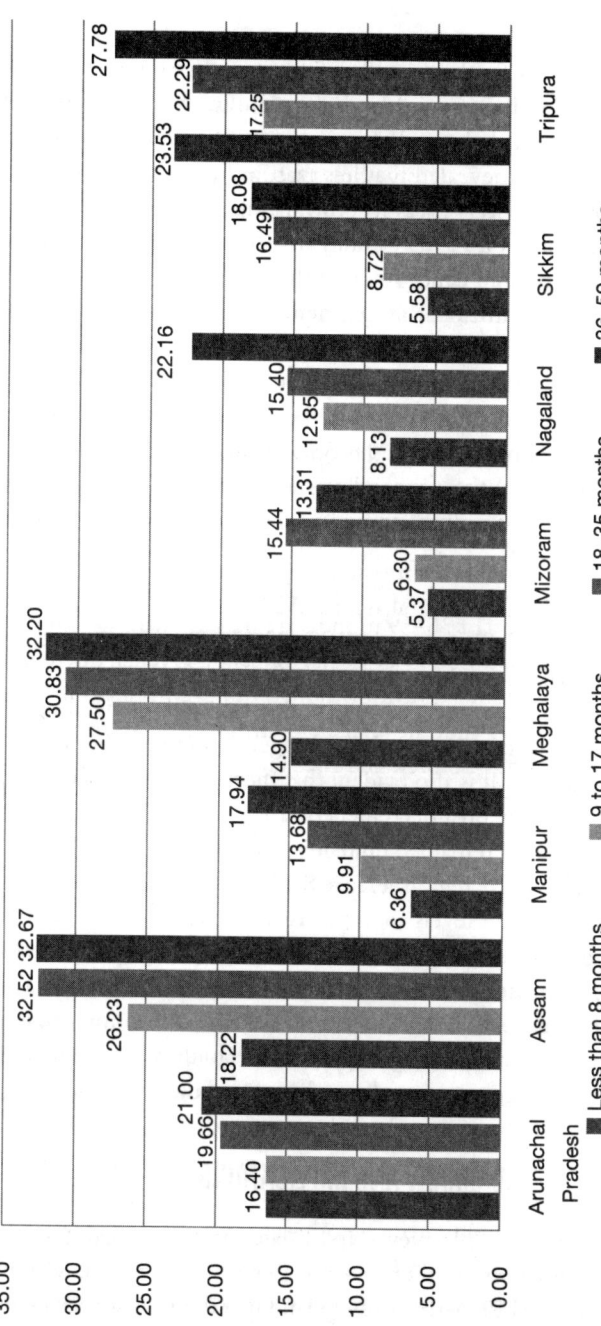

Figure 8.11 *Percentage of Underweight Children according to age, 2015–2016*

Source: Author's calculation from IIPS (2017).

Note: Underweight children are defined according to weight-for-age (% below −2 standard deviation).

breastfed for the first 6 months of life with no other liquids or food. However, liquids and semi-solid foods are often introduced in the diet before the recommended age of 6 months in several states of India. The NFHS data have revealed that less than half the children under 6 months of age are exclusively breastfed in India, and more than one-fifth of the children aged 18–23 months are not breastfed at all. Almost one-fifth of the children aged 4–5 months are given complementary foods, contrary to nutritional recommendations. Some children are weaned before they are 1 year old, and the pace of weaning acceler-ates beyond 12 months of age. According to the recent CNNS, in 57 per cent of the overall children born in the 2 years prior to the survey, breastfeeding was initiated within 1 hour of birth, 58 per cent of infants under the age of 6 months were exclusively breastfed, and 83 per cent of children aged 12–15 months continued to be breastfed at age 1 year.

The median duration of breastfeeding in India remains at 29.6 months, with 33 months in rural areas and 24.4 months in urban areas, according to the NFHS-4 survey (IIPS, 2017). This means that, on average, about half the children in India stop breastfeeding around the age of 30 months. However, the median duration of breastfeeding has been found to be about 36 months or longer in some of the states in NE India (Table 8.3). It is also evident that there are wide variations in the median duration of breastfeeding period across the NE Indian states, and the recorded level remained quite low for Nagaland in comparison to the other states of the region. Figure 8.12 reworks the age classifica-tion of under-nutrition levels so as to organize the data for only two relevant age groups, namely, the breastfeeding age group (<35 months) and the age group after the end of breastfeeding (36–59 months). This exploration clearly reveals that the extent of under-nutrition remains significantly higher in the age group after the children are weaned in comparison to the age group with any breastfeeding.

SUMMARY AND IMPLICATIONS

The National Nutrition Survey (NNS) data recently revealed in the context of north-eastern states that while states like Mizoram, Sikkim, Manipur, Arunachal Pradesh and Nagaland had the lowest prevalence

Table 8.3 Median Duration of Any Breastfeeding (Months) in North-east India (2014–2015)

Arunachal Pradesh	Assam	Manipur	Meghalaya	Mizoram	Nagaland	Sikkim	Tripura	All-India
31	>36	>36	29.3	29.8	18.5	32	>36	29.6

Source: IIPS (2017): NFHS-4.

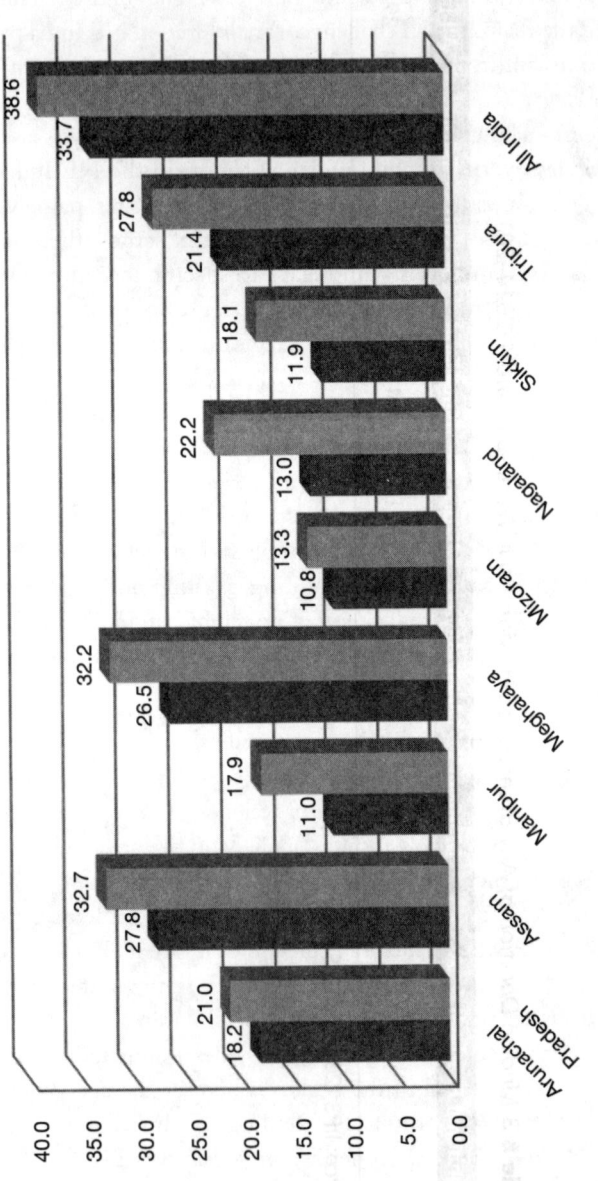

Figure 8.12 *Percentage of Underweight Children before and after Breastfeeding Age, 2015–2016*

Source: Author's calculation from IIPS (2017).

Note: Underweight children are defined according to weight-for-age (% below −2 standard deviation).

of underweight children, the same states also lagged in indicators like child stunting, child wasting and anaemic or overweight children. This chapter probed the malnutrition challenges for children in NE India by examining various anthropometric indicators. It is apparent that some of the north-eastern states have done better than the all-India level in respect of specific malnutrition indicators. However, our analysis also reveals the overall severity of child under-nutrition in the NE India while disclosing the variations within the region. A few states, namely, Mizoram, Nagaland and Sikkim, have outperformed the others in enhancing child nutrition levels with regard to specific indicators for the region. Overall, there is an indication of progress; however, the results also highlight the challenges in the region. Table 8.4 provides information on the gap between projected malnutrition prevalence and targets in the states of NE India from the results of the State-Level Disease Burden Initiative (2019). It can be seen that Sikkim has no gap with regard to the child stunting target, and Table 8.4 also indicates impressive performances in almost all the indicators. While most of the NE Indian states were placed better than the all-India level with regard to many malnutrition indicators like stunting, wasting and anaemia, they lagged behind in the prevalence of overweight children. On the other hand, states like Assam, Manipur, Meghalaya and Tripura remain behind the target with regard to several indicators.

The focus on the intensity of malnutrition among children below 5 years of age in different age groups has been the particular concern of this chapter. Our results revealed that the prevalence of malnutrition in the region sets in during the early months, namely, in the first 8 months of a child's life, which increases thereafter and attains a maximum value at the age group of 36–59 months. The rearrangement of the under-nutrition data for the two pertinent age groups of less than 35 months (any breastfeeding) and 36–59 months (after the end of breastfeeding) clearly revealed higher under-nutrition after the children are weaned, in all the states of the region. Our analysis provides a clear indication that the under-nutrition level in the region is high at the age group successive to the infant age group. The findings of this chapter also revealed that although there is no gender or social class bias against female children, significant variations in the prevalence of malnutrition

Table 8.4 Gap Between Projected Malnutrition Prevalence and Targets in North-east India

States	Gap Between Projected Low Birthweight and Target (%)		Gap Between Projected Child Stunting and Target (%)		Gap Between Projected Child Wasting and WHO and UNICEF 2030 Target (%)	Gap Between Projected Child Underweight and NNM 2022 Target (%)	Gap Between Projected Child Anaemia and NNM 2022 Target (%)	Gap Between Projected Child Overweight and WHO and UNICEF 2030 Target (%)
	NNM 2022 Target	WHO and UNICEF 2030 Target	NNM 2022 Target	WHO and UNICEF 2030 Target				
Arunachal Pradesh	9.4	3.8	3.1	3.3	14.4	8.4	15	25.5
Assam	8.8	2.4	8.2	4.3	8.3	6.3	6.1	12.1
Manipur	8.6	0.6	3.7	5.4	3.6	8.2	10.5	24.1
Meghalaya	8.9	2.4	17.3	14.1	5.3	2.6	9.1	14.9
Mizoram	8.3	1.3	0.6	2.7	10.1	8.5	9.0	16.0
Nagaland	9.2	2.6	2.9	4.7	7.6	8.2	10.2	17.9
Sikkim	8.5	No gap	No gap	1.8	2.1	8.2	11.1	20.1
Tripura	8.7	2.1	0.9	2.1	10.4	6.0	10.0	18.3
All-India	**8.9**	**2.8**	**9.6**	**5.2**	**10.4**	**4.8**	**11.7**	**14.5**

Source: The India State-Level Disease Burden Initiative (2019).

rates persisted between the rural and urban areas or, for that matter, across different social classes in the region.

While the analyses on child nutrition in India generally put emphasis on the underweight children, the growing prevalence of overweight children in recent times has become a concern for many states. Overweight or obesity in children can cause several impairments in the nutritional level of children and is sometimes a major cause of non-communicable diseases and respiratory symptoms. Although micronutrient deficiencies are considered to determine the prevalence of child malnutrition, there exist very little statistics on micronutrient status and deficiencies at the state level in India. The occurrence of infectious diseases and under-five mortality is usually considered to be a result of child under-nutrition in developing countries, as well as in India. It is argued that if a child is malnourished, the mortality risks associated with respiratory infections, diarrhoea, malaria, measles and other infectious diseases are increased. The India State-Level Disease Burden Initiative (2019) has accordingly identified low birthweight of children as the biggest contributor to the disease burden among various malnutrition indicators in India, followed by stunting, underweight and wasting. A further extension of this study could take up the topic of whether the result of the changing prevalence of under-nutrition along with age remains consistent with the divergence between infant and child mortality rates in the region.

REFERENCES

Ao, M., & Lhungdim, H. (2014, February 8). Re-estimating malnourishment and inequality among children in North-east India. *Economic & Political Weekly, 49*(6), 53–63.

Chyne, D. A. L., Meshram, I. I., Rajendran, A., Kodali, V., Getti, N., Roy, P., Kuhnlein, H. V., & Longvah, T. (2017). Nutritional status, food insecurity and biodiversity among the Khasi in Meghalaya, North-East India. *Maternal and Child Nutrition, 3*(S3). https://doi.org/10.1111/mcn.12557

Das, T., & Guha, P. (2017, April–June). Direction of uneven health-care expenditure: Evidence from Northeast India. *Indian Journal of Public Health, 61*(2). www.ijph.in. https://doi.org/10.4103/ijph.IJPH_315_15

International Institute of Population Sciences (IIPS). (2007). *National family health survey (NFHS-3), 2005–06, state fact sheets.* IIPS.

Government of India. (2019). *Comprehensive national nutrition survey*. UNICEF and Population Council, Ministry of Health and Family Welfare.

International Institute of Population Sciences (IIPS). (2017). *National family health survey (NFHS-4), 2015–16, state fact sheets*. IIPS.

India State-Level Disease Burden Initiative Malnutrition Collaborators. (2019, September 18). The burden of child and maternal malnutrition and the trends in its indicators in the states of India: The global burden of disease study 1990–2017. *Lancet Child & Adolescent Health*. https://doi.org/10.1016/S2352-4642(19)30273-1

Mondal, N., & Terangpi, M. (2014). Prevalence of under-nutrition among tribal adolescents of KarbiAnglong district of Assam, Northeast India, Sri Lanka. *Journal of Child Health, 43*(3), 154–157.

Rengma, M. S., Bose, K., & Mondal, N. (2016). Socio-economic and demographic correlates of stunting among adolescents of Assam, North-east India. *Anthropological Review, 79*(4), 409–425.

Ruel, M. T., Haddad, L., & Garrett, J. L. (1999). Some urban facts of life: Implications for research and policy. *World Development, 27*(11), 1917–1938.

von Braun, J., McComb, J., Fred-Mensah, B., & Pandya-Lorch, R. (1993). *Urban food insecurity and malnutrition in developing countries: Trends, policies and research implications*. International Food Policy Research Institute.

World Health Organization (WHO). (2006). *Child growth standards, length/height-for-age, weight-for-age, weight-for-length, weight-for-height and body mass index-for-age: Methods and development*. Department of Nutrition for Health and Development, WHO.

World Health Organization (WHO). (2009). *Child growth standards, growth velocity based on weight, length and head circumference: Methods and development*. Department of Nutrition for Health and Development, WHO.

SECTION V

Poverty, Unemployment and Food Security

Chapter 9

Poverty in North-east India
An Overview

Joydeep Baruah

In this chapter, an attempt has been made to provide an overview of the poverty scenario in the eight states of North-east (NE) India, namely, Arunachal Pradesh, Assam, Manipur, Meghalaya, Mizoram, Nagaland, Tripura and Sikkim. As per Census 2011, the eight states together cover nearly 8 per cent of the total geographical area of the country and accommodate close to 4 per cent of the country's total population. These states are enormously diverse in terms of geography, demography and economic structures, besides historical contexts. For instance, during the colonial times, the British administered the region through four different mechanisms, that is, Assam, which then included the present Meghalaya, Nagaland and Mizoram as districts, was a directly governed province under the colonial rule, Manipur and Tripura were two princely states, and a large part of the region was also placed under 'excluded' and 'partially excluded' areas, while Sikkim was a British 'protectorate'. Notably, the Indian Council Act 1919 put 'all the backward tracts of Assam' as partially excluded areas. Subsequently, the Government of India Act, 1935, placed Balipara Frontier Tract, Sadiya Frontier Tract and Lakhimpur Frontier Tract, which later on formed the North-East Frontier Agency (NEFA) and subsequently came to be known as Arunachal Pradesh, Naga Hills District, Lushai

Hills District (present Mizoram) and North Cachar Hills under the 'Excluded Areas', whereas the Garo Hills District, Mikir Hills District and the British portion of Khasi and Jaintia Hills District, excluding Shillong Municipality and Cantonment areas, came to be known as the 'Partially Excluded Areas'.[1] The so-called backward tracts were the areas mostly covered by hills and inhabited by indigenous tribal communities; it may be mentioned that the hill–valley dichotomy, as well as interconnections, determine, to a large extent, the overarching structure of the economy of the region.

The present chapter deals with 'deprivation(s)'—officially measured in India through a 'poverty line' derived on the basis of consumer expenditure data supposedly representing deprivations in 'fixed calorie norm' necessary for an 'acceptable life'. As such, the analysis presented in the chapter heavily draws on published data and 'official' estimates of poverty. Nonetheless, several significant deprivations other than consumption are also highlighted. The chapter also presents a set of estimates and results obtained from the analyses of unit-level data of the 68th round of consumption expenditure survey conducted by the National Sample Survey Office (NSSO) for the eight north-eastern states. Further, given the vast diversities *within* the region, this chapter does not wish to make any generalizations as such. Contrarily, it intends to highlight some of the key aspects and issues of poverty in the region, in general, given those diversities. Focus, however, remains in deciphering the broad messages emanating from such analyses.

POVERTY SCENARIO SINCE THE 1990s

Estimation of poverty in India has been primarily done by the erstwhile Planning Commission based on the recommendations of various working groups, task forces and expert groups. These include recommendations of the working group of 1962, task force of 1979 under the chairmanship of Y. K. Alagh, expert groups of 1993 under D. T. Lakdawala and the expert group of 2009 under S. D. Tendulkar, as

---

[1] Government of India Act 1935; the full text of the Act of 1935 can be accessed at https://archive.org/stream/excludedareas035320mbp/excludedareas035320mbp_djvu.txt

well as that of 2014 under C. Rangarajan. Even though the Rangarajan Committee is the latest one in the league, discussions on poverty in India often use the poverty line derived as per the recommendations of the Tendulkar Committee. One of the relative advantages of Tendulkar's poverty lines is that those are available 1993–1994 onwards for almost all the quinquennially conducted rounds of NSSO consumption expenditure surveys.[2] As such, the official poverty ratios are also available for the periods starting from 1993–1994. The last officially released round of consumption expenditure survey was carried out in 2011–2012. The poverty ratios for the eight north-eastern states between 1993–1994 and 2011–2012 are presented in Table 9.1.

Like in the case of India (Dev & Ravi, 2007; Sen & Himanshu, 2004), there is an overall decline in the poverty headcounts between 1993–1994 and 2011–2012 in the north-eastern states barring Mizoram, where the poverty headcounts doubled. As shown by the data, this increase in poverty in Mizoram in 2011–2012 primarily comes from the rural areas.

Given the relatively low rate of urbanization in the region, in general, decline in overall poverty relies on improvement in rural areas. Yet, in some of the hill states like Meghalaya and Sikkim, decline in urban poverty is also prominent. Notwithstanding, improvement in rural poverty is critically important in the region for lowering the overall poverty headcounts. This, in turn, depends on the performance of the agricultural sector in the region, since the majority of rural masses still depend on agriculture directly as well as indirectly. Census data on workers, for instance, reveal that while the agriculture-dependent population as a share of the total workers has been gradually declining in the region, still, an overwhelming majority of people are engaged in agricultural activities for livelihood. Moreover, the agriculture-dependent population in absolute numbers is constantly on the rise. Such trend is visible in Table 9.2.

However, the agriculture in the region, particularly in the hills, is constrained by geographical and various institutional factors.

---

[2] These are provided by the Tendulkar Committee and the Rangarajan Committee in their reports.

Table 9.1 *Poverty Ratios in the North-eastern States*

States/Year	1993–1994			2004–2005			2009–2010			2011–2012		
	Total	Rural	Urban	Total	Rural	Urban	Total	Rural	Urban	Total	Rural	Urban
Arunachal Pradesh	54.5	60.0	22.6	31.1	33.6	23.5	25.9	26.2	24.9	34.7	38.9	20.3
Assam	51.8	54.9	27.7	34.4	36.4	21.8	37.9	39.9	26.1	32.0	33.9	20.5
Manipur	65.1	64.4	67.2	38.0	39.3	34.5	47.1	47.4	46.4	36.9	38.8	32.6
Meghalaya	35.2	38.0	23.0	16.1	14.0	24.7	17.1	15.3	24.1	11.9	12.5	9.3
Mizoram	11.8	16.6	6.3	15.3	23.0	7.9	21.1	31.1	11.5	20.4	35.4	6.4
Nagaland	20.4	20.1	21.8	9.0	10.0	4.3	20.9	19.3	25.0	18.9	19.9	16.5
Tripura	32.9	34.3	25.4	40.6	44.5	22.5	17.4	19.8	10.0	14.0	16.5	7.4
Sikkim	31.8	33.0	20.4	31.1	31.8	25.9	13.1	15.5	5.0	11.3	9.9	3.7
India	45.3	50.1	31.8	37.2	41.8	25.7	29.8	33.8	20.9	21.9	25.7	13.7

Source: The Planning Commission, Government of India (2009).

Note: Estimates for 1993–1994 and 2004–2005 are taken from the report of the Tendulkar Committee, and those for the other two periods are taken from the report of the Rangarajan Committee.

Table 9.2 *Share of Cultivators and Agricultural Labourers (Main + Marginal) to Total Workers*

States/Year	Cultivators		Agricultural Labourers	
	2001	2011	2001	2011
Arunachal Pradesh	57.8	51.5	3.9	6.2
Assam	39.1	30.3	13.2	15.4
Manipur	40.2	42.1	12.0	8.8
Meghalaya	48.1	41.7	17.7	15.2
Mizoram	54.9	45.5	5.7	8.6
Nagaland	64.7	55.2	3.6	4.7
Tripura	27.0	20.1	23.8	22.2
Sikkim	49.9	38.1	6.5	8.4
India	31.7	24.6	26.5	29.9

Source: Census of India (2001, 2011).

Data reveal that since 1990–1991, gross sown area in the region has largely remained unchanged except in a few cases of limited increase (Table 9.3). Besides, agriculture in the region is also characterized by low cropping intensity (Table 9.4) and also relatively low yield rates (Table 9.5). This limits the scope of the agricultural sector and prospects of agricultural income.

During the period, unemployment rates have also shown a steady rise in the region (Table 9.6). The rates have shown a sharp increase in Nagaland and Tripura, more so in urban areas. While the unemployment–poverty linkage is obvious, the relation is not at all straightforward. It is believed that productivity and rate of growth of real wage are more critical for reduction in poverty rather than employment per se (Deaton & Dreze, 2002; Sundaram, 2007). Notwithstanding, reduction in poverty rates, coupled with increasing rates of unemployment in the region, since the 1990s points to other 'exogenous' factors.

It appears that one of the plausible and critical 'exogenous' factors in bringing down poverty, especially during the latter part of the

Table 9.3 *Gross Sown Area (in Thousand Hectares)*

States/Year	1990–1991	2000–2001	2010–2011	2014–2015
Arunachal Pradesh	247	242	278	299
Assam	3,807	4,092	4,160	4,083
Manipur	201	209	348	383
Meghalaya	240	277	338	343
Mizoram	85	82	121	145
Nagaland	211	336	452	500
Tripura	463	301	470	483
Sikkim	149	117	152	136
India	185,742	185,340	197,683	198,360

Source: Reserve Bank of India (2019).

Table 9.4 *Cropping Intensity (in %)*

States/Year	1990–1991	2000–2001	2010–2011	2014–2015
Arunachal Pradesh	165.4	147.6	130.5	132.8
Assam	140.7	146.5	148.0	144.4
Manipur	143.6	100.0	100.0	100.0
Meghalaya	118.9	120.1	119.0	120.0
Mizoram	130.4	100.0	100.0	100.0
Nagaland	110.9	111.6	124.9	130.3
Tripura	167.0	107.4	184.0	189.3
Sikkim	157.0	149.7	196.2	176.0
India	130.0	131.6	139.6	141.6

Source: Reserve Bank of India (2019).

Table 9.5 *Yield of Rice (in kg/ha)*

States/Year	1990–1991	2000–2001	2010–2011	2014–2015
Arunachal Pradesh	1,170	1,119	1,925	2,241
Assam	1,313	1,511	1,843	2,093
Manipur	1,742	2,431	2,453	1,488
Meghalaya	1,155	1,679	1,912	2,703
Mizoram	1,244	1,998	1,160	1,643
Nagaland	1,195	1,533	2,102	2,326
Tripura	1,830	2,129	2,655	2,903
Sikkim	1,360	1,408	1,727	1,818
India	1,740	1,901	2,239	2,391

Source: Reserve Bank of India (2019).

Table 9.6 *Unemployment Rate, Usual Status (per 1,000)*

States/Year	1993–1994		1999–2000		2004–2005		2009–2010		2011–2012	
	R	U	R	U	R	U	R	U	R	U
Arunachal Pradesh	10	26	5	29	9	12	13	34	17	48
Assam	52	89	39	97	26	72	39	52	45	56
Manipur	10	42	19	67	11	55	38	48	26	71
Meghalaya	2	17	4	46	3	35	4	51	4	28
Mizoram	10	5	9	30	3	19	13	28	18	50
Nagaland	14	68	24	91	18	55	106	92	151	238
Tripura	23	85	12	58	133	280	92	171	105	252
Sikkim	7	31	28	75	24	37	43	–	10	23
India	12	45	15	47	17	45	16	34	17	34

Source: NSSO Employment and Unemployment Survey Reports, various rounds.

Notes: Employment figures are the sum of principal status and subsidiary status. R = Rural, U = Urban.

2000s, has been manifold increases in the social sector expenditure in the region during the period. The period witnessed the proliferation of several centrally funded big-ticket central sector schemes (CSSs). The period also witnessed the implementation of the National Rural Employment Guarantee Scheme. Many of these schemes started 2004–2005 onwards. Social sector expenditure post 2004–2005 has been presented in Table 9.7.

It is evident from Table 9.7 that from 2005–2006 onwards, there has been a massive increase in social sector expenditure. The percentage increase in social sector expenditure per capita provides an idea of the kind of interventions undertaken during the period. Public investment of this order definitely has the capacity to have an impact on poverty. However, it is also seen that there are vast variations in the extent of poverty reduction among the states. This, invariably, highlights specificities and diversities *within* the states. Besides, the way in which the public investment is delivered matters more than the extent of investment in lowering the poverty (Thorat & Fan, 2007). Nonetheless, given the limitations of the region's agricultural sector and rising unemployment, public investment, particularly, massive increase in social sector expenditure, has created a favourable condition for reduction in poverty in the region since the 1990s, which is evident from the 'official' estimates of poverty in the eight states of the NE. This, however, comes with the problem of growing fiscal deficit for the states, which is also evident from Table 9.7.

POVERTY SITUATION IN THE NORTH-EAST: A DECOMPOSITIONAL ANALYSIS

To better understand the poverty situation in the north-eastern states, a decompositional analysis has been conducted using the class of Foster–Greer–Thorbecke (FGT) measures (Foster et al., 1984; Foster et al., 2013). The analysis has been carried out using the unit-level data of the consumption expenditure survey of NSSO's 68th round (2011–2012) and using Tendulkar's poverty line for the year 2011–2012. The class of FGT measures provides three indices, namely, poverty headcounts, poverty gap and squared poverty gap, which offer three different

Table 9.7 *Social Sector Expenditure (SSE) (in Crores)*

State/Year	Gross Fiscal Deficit		SSE		SSE per Capita*		Change (in %)	
	2005–2006	2017–2018	2005–2006	2017–2018	2005–2006	2017–2018	SSE	SSE per Capita
Arunachal Pradesh	256	313	741	5,475	6,754	39,566	638.4	485.8
Assam	(-)356	9,292	4,452	27,844	1,670	8,923	525.4	434.2
Manipur	271	339	938	4,298	4,093	15,050	357.8	267.7
Meghalaya	179	137	767	4,575	3,308	15,421	496.4	366.2
Mizoram	397	320	722	3,814	8,127	34,768	427.9	327.8
Nagaland	306	446	804	4,479	4,040	22,636	457.2	460.3
Tripura	110	2,071	1,121	5,867	3,505	15,971	423.2	355.6
Sikkim	149	461	500	2,274	9,253	37,221	354.3	302.2

Source: State Finance: A Study of Budgets, Reserve Bank of India, relevant years.

Note: *Based on Census 2001 and Census 2011 populations, respectively. Values in ₹.

(-) Indicates surplus.

insights into the poverty situation. The poverty headcount is a common measure denoted by the ratio of the poor to the total population. The ratio is given as the average of the income of the poor to the poverty line. The poverty gap ratio is the mean shortfall of the total population from the poverty line (counting the non-poor as having zero shortfall), expressed as a percentage of the poverty line. Therefore, the poverty gap ratio depicts the extent or depth of poverty, indicating how poor the poor are. On the other hand, the squared poverty gap index measures the severity of poverty for each area. By squaring the poverty gap for each household or individual, this measure gives greater weight to those that fall far below the poverty line than those that are closer to it. The three measures for the region are given in Table 9.8.

It is found that there is a wide variation in poverty headcounts, extent of poverty and severity of poverty in the region. In rural areas, it is found that poverty in Arunachal Pradesh, Mizoram and Manipur is higher on all counts, that is, in terms of headcounts, depth and severity. However, the situations in Sikkim and Meghalaya are relative better. In Assam, though the headcount is high, the extent and severity of poverty are not too high relative of those of India. However, poverty in urban areas of Arunachal Pradesh, Assam and Manipur are found to be higher compared to those of other states and the country as a whole. Poverty is found to be less in the urban areas of Mizoram than in the rural areas. It emerges that both in rural and urban areas, Sikkim, Meghalaya and Tripura have less poverty incidences and depth. Overall, poverty is found to be prominently visible in Arunachal Pradesh, Manipur and Assam.

One of the useful properties of the FGT class of measures is that it is decomposable for various subgroups within a population. As such, three decompositions were carried out according to social groups, religion and type of households by economic activities for both rural and urban areas.

While analysing poverty across social groups and religion, it is important to understand the population compositions in the north-eastern states. A synoptic view of the population composition in the region based on Census 2011 is provided in Table 9.9. Barring Assam, Tripura, Manipur and Sikkim, an overwhelming share of the

Table 9.8 *Headcount, Poverty Gap and Squared Poverty Gap in the North-east (2011–2012)*

States	Rural				Urban			
	HCR %	Poverty Gap %	Squared Gap %	Poverty Line (MPCE in ₹)	HCR %	Poverty Gap %	Squared Gap %	Poverty Line (MPCE in ₹)
Arunachal Pradesh	38.9	10.37	3.6	930	20.3	5.4	2.3	1,060
Assam	33.9	5.8	1.4	828	20.5	3.8	0.9	1,008
Manipur	38.8	6.6	1.6	1,118	32.6	6.1	1.7	1,170
Meghalaya	12.5	1.6	0.3	888	9.3	1.5	0.2	1,154
Mizoram	35.4	7.5	2.4	1,066	6.4	0.6	0.1	1,155
Nagaland	19.9	3.8	1	1,270	16.5	1.7	0.3	1,302
Tripura	16.5	2.2	0.4	798	7.4	1.7	0.5	920
Sikkim	9.9	0.9	0.1	930	3.7	0.4	0.1	1,226
India	25.7	5	1.5	816	13.7	2.7	0.8	1,000

Source: The author.

Note: Data from the NSSO 68th round survey is used. HCR=Headcount ratio; MPCE=monthly per capita consumer expenditure.

Table 9.9 A Synoptic View of the Population Composition of the North-eastern States

State	Recognized Number*		Population (in %)**				
	SC	ST	SC	ST	Hindu	Muslim	Christian
Arunachal Pradesh		101	–	68.79	29.04	1.95	30.26
Assam	16	23	7.15	12.45	61.47	34.22	3.74
Manipur	7	29	3.41	40.88	41.39	8.40	41.29
Meghalaya	16	14	0.58	86.15	11.53	4.40	74.59
Mizoram		5	0.11	94.43	2.75	1.35	87.16
Nagaland		20	–	86.48	8.75	2.47	87.93
Tripura	32	19	17.83	31.76	83.40	8.60	4.35
Sikkim		6	4.63	33.80	57.76	1.62	9.91

Source: *Relevant Notification, Government of India, from time to time; **Census 2011.

Note: Buddhists in Sikkim 27.39%, Arunachal 11.77%, other 26.20%.

population in the other states belong to the Scheduled Tribes (STs). On the other hand, the Scheduled Caste (SC) population has a sizeable presence only in Tripura, followed by Assam. Similarly, the population of Nagaland, Mizoram and Meghalaya are mostly Christians. Muslims have a distinct presence only in Assam. Sikkim and Arunachal Pradesh have a distinct presence of Buddhists.

Tables 9.10 and 9.11 provide data on poverty incidences in the NE by social groups and religion. These provide useful insights into the poverty situation in the region. Clearly, SCs and OBCs are marginal in Nagaland, Mizoram, Manipur and Arunachal Pradesh. However, the incidence of poverty, particularly in rural areas, is found to be higher among those in these states. This is indicative of a specific process of deprivation and marginalization in the region. A similar process is also visible in the case of religion. In Mizoram, for instance, where close to 90 per cent of the population is Christian, poverty headcounts are found to be higher among 'Hindus' and 'Others'. In Assam, however,

Table 9.10 *Poverty Headcounts in the North-east by Social Groups, 2011–2012 (in %)*

States	Rural				Urban				Total*			
	ST	SC	OBC	Others	ST	SC	OBC	Others	ST	SC	OBC	Others
Arunachal Pradesh	33.9	23.3	81.1	40.4	21.1	–	26.5	18.2	32.1	17.1	74.5	32.4
Assam	33.4	28.2	34.4	34.8	15.6	30.5	10.9	21.2	33.0	28.7	32.6	32.7
Manipur	43.4	60.5	30.6	59.8	24.1	33.0	33.6	27.3	43.9	45.3	31.7	44.6
Meghalaya	12.9	–	–	4.5	10.3	–	2.2	6.9	10.6	–	1.7	5.8
Mizoram	32.9	–	84.5	31.8	6.5	0.0	0.0	4.9	17.4	–	63.6	26.2
Nagaland	19.4	81.6	46.3	89.5	16.9	11.8	0.0	14.8	40.5	15.5	41.2	15.9
Tripura	25.9	9.4	4.9	11.8	7.6	14.6	6.2	4.2	24.9	10.3	5.2	9.5
Sikkim	8.0	28.2	10.8	0.0	1.6	0.0	3.3	7.1	10.1	15.2	9.0	4.4
India	**42.7**	**32.2**	**24.1**	**14.9**	**23.3**	**21.6**	**16.2**	**7.4**	**41.4**	**29.7**	**21.8**	**11.5**

Source: The author.

Note: Data from the NSSO 68th round survey is used.

*Total is derived as a weighted average of rural and urban poverty ratios.

Table 9.11 Poverty Headcounts in the North-east by Religion, 2011–2012 (in %)

States	Rural				Urban				Total*			
	Hindu	Muslim	Christian	Others	Hindu	Muslim	Christian	Others	Hindu	Muslim	Christian	Others
Arunachal Pradesh	51.6	8.5	39.8	32.9	19.4	24.4	22.4	18.8	40.7	22.8	37.4	30.6
Assam	29.9	40.2	46.6	15.8	18.7	30.9	25.3	1.7	28.2	39.5	45.5	9.3
Manipur	35.3	30.1	43.8	35.7	30.4	41.6	25.9	38.7	33.3	34.1	43.3	36.8
Meghalaya	10.9	6.1	12.9	10.9	7.4	–	10.2	9.3	8.7	4.8	12.4	10.9
Mizoram	91.3	–	28.8	58.4	0.8	13.7	6.4	–	44.2	13.4	17.6	57.7
Nagaland	28.3	–	19.9	–	14.1	–	16.9	–	15.6	–	18.9	–
Tripura	15.6	20.9	19.4	4.8	6.7	20.2	–	–	13.9	20.8	18.6	4.6
Sikkim	8.4	–	7.3	12.2	2	26.1	5.4	2.2	6.6	18.0	6.8	11.1
India	**26.2**	**28.1**	**16.4**	**6.8**	**12.2**	**22.9**	**5.1**	**8.9**	**22.0**	**26.2**	**12.0**	**7.6**

Source: The author.

Note: Data from the NSSO 68th round survey is used.

*Total is derived as a weighted average of rural and urban poverty ratios.

poverty is found more among Muslims relative to people of other religions. In Arunachal Pradesh, clearly, poverty is found to be significant among the Buddhists, given the composition of the population in the states.

Another important result that surfaced from the decompositional analysis relates to poverty by the types of activities. In rural areas, incidences of poverty are found to be higher among the casual labourers—both in agriculture and non-agriculture—in all eight states. In Mizoram, incidences of poverty are also found to be more in households self-employed in agriculture. Arunachal Pradesh, Assam and Manipur also show considerably high poverty incidences among the regular wage earners (Table 9.12). Similarly, in urban areas too, poverty is found to be relatively higher among the casual labourers. Higher poverty among the self-employed is also observed in urban areas (Table 9.13). It was also found that the poverty gap, that is, the 'depth' of poverty, is also the greatest among the casual labourers— both in rural and in urban areas.

The results throw up quite a number of issues. First, it is indicated that while employment, *ipso facto*, is important for lowering poverty in general, in practice, the 'type' of employment matters most, as adequacy and security are linked to it, which impact poverty in concrete terms. Second, a higher incidence of poverty among regular salary and wage earners indicates towards 'working poor', where income earned is not sufficient to maintain acceptable standards of living. Third, higher incidences of poverty among the self-employed can be a sign of 'disguised' unemployment, where non-availability of remunerative employment options compel people to resort to myriad types of self-employment, including in agriculture. Last, as per the definition of NSSO, the category of 'others' also includes those households 'without any economic activities'; therefore, a higher incidence of poverty among these categories is self-explanatory. However, low poverty ratios among them indicate support system and social capital in rural areas, particularly in the hills and among the tribal populations, which facilitates the lowering of poverty quite effectively.

Table 9.12 *Poverty Headcounts in the North-east by Type of Activity (Rural), 2011–2012 (in %)*

States	Self-employed in Agriculture	Self-employed in Non-agriculture	Regular Wage/ Salary	Casual Labour in Agriculture	Casual Labour in Non-agriculture	Others
Arunachal Pradesh	41.8	37.1	19.6	71.7	76.6	24.3
Assam	32.9	29.3	28.2	68.2	37.9	11.1
Manipur	54.7	23.3	17.6	73.7	42.5	31.9
Meghalaya	15.9	1.1	1.5	38.1	9.9	4.1
Mizoram	46.6	9.5	3.1	–	53.8	9.5
Nagaland	33.3	3.2	0.0	–	0.0	16.1
Tripura	9.9	4.9	6.9	47.4	22.9	8.6
Sikkim	14.2	3.6	0.3	20.4	17.8	0.0

Source: The author.

Note: Data from the NSSO 68th round survey is used.

Table 9.13 *Poverty Headcounts in the North-east by Type of Activity (Urban), 2011–2012 (in %)*

States	Self-employed	Regular Wage/Salary	Casual Labour	Other
Arunachal Pradesh	23.2	13.4	26.5	45.1
Assam	29.7	7.3	45.7	12.8
Manipur	40.8	13.3	57.2	40.5
Meghalaya	11	7.7	14.7	3.5
Mizoram	9.2	0.7	16.1	26.2
Nagaland	27	7.6	30.6	24.3
Tripura	8.9	3.3	16.8	1.8
Sikkim	6.2	2.4	6.9	0

Source: The author.

Note: Data from the NSSO 68th round survey is used.

CHANGE IN POVERTY BETWEEN 2004–2005 AND 2011–2012

In this section, changes in poverty in the north-eastern states are examined in some detail for the period between 2004–2005 and 2011–2012.[3] It is evident from the data that between 2004–2005 and 2011–2012, poverty has declined in India—both in rural and urban areas. However, total poverty has increased in three north-eastern states, namely, Nagaland, Mizoram and Arunachal Pradesh, during the same period. It is further observed that the increase in poverty is profound in Nagaland across rural and urban areas. The increase in poverty in Mizoram, however, is sourced to rural areas, whereas urban poverty in the state has recorded a decline. Similar is the case with Arunachal Pradesh. In general, with the only exception of Nagaland, urban poverty has shown a secular decline during the period, relative to rural

---

[3] There is a problem of data inadequacy for the north-eastern states, since NSSO consumption expenditure surveys 'clubbed' data for the states other than Assam in most of the earlier rounds.

poverty. It is also noticed that in Tripura and Sikkim, the decline in poverty—both rural and urban—is overwhelming (Table 9.14).

Notwithstanding the decline in poverty ratios in the region between 2004–2005 and 2011–2012, it is observed that the absolute number of poor has not declined much. During the period, in the eight states taken together, the number of poor has reduced by only about 50,000. In India, however, the number of both rural poor and urban poor has significantly declined during the same period (Table 9.15). It is also observed that only in two states, Sikkim and Tripura, have the numbers of poor recorded a decline in rural as well as urban areas, whereas the number of urban poor has declined massively in Meghalaya, contributing to an overall decline.

In order to draw further insights on the *process* of decline of poverty in the region between 2004–2005 and 2011–2012, change (or growth) in the average monthly per capita consumption expenditure (MPCE) and inequality (Gini coefficient) in its distribution have been examined over the period for the eight states in the line of a growth and distribution decompositional analysis framework (Ravalliion & Datt, 2002). The results are presented in Table 9.16.

Table 9.17 provides an important insight into the *process* of poverty reduction. While the growth in mean MPCE is definitely important for reduction in poverty, improvement in the distribution of MPCE in terms of reduction of inequality is extremely important for reduction in poverty. Without any change in the overall inequality, any increase in mean MPCE will reduce poverty. However, if an increase in mean MPCE is accompanied by an increase in inequality, then the poverty decline in poverty ratio *will not be adequate enough to result in a decline in the absolute number of poor*. It is observed that improvement in inequality is seen in Sikkim and Tripura in both rural and urban areas and also in Meghalaya in urban areas, wherein there has been a decline in the absolute number of poor. Contrarily, in Arunachal Pradesh, even though the mean MPCE records a massive increase, poverty did not decline, due to the worsening of inequality of the distribution. For a region like the NE which is marked by several growth constraints, distributive justice holds a critical role in poverty reduction.

Table 9.14 *Change in Poverty Ratios in the North-east Between 2004–2005 and 2011–2012*

States	Rural (R)		Urban (U)		Total (T)		Change in Poverty		
	2004–2005	2011–2012	2004–2005	2011–2012	2004–2005	2011–2012	R	U	T
Arunachal Pradesh	33.6	38.9	23.5	20.3	31.1	34.7	15.8	−13.6	11.6
Assam	36.4	33.9	21.8	20.5	34.4	32.0	−6.9	−6.0	−7.0
Manipur	39.3	38.8	34.5	32.6	38.0	36.9	−1.3	−5.5	−2.9
Meghalaya	14.0	12.5	24.7	9.3	16.1	11.9	−10.7	−62.3	−26.1
Mizoram	23.0	35.4	7.9	6.4	15.3	20.4	53.9	−19.0	33.3
Nagaland	10.0	19.9	4.3	16.5	9.0	18.9	99.0	283.7	110.0
Tripura	44.5	16.5	22.5	7.4	40.6	14.0	−62.9	−67.1	−65.5
Sikkim	31.8	9.9	25.9	3.7	31.1	11.3	−68.9	−85.7	−63.7
India	**41.8**	**25.7**	**25.7**	**13.7**	**37.2**	**21.9**	**−38.5**	**−46.7**	**−41.1**

Source: The Planning Commission, Government of India (2014).

Table 9.15 *Change in the Number of Poor in the North-east Between 2004–2005 and 2011–2012 (in Lakhs)*

States	Rural (R)		Urban (U)		Total (T)		Change in No. of Poor (%)		
	2004–2005	2011–2012	2004–2005	2011–2012	2004–2005	2011–2012	R	U	T
Arunachal Pradesh	2.9	4.2	0.7	0.7	3.6	4.9	44.8	0.0	36.1
Assam	88.8	92.1	8.4	9.2	97.3	101.3	3.7	9.5	4.1
Manipur	6.6	7.4	2.1	2.8	8.7	10.2	12.1	33.3	17.2
Meghalaya	2.7	3.0	1.2	0.6	3.9	3.6	11.1	−50.0	−7.7
Mizoram	1.1	1.9	0.4	0.4	1.4	2.3	72.7	0.0	64.3
Nagaland	1.7	2.8	0.2	1.0	1.9	3.8	64.7	400.0	100.0
Tripura	12.3	4.5	1.3	0.8	13.7	5.2	−63.4	−38.5	−62.0
Sikkim	1.6	0.4	0.2	0.1	1.8	0.5	−75.0	−50.0	−72.2
India	3,266.6	2,166.6	807.6	531.2	4,076.1	2,697.8	−33.7	−34.2	−33.8

Source: The author.

Note: Data from the NSSO 68th round survey is used.

Table 9.16 *Mean MPCE and Inequality in MPCE Between 2004–2005 and 2011–2012*

States	Mean MPCE (in ₹)				Inequality in MPCE (Gini)			
	Rural 2004–2005	Rural 2011–2012	Urban 2004–2005	Urban 2011–2012	Rural 2004–2005	Rural 2011–2012	Urban 2004–2005	Urban 2011–2012
Arunachal Pradesh	829	1,767	980	2,370	0.306	0.386	0.235	0.345
Assam	594	1,117	1,291	2,391	0.193	0.216	0.311	0.353
Manipur	668	1,399	792	1,518	0.152	0.197	0.165	0.203
Meghalaya	730	1,403	1,520	2,554	0.149	0.176	0.261	0.232
Mizoram	906	1,436	1,368	2,523	0.186	0.249	0.229	0.249
Nagaland	1,103	1,813	1,671	2,394	0.176	0.195	0.224	0.231
Tripura	538	1,252	1,127	2,240	0.226	0.212	0.314	0.296
Sikkim	867	1,615	1,421	2,941	0.254	0.197	0.246	0.199
India	**629**	**1,417**	**1,287**	**2,913**	**0.281**	**0.287**	**0.364**	**0.377**

Source: The author.

Note: Data from the NSSO 68th round survey is used.

Table 9.17 Growth of Mean MPCE and Change in MPCE Inequality Between 2004–2005 and 2011–2012

States	Growth of MPCE (%)		Change in MPCE Inequality (%)	
	Rural	Urban	Rural	Urban
Arunachal Pradesh	113.1	141.8	26.1	46.8
Assam	88.0	85.2	11.9	13.5
Manipur	109.4	91.7	29.6	23.0
Meghalaya	92.2	68.0	18.1	−11.1
Mizoram	58.5	84.4	33.9	8.7
Nagaland	64.4	43.3	10.8	3.1
Tripura	132.7	98.8	−6.2	−5.7
Sikkim	86.3	107.0	−22.4	−19.1
India	**125.3**	**126.3**	**2.1**	**3.6**

Source: The author.

Note: Data from the NSSO 68th round survey is used.

ADDITIONAL DIMENSIONS OF DEPRIVATIONS

Poverty does not only involve income and/or consumption deprivations. While income is important for overcoming *other* dimensions of deprivations, there are non-income dimensions of deprivations as well. Besides, there can be deprivations independent of income also. Some of the important dimensions include nutritional and health outcomes and basic amenities. Table 9.18 presents the most recent data on select indicators related to some of these dimensions.

It is observed from Table 9.18 that barring a few exceptions, in general, deprivations in nutritional and health outcomes, as well as in access to basic amenities, are relatively less in the region. However, access to services is one area where deprivations are visibly high. This might be due to the difficult terrains which constrict access to and delivery of services. Therefore, deprivations in access to various services need attention.

Table 9.18 Select Indicators of Deprivation in the North-east

	Arunachal Pradesh	Assam	Manipur	Meghalaya	Mizoram	Nagaland	Tripura	Sikkim	India
Nutritional and health outcomes									
Children under 5 underweight	19.4	29.8	13.8	28.9	12.0	16.7	24.1	14.2	35.8
Women with below-normal body mass index (BMI)	8.5	25.7	8.8	12.1	8.4	12.3	18.9	6.4	22.9
Men with below-normal BMI	8.3	20.7	11.1	11.6	7.3	11.5	15.7	2.4	20.2
Anaemia among children under 5	54.2	35.7	23.9	48.0	19.3	26.4	48.3	55.1	58.6
Anaemia among women	43.2	46.0	26.4	56.2	24.7	27.7	54.5	34.9	53.1
Anaemia among men	18.6	25.4	26.0	32.4	27.0	32.7	27.4	15.7	52.7
Infant Mortality Rate (per 1,000 live births)	23.0	48.0	22.0	30.0	40.0	30.0	27.0	30.0	41.0
Under-5 mortality rate (per 1,000 live births)	33.0	56.0	26.0	40.0	46.0	37.0	33.0	32.0	50.0

(Continued)

Table 9.18 *Continued*

	Arunachal Pradesh	Assam	Manipur	Meghalaya	Mizoram	Nagaland	Tripura	Sikkim	India
Access to healthcare									
Mothers having full ante-natal care	3.5	18.1	33.9	23.5	38.3	2.4	7.6	39.0	21.0
Institutional Birth	52.2	70.6	69.1	51.4	79.7	32.8	79.9	94.7	78.9
Children fully immunised	38.2	47.1	65.8	61.4	50.7	35.4	54.5	83.0	62.0
Access to basic amenities									
Household with electricity	88.7	78.2	92.4	91.4	95.9	97.0	92.7	99.4	88.2
Household with improved drinking water source	87.5	83.8	41.6	67.9	91.4	80.6	87.3	97.6	89.9
Household with sanitation facility	61.3	47.7	49.9	60.3	83.3	75.1	61.3	88.2	48.4
Household with clean fuel for cooking	45.0	25.1	42.1	21.8	66.1	32.8	31.9	59.1	43.8

Source: State Fact Sheets, NFHS-4, 2015–2016.

Of late, there have been serious attempts at looking at poverty through a multidimensional framework. In fact, multidimensional poverty reduction has got a place in the Sustainable Development Goals globally. One of the widely used multidimensional frameworks is that of Multidimensional Poverty Index (MPI). The framework treats those as multi-dimensionally poor who are *simultaneously deprived* in one-third of the dimensions covering health, education and basic amenities. Like the class of FGT measures, this framework also provides headcounts, that is, number of those who are multi-dimensionally poor and intensity of poverty, that is, the average number of dimensions of deprivations. MPI is obtained as the product of the headcount and intensity, which provides information on the extent of multidimensional poverty, that is, the proportion of deprivations out of all the possible deprivations currently suffered by the poor (Alkire et al., 2015). The scenario of the multidimensional poverty in the north-eastern states is presented in Table 9.19. It clearly shows an improvement in the multidimensional poverty situation in the region. There is a distinct decline in the incidence, intensity and extent of multidimensional poverty in the region during the period between 2005–2006 and 2015–2016.

CONCLUSION

In the chapter, an overview of the situation of poverty in the eight north-eastern states has been provided. The chapter shows that since the 1990s, in general, and during the last 5–10 years, in particular, there has been a decline in incidences of poverty—both consumption as well as multidimensional poverty—in the region. It is also argued that given the high dependence on agriculture, the sector's role in poverty reduction remains vital. However, the scope of the agriculture sector in the region is severely constrained by specific geographical and institutional factors. Therefore, the role of public investment, especially in the social sector, is extremely critical for the region. It is further shown that poverty in the region has visible gradients with respect to social and religion groups indicating certain processes of marginalization. Besides, poverty is also related to types of economic activities adopted by households. It is argued that the quality of employment is more important than employment *per se* in reducing poverty. Finally, the chapter shows that reduction in poverty ratio does not necessarily imply reduction in the

Table 9.19 Multidimensional Poverty Situation in the North-east Between 2005–2006 and 2015–2016

States	2005–2006			2015–2016			Change (%)	
	MPI	Incidence	Intensity	MPI	Incidence	Intensity	MPI	Incidence
Arunachal Pradesh	0.309	59.7	51.8	0.106	24.0	44.1	−0.203	−35.7
Assam	0.312	60.7	51.4	0.16	35.8	44.6	−0.152	−24.8
Manipur	0.207	45.1	45.8	0.083	20.7	40.3	−0.123	−24.4
Meghalaya	0.334	60.5	55.2	0.145	32.7	44.5	−0.188	−27.8
Mizoram	0.139	30.8	45	0.044	9.7	45.2	−0.095	−21.2
Nagaland	0.294	56.9	51.6	0.097	23.3	41.7	−0.196	−33.6
Tripura	0.265	54.4	48.6	0.086	20.1	42.7	−0.179	−34.3
Sikkim	0.176	37.6	46.7	0.019	4.9	38.1	−0.157	−32.7
India	**0.279**	**54.7**	**51.1**	**0.121**	**27.5**	**43.9**	**−0.158**	**−27.2**

Source: Global MPI Report 2018, Oxford Poverty and Human Development Initiatives.

absolute number of poor, which is the most critical aspect of eradication of poverty. In order to obtain a reduction in the number of poor along with the decline in poverty headcount ratio, it is essential to improve the distributional inequality. The chapter, therefore, concludes that overcoming the geographical and institutional constraints in agriculture, expanding public investment in the social sector, improving the scope of quality employment and addressing inequalities could form an effective strategy for the eradication of poverty in the region.

REFERENCES

Alkire, S., Foster, J. E., James E., Seth, S., Santos, M. E., Roche, J. M., & Ballón, P. (2015). *Multidimensional poverty measurement and analysis* (1st ed.). Oxford University Press.

Census of India. (2001). https://censusindia.gov.in/2011-common/census_data_2001.html

Census of India. (2011). https://censusindia.gov.in/Tables_Published/D-Series/Tables_on_Migration_Census_of_India_2001.aspx/D-Series_link/D3_India.pdf

Deaton, A., & Dreze, J. (2002). Poverty and inequality in India: A re-examination. *Economic and Political Weekly, 37*(36), 3729–3748.

Dev, M. S., & Ravi, C. (2007). Poverty and inequality: All India and states 1983–2005. *Economic and Political Weekly, 42*(6), 509–521.

Foster, J., Greer, J., & Thorbecke, E. (1984). A class of decomposable poverty measures. *Econometrica, 52*(3), 761–765.

Foster, J., Seth, S., Lokshin, M., & Sajaia, Z. (2013). *A unified approach to measuring poverty and inequality*. The World Bank.

Planning Commission. (2009). Report of the expert group to review the methodology for estimation of poverty, Government of India.

Planning Commission. (2014). Report of the expert group to review the methodology for estimation of poverty, Government of India.

Ravalliion, M., & Datt, G. (2002). Why has economic growth been more propoor in some states of India than others. *Journal of Development Economics, 68*(2), 381–400.

Reserve Bank of India. (2019, March 3). *Handbook of statistics on Indian states 2018–19*. https://m.rbi.org.in/Scripts/AnnualPublications.aspx?head=Handbook+of+Statistics+on+Indian+States

Sen, A., & Himanshu. (2004). Poverty and inequality in India I. *Economic and Political Weekly, 39*(38), 4247–4263.

Sundaram, K. (2007). Employment and poverty in India 2000–2005. *Economic and Political Weekly, 42*(30), 3121–3131.

Thorat, S., & Fan, S. (2007). Public investment and poverty reduction: Lessons from China and India. *Economic and Political Weekly, 42*(8), 704–710.

Chapter 10

Unemployment and Outmigration for Work from North-east India
How Does It Ensure Well-being?

Kalyan Das

INTRODUCTION

A host of indicators like youth unemployment rate, lack of basic amenities for living, declining agriculture land per rural household,[1] etc., reveal that the states of North-east (NE) India have reached the limit of their carrying capacity at the present state of development. This thinly populated, land-abundant region in a short span of time has become a region facing a crisis of natural resources. Census of India (2001) showed that the net migration rate in the states of Assam, Manipur, Mizoram and Nagaland had already become negative, with

---

[1] There are some explanations for choosing these indicators. Youth unemployment is a better reflective indicator of crisis than the overall unemployment rate; after a certain age, people are forced to work at survival or market-clearing wage. In many households, returns from livelihood avenues are not enough to go for amenities such as electricity and liquefied petroleum gas (LPG) because of high initial connection and installation costs. A population gets doubled every 35 years if the rate of population growth is 2.0, which puts enormous stress on its resources.

more people migrating away from their respective states than the total number of in-migrants during 1991–2001 (see Table 10.1). Partially released data of Census 2011 show that the proportion of the migrant population that has moved within the country—intra-district, inter-district and inter-state—for work and business is very high[2] in Nagaland (25.5% of the total migrants), Arunachal Pradesh (24.5%) and Mizoram (20.2%) compared to the all-India average of 11.2 per cent. The figures for Assam (8.7%), Meghalaya (9.2%), Manipur (6.0%) and Tripura (9.5%), though low, cannot be considered insignificant,[3] reflecting the crisis of resources in the region. Field observations and interactions, within as well as outside the region, indicate that the magnitude of outmigration for work from NE India is high. A study, conducted by the Gulati Institute of Finance and Taxation for Government of Kerala (Narayana & Venkiteswaran, 2013) on Domestic Migrant Labour in Kerala, estimated the presence of a minimum of 4.32 lakh migrant workers from Assam alone in Kerala. A factory manager, in September 2010, reported the presence of about 8,000 youths from Assam from 400 plywood factories in and around Perumbavoor (Das & Chutia, 2011) in Ernakulam district. A repeat visit in 2017 confirmed the rising magnitude of workers from Assam.

One of the prime factors that led to the limits of carrying capacity of the region was the massive population growth; although birth rate has witnessed a decline in recent years, it is emerging as a bigger determinant of population growth than immigration. National Family Health Survey-4 (NFHS-4) data of 2015–2016 indicate that fertility rates in the states of the region, except Tripura and Arunachal Pradesh, are higher than the all-India average (Table 10.1). The limit of the carrying capacity of the region also arises due to (a) the fragile hill ecosystem and ecology, which sets limits on expanding the provisioning; (b) approach as well as capabilities of the state to regulate and govern the existing resources; and (c) environmental externalities stressed by anthropogenic factors.

The rising trend of outward migration of the people from this region warrants an analysis of the trend in migration, the location of

---

[2] Marriage, in particular, accounts for a larger share of migrants.

[3] The worker population ratio (33.2%) of the region indicates that one worker or one out-migrant for work supports two family members on an average.

Table 10.1 Some Indicators on the State of Development of States in the North-east Region

States	Youth Unemployment Rate (2017–2018) (15–29 Years Old) 1*	Household with No Electricity Connection (in %) (2011) 2*	Household with No LPG as Fuel (in %) (2011) 3*	Net Immigrants (in Numbers) (2001) 4*	Migration for Business and Work (in %) (2011) 5*	Fertility Rate (2015–2016) 6*
Arunachal Pradesh	26.1	34.3	70.8	59,505	24.5	2.1
Assam	27.0	72.9	81.0	(–)154,654	8.7	2.2
Manipur	35.7	30.7	72.4	(–)26,298	6.0	2.6
Meghalaya	5.1	39.1	88.2	13,300	9.2	3.0
Mizoram	28.6	15.8	47.5	(–)9,126	20.2	2.3
Nagaland	56.0	18.4	80.0	(–) 18,243	25.5	2.7
Tripura	19.9	31.6	82.2	16,767	9.5	1.7
India	17.8	32.7	71.5	–	11.2	2.2

Sources: 1*: Calculated based on NSSO unit-level data, taking the 2011 population census data as weights; 2* and 3*: Housing Tables: Census of India, 2011; 4*: Migration Tables: Census of India, 2001; 5*: Migration Tables: Census of India, 2011; 6*: NFHS-4.

Note: LPG = Liquefied petroleum gas.

the destination and how migrants submit and adapt themselves in the labour markets of the country that have increasingly become less labour-friendly with with less stringent enforcement of labour laws and welfare provisions. The outward migration of some from their region, though aspirational, is distressed as well, caused by environmental degradation and subsequent disruptions of their living spaces and shrinking livelihood avenues. The disruptions are often sudden, leaving little time to decide where to relocate. The question that arises in such situations is how out-migrants gain from migration. This requires discussions on the nature of jobs they get at their destination, their remittances and well-being, and other social costs of migration. It requires understanding the determinants of the *push* in *weak pull* situations[4] and how these determinants could be addressed and ameliorated through regulatory measures. One important aspect, however, is that outmigration from a region not only reduces the stress on natural resources but also brings remittances.

This chapter makes an attempt to understand the following questions:

1. Is NE India in a position to address the problem of huge unemployment?
2. Would generation of additional employment put further stress on its natural resources?
3. What went wrong with this resource-rich region that it has come to face such a situation?
4. Is outmigration a way out to reduce pressure on local resources?
5. Does migration lead to an increase in the well-being of the migrant people?

RISING LABOUR FORCE AND UNEMPLOYMENT

The livelihood sectors of the NE region have shown transformational changes,[5] from that of heavy dependence on farm activities to various

---

[4] Migrants migrating for work are likely to be better off at the place of destination. The pull, however, is considered weak if the earning at the destination fails to ensure the basic indicators of living.

[5] Rural workforce from 1993–1994 (National Sample Survey Office [NSSO] 50th round) to 2011–2012 (NSSO 68th round) in the agriculture sector declined by 8.5 per cent in Arunachal Pradesh from 86.4 per cent, in Assam by 17.2 per cent

kinds of petty non-standard jobs primarily in the services sector; a large proportion of jobs, as observed, fail to ensure even a threshold of minimum income.[6] There is apparently a crisis of the self-employed as well as of the employed, with increasing insecurities in the labour market within the NE region.[7] The state of uncertainties and anxiety to ensure an a threshold income has forced many people to look for avenues of employment outside the region.[8]

The region, the population of which has increased from 4.5 million in 1901 to about 45 million in 2011, has changed its character from that of land abundance to land scarcity. Earlier, the abundant land was able to meet the requirements of most of the people; the industrial (primarily household) sector was small and was only fulfilling certain basic needs. The establishment of various departments and administrative centres

---

from 79.2 per cent, in Manipur 18.3 per cent from 63.8 per cent, in Meghalaya 19.7 per cent from 86 per cent, in Mizoram 13.1 per cent from 88.9 per cent, and in Tripura 16.8 per cent from 47.6 per cent; Nagaland was the exception, with a marginal rise of 1.8 per cent from 74.9 per cent. The declines reflect the unaccommodating nature and unattractiveness of the agriculture sector to ensure livelihood of the rural people.

[6] Though wage rates (of male casual workers) have been higher than the national average in the states of the NE region (except Assam), the Periodic Labour Force Survey of NSSO, 2017, now shows lower wage rates in urban areas of Nagaland and Tripura, and in those of Assam. Increasing gender disparity in earning, even in the case of regular wage earners, in all the states of the region (except Arunachal Pradesh) from 1993–1994 to 2011–2012 (NSSO rounds) requires an in-depth analysis to understand the crisis inherent in livelihood sectors. The question is how the low wages of women explain the livelihood crisis of a particular place.

[7] Though quality of employment is assessed by the categories of self-employed, regular salaried and casual works, with casual works having the presence of anxieties and insecurities, now, people engaged in the other two types are also not free from anxieties and insecurities with the rising informalization of the economy and inappropriate workplace regulation.

[8] Interactions with out-migrants for work reveal that their decision to migrate to distance places of the country is not driven by the wage factor alone, though it is said that more than a 30 per cent wage difference is necessary to drive migration (Mansoor & Quillin, 2006); it is in pursuit to get a job which ensures continuity at least for a few years. Seeking and asking for intermittent jobs in home states not only creates stress, but it also creates a dependency syndrome through seeking a favour from an employer or agents.

and welfare measures of the state generated a handful of government jobs. The expansion in government jobs was not commensurate with the population growth, and the failure to drive the agriculture and industrial sectors, along with the increasing population, resulted in a serious livelihood crisis in the region.

Consequently, the unemployment rate of the region (overall 8.3%) is not only higher than the national average of 6.1 per cent but has also been its highest since 1993–1994 (National Sample Survey Office [NSSO] 50th round). The unemployment rate of the region is higher than the national average both in rural and urban areas. As against 5.3 per cent rural unemployment and 7.8 per cent urban unemployment, the corresponding rates for the region are 8.2 per cent and 8.8 per cent, respectively. In some states, it is much higher. For example, the overall unemployment rate is 10.1 per cent in Mizoram, 11.6 per cent in Manipur and 21.4 per cent in Nagaland. The youth unemployment rate is much higher in the region, thereby showing the gravity of the situation.

EDUCATED AND SKILLED IN THE LABOUR MARKET

Education is important for two reasons: (a) attainment of knowledge, which boosts self-esteem, provides respectability in society and improves quality of life; and (b) development of capability required for getting into employment and occupations of choice. While the first is beyond the purview of this chapter, the second requires to be explored. Looking at the available data on work participation and unemployment and, more specifically, the youth unemployment rate in the states of the region, the important questions that arise are (a) whether there are enough jobs available in the largely self-contained farm-dependent hill ecosystems of the region; and (ii) how recent developments and structural shifts (refer to footnote 5) in ecological, economic and social settings, partly induced by the market and partly by state policies, are able to specifically meet job aspirations of the youth.[9]

---

[9] The need is to assess the changes in the structure of the economy, people's aspirations to get engaged in the services sectors of health and education created

This chapter analyses unemployment data to show that the economy of the NE region is unable to absorb the labour force at the present state of development, although knowledge and skills acquired through education have helped a section of educated and skilled workers to explore opportunities in national and international labour markets, even as a section of the population is forced to work in non-standard jobs outside the region or remain unemployed.

In 2011–2012, the work participation rate (WPR) of graduates and above, including diploma holders, was 77.7 per cent for rural males, 33.4 per cent for rural females, 78.1 per cent for urban males and 30.4 per cent for urban females in the NE region. This, however, varied across the states (Meghalaya with the highest at 96.7% to Nagaland with the lowest at 45% for rural males; Meghalaya with 83.4% to Nagaland with 17.4% for rural females; Arunachal Pradesh with 85.8% to Nagaland with 63.5% for urban males; and Mizoram with 66.6% to Arunachal Pradesh with 16.6% for urban females).

The segregation of the WPR data of diploma holders, graduates and postgraduates reveals that diploma holders (WPR 54.7% in rural areas to 78.4% in urban areas) have higher chances to getting absorbed than graduates (rural 64.4%, urban 58.8%) and postgraduates (rural 62.1%, urban 68.9%), particularly in urban areas of the region, as per the NSSO data of 2011–2012. Thus, the chance of getting employed in an economic activity after acquiring higher education is limited, though a section may opt out of the labour market for various reasons. In this regard, unemployment data give a clearer picture than the WPR. Data indicate that the unemployment rate of graduates and above, including that of diploma holders, in the NE region was much higher (16.4%) than the national average (7.6%) in 2011–2012. There were, however, significant variations in the unemployment rates of educated and skilled workers across the states (Nagaland with 49.5% to Arunachal Pradesh with 4%).

Further, the unemployment rate of graduates (15–29 years old) and above in the NE region (rural 44.0%, urban 45.5%) was much higher

---

in state and private sectors and the compulsion to get engaged in the varied nature of informal jobs associated with the utility, construction and transport sectors.

than the national average (21.0% in rural and 17.8% in urban areas). Employment possibilities seem to be better for diploma holders (78.4% in urban areas), much above the national average (59.2%), than for those with a postgraduate degree (68.9%) in the region. Studies[10] on employment possibilities in the region suggest low demand for graduates. There is a preference for technical, professional degree holders in the labour market. It, thus, appears that while education provides knowledge, skill matters the most in finding a livelihood and ensuring employability. It has often been observed that even after the attainment of higher education,[11] people opt for skill development training. The key issue here is promoting those sectors of the economy of the region which would provide employment.

INCREASING LIVELIHOOD OPPORTUNITIES: WHERE DID IT GO WRONG?

This chapter analyses possibilities of increasing livelihood opportunities in the NE region without deleterious impacts on ecology and environment. It does not take up debates on the industrialization process initiated in the region by the colonial administration through the exploration and exploitation of oil, coal, timber and tea. The colonial policy targeted at natural resource–extracting industries (Roy, 2000). The positive point was that the initiatives created an environment for industrialization in the region, particularly in the plains, a large part of which comes under part of the state of Assam. Immigration of labour

---

[10] An evaluative study of the beneficiaries of a skill development programme of the Ministry of Social Justice and Empowerment in the states of Assam and Manipur, conducted by OKD Institute in 2007, brings out the deficiencies in the formal educational system and importance of skill development programmes, both for upper-end and lower-end jobs. The level of fulfilment of expectations from the training, however, varied significantly across the beneficiaries. Low salary, meagre earnings and jobs unrelated to the acquired skills are the main reasons mentioned for non-fulfilment of the expectations.

[11] Presently, a large section of the youth are undergoing skill development programmes under the Pradhan Mantri Kaushal Vikas Yojana (PMKVY). Data would reveal that many of the participants of the programmes are graduates or postgraduates.

from outside the NE region shows that indigenous inhabitants were able to meet their requirements without any problem. However, in the present context of unemployment, it is relevant to understand the reasons for failure of the governments in the post-Independence period to carry forward the industrialization process.

In the post-Independence period, at various stages, the Government of India recognized the need to pay special attention to infrastructural development and boost the industrialization process in the region. Various committees constituted for this purpose (L. C. Jain Committee in 1990 and S. P. Shukla Committee in 1997) placed emphasis on the development of road, rail, power and social sector infrastructure. The recommendations of the Borthakur Committee Report in 1994 led to two important outcomes in the region. First, the formation of a specialized financial institution in 1996, the North Eastern Development Finance Corporation Ltd. (NEDFL); and second, the adoption of North East Industrial Policy (NEIP) in 1997.

The subsidy-laden NEIP, 1997, expanded as the North East Industrial and Investment Policy, 2007, was planned to usher in the industrialization process in the region but failed to derive the desired result. Data show that ₹5,534 million was disbursed by NEDFI as capital investment subsidy to 1,365 industrial units (each unit received an average subsidy of ₹4.05 million) and ₹25,503 million as transport subsidy to 9,650 industrial units (average subsidy of ₹2.6 million to each unit) during April 2000–March 2015 in the various states of the region. Moreover, 2,204 units received interest on working capital subsidy at an average of ₹0.86 million.

In the period mentioned above, 29,318 jobs were added in Assam, 4,032 jobs in Manipur, 1,168 in Meghalaya, 38,518 jobs in Tripura and (-) 2,528 jobs in Nagaland. Estimates show that to create one industrial job, a subsidy amount of ₹0.51 million was utilized in Assam. This figure for Meghalaya was ₹1.18 million (Das, 2017). The per capita net value addition of workers in the states also remained low compared to the national average, barring in Meghalaya. Nevertheless, the share of average wages to the average net value addition remained low compared to the national average. The proportion of casual or contract workers employed in the organized sector of the industries in the states of the region also support this phenomenon. The Annual Survey of Industries data of 2012–2013 indicated that 90 per cent industrial workers in Tripura, 67 per cent in Manipur, 63 per cent in Meghalaya and 32 per cent in Nagaland were contract workers, not directly in the payroll of the industries. This figure for the country as a whole was 34 per cent. The low share of wages in total value addition and high proportion of contract workers are a reflection of the weak regulatory interventions of the state and a constrained situation on the employment front.

The third all-India census of small-scale industries of 2001–2002 revealed that out of 22.62 lakh units permanently registered in the NE region, 39 per cent were found to be closed at the time of the third census. The proportion of registered closed units in the states of the region were found to be 49.3 per cent in Arunachal Pradesh, 41.7 per cent in Assam, 21 per cent in Manipur, 49.6 per cent in Meghalaya, 32.5 per cent in Mizoram, 18.5 per cent in Nagaland and 52.9 per cent in Tripura. The reasons for the closure of industries were not elicited by the census. However, a sample survey, conducted in 2000–2001 to draw out the causes of closure, revealed three main reasons: (a) the problem of market access; (b) the problem of finance; and (c) the competition faced in the market. It is estimated from the NSSO 2001 survey on the unorganized manufacturing sector of India that the employment intensity of the unorganized manufacturing sector (Own Account Enterprises; Non-Directory Manufacturing Establishments; and Directory Manufacturing Establishments) was 1.8 persons in the NE region as a whole. It may be concluded that the closed manufacturing industrial units could have supported the livelihood of an additional 15.87 lakh people in the region.

A few specific cases further show the failure of the state to ensure sustainable livelihood. It has been commented that the developments to take initiatives have moved so fast that the regulatory models of the country have been unable to catch up with them to ensure sustainability (Manju & Kohli, 2015). There are two specific examples of unplanned initiatives (or initiatives not following appropriate work plans) in the NE region—how continuing livelihood came to an abrupt halt because of interventions from the Supreme Court of India (regarding the wood-based industries of the region, in 1996) and the National Green Tribunal (regarding coal mining in Meghalaya, in 2014). Such an abrupt end of industries leads to tremendous hardships for those employed in these industries.

Between 1995–1996 and 2001–2002, the number of timber units in the NE region declined from 461 to 136, and direct employment in these industries from 17,126 to 1,146. In addition, the Supreme Court ban on timber felling had an effect on paper and paper products manufacturing units of the region accounting for the loss of about 4,000 jobs during this period. (Annual Survey of Industries, 1995–1996 and 2001–2002).

Commercial coal mining activities in Meghalaya developed after a group of entrepreneurs explored the possibilities. Once the negative environmental externalities started to emerge, a ban was imposed to control the activities of mining. The sudden ban not only led to a serious crisis on the livelihood front for the miners and transporters but also resulted in the collapse of the market that flourished around mining activities.

However, there are instances of states giving consideration to the sustainability factor through their policy interventions to raise livelihood opportunities. The government of Mizoram adopted a New Land Use Policy (NLUP) in 2011, with a financial provision of ₹12,698 million, to ensure livelihood other than from shifting agriculture.[12] The nature of activities in the initiatives under the NLUP, 2011, are in agriculture (wet rice, terrace, palm oil, sugarcane), horticulture, pisciculture, mulberry silk rearing, animal husbandry, soil and water conservation, rubber, coffee and broom grass plantations, micro-enterprises in the non-farm sector and handloom and bamboo plantations. This has created opportunities for diversified livelihood options. The Rubber Board of India had made a plan to extend cultivation of rubber to 141,000 ha

---

[12] Two idealistic paradigms (see National Afforestation and Eco-Development Board- www.naeb.ni.in) in the context of shifting cultivation now operate at the policy and institutional levels. The dominant perspective is that shifting cultivation is a wasteful and ecologically dysfunctional system, detrimental to forests and soil, and hence needs to be eradicated by inducing cultivators to adopt other forms of livelihood. The other paradigm, playing a more dominant role in the recent period, is that shifting cultivation is a legitimate practice that ensures the survival of people living on marginal lands and, hence, should be allowed to carry on as it is without external influence.

of land in the NE region and reached the target in 2012–2013 (*Shillong Times*, 2014). An exploratory survey by the Rubber Board of India in the early 1960s had identified a vast land area of about 450,000 ha in the NE region with potential for rubber cultivation (Mohanan et al., 2003). Studies in Mizoram map the potential areas for rubber plantations at 29 per cent of the total geographical area of the state (Lallianthanga et al., 2014). The Rubber Board's perception, of utilizing the hills of the NE region for rubber plantation expansion and provisioning of subsidy to drive land use changes, etc., requires a review to prevent market-linked livelihood shocks and an ecological crisis due to accelerated suction of groundwater and greater water losses through rubber evapotranspiration arising out of mono-cultural activities.

Commodity boards of several plantation crops of India have come out with provisioning to attract the farmers and investors. It has been observed that rubber, cashew and spice plantations compete for the same space, and the provisioning of subsidies in a certain crop or plantation eliminate other crops from the process. In such competitive drives, two factors are often ignored—one is that of the market[13] of the produces and the other is the ecological factor.

A CASE OF COMPETING LAND USE AND PROBABLE OUTCOME

The farmers in the Garobadha and Ampata areas of West Garo Hill district of Meghalaya initiated cashew nut cultivation in the late 1980s. The production boom led to the establishment of 15 cashew nut–processing factories in the neighbouring Mankachar area and 7 in the Phulbari area. These factories are in operation for 8–9 months in a year.

A field visit revealed the unwillingness of the cashew nut farmers to continue. The prime reasons for this are provisioning of subsidies for rubber plantations and other pecuniary supports received from the Rubber Board.

---

[13] The market, even though internal, is affected by the bilateral trade agreement and relationships between two countries. The Government of India's gesture to relax the import duty on bamboo sticks sourced from Vietnam to 10 per cent from the earlier rate of 30 per cent has an impact on the bamboo-based livelihood sector in the NE region, particularly in Tripura.

A field visit in September 2015 revealed the unwillingness of the cashew nut farmers to continue operation. The prime reason for this is provisioning of subsidies for rubber plantations and other pecuniary supports received from the Rubber Board.

MARKET AS AN INSTITUTION FOR DEVELOPMENT AND LIVELIHOOD EXPANSION

Some of the constraints in bulk marketing of the hill produces (ginger, for example) are grading of the products, time consumed in grading and lack of premium prices even for the graded products. Lack of approach road, lack of market information, over-reliability on selling locally, peak-period gluts, lack of processing and storage facilities, etc. are emerging as constraints (Tripathi et al., 2007). The result is that people who take initiatives and make efforts for procurement from interior areas derive greater benefits than the farmers.[14]

The initiatives of North Eastern Regional Agricultural Marketing Corporation Ltd. (NERAMAC) in 2009[15] tried to focus on the creation of value chain of the agriculture products of the region through primary processing, upholding locality-specific diversification of production, with a flexible processing structure. A flexible structure accommodating diversified produces is important to ensure processing activity and ensure jobs round the year.

Flexible and feasible combinations of primary processing units, such as in Bomdila (apple, tomato, kiwi), Churachandpur (pineapple, passion

---

[14] Tripathi et al. (2007) find that the producer's share is lowest (38%) if the product is disposed through layers of intermediaries—where village-level collectors, traders, wholesalers and retailers take their respective shares. This mode of marketing, however, is efficient on the grounds of final disposition of the products compared to the modes of: (II) sale of the products at local markets by the producers (from where the agents and other retailers procure them); (III) selling through the commission agents at large markets; and (IV) selling at local markets, from where the small traders procure directly.

[15] Techno-Economic Feasibility Study for setting up collection and procurement centres of Horticulture products in Northeast India (2009). A study conducted for North Eastern Regional Agriculture Marketing Corporation Limited, OKD Institute of Social Change and Development.

fruit, ginger), Nongpoh (ginger, pineapple, guava, banana) etc., would have provided year-long employment and ensured processing of fruit throughout the year. The initiative of NERAMAC failed to take off for certain reasons; thus missed a State-initiated opportunity to create a value chain of agro–horticultural products which, in addition to making provisioning of direct jobs, had probability to drive supplementary activities in secondary and service sectors.

Overall, it appears that there is a lack of willingness, as well as of capabilities, of the existing systems of the state to regulate and govern the available resources, and a relative failure to develop market as an institution in the hill economy and, thus, generate remunerative livelihood.

The NE region may adopt two kinds of approaches. The first one is to restrict population congestion in the fragile ecological region to reduce pressure on resources. The second is to limit the consumption level of certain goods (extraneous) in order to ensure sustainability and accommodative capacity. The first point has significance for easing the population burden of the states of the region.

OUTMIGRATION FOR WORK AND ITS IMPACTS

This section shall try to provide an understanding of a few aspects on the outcomes of migrating for work.

Movement to Distant Locations: Case of Entry at Ease

It is interesting to know why workers from the NE region travel to and work in the distant places of Tamil Nadu, Kerala, Gujarat, Karnataka, Delhi and many other pockets of the country where average wage rates are low compared to their own region. Interaction[16] with the workers revealed that the prime driver was the need of a regular job, with the workers indicating that it was easy to get a lower-end job in the destinations. The process, however, involved three factors—one had

---

[16] This chapter draws information from data collected for an in-house study on out-migration conducted at OKD Institute of Social Change and Development, Guwahati, during 2017–2018.

to make the effort to reach the destination (undertake the long train journey in an unreserved compartment, with anxieties of uncertainties in an unknown world), get the required recommendation from fellow workers and be willing to accept a wage determined by the employer.

Field interactions show that it is not educational attainment levels but skills and perseverance that matter to sustain in the job, employment and labour markets. Not much time is required to get accustomed to a semi-skilled job in a plywood-, biscuit-, ice- or even a motor parts—manufacturing unit. This is the reason why the distressed unemployed youths, irrespective of their level of education, crowd in all forms of jobs, making it difficult to draw a linear linkage of the types of jobs and education attainment levels of the migrant workers in all informal and non-standards jobs across unorganized and even organized sectors.[17] The skills required to work in a plywood factory can be acquired in about 2–3 months' time. The field visit revealed the preference of employers for workers from Assam. For example, in the plywood factories of Perumbavoor, Kerala, workers from Assam now account for 80 per cent of the total number of workers. The presence of workers from Assam is also reported in rubber, plastic and spice factories, as well as in non-standard jobs of the hotel and hospitality sector. What makes workers from Assam prefer standard jobs in Kerala? The employer mentioned that these workers were liked because of their amiable nature, industrious character, efficiency and ability to withstand long hours of work. Workers in plywood factories work for 12 hours in a shift, 6 days a week, with Sunday being the rest day, primarily for the maintenance of machines. Interaction with the workers revealed that having no requirement to spend time with their family, they were willing to work extra hours to earn an additional income.

Evidence indicates that apart from individual initiatives, passages for the workers are created by friends and relatives. Labour contractors

---

[17] Two supportive evidences substantiate this conclusion. The first, as discussed in section II, is that NSSO data reveal a very low work participation rate (WPR) of rural persons with graduate and postgraduate degrees in the NE region; a significant section now have moved to non-standard jobs outside the region. The second is that of subcontracting work organizations, which delink a large section of workers from the management to evaluate their educational levels.

play a decisive role in ensuring the entry of fellow workers from their native place. In plywood factories, for example, all the units, peeling, drying, assembling, pressing and finishing, have to operate simultaneously. Each unit of the production component is headed by a labour contractor, who is responsible for recruiting employees, bargaining on and setting the wage and running the unit of production. The labour contractor also shares the work, being part of the production unit with responsibility for the quality of the products. In one factory, there could be several groups of workers, each headed by a labour contractor.

Interaction with the workers revealed that the lack of avenues for regular and decent sources of income back in their villages and neighbouring towns (non-linear route now has turned into linear route, unlike many migration streams with the direct arrival of workers at the present workplace) forced them to move to distant places. There are several factors for the push: lack of land and other resources, degraded land and frequent waves of floods rendering them distressed, with no sustainable sources of income, unremunerative agriculture, etc. The process of movement had started in the late 1990s; some youths facing harsh conditions for survival reached the metros of Bangalore and Chennai and, eventually, carved out a niche for themselves into the lower-end jobs in the industries of Kerala—primarily in plywood and rubber factories. The numbers shot up in geometric progression as the youths back in their villages heard about the availability of jobs and regular income outside the state.

The state of Kerala, though, has not gained much from the inflow of foreign direct investments like the states of Maharashtra, Seemandhra, Telangana, Gujarat and Tamil Nadu; the remittance of its diaspora has probably driven the investment in the industrial sector.[18] Moreover, the high human development, as well as the low birth rate, in Kerala has created a vacuum in labour supply in non-standard jobs. The message of availability of jobs in Kerala reached distressed youths in the villages of the states of the NE region of India. The youths who visit their home during festivals and other occasions create some impact of

---

[18] We find enough literature on remittance-induced construction sector boom in Kerala in the 1970s and 1980s.

their acquired well-being; they create the passage for their friends and relatives to the locations of the country where they have got a job.

Conditions of Work, Earning, Remittance and Outcomes

A worker in a plywood factory could earn ₹3,000 a week and ₹12,000 a month. There is an overtime allowance of ₹40 per hour. A security guard in Bangalore could earn ₹12,000 to ₹15,000 a month. As reported, many workers in industrial units get free accommodation.[19]

Though many workers work on time rates in manufacturing units, employers now have introduced the practice of piece rates. The practice of subcontracting now delinks a large chunk of workers from the management. The labour contractors are responsible for recruiting the workers, mostly from their own villages, and getting the job done. It is up to the labour contractor how he keeps his workers happy, as well as extracting maximum output from them. The workers paid on a work-rate basis, thus, put in efforts to produce more for their own benefit.

The workers in manufacturing units, as revealed, enjoy their job. It can, however, be mentioned that the workers work in an unregulated environment where labour laws are not applicable. They are happy to earn through their hard work their wages, which are decent from their perspective and help support their families back home. Some of them would come for a few months to earn some quick money and meet certain household commitments, while some others would return every year during the non-agriculture season, even as a few would be engaged at the workplace for years. Facilities of electronic money transfer to their homes and cellular phone services have made access to their families easy, fast and convenient.

Remittances and Outcomes

The survey on domestic migrant labour conducted for the government of Kerala (2013) estimated annual remittances made by 25 lakh migrant

---

[19] It helps extract work from migrant workers; though overtime allowance is paid, there is importance placed on getting work done on time.

workers at ₹16,076.16 crore, the per capita annual remittance standing at ₹64,000. Our interactions with the migrant workers also revealed that, on an average, a migrant worker sends a remittance to the tune of ₹5,000–6,000 per month.

Mr PC, aged 32, earns ₹16,000–20,000 a month as a worker-cum–labour subcontractor in a plywood factory in Perumbavoor and remits ₹3,000–4,000 per month (interview conducted in September 2017). PC has been in Kerala since 2009, and his savings have helped him buy a plot of land in Dhemaji town of Assam, pay a down payment to procure a light commercial vehicle for his elder brother and also construct a semi-*pucca* house. Six years of work in a factory of disposal goods, with a monthly salary of ₹10,000 and overtime earning of ₹2,000, has helped Mr LG (46 years old) remit ₹5,000 home every month and marry off two daughters.

Back home, families of migrant workers use the remittances for meeting day-to-day consumption needs and medical and educational expenses, as well as charges for utilities like phone, gas and electricity, besides TV. These items have now become part of their essential household expenditure. In the case of a large section of workers, the remittance money is primarily utilized for home renovation and construction.

The regular nature of the earning, remittance and spending pattern generates a few issues for discussion. The labour market at the place of destination, though unregulated, has been able to ensure uninterrupted work.

There are also evidences to indicate that remittances have led to house-construction activities in the rural areas of the region. In rural areas of the states in the region, NSSO data reveal a rise in construction activities, particularly in Manipur (23%) and Tripura (43%), wherein a significant section of rural workers were engaged in construction activities during 2011–2012. Though the state-supported rural employment programme (Mahatma Gandhi National Rural Employment Guarantee Act [MGNREGA]) is a factor, particularly in Tripura, it requires an assessment of contribution of remittances to the growth of rural construction activities. Information on the use of remittances to procure inputs for agricultural operations reveals the contribution of migrant workers to drive the agriculture sector of the region.

Economic Un-freedom to Freedom!

One of the discussion points is that the outward movement for work ensures economic freedom[20] or the independence of the migrant workers and, thus, contributes to the well-being of their households. Even though migrants are free to use their labour power, there are gradations of freedom and unfreedom (Brass, 2016). The apparent economic freedom at new destinations (it is relative), however, needs to be looked at from a much wider perspective and through various dimensions. There are criteria that make migrant labourers unfree. First, the movement is out of their compulsion (they are forced to leave and, in most cases, are involuntary to the non-standard jobs).[21] Second, wages at the destination are higher than the wages at the origin but often do not exceed subsistence wages and/or market-clearing wages at the destination and do not come under workplace regulations and labour laws of the state. The advantage, however, is that there is a congenial environment for investment that has ensured continuous work. Third, the conditions at the workplace are not conducive. Migrant workers are, thus, like unfree labour the conditions at work are more easily framed and enforced and thus the migrant workers are unfree labour in a production space, which follows a low road approach.[22]

---

[20] There are complexities involved in defining the term 'freedom' for a person moving from joblessness to job, employment and labour market security. Though income security thus derived ensures economic freedom, the freedom comes at a cost of alienation from families, exposure to risks and hazards at work and invasion of personal dignity. The concern is how a worker balances the constraints and economic independence. Field interactions revealed joblessness and uncertainty of getting a job in the place of origin, and seeking a personal favour to get a job invades into workers' dignity. The constraints, particularly for women workers, are of a specific nature.

[21] This is also revealed by their willingness to return after a certain point of time.

[22] Low-road approach is seeking competitiveness through low labour costs at a deregulated labour market environment (Sengenberger & Pyke, 1992) Industrial District and Local Economic Regeneration, IILS, Geneva.

Field interactions reveal the presence of traits of unfreedom in migrant workers. For Mr NC (25 years old), the solace gained from the monthly earning of ₹12,000 from his security-guard job in Bangalore and the remittance have helped him reconstruct his house, damaged by floods, and negate the family alienation factor to some extent. Mrs E's (29 years old) present job at a spa in Kerala fetches her ₹15,000 per month, which is much higher than what she could earn (₹4,000) from her tailoring job in Imphal West district. Her decision to move comes at the cost of her being away from her husband, whose earnings from the motor repair shop are a meagre ₹4,000. On the other hand, Ms DG (27 years old) never received the promised monthly salary of ₹10,000 and was paid only ₹3,000 per month for survival. The contract, signed with a surety bond of ₹50,000, compelled her to work for 2 years at a beauty parlour in Hyderabad.

Migrant workers face all possible adversities and adapt in the process to generate a threshold income. One of the criteria to assess whether a migrant labour is free or unfree is the labourer's command in the labour market—how he/she ensures a job, whatever may be the form in the place of work, dictating his/her own terms on the wage factor. This is, however, not the case.

The outward movement for work has surely taken the form of submission to the coercive labour market, and though unskilled,[23] the workers find it easy to enter certain categories of jobs yielding relatively better wages and income. It can be said that the out-migrants for work take a rational decision on the wage factor (the arguments of neo-classical approach by Harris & Todaro [1970]) and a decision on relative costs and benefits arising from a continuous job with little possibility of termination.

CONTINUITY AND WELL-BEING

Migrant workers plan to work for a short period at the place of destination, which might, however, vary from 2–3 years to 10–15 years.

---

[23] In contemporary production spaces, the sophisticated machines needs operators, not specialized skilled workers. A person with a minimum, basic understanding could easily acquire the skills for the operational tasks.

Their only concern is to remit money to their homes and save for a better future. Their priority is to meet the immediate needs, including the expenses on the education of their children, and their long-term goal is to invest in house construction/renovation and set up avenues for self-employment at their native places. They would finally like to settle down in their own enterprises at home after working for years as a migrant labourer.

The study on domestic migrant labour, conducted for the government of Kerala (2013), recommended the need for improved housing and living conditions of migrant workers, ensuring their health and providing them social security benefits and employment security. It also recommended promoting good relations between migrant workers and local communities. Most of the workers in Kerala revealed the support received from the employers in case of unforeseen events and the local community's cordiality towards them.

Apart from protecting casual labourers and providing them proper social security, there is a need to regulate self-employed industries, mainly to protect the labourers from precarious conditions.

REFERENCES

Brass, T. (2016). *Labour regime change in the twenty-first century—Unfreedom, capitalism and primitive accumulation.* Aakar Books.

Census of India. (2001). https://censusindia.gov.in/Tables_Published/D-Series/Tables_on_Migration_Census_of_India_2001.aspx/D-Series_link/D3_India.pdf

Census of India. (2011). https://censusindia.gov.in/Tables_Published/D-Series/Tables_on_Migration_Census_of_India_2001.aspx/D-Series_link/D3_India.pdf

Das, K. (2017). Understanding Sluggish industrial process in Northeast India. In D. K. Mishra & Vandana Upadhyay (Eds.), *Rethinking economic development in Northeast India* (pp. 273–314). Routledge.

Das, K., & Chutia, D. (2011, February 6). Outward bound. *The Assam Tribune.*

Harris, J. R., & Todaro, M. P. (1970) Migration, unemployment and development: A two-sector analysis, *The American Economic Review, 60*(1), 126–142.

Lallianthanga, R. K., et al. (2014, January–April). Mapping of potential areas for rubber plantations in Mizoram. *International Journal of Geology, Earth and Environmental Sciences, 4*(1), 150–155.

Manju, M., & Kohli, K. (2015, December 12). Environmental regulation in India, moving 'forward' in the old direction. *Economic and Political Weekly, 50*(50), 20–23.

Mansoor, A., & Quillin, B. (2006). *Migration and remittance.* World Bank.

Mohanan, K. G., Krishnakumar, A. K., & Lalithakumari, E. (2003). An overview of rubber plantation development in North-east India. In C. Kuruvilla Jacob (Ed.), *Global Competitiveness of Indian Rubber Plantation Industry* (pp. 359–368). Rubber Research Institute of India.

Narayana, D., & Venkiteswaran, C. S. (2013). *Domestic migrant labour in Kerala,* Gulati Institute of Finance and Taxation; submitted to Labour and Welfare Department, Government of Kerala.

Roy, T. (2000, April 22). De-industrialisation: Alternative view. *Economic and Political Weekly, 35*(17), 142–147.

Sengenberger W., & Pyke, F. (Eds.) (1992). Industrial districts and local economic regeneration: Research and policy issues. In *Industrial district and local economic regeneration* (pp. 3–29). International Institute of Labour Studies.

Shillong Times (2014, October 31). Rubber cultivation in northeast vital to meet demand. http://theshillongtimes.com/2014/10/31/rubber-cultivation-in-northeast-vital-to-meet-demand/

Tripathi, A. K., et al. (2007). *Production and marketing of selected high value crops in Meghalaya.* Division of Agriculture Economics, ICAR, NEH Region, Umium.

Chapter 11

Public Food Distribution System in the Riverine Villages of Assam
A Cross-sectional Analysis

Rajshree Bedamatta and
Mahsina Rahman

INTRODUCTION

Rural Assam, like other eastern states of India, spends most of its food consumption–related incomes on cereals. The various consumer expenditure rounds of the National Sample Survey Office (NSSO) show that, on an average, a person in Assam spends more on cereals than people in many other states of India. The period between 2004–2005 and 2009–2010 throws up some interesting findings with regard to rural Assam. The average monthly per capita consumption of cereals was 13.4 kg in 2004–2005 and 12.6 kg in 2009–2010. The monthly per capita consumption expenditure on cereals increased from ₹134.81 to ₹207.81 during the same period. Further, contrary to the pattern emerging from the other states, where a decline in cereal intake is also accompanied by a decline in poverty ratios, in Assam, there seems to be an opposite pattern—a decline in cereals intake is accompanied by an increase in poverty ratios (Government of India, 2007, 2011, 2013a, 2013b). Thus, food expenditure has continuously taken a major share of the consumer's total monthly household expenditure, and the money spent on food takes away the major share of household income. When the sources of household income are irregular, as in the case of agricultural incomes and non-salaried families of the rural areas, the impact of this expenditure falls heavily on their general living conditions.

The decline in cereal intake in Assam has its impact on malnutrition. In Assam, 36 per cent of children under the age of 5 years are stunted. The nationally representative National Family Health Surveys (NFHS-3 and NFHS-4) show that between 2005–2006 and 2015–2016, the rates of wasting among children increased by 3 percentage points (from 14% to 17%). Wasting is an indicator of acute malnourishment among children with direct linkages to short-term food insecurity conditions. Malnourishment rates among adults are equally high in Assam. The NFHS-4 (2015–2016) survey results report 39 per cent of women and 34 per cent of men in Assam being either too thin or overweight or obese.

Assam has had a history of food-related disturbances/civic riots. Reports show that immediately following the Bengal famine of 1943, Western Assam saw violent food riots resulting in peasants breaking down granaries of landlords and forcibly distributing rice among the small peasant households. Saikia (2010) traces the reasons for food riots to after-war shocks, severe floods and disputes among peasants and landlords. There are very few published studies reflecting the state of food policy in Assam during the period from the 1970s to the 1990s. Post the 1990s, the very few empirical studies on the public distribution system (PDS) that we could refer to spoke about high errors of exclusion, lack of awareness regarding entitlements, high price of PDS commodities compared to the open market price of rice, and so on (Priyadarshini, 2006; Sengupta, 2006).

This chapter is based on a cross-sectional study of 96 rural households from two revenue villages located in Jorhat and Dhubri (the so-called Upper Assam and Lower Assam, respectively) districts of Assam. The primary objective of this chapter is to investigate whether or not the public distribution system of food contributed significantly to the cereal consumption needs of the sample households. The analysis carried out here shows some significant results with regard to PDS's contribution to household-level food security, based on which this chapter argues for a more inclusive PDS. However, while this chapter argues for a better PDS in rural Assam, it also highlights some of the crucial problems of pricing that the PDS in Assam is facing, which need to be addressed at an administrative level.

The second section of this chapter discusses price-based geographical targeting of PDS in Assam. The third section describes the study area and the details of sample households. The functioning of targeted PDS is described in the fourth section. The fifth section discusses the pooled ordinary least squares (OLS) regression and quantile regression models and results. The sixth section carries the conclusion.

PRICE-BASED GEOGRAPHICAL TARGETING OF THE PDS IN RURAL ASSAM

Assam follows price-based geographical targeting of the PDS. Food distribution in Assam takes place through the network of Gram Panchayat Samabaya Samitis (GPSSs), otherwise called Panchayat-run cooperative societies, and the network of fair price shops (FPSs).[1] Unlike many other states of India, Assam does not maintain a state buffer.[2] Thus, the

---

[1] Panchayats are village-level councils that have a pan-Indian existence. Panchayats or Panchayati Raj Institutions (PRIs) are best known as units of local government established by the Indian Constitution as the third level of India's federal democracy through the 73rd Amendment Act of 1992. The statement of objects and reasons on PRIs of India can be found on https://www.india.gov.in/my-government/constitution-india/amendments/constitution-india-seventy-third-amendment-act-1992.Fair price shops are also known as ration shops that are legally mandated to sell public distribution system (PDS) commodities in India. They are one of the crucial actors in the regulated market of India that sell subsidized food grains to households.

[2] Given the federal character of the Indian State, PDS is both a state and a union subject. While policy formulations regarding the design of PDS are made by the union government, states exercise their autonomy in operational matters. Food grains distributed through the network of fair price shops are stored in granaries maintained by either the state governments or the union government. Since the Government of Assam does not maintain a state buffer, the union government provides storage facilities through granaries operated by the Food Corporation of India.

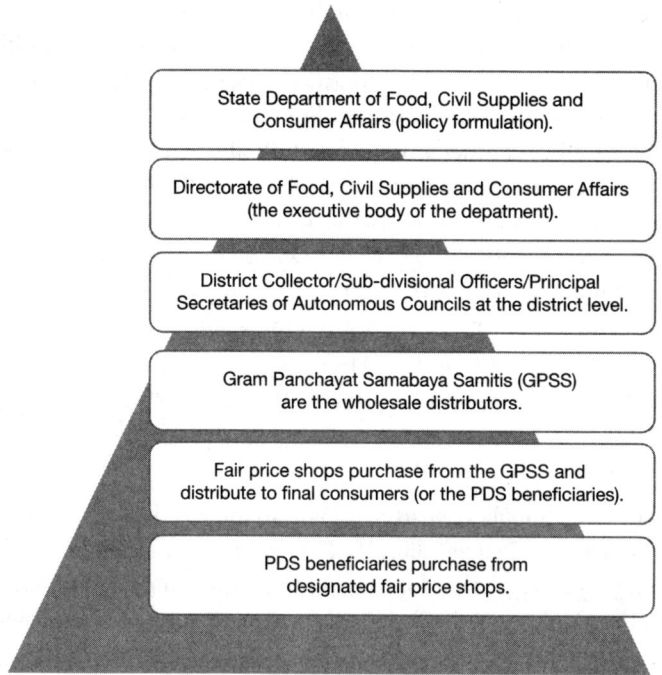

State Department of Food, Civil Supplies and Consumer Affairs (policy formulation).

Directorate of Food, Civil Supplies and Consumer Affairs (the executive body of the depatment).

District Collector/Sub-divisional Officers/Principal Secretaries of Autonomous Councils at the district level.

Gram Panchayat Samabaya Samitis (GPSS) are the wholesale distributors.

Fair price shops purchase from the GPSS and distribute to final consumers (or the PDS beneficiaries).

PDS beneficiaries purchase from designated fair price shops.

Figure 11.1 *Flow Chart of the Public Distribution System*
Source: The author.

Food Corporation of India (FCI) is the major actor for procurement and storage in the absence of any other decentralized procurement mechanisms. GPSSs are the wholesalers from whom private dealers or FPSs purchase the PDS items for distribution to end consumers (Figure 11.1).

The Department of Food, Civil Supplies and Consumer Affairs (henceforth Civil Supplies department), Government of Assam, fixes the transportation charge and profit margin for the GPSSs and FPSs over and above the central issue price (CIP)[3] of rice allotted by the

---

[3] The central issue price is the price fixed by the union government at which the PDS commodities will be made available to the state governments. Similarly, the state governments fix the state issue price (SIP), which is the price at which

Government of India. Depending on the margins fixed, the state issue price (SIP) is fixed for different gradations (depending upon quality) of rice.[4] There is, however, a norm of maintaining the SIP within a range of ₹0.50 above the CIP for poor families or below-poverty-line (BPL)[5] families. In other words, if the CIP of BPL rice is fixed at ₹6.20, the SIP must be maintained at a range within ₹6.20 to ₹6.70. Based on discussions with the various state- and district-level functionaries in Assam, it was found that the SIP of PDS items is usually kept open (not fixed uniformly), as no strict instructions are officially provided to the GPSSs and FPSs. Therefore, distributing agencies add the rising fuel price to transportation costs and push the price burden to end consumers. This was corroborated during the field work, as many households were not aware of the price of PDS rice or quoted different rates than what was fixed for the PDS.

The Civil Supplies department officials informed that transportation charges were revised periodically. However, information on this is not available on the public domain. According to information gathered from the Civil Supplies offices at the state and district levels, transportation charges were revised in the state only thrice since January 1987, and profit margins were revised only twice and continued to hold till at

---

PDS commodities will be made available to the wholesalers (the Gram Panchayat Samabaya Samitis [GPSSs] in our case).

[4] Two gradations of rice are usually distributed through the PDS: common rice (relatively low-priced) meant for poor families and Grade A rice (relatively high-priced) meant for non-poor families. However, both common rice and Grade A rice are subsidized. For more on this, see Bedamatta (2016).

[5] India follows a poverty line criterion for identifying poor and non-poor households. The criterion of poverty line has undergone various changes over the course of the last two decades. We have moved from income poverty to household consumption expenditure poverty and asset-scoring methodologies. Based on the poverty line criterion, the poor households are termed below poverty line (BPL) and non-poor households are termed above poverty line (APL). Post the National Food Security Act (NFSA), 2013, which has been operational in the states since 2016–2017, there has been a renaming of BPL and APL households to *priority households* and *non-poor households*. Accordingly, instead of a BPL card, a priority household now possesses a priority card. The terminologies APL households and APL cards are no longer in use.

least 2015, which was the year during which this study was undertaken (also see Government of Assam, n.d.).

Further, the transport charges were fixed based on a geographical location classification and a distance slab. The geographical classification followed is plain, riverine and hill areas. The distance slabs are 0–5 km, >5–10 km, >10–30 km, >30–50 km and >50 km. Thus, the SIP fixed, as mentioned earlier, could vary across different locations within the state depending on whether they appeared in the category of plain, riverine or hill areas. Thus, based on three geographical locations and five different distance slabs, there are 15 different SIPs in Assam (Table 11.1).[6]

Table 11.1 shows the SIP and CIP of PDS rice distributed among the BPL households in rural Assam from 1997 onwards. The upper slot shows price revisions between 1997 and 2008 and the lower slot shows those between 2008 and 2015. Assam does not provide a state subsidy to any of its consumers in any of the geographical locations. This has price implications for vulnerable households in the riverine and hill areas. Even if geographical targeting is justified on the assumption that riverine- and hill-area distribution costs are higher, end consumers in disadvantageous locations seem to be paying higher than those in the plain areas. BPL families in the hill and riverine areas bear a higher burden of price than a similar family in the plain areas. Such a practice is counter-intuitive.

THE STUDY AREA AND PROCEDURE OF DATA COLLECTION

A multi-stage sampling method was followed for carrying out the sample survey. The primary stage unit (PSU) was the selection of districts based on district-level ranking of food security following the World Food Programme (WFP) framework of food insecurity. The second stage unit (SSU) was the selection of community development (CD) blocks. Revenue villages from the chosen CD blocks were

---

[6] Appendix Table 11A.2 shows the Indian state-wise distribution of SIPs. The SIPs, as calculated, have remained the same even after 2015. However, since the price-related investigations were carried out in 2015–2016, we cannot conclusively claim if revisions have not been carried out after 2015.

Table 11.1 *Geographical Location and Distance Slab-wise Issue Price of PDS Rice Meant for BPL Families, Rural Assam (1997–2015)*

Distance Slab (in km)	SIP, 1997–2008			Year	CIP
	Plain	Riverine	Hill	01.12.1997 to 28.01.1999	3.50
0–5	6.31	6.32	6.37	29.01.1999 to 31.03.2000	3.50
>5 to 10	6.33	6.34	6.38	01.04.2000 to 24.07.2000	5.90
>10 to 30	6.35	6.36	6.40	25.07.2000 to 11.07.2001	5.65
>30 to 50	6.37	6.38	6.42	12.07.2001 to 31.03.2002	5.65
>50	6.38	6.40	6.43	01.04.2002 to 30.06.2002	5.65
				01.07.2002 to 18.02.2008	5.65
SIP, 2008–2009 and Continuing					
0–5	6.51	6.52	6.62	2008–2009	5.65
>5 to 10	6.54	6.56	6.63	2009–2010	5.65
>10 to 30	6.58	6.60	6.68	2010–2011	5.65
>30 to 50	6.61	6.64	6.71	2011–2012	5.65
>50	6.64	6.68	6.74	2012–2013	5.65
				2013–2015*	5.65

Source: Economic Survey, Government of Assam (2004–2005; 2005–2006; 2006–2007; 2007–2008; 2008–2009, 2009–2010; and 2010–2011); Government of Assam (2010a).

Note: State issue price is calculated by the authors based on the transport costs and profit margins meant for each of the geographical locations based on discussions with officials at the Department of Food, Civil Supplies and Consumer Affairs, Government of Assam. The central issue price is as has appeared in various issues of the Economic Survey of Government of India, gathered from www.indiastat.com, browsed on 30 June 2017.

*Between 2013 and 2015, National Food Security Act was implemented in Assam in a phased manner. Revisions in state issue prices of rice were gradually introduced.

selected, based on discussions with government functionaries at the district and block levels. The final stage unit (FSU) was the revenue village from where households were selected following the method of simple random sampling without replacement.

A district ranking of food security, based on WFP's widely approved dimensions of food availability, accessibility and absorption, was prepared. After controlling for data availability issues, the indicators under each of these dimensions that were considered for the district ranks were per capita net cereal production, percentage of BPL households to total rural households, per capita net district domestic product (at 1999–2000 constant prices), percentage of agricultural labourers to total workers in rural areas, under-five mortality rate (U5MR) in rural areas and access to safe drinking water in rural areas. This study followed a Borda ranking procedure to come up with the overall ranks. The cumulative ranks showed that Dhubri district (representing Lower Assam) ranked the lowest in all the dimensions of food security, while Jorhat district (representing Upper Assam) was the best ranked. Therefore, in order to assess the contribution of the PDS to household food security, two villages from these two districts were chosen.

Various rounds of discussions were carried out at the district offices of Food and Civil Supply and Health Services in order to identify blocks and revenue villages where the household survey questionnaires could be administered. The Civil Supply offices of both Dhubri and Jorhat districts provided a list of 'model PDS villages' where targeted PDSs were identified as being implemented successfully. However, in order to identify the shortcomings of the system, instead of considering the model villages, it was decided to choose areas that were officially identified as having adverse health outcome indicators, and therefore, the need for food-based interventions was considered significant. The Directorate of Health officials indicated blocks and revenue villages with adverse health outcome indicators.

From the official records of the Joint Directorate of Health in Dhubri and various development reports, including the Human Development Report of Assam 2014, it was learnt that the problem of hunger is acute in the riverine (*char*) areas affected by floods. It was, therefore, decided to select a riverine village that would have the additional characteristic of being regularly flood-affected and yet accessible from the main town of Dhubri. Birsingjarua CD block was chosen, as it was closely located to Dhubri town. From this block, revenue village Chaudhurirchar was selected in consultation with the health officials, as, according to them, the dependence on the PDS of this village was particularly high. Besides, since Dhubri was highly affected by floods and soil erosion, studying a *char* village assumed significance, as it was felt that people's dependence on the PDS would be relatively high. Further, this would also provide an opportunity of making an evidence-based analysis of price-based geographical targeting for riverine areas.

As per census records of 2011, Chaudhurirchar Part-1 and Part-2 appear as two separate revenue villages. During the field survey in 2015, it was found that the total number of households in Part-1 was 11, whereas Census 2011 recorded 30 households. In Chaudhurirchar Part-2, the total number of households during house listing was 116, and the census record showed 113. Both these revenue villages were studied by clubbing them together as Chaudhurirchar revenue village. Combining Part-1 and Part-2 did not pose any problem, as there were no significant differences in the socio-economic conditions of families living in both the villages. During the course of investigation, it was learnt that a large numbers of households had been displaced from these villages due to regular floods and soil erosion, which happens to be an important characteristic of a riverine village.

Similarly, in Jorhat, hunger and malnutrition were identified as being high in the riverine areas; these were also the areas that were predominantly tribal and had a high presence of tea garden labour. Based on similar consultations with the health officials of Jorhat, Kumargaon revenue village from the Jorhat North West CD block was chosen. Kumargaon is also a riverine village that is severely flood- and erosion-affected. While the census records the name of this village as Kumargaon, residents mention the name as Vitorkokilakumargaon. After validating with the census data and based on discussions with the village headman, it was decided to go by the

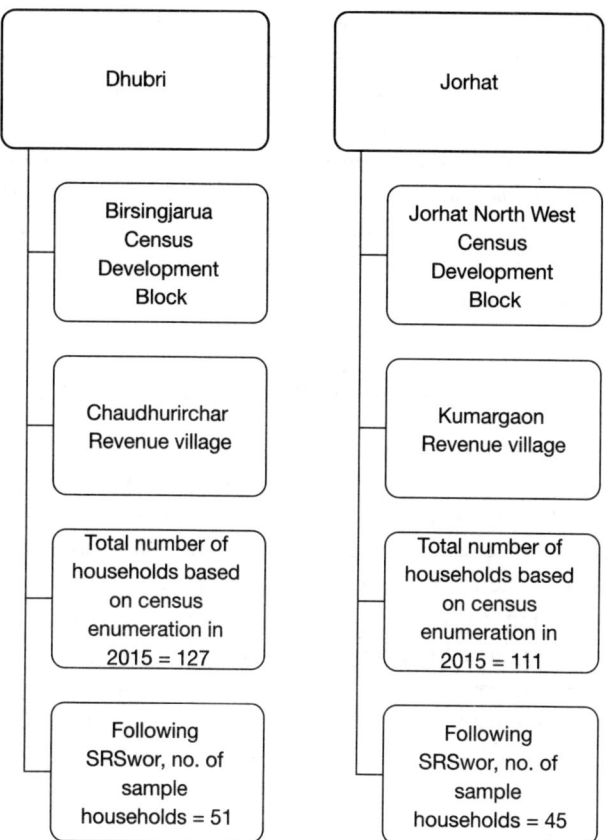

Figure 11.2 *Flow Chart Showing Sample Study Area Details*
Source: The author.

census name of Kumargaon. The study location details are shown in a
flow chart (Figure 11.2).

Sample Design

The survey was carried out in two phases. In the first phase, a complete
enumeration of all households in both revenue villages was done with
the help of a structured questionnaire, where information on household
size, education, marital status, occupation status, ownership of ration

cards, status of households having access to various kinds of food-based welfare programmes, landholding position of the households and households having access to two square meals a day was collected. According to this house-listing survey, the total count of families in Chaudhurirchar was 127 and that in Kumargaon 111. Based on the house-listing count, 40 per cent of families were selected for a detailed survey following the method of simple random sampling without replacement in each revenue village. A total of 51 households in Chaudhurirchar village and 45 households in Kumargaon village were surveyed.

Assam's Riverine Villages

Assam's riverine areas are an integral part of the fluvial process of the Brahmaputra and its tributaries. Because of their typical geographical formation, the locations of the riverine or *chars* are very unstable and can be wiped out by erosion during recurrent floods. These areas are subject to erosion on the upstream and deposition on the downstream, due to which they shift downstream. The riverine areas are, therefore, in great danger of changing locations after every flood. Though the riverine areas have a history more than 100 years old, information relating to the dwellers is minimal and still forthcoming. The Directorate of Char Area Development of Assam carried out two socio-economic surveys on the *char* areas, and these happen to be the only source of official information on *chars*. The first socio-economic survey of *char* areas was carried out in 1992–1993, and then it was repeated in 2003–2004. The result of the first survey report shows that Barpeta district has the highest number of *char* villages and population, followed by Dhubri and Jorhat districts. The second survey report shows that Dhubri district has the highest numbers, followed by Jorhat and Barpeta. The Directory of Char Areas (2007–2008), Government of Assam, cited in Government of Assam (2016), estimates *char* areas at 5 per cent of the total area of the state, spread across 14 districts and comprising a total of 2,300 villages (Government of Assam, 2016).

Chaudhurirchar Village

Chaudhurirchar meets the Gauranga tributary of River Brahmaputra. It is located at a distance of 35 km from Dhubri town in the Fulkatri

Table 11.2 *Demographic Profile of Chaudhurirchar Revenue Village, 2011 and 2015*

Indicator	2011		2015	
	Number	Percentage	Number	Percentage
Households	143	–	127	–
Muslim households	–	–	107	80
Hindu households	–	–	26	20
Population	743	–	713	–
Male population	387	52	368	52
Female population	356	48	345	48
Sex ratio	920	–	938	–
Juvenile sex ratio	938	–	1254	–
Male literacy	159	49	144	48
Female literacy	119	40	109	45
Total literacy	278	45	253	45

Source: Registrar General of Census of India, 2011; and survey data, 2015.

Gram Panchayat. The village has a mix of both Hindu and Muslim families. Muslim families constitute 80 per cent of the total. All Hindu families identify themselves as belonging to the Other Backward Castes (OBC) group. The language spoken by the villagers is known as Bhatia, a dialect of Bengali. Table 11.2 depicts the demographic details of Chaudhurirchar village, based on information from Census 2011 and the survey conducted in 2015. There was a decline in the numbers of households and the total population of the village between 2011 and 2015, which could be attributed to displacements on account of floods and flood-related erosions. A sizeable difference in the juvenile sex ratio between that reported in Census 2011 and that estimated from the survey was also found. The reported ratio in 2011 was 920, while that estimated from the survey was 1,254. The survey estimate of juvenile sex ratio also matched with the records of the village Accredited Social Health Activist (ASHA). Therefore, the discrepancy with regard to the census data is unexplained.

In Chaudhurirchar, overall dependence on agriculture was very low. The share of the population employed in agriculture either as cultivators (6%) or as hired wage workers (3%) was very low. This was largely due to low operational holdings of land and loss of agricultural land to floods and erosion. The opportunities for non-agricultural incomes were also very limited. As such, people in the economically active age group were generally active seeking work in any kind of engagement that they could have recourse to. Of the total population, 22 per cent were engaged in household works, and all of them were women. About 29 per cent of the population were children, who were enrolled in school. About 15 per cent of the population were out of the labour force and entirely dependent on family incomes. The regular salaried formed 3 per cent, and the daily wage workers in agriculture and non-agriculture 9 per cent. Such workers reported working mostly as helpers in construction sites in Kokrajhar and Bongaigaon districts. Some travelled to Meghalaya and Guwahati on a weekly, fortnightly or monthly basis. About 8 per cent of the population were engaged in petty trade as puffed rice sellers and wood collectors. Of the working age group population in Chaudhurirchar, 57 per cent never attended school. Almost half the village (49% of households) was either landless or near-landless, with very small patches of operational holdings of land (Table 11A.1).

Kumargaon Village

The inhabitants of Kumargaon village belong to the potter community, and the village is named after them. The village is located about 15 km away from Jorhat town and has all Hindu families from the OBC group. An embankment of the River Brahmaputra runs through the village, bisecting it, with one part of the village protected by the embankment and the other left to the mercy of floods. The embankment also serves as the main road of the village. Like Chaudhurirchar, the demographic details of Kumargaon also showed a massive decline in the count of numbers of households as compared to the Census 2011 figures. The village headman blamed it on displacements due to flood-related erosion of land and lack of employment opportunities resulting in families migrating from the village. Census 2011 recorded

Table 11.3 Demographic Profile of Kumargaon Revenue Village, 2011 and 2015

Indicator	2011		2015	
	Number	Percentage	Number	Percentage
Households	163	–	111	–
Population	756	–	477	–
Male population	397	53	242	51
Female population	359	47	235	49
Sex ratio	904	–	971	–
Juvenile sex ratio	942	–	615	–
Male literates	351	88	189	88
Female literates	299	83	174	79
Total literates	650	86	363	83

Source: Registrar General of Census of India, 2011; and survey data, 2015.

Kumargaon's population count as 756, while the survey conducted for this study in 2015 indicated the count as 477.

Another alarming feature of this village was the extremely adverse child sex ratio. The ratio reported in 2011 was 942, while the survey of 2015 showed the ratio as 615. Since this was an incredibly low ratio, it was cross-checked with the child sex ratio data with the Anganwadi Worker (AWW) of the village by carrying out a random check of the 2012–2013 record. In that year, of the 26 pregnant women, 23 gave birth to male children. During the period of investigation, it was learnt that this was due to sex-selective abortions carried out in the village. Table 11.3 depicts the demographic profile of Kumargaon village.

Compared to Chaudhurirchar, educational attainments were much better in Kumargaon. Above 41 per cent of the population had attained secondary level education, 21 per cent had reached the higher secondary level, with slightly more than 2 per cent reaching graduation and post-graduation levels. Landless and near-landless population were 23 per cent, while 63 per cent had some marginal landholdings. In both villages, medium and large landowning categories did not exist at all.

Table 11.4 *Major Crops Cultivated in Chaudhurirchar and Kumargaon Revenue Villages*

Crop	Month of Sowing	Month of Harvesting	Source of Irrigation
		Chaudhurirchar	
Summer paddy (IRRI)	November–December	May–June	Shallow tube well
Winter paddy (*sali*)	April–May	October–November	Rainwater
Jute	March	September	Rainwater
Urad dal	October	January	Rainwater
Mustard	October–November	January	Rainwater
		Kumargaon	
Winter paddy (*sali*)	April-May	October–November	Rainwater
Mustard	October–November	January	Rainwater

Source: Survey data, 2015.

In spite of the persisting problem of erosion, agricultural land was cited as one of the crucial assets that people tried to retain. Thus, landless and near-landless households exhibited higher vulnerability to poverty and food insecurity traps.

Crops Cultivated in the Study Villages

The main food crop cultivated in Chaudhurirchar was summer paddy (most cultivated were IRRI and its different varieties) and black gram (*matikalai*). Among non-food items, jute (*pata*) and mustard seeds were widely cultivated. Paddy was mostly confined to household cultivation, though the cost of cultivation reported by the households was very high. A majority of the households cultivated IRRI paddy, because the yields per acre were reportedly higher and it was also found more suita-ble for flood-affected areas. Cultivation began in November–December and crops could be harvested at the end of May, which was just before the starting of the monsoon season.

In Kumargaon, winter paddy, or *sali,* was the main crop cultivated, while a few households cultivated mustard seeds. As noticed from the landholding status, farming was at the subsistence level, and cultivation was mostly for self-consumption. This gave the households food support for some months or for the whole year, depending upon their landholding capacities. Jute, black gram and mustard seeds were grown for commercial purposes, as they fetched relatively higher returns compared to paddy. Summer paddy (IRRI) cultivation required more water, as well as involved other input costs for the purchase of chemical fertilizers and high-yielding variety (HYV) seeds. The source of irrigation was shallow tube wells used to lift groundwater, and consequently, the cost of irrigation was also high. However, winter paddy did not require large investments, but the yield rates were low.

Basic Infrastructure, Water and Sanitation

The eastern and southern parts of Chaudhurirchar village remain submerged during the monsoons. The villagers have to negotiate muddy, waterlogged roads during the entire monsoon season. They use wooden boats and boats made from banana plants' trunks for commuting in the village. The nearest market, Fulkatri, which is located at a distance of about 6 km from the village, gets severely inundated during floods. The main road of the village also gets damaged due to floods, making the communication pathetic during the monsoons. In Kumargaon village too, the roads remain in a bad condition. The nearest market is Jorhat, which is 15 km from the village (Table 11.5).

There is no concrete housing in Chaudhurirchar village. People construct houses out of tin roofs to cope with the floods, but this adds to the heat in these dwelling units, resulting in oppressive conditions. In Kumargaon, semi-*pucca* and *kachcha* houses outnumber the *pucca* ones. Houses are densely clustered, due to the fragmentation of landholdings. Besides, those households that are more exposed to floods have to bear repairing costs every year. The main sources of drinking water in both villages are hand pumps. In Chaudhurirchar and Kumargaon,

Table 11.5 *Availability of Basic Infrastructure in Chaudhurirchar and Kumargaon Revenue Villages*

Availability of Infrastructure	Chaudhurirchar	Kumargaon
Electricity	123 households	107 households
Safe drinking water	120 households	83 households
Sanitation	47 households	52 households
School/college	One primary school/one middle school	One primary school
Distance from nearest town	35 km (approx.)	15 km (approx.)
Distance from primary health centre	70 km	2 km
Distance of nearest market	Fulkatri at 6 km	Jorhat at 15 km

Source: Survey data, 2015.

120 and 83 families, respectively, had their own hand pumps. During floods, as a result of groundwater contamination, drinking water supplies are badly hit. The affected families are largely dependent on their better-off neighbours.

FUNCTIONING OF THE PDS IN ASSAM'S RIVERINE VILLAGES

Number of Beneficiary Families

There were four categories of ration card holder families in the study villages during the time of survey: Antyodaya Anna Yojana (AAY), Below Poverty Line (BPL), Above Poverty Line (APL) and Mukhya Mantri Anna Surakhya Yojana (MMASY). Data on ration cards held were collected during the house-listing count. In Chaudhurirchar, nearly 35 per cent of the families held a BPL card, while the corresponding figure for Kumargaon was 20 per cent. The average monthly per capita expenditure (MPCE) of an AAY family in Chaudhurirchar was ₹528, of which ₹278, or more than half, was spent on food. A similar family in Kumargaon had an MPCE of ₹1,592, of which ₹629, or more than a quarter, was spent on food. The monthly consumption expenditures of BPL families in the two villages were ₹879 and ₹1,607, respectively. The corresponding figures for food expenditures were ₹554 and ₹922, respectively (Table 11A.3).

Source of Cereals

The data on monthly consumption of rice show that in both the villages, families consumed rice from three main sources: from the *open market*, from the *home-grown stock* and from the *PDS*. In Chaudhurirchar, about 8 per cent of the households were completely dependent on the PDS for their monthly rice consumption. About 33 per cent of families consumed rice from the open market, and an equal percentage of families consumed rice from the combined sources of the PDS and the open market. Around 24 per cent of the families in Chaudhurirchar consumed only home-grown rice. None of the households in this village consumed from the combined source of the PDS and home-grown stocks, which indicates that those who consumed entirely from the PDS do not have any home-grown stock. These are the households that are more susceptible to the vagaries of market forces, as well as to fluctuations in PDS supplies and prices (Table 11.6).

In Kumargaon village, the majority of the households were dependent on the combined sources of the PDS and the open market. A sizeable proportion of families were also dependent on the combined sources of the PDS and home-grown stocks, and the number of families that were entirely dependent on the PDS for survival were about half that in Chaudhurirchar.

Utilization of PDS Rice

The study investigated the actual amount of food received by the households and price paid for it, as against the official entitlement and the SIP meant for riverine villages in Assam. Data collection was based on what could be recalled by the respondent families, because the BPL and APL cards were submitted at the block office, as the official process of selection of beneficiaries for National Food Security Act (NFSA),

Table 11.6 *Household Consumption of Rice from Different Sources in the Study Villages*

Source	Chaudhurirchar		Kumargaon	
	Number	Percentage	Number	Percentage
Only from the PDS	4	7.8	2	4.4
Only from the home-grown stock	12	23.5	8	17.8
Only from the open market	17	33.3	7	15.6
From the PDS and the home-grown stock	0	0	12	26.7
From the PDS and the open market	17	33.3	15	33.3
From the home-grown stock and the open market	1	2	0	0
From all three sources	0	0	1	2.2

Source: Sample survey data, 2015.

2013, had begun during the survey period. Some families still held (the now-discontinued) MMASY cards.[7] APL families of Chaudhurirchar village never received printed cards. They received their monthly entitlements based on the list of names in the register held with the fair price shop that had been operational since 1997.

The quantity entitlement of rice for AAY families was 35 kg per month, and the SIP fixed for this category of cardholders was ₹3 per kilogram. Similarly, the quantity entitlement of BPL families was 33.33 kg within the price range of ₹6.52 to ₹6.68 that depended on the distance slabs. However, the actual amount of rice purchased by the families of both these categories of cardholders was 30 kg. The AAY

---

[7] For more details on Mukhya Mantri Anna Surakhya Yojana (MMASY), see Government of Assam (2010b).

families paid ₹3 per kg, whereas the BPL families paid ₹7 per kilogram. The FPS dealer of Chaudhurirchar admitted to selling off the rest of the entitled rice at the rate of ₹16 per kg to meet the logistics of transportation. Thus, 3.33 kg of rice per BPL family and 5 kg of rice meant per AAY family were leaked out of the system. The BPL families of the village did not seem to have accurate knowledge about their actual quantity and price entitlements from the PDS. The AAY families, on their part, were strangely convinced that they had to forego the 5 kg of entitled rice as the FPS had to meet the costs of transportation to ensure that the subsidized rice reached the families. During the period of the survey, the APL families did not draw any rice from the PDS. The last reported purchase by the APL families was 4–5 months preceding the date of our survey. The APL families in rural Assam were entitled to purchase 10 kg of rice at a rate ranging from ₹9.02 to ₹9.18 per kg in the riverine areas. The quantity entitlement as reported by the households was 9 kg per month at the rate of ₹13.5. Table 11.7 summarizes the official and actual price and quantity entitlements of PDS rice in Chaudhurirchar riverine village.

In Kumargaon village, the first phase of NFSA, 2013 roll-out had started. The existing ration cards were being replaced with new NFSA cards. All AAY families in this village received their full quantity entitlement at the allotted price of ₹3 per kg. The BPL families were informed that their quantity entitlement was 32 kg instead of 33.33 kg. The APL families in Kumargaon, like in the previous village, did not receive their rice quota regularly, but the reported quantity and price entitlements were 9 kg of rice bought at the rate of ₹12 per kg. The MMASY families and BPL families were charged the same price of ₹7 per kg. The BPL and AAY variety rice were reportedly sold in these villages at the open market price of ₹16 to ₹17 per kg. The market price of APL variety of rice was in the range of ₹18 to ₹20.

As such, what was the subsidy lost by the households due to the systemic failure of rice not being made available as per entitlements? AAY families in Chaudhurirchar not getting their full quantity entitlement have been losing 5 kg at ₹16 per kg or ₹80 per family per month. Since the number of families holding AAY cards in this village was 20, the total subsidy loss was to the tune of ₹1,600. Similarly, a BPL family in

Table 11.7 Quantity and Price Entitlements of PDS Rice and Actual Purchase Reported

Type of Card	Quantity Allotted (in kg)	CIP (₹/kg)	SIP for Riverine Villages (₹/kg)	Actual Quantity Received (in kg)			Actual Price Paid (₹/kg)	
				Chaudhurirchar	Kumargaon		Chaudhurirchar	Kumargaon
AAY	35	3	3	30	35		3	3
BPL	33.33	5.65	6.52–6.68	30	32		7	7
APL	10	8.3	9.02–9.18	9	9		13.5	12
MMASY	5	5.65	7	5	5		7	7

Source: Sample survey data, 2015.

this village was losing 3.33 kg at ₹16 per kg or ₹53.3 per family. Given the amount and nature of leakages in both villages, loss of subsidy to families was higher in Chaudhurirchar than in Kumargaon. The records of the FPS owners were checked and it was found that the dealers entered the exact official rates and figures against each beneficiary. The reported quantity and price based on the household survey were as mentioned above.

After the Rolling Out of the National Food Security Act, 2013

The National Food Security Act, 2013, identified all BPL families as *priority households,* and the coverage of families in this category was also set to increase. The AAY families were to continue, as earlier, with the 35 kg and ₹3 per kg quantity and price entitlements, respectively (Government of Assam, 2017). The survey was followed up with subsequent short visits to observe post-NFSA changes in the years 2016 and 2017. It was found that the AAY families continued to receive the same 30 kg at ₹3 per kg. The priority households (who were the erstwhile BPL families with the same coverage) received 5 kg less than their entitlements. In Kumargaon, the quantity purchased by AAY families was 35 kg but the price charged was ₹4 per kg. The priority households received 5 kg per person at the rate of ₹4 per kg. The discrepancies relating to price and quantity entitlements were all attributed to the need for meeting transport costs by the FPS dealers.

CONTRIBUTION OF THE PDS TO HOUSEHOLD CEREAL CONSUMPTION NEEDS

An ordinary least squares (OLS) regression and quantile regression was carried out to explain factors that contribute to deficiency in food grain consumption at the household level. Food grain deficiency here means the difference in the actual level of consumption and specified norms. Here, the norms specified by the then–National Advisory Council of India 2011,[8] following Bhattacharya et al. (2016), were applied.

---

[8] The National Advisory Council of India was formed in 2000 and was operational between 2000 and 2014. It was an advisory body comprising a mix of

A 40 per cent random sample of households from the house-listing count was drawn. Accordingly, 51 sample households were chosen for Chaudhurirchar and 45 for Kumargaon. However, there were a few households from vulnerable groups such as landless, agricultural labour and casual labour not possessing ration cards. Eight such households in Chaudhurirchar and seven in Kumargaon were identified. As these households could not be a part of the sample during the random selection, they were purposively added for the regression analysis. Finally, the total sample for Chaudhurirchar was 59 and that for Kumargaon 52. The village data were pooled, and the observations totalled 111.

The Dependent Variable

FDEV, or food grain deviation, is defined as the deviation of the actual consumption of food grains from a required threshold limit.

The threshold limit has been based on the National Advisory Council (NAC) 2011 norms of monthly per capita consumption of food grains. The NAC 2011 had recommended that monthly requirement of food grains should be at least 7 kg of cereals per capita per month for an adult member. The required norm is then adjusted to NSSO-provided consumer units, as food requirements vary across sex, age, physiological status and activity level. For example, a normal male person doing sedentary work and belonging to the age group 20–39 years is considered as one consumer unit, which is a standard numeraire. Similarly, a person of a given age, sex and activity level is converted into an appropriate number of consumer units based on his/her respective calorie requirement relative to the calorie requirement of the numeraire. Thus, the NAC's norm of the 7 kg per capita per month threshold is converted into per consumer unit as follows.

FDEV or food grain deviation is calculated as:

---

economists, bureaucrats, politicians and industrialists that provided key inputs and was instrumental in drafting the Right to Information Act, Right to Education Act, Employment Guarantee Act and Food Security Bill.

7 kg × average consumer unit of the household = x,

where average consumer unit = $\dfrac{\text{total consumer units of the household}}{\text{total size of the household}}$.

Thus, FDEV = actual amount of rice consumed per consumer unit, where rice per consumer unit is

$$\frac{\text{Total rice consumed by the household}}{\text{Total consumer units of the household}}.$$

In other words, FDEV is how much more (or less) quantity of rice (in kg) is consumed by a person than the threshold limit of the household per month. Thus, if the amount is >0 then the household is food secure, and if it is ≤0 then the household is food insecure. It is a normalized figure for monthly per capita consumption of rice.

Independent Variables

1. **OH_Land, or size of operational holdings of land,** is the main determinant of food security of the rural households. It is assumed that there is a positive relationship between households' food grain security and the size of the operational holding.
2. **FDI, or food diversity index,** has been calculated to measure dietary diversity or to assess the typical dietary pattern of the household or individuals or to assess the food security situation of rural agriculture-based societies. This variable will also bring out the importance of welfare interventions during the periods of intense food shortages such as immediately prior to harvest or after emergencies and natural disasters. The FDI variable will also show the seasonality of food security in both the flood-affected villages. Dietary diversity, in turn, is measured by a proxy indicator of food diversity index or what is called entropy index. The formula to compute FDI or entropy index is as follows:

$$h_i = -\sum_{j=1}^{k} P_{ij} \ln\left(P_{ij}\right),$$

where k=number of food groups and P_{ij}=proportion of population consuming the food groups. The range of this entropy index is between 0 and ln (n). A higher value of index implies more diversified food consumption by the households. In our study, nine broad food groups are considered following the manual on Dietary Guidelines for Indians (National Institute of Nutrition, 2011). They are: cereals, pulses, non-vegetarian foods like meat and fish, seasonal vegetables, milk, fresh fruits, sugar products, edible oil and salt. The value of entropy index is bounded between 0 and 2.197, as $n=9$.

MPCE, or monthly per capita consumption expenditure, is the proxy income variable of the household. MPCE is the sum total of MPCE for food and non-food. The reference period for food consumption expenditure is 30 days and that for non-food consumption expenditure is 365 days. The relationship between FDEV and MPCE can be both positive and negative. The response of MPCE to FDEV has been severely contested. However, it has been noticed that the general calorie consumption puzzle and food budget–squeezing argument may not hold true for cross-sectional studies. Food budget of the households are largely cereal-laden, particularly under conditions of poverty, lack of employment opportunities and seasonal food insecurity. Therefore, MPCE is expected to have a positive relationship with FDEV.

3. **Adult_literate, or number of literate adult members in the household,** is the sum total of adult literate members in the household. There should be a negative relation between this variable and cereal consumption of households, as it is assumed that with the increase in education level, people tend to do less manual work and, therefore, cereal consumption comes down.

4. **ICDS_dummy:** Households that have children having access to the Integrated Child Development Services (ICDS) programme.

5. **MDM_dummy:** Households that have children having access to the Mid-Day Meal (MDM) programme.

6. **Ration card dummies:** RC_1=1 if households have AAY cards, 0 otherwise; RC_2=1 if households have BPL cards, 0 otherwise; RC_3=1 if households have APL and MMASY cards, 0 otherwise; and RC_4=1 if households have no cards, 0 otherwise.

7. **Village_dummy** is 1 if Kumargaon and 0 otherwise.

A pooled quantile regression has been fitted to study the effect of the explanatory variables on FDEV. Quantile regression measures the effects of explanatory variables across the distribution of the dependent variable. Justification for using a quantile regression along with OLS is that it may give a significantly different coefficient from the OLS coefficient, which means OLS coefficient is outside the quantile regression coefficient confidence interval when there is heteroscedasticity in the data. The Breusch–Pagan test was conducted to check the presence of heteroscedasticity in the pooled data, which shows the value of χ^2, and the p-value is 0.0123, which is less than 0.05, and because of this, the quantile regression measure has been adopted to see the difference of impact of the explanatory variables across different quantiles of the dependent variable. OLS model the relationship between explanatory variables and the conditional mean of Y variable, whereas quantile regression measures the relationship between explanatory variables and conditional quantiles of Y variable, rather than just the conditional mean of Y variable. OLS regression equation, in our model, has the following form:

$$\text{FDEV}_{ij} = \alpha + \beta 1 \text{OHland}_{ij} + \beta 2 \text{FDI}_{ij} + \beta 3 \text{MPCE}_{ij} + \beta 4 \text{Adult } literate_{ij}$$
$$+ \beta 5 \text{ICDS\_} dummy_{ij} + \beta 6 \text{MDM\_} dummy_{ij}$$
$$+ \beta 7 \text{rationcard\_} dummy_{ij} + \beta 8 \text{village\_} dummy_{ij} + \varepsilon_{ij}$$

where FDEV_{ij} is the food grain deviation of the ith household for jth village. The empirical specification of quantile regression is

$$\text{FDEV}_i = X'_i \beta_q + e_i,$$

where X'_i is the vector of determinants of food grain deviation.

$$(\beta_q) = \sum_{i:\text{FDEV} \geq X'_i\beta}^{N} q \,|\, \text{FDEV}_i - X'_i\beta_q \,|\, + \sum_{i:\text{FDEV} \leq X'_i\beta}^{N} (1-q) \,|\, \text{FDEV}_i - X'_i\beta_q \,|.$$

In the case of the above-mentioned equation, the weighted absolute value of the residuals is minimized, unlike in OLS, where the sums of the squared residuals are minimized. For the *j*th regressor, the marginal effect is the coefficient for the *q*th quantile.

$$\frac{\partial Q_q \ (\text{FDEV} \mid X)}{\partial x_j} = \beta_{qj}.$$

Results and Discussion of the Pooled Regression Following the OLS and Quantile Regression Models

In the quantile regression model, the 25th quantile is the lowest quantile, the 50th is the median quantile and the 75th is the highest quantile class of the dependent variable FDEV. The 25th quantile class is the most food grain–insecure class, and the 75th quantile class is the least food grain–insecure class. For pooled quantile regression, the key variable is ration card_dummy, where the reference variable is RC_3, or households having APL cards and MMASY cards, which are comparatively well-off households in some form or the other. The results of the other categories of households are interpreted in terms of the RC_3 variable.

BPL households show positive and significant contribution in the 50th and 75th quantiles but no significant impact on the lowest quantile, which means that BPL allocation is not sufficient for most food-insecure households. The RC_4 dummy has a negative and significant association for OLS as well as for the 25th and 50th quantiles, which shows that the most food-insecure households (or those that do not have any access to the PDS) need some kind of public food intervention. The regression results are presented in Table 11.8.

The other important explanatory variables are OH_Land, FDI and MPCE and dummies for ICDS and MDM beneficiary households. The variable OH_Land is positive and significant for OLS and all the quantiles, and this implies that possession of land is advantageous for gaining household food security. The food diversity index does not show any significant association with the variable FDEV. A causal relationship would be expected if FDI were to be regressed on nutritional outcomes rather than on cereal intake. The MPCE variable also shows a positive and significant effect for both OLS and all the quantile classes of

Table 11.8 *Factors Contributing to Food Grain Deviation from the Norm, Pooled for Chaudhurirchar and Kumargaon (OLS and Quantile Regression Results)*

Independent Variable	Quantiles			OLS
	25th	50th	75th	
OH_Land	0.579*	0.00738***#	1.1**	0.084**
	−0.001	−0.003	−0.003	−1.87
FDI	−2.52	−1.68	−4.3	−5.97
	−1.3	−2.43	−2.4	(−2.18)
MPCE	0.002519*	0.002137***#	0.003529**	0.002614***
	−0.0005	−0.0008	−0.35	−0.001
Village_dummy	−1.5	−1.94976	−2.6358	−1.08395
	−0.73	−1.28	−1.27	−1.2
Adult_literate	−0.05	−0.339	−0.93	−0.8021849*
	−0.11	(−0.70)	(−1.05)	(−1.52)
ICDS_dummy	1.3	1.2	1.6	2.248*
	−0.79	−0.91	−0.67	−1.52
MDM_dummy	−1.08	−3.35**	−4.07*	−3.9**
	(−0.74)	(−2.01)	(−1.49)	(−2.80)
RC_1	0.4	1.2	−0.04	1.3
	−1.1	−2.2	−2.23	−0.64
RC_2	0.31	2.1*	4.2*#	2.85
	−1.1	−1.8	−1.9	−1.61
RC_4	−7.66***	−6.4**	−4.1	−5.578**
	(−3.39)	(−3.35)	−1.5	(−2.79)
Constant	1.98**	3.15**	6.43***	4.56
	−1.1	−1.7	−1.48	−2.87
Pseudo R^2	0.26	0.39	0.17	R^2=0.29**

Source: Survey data, 2015.

Note: Absolute value of *t*-statistics based on robust standard error in parentheses.

*, ** and ***significant at 10%, 5% and 1% level, respectively.

represents significantly different quantile regression coefficient from OLS coefficients.

food grain deviation, implying that an increase in MPCE also increases households' food security. The variable Adult_literate shows a negative and significant association at the 10 per cent level for OLS but is not significant for any of the quantiles. Similarly, ICDS_dummy shows a positive and significant association in OLS but not in the quantiles. However, MDM_dummy shows a negative and significant association with OLS in the 50th and 75th quantiles of food grain deviation class. MDM_dummy, which should show a positive contribution to household food security status, is negative here, and we feel that it may not be generalized from this case, as only a fraction of population has been considered. The results of the multicollinearity test for the independent variables are presented in Table 11A.4.

From the village data, it is clear that very few households can entirely rely on PDS rice for their monthly consumption, because PDS rice cannot give them month-long support. Thus, the households have to rely either on the open market or on the home–grown stock of rice. However, in both the study villages, the majority of the households are marginal landholders, and their home–grown stocks last only 2–3 months in a year. As such, the households rely on a combination of all sources for their monthly rice consumption. In both the villages, a targeted PDS is mainly available to BPL and AAY households.

CONCLUSION

The chapter studied food–based welfare programmes in two riverine villages of rural Assam, with particular focus on the public distribution system of food. The ICDS and MDM programmes meant for young non–school–going–age and school–going–age children were also taken as variables. The riverine villages of Assam have special significance, given the peculiarity of their geographical formation. They were chosen for two main reasons. The first was to investigate how price–based geographical targeting of the PDS has been in operation in these villages, and the second, given their specific vulnerability to food insecurity, was to investigate the contribution of food–based welfare programmes to overall household food security.

Assam's price-based geographical targeting, according to distance slabs in plains, hills and riverine areas, is one of its kind in India. The different ranges of SIPs specified have created information distortions at the ground level. The administrative costs of distribution, particularly in terms of transportation, have not been tamed effectively. This is giving rise to leakages at the FPS level. Further, keeping transport costs open to manipulation by the GPSS–FPS nexus results in a massive loss of subsidy meant for the rightful beneficiaries. It is argued that unless the loopholes with regard to transport costs are effectively tackled through administrative measures at the appropriate levels, the NFSA, 2013–mandated distribution of food to priority households will fall short of the target quantity.

Another facet of the above problem of information distortions with regard to the price of PDS rice is awareness among beneficiaries. The beneficiaries are ignorant about their actual price and quantity entitlements, as prices keep changing at every 5 km. The involvement of private dealers in the distribution of PDS rice and provision for variations in issue price increase the scope of leakages and corruption. While geographical targeting as policy prescription has been followed in different countries of the world, including in Indian states, Assam's geographical targeting policy is complex, with adverse consequences for end users.

The pooled quantile and OLS regression results explaining the factors affecting the food grain deviation (FDEV) show the BPL families having a positive and significant contribution in the 50th and 75th quantile classes of FDEV but no impact on the lowest quantile class, which means that BPL allocation is not sufficient for the most food-insecure households. Another way of arguing that would be that BPL allocation is the crucial factor that ensures some amount of food to the most food-insecure families. Families' pooled regression also showed that families drawing food from all sources, including from the PDS, were the only category that faced less food grain consumption deviation from the norm. In other words, they are the most food-secure compared to all the other categories of families. The ICDS and MDM programmes were found to be fully utilized in both the study villages. Lack of basic infrastructure and irregularity of funds were major problems. The dependence on and demand for food-based welfare programmes are not only extremely high but are also critical for food security in a state like Assam.

Policy interventions are urgently required for systematizing the pricing mechanism worked out through the network of GPSSs. These rural cooperatives form the backbone of essential commodities' distribution in Assam. Assam is the only state in India that has not formed a Civil Supplies Corporation that can effectively look into the matters of distribution. Given the above and the fact that the Government of Assam does not maintain a state pool of food grains, food supply management in the state is full of challenges.

The usual limitations of a cross-sectional analysis apply to this study. The findings, as such, cannot be generalized to the whole of Assam. The study, however, does provide a partial view of PDS functioning, as well as the performance of food-based welfare programmes in the riverine villages. The serious fallout of discriminatory pricing, based on distance slabs, in the riverine areas have been examined in detail. The study could not examine allocation and off-take data on rice, as the data were not maintained systematically by the Department of Food, Civil Supplies and Consumer Affairs. Assam being prone to regular floods, allocations are done on special, *ad hoc* and special *ad hoc* bases. Records on these are scattered and could not be compiled conclusively. Furthermore, this study could not examine the nutritional impact of food supplied through food-based welfare programmes.

APPENDIX A

Table 11A.1 *Distribution of Households by Occupation Category and Size Class of Landholdings, Chaudhurirchar and Kumargaon (in %)*

Occupation Category	Chaudhurirchar	Kumargaon
Cultivator	6.1	4
Labourer in agriculture	2.8	Nil
Labourer in non-agriculture	9.1	16
Self-employed in non-agriculture	4.9	3

Occupation Category	Chaudhurirchar	Kumargaon
Petty trader	7.7	14
Salaried	3.2	6
Currently enrolled in school	29.3	21
Household work[1]	21.5	25
Reported out of labour force[2]	15.1	11
Size Class of Landholdings		
<0.005	49	23
>0.005 to <2.47	43	63
>2.47 to <4.95	4	7
>4.94 to <9.88	4	7

Source: Survey data, 2015.

Note: 1. Non-school-going-age population reporting primary activity as household work.
   2. Infants and young children + school-going-age population + non-school-going-age population reporting unemployment and not actively seeking work in the 6 months preceding the survey month.

Table 11A.2 State-wise Distribution of State Issue Price at Fair Price Shops

State	BPL Common rice	AAY Common rice	APL Rice Grade A
Andhra Pradesh	2	2	–
Arunachal Pradesh	6.15	3	8.8
Assam	6.27–6.67	3	9.17–9.43
Bihar	6.78	3	9.14
Chhattisgarh	6.15	3	8.95
Gujarat	3.00–6.70	3	–
Himachal Pradesh	6.85	3	9
Jammu and Kashmir	6.25	3	9.6

(Continued)

Table 11A.2 *Continued*

State	BPL Common rice	AAY Common rice	APL Rice Grade A
Jharkhand	6.15	3	8.3
Karnataka	3	3	9.4
Kerala	2	2	8.9
Madhya Pradesh	4.5	3	–
Maharashtra	6	3	9.6
Manipur	6.2	3.47	8.95
Meghalaya	6.15	3	8.80–10.00
Mizoram	6.15	3	9.5
Nagaland	6.15	3	8.30
Odisha	2	2	9.3
Rajasthan	6.3	3	9
Sikkim	4	Free of cost	9
Tamil Nadu	1	1	1
Tripura	6.15	3	9.6
Uttar Pradesh	6.15	3	8.45
Uttarakhand	6.15	3	–
West Bengal	2	2	9

Source: www.indiastat.com, browsed on 30 June 2017.

Table 11A.3 *Number of Beneficiary Households, by Card, by Household Characteristics and by Share of Expenditure on Various Heads, Chaudhurirchar and Kumargaon*

Households by Characteristics and Expenditure Status	Chaudhurirchar					Kumargaon				
	APL	BPL	AAY	MMASY	No Card	APL	BPL	AAY	MMASY	No Card
Number of households	25	44	20	20	18	19	23	37	19	13
Proportion of households (%)	19.7	34.6	15.7	15.7	14.2	15.4	19.8	33.4	17	11.7
Average household size	5	5	4	7	4	5	5	4	4	4
Average land size owned (in acres)	2.3	0.6	0.4	1.5	0.3	2.2	0.7	1.6	0.7	1.5
Access to proper sanitation (%)	83	63	50	73	50	25	40	50	86	75
Average MPCE (in ₹)	1,558	879	528	1,544	1,021	2,264	1,607	1,592	2,075	2,578
Average MPCE: food (in ₹)	857	554	278	735	703	1,000	922	629	1,132	1,199
Average MPCE: non-food (in ₹)	700	325	249	809	318	1,264	685	963	943	1,379
Average MPCE: cereal (in ₹)	367	210	106	335	298	272	238	156	284	273
Average MPCE: non-cereal (in ₹)	487	342	170	397	402	726	681	471	846	923
Share of expenditure: house repairing (in ₹)	21	14	10	20	7	14	28	19	28	15
Share of expenditure: health (in ₹)	21	20	34	19	42	35	20	25	10	19
Share of expenditure: education (in ₹)	9	11	10	12	0	7	3	11	7	5
Share of expenditure: transport (in ₹)	9	9	13	6	4	9	4	4	8	7

Source: Survey data, 2015.

Table 11A.4 *Multicollinearity Test Results*

Variable	VIF	1/VIF
FDI	2.48	0.404
MPCE	2.36	0.423
OH_Land	1.38	0.727
Adult_literate	1.28	0.778
RC_4	1.8	0.556
RC_1	1.67	0.600
RC_2	1.55	0.646
MDM_dummy	1.3	0.772
ICDS_dummy	1.42	0.703
Village_dummy	1.32	0.758
Mean VIF	1.70	

Source: Based on author's calculations.

REFERENCES

Bedamatta, R. (2016). Two decades of geographical targeting in food distribution: Drawing lessons from an Indian State. *Indian Journal of Human Development, 10*(3), 366–383.

Bhattacharya, P., Mitra, S., & Siddiqui, M. Z. (2016). Dynamics of food grain deficiency in India. *Margin: The Journal of Applied Economic Research, 10*(4), 465–498.

Government of Assam. (2004–2005). *Economic survey.* Directorate of Economics and Statistics, Planning and Development Department.

Government of Assam. (2005–2006). *Economic survey.* Directorate of Economics and Statistics, Planning and Development Department.

Government of Assam. (2006–2007). *Economic survey.* Directorate of Economics and Statistics, Planning and Development Department.

Government of Assam. (2007–2008). *Economic survey.* Directorate of Economics and Statistics, Planning and Development Department.

Government of Assam. (2008–2009). *Economic survey.* Directorate of Economics and Statistics, Planning and Development Department.

Government of Assam. (2009–2010). *Economic survey.* Directorate of Economics and Statistics, Planning and Development Department.

Government of Assam. (2010–2011). *Economic survey.* Directorate of Economics and Statistics, Planning and Development Department.

Government of Assam. (2010a). *At a glance.* Internal Report, Directorate of Food, Civil Supplies and Consumer Affairs.

Government of Assam. (2010b). *Innovative scheme, Mukhyo Mantrir Anna Suraksha Yojana, guidelines.* Internal Report, Directorate of Food, Civil Supplies and Consumer Affairs.

Government of Assam. (2016). *Assam human development report 2014.* Planning and Development Department.

Government of Assam. (2017). *Steps for operationalisation of National Food Security Act 2013 in Assam.* http://fcsca.assam.gov.in/information-services/detail/guideline-for-selection-of-beneficiaries-under-nfsa

Government of Assam. (n.d.). *Guidelines and measures adopted for implementation of targeted public distribution system (TPDS).* Internal Report, Directorate of Food, Civil Supplies and Consumer Affairs.

Government of India. (2007). *Public distribution and other sources of household consumption, 2004–05* (61st round, Report No. 510, Vol. 1). National Sample Survey Organisation, Ministry of Statistics and Programme Implementation.

Government of India. (2011). *Level and pattern of consumer expenditure, 2009–10* (66th round, Report no. 538). National Sample Survey Organisation, Ministry of Statistics and Programme Implementation.

Government of India. (2013a). *Perceived adequacy of food consumption in Indian households, 2009–10* (66th round, Report no. 547). National Sample Survey Organisation, Ministry of Statistics and Programme Implementation.

Government of India. (2013b). *Public distribution system and other sources of household consumption, 2009–10* (66th round, Report no. 545). National Sample Survey Organisation, Ministry of Statistics and Programme Implementation.

Priyadarshini, S. (2006). Food security: A case study of Assam. In D. Basu, Kulkarni, B. Francis, & B. Dutta-Ray (Eds.), *Agriculture, food security, nutrition, and health in North-east India* (pp. 173–183). Mittal Publications.

Saikia, A. (2010). The moneylenders and indebtedness: Understanding the peasant economy of colonial Assam, 1900–1950. *Indian Historical Review, 37*(1), 63–68.

Sengupta, K. (2006). Effectiveness of targeted public distribution: A case study of Silchar town of South Assam. In D. Basu, Kulkarni, B. Francis, & B. Dutta-Ray (Eds.), *Agriculture, food security, nutrition, and health in North-East India.* (pp. 173–184) Mittal Publications.

SECTION VI

Governance

Chapter 12

Nation State and North-east India
From Exclusion to Autonomy

Bhupen Sarmah and Joseph K. Lalfakzuala

The discrete political units of India's North East (NE) emerged in the process of normalization of colonial governance that was structured and territorially arranged, essentializing the sociocultural, economic, geographic and linguistic differences. Consolidation of the colonial state in the valleys required the spreading out of colonial administration to the hills, on the one hand, and the construction of a sociocultural and political binary between hills and valleys, on the other hand. Colonial articulation of the differences was gradually normalized through political and administrative mechanisms. The partition and independence resulted in the formation of the idea of the 'North East', an assemblage of the colonial administrative dispositions, implying a political reality of geopolitical significance for the emerging nation state. The transformation of the 'colonial administrative units' categorized as the 'North-East Frontier Agency (NEFA)' to political units of the nation state still constitutes an agenda for serious academic engagement, because of the perceptible resistance revealed by the process. This chapter makes an attempt, essentially, to analyse the transformation of the 'colonial administrative units' to the political units of the nation state, locating the frontier space in its own historicity.

Despite geographical encumbrances, the states that emerged in the valleys of the region long before colonial interventions had never been entirely cut off from the politico-economic and cultural influences of both Southeast Asia and the Indian subcontinent. With the influences of both Indo-Aryan and Indo-Mongoloid political and cultural traditions, the region witnessed the emergence of myriad proto-state formations centring around different cultural identities, such as the Chutiya, the Tai-Ahom, the Koch, the Dimasa (Kachari), the Tripuri, the Meitei (Manipuri), the Khasi (Khyriem), the Pnar (Jaintia), etc. Gradual adoption of wet rice cultivation and petty commodity production, to a limited extent, helped crystallization of the pre-colonial states since the 16th century (Bhattacharjee, 2010, pp. 2015–2069; Guha, 1987, pp. 143–172), and Ahom, Jaintia, Cachar, Tripura and Manipur survived as sovereign states till the early 19th century. The process of political crystallization of the pre-colonial valley states also required close interactions with their non-state counterparts in the surrounding hills.

The historiography of the Ahom state, since its inception in the eastern corner of the Brahmaputra Valley and gradual expansion, provides abundant instances of not only sociocultural integration of a multitude of religious and cultural identities and traditions but also myriad forms of negotiation with the chiefs of the surrounding cultural communities. Through sustained negotiations, the Ahom state maintained peaceful relations with the neighbouring Naga communities on the south of the valley. The organized state shared natural resources with the Nocte Nagas of the low hills adjoining the plains of Sibsagar and Lakhimpur, and it also developed friendly relations with other Naga communities by extending military support to their chiefs. The hill communities on the north of the valley also first came into contact with the organized Ahom state in the early part of the 16th century (Devi, 1968, pp. 19–52).

Besides the well-known history of the Ahom state, the state formed by the Dimasas, also called the Kacharis, provides a unique example of sociocultural interactions among the people of the plains and the hills. Emerging as a tiny state in the Brahmaputra Valley, the Dimasas' state gradually became a fairly large and sophisticated Hinduized state (Bhattacharjee, 1987, pp. 177–206) which reached its climax in the middle of the 18th century, with its territory expanded over vast plain.[1] Similarly, the political structure organized by the Khasis and the Jaintias took the shape of autonomous *Syiemships* in the early 16th century on the west of the Dimasa state and included, besides the Khasi and Jaintia Hills, the plains south of the hills and north of Barak River in the erstwhile Sylhet district, now part of Bangladesh (Bareh, 1964, pp. 30–70; Syiemlieh, 1989, pp. 10–60). The state formed by the Meities covering the wide, fertile Imphal Valley encircled by mountains, inhabited by a large number of communities, had marginal influence over the communities living in the hills. However, a major part of the history of Manipur is devoted to the interactions between the dominant Meitei and the surrounding hill communities. Their inter-actions, struggle for supremacy and subsequent fusion into a common ethno-linguistic identity as the Meitei and extension of their power and authority constituted the essence of the history of Manipur (Hassan, 2008, pp. 109–137).

The erstwhile princely state known as 'Hill Tipperah', which emerged in the early 15th century, was gradually expanded to include a substantial part in the plains in the west from Chittagong to Sylhet. Of the four major communities—the Kukis, Tripuris, Riangs and Jamatias—inhabiting the hills, the Tripuris, for their concentration in the western part adjoining plains of Bengal, were the first to come in contact with the neighbouring Bengali people. Besides having trade relations with Bengal, the rulers of Tripura could consolidate author-ity over other non-tribal communities (Ganguly, 1994, pp. 394–414). With economic consolidation and administrative sophistication, the state expanded towards the west beyond the hills, also occupying a sizeable part of Bengal. The Mughals, through a series of wars, how-ever, pushed the Tripuris back. The position of the Tripuri king was

---

[1] The Dimasa state included a part of Nagaon (Hojai–Davaka area) and the Cachar, besides the North Cachar Hills of Assam, Dayung–Dhansiri Valley in Nagaland and the Jiriri Frontier area in Manipur.

reduced to a *zamindar* of the estate called 'Chakle Roshnabad' bordering Hill Tipperah (Mackenzie, 1985, p. 272; Bhattacharyya, 1986, p. 25).

Following from the above, one can argue that the geographical space which appeared as terra incognita in the initial phase of colonialism in India cannot be considered entirely as a non-state category nor can it be imagined as a periphery of any 'main land'. With their territorial fluidity, the states that emerged in the region were dependent on close interactions between the settled agricultural communities of the valleys and the shifting cultivators of the surrounding hills, had a network of relations across the valleys (Chatterjee, 2013, p. 38) and allowed the migration of people and ideas without the notion of exclusion. The high lands, though, remained free from the visible cultural influences of both Hindus and Muslims and maintained connections with Southeast and East Asia (Ludden, 2019, pp. 24–36).

EXCLUSION AND COLONIAL GOVERNMENTALITY

The geographical space that became the 'North Eastern Frontier' of colonial India became the site of colonial intervention immediately after annexation of the Chittagong Hill Tract in 1760 followed by the assault on Tripura in 1761.[2] However, colonial interventions in rest of the 'state space'[3] began only after the Burmese invasions of Assam, Manipur and Cachar plains (1817–1824). Internecine conflicts within the royal families of Assam and Manipur, besides the worsening of Anglo-Burmese relations, brought the organized states under British control after the defeat of Burma and signing of the treaty of Yandaboo

---

[2] For the default of the Tripura king in payment of revenue, the East India Company occupied Chakla Roshnabad in 1765, and it was permanently settled in favour of the Tripura king in 1793. Since then, the British colonizers recognized the king of Tripura as the independent ruler of Hill Tipperah and a *zamindar* of Chakla Roshnabad, the estate which became an integral part of British India (Ganguly, 2006, pp. 395–397).

[3] It implies the medieval kingdoms of Manipur, Jaintia, Cachar and Assam. After the acquisition of the Diwani of Bengal in 1765, the region was undisturbed by colonialism primarily because of the poor revenue-yielding potential of the sparsely populated semi-feudal states.

in 1826. Although Assam Proper[4] was annexed in 1826, direct colonial administration was uniformly introduced and stabilized over the entire erstwhile Ahom kingdom after explorations of various economic potentials, especially of tea, during the first decade of colonial occupation (Guha, 1991, pp. 159–175). Subsequently, the kingdoms of Jaintia, Cachar and all the petty independent states of the Khasi Hills were annexed. Further annexation of the remaining hills was subsequently completed step by step in the face of stiff resistance (Guha, 2006, p. 1). For the convenience of the colonial administration, the contiguous hills and plains gradually annexed were also brought under the British province of Assam. In the process, the territory of Assam was substantially expanded,[5] and the British province that came to be known as Assam took shape in the last quarter of the 19th century, and territorially, it included almost the entire present NE India, excluding the two princely states of Manipur and Tripura. The administrative arrangement in the British province was also in a flux and kept changing almost till the end of colonialism in India.[6]

Colonial interventions in the frontier space between China and Burma were initiated after six decades of the assault on Tripura when the British private capital enthusiastically responded to the prospects of tea plantation in the Brahmaputra Valley. Though the Ahom state was annexed in 1826, Assam Proper was brought under direct colonial rule a decade after, followed by the establishment of the Assam Tea Company in 1838. When the tea plantation, with a rapid growth during the

---

[4] That is, the five districts of Kamrup, Darrang, Nowgong, Sibsagar and Lakhimpur.

[5] The Cachar plains annexed in 1830, Khasi Hills in 1833, Jaintia plains in 1835, areas under present Karbi Anglong and North Cachar in 1838 and 1854, respectively, Naga Hills during 1866–1904, Garo Hills in 1872–1873 and Lushai Hills in 1890.

[6] In 1853, district administration was introduced in the province, and in 1874, Assam was placed under a Chief Commissioner by taking away its control from the Lieutenant Governor of Bengal. In 1905, it became part of the Lieutenant Governor's Province of East Bengal and Assam, and in 1912, Assam was separated and converted to Chief Commissionership with a legislature. Finally, in 1921, it became a Governor's province as per the provisions of the Government of India Act, 1919.

next three decades, could be established firmly, oil and coal appeared in the hinterland to lure the colonial capital more (Goswami, 1991, pp. 354–360). The pre-capitalist valley economy was restructured by the commodification and privatization of land, commodification of labour, monetization of revenue, exchange and taxation, etc., essentially to meet the increasing demands of colonial capital. With deep penetration of colonial capital backed by the 'Planters Raj',[7] the erstwhile Brahmaputra Valley–based Ahom kingdom, surrounded by hills on three sides, was pushed towards a massive transformation, significantly influencing the everyday life of the colonial subjects.

Colonial interventions in Tripura and Manipur, the two princely states, were primarily administrative in nature, albeit paving the road for monetization of revenue in the valleys and imposition of house tax in the hills (Allen, 2005, p. 118; Kamei, 2016, p. 17). The Imphal valley and the surrounding hills were annexed, essentially for creating a buffer against the hostile Burmese. The valley state was, therefore, protected, albeit the old structure was reformed. Significant changes included the monetization of land revenue, settlement of agricultural land and introduction of the colonial administrative and judicial system. The hill communities beyond the valley state were controlled and subdued through the Raja without being brought into the fold of colonial governmentality. The segregation was justified on the basis of the cultural differences between the people of the hills and the valleys (Dun, 1992, p. 13). The rebellion of the Kuki chiefs (1917–1919), nevertheless, led to certain cosmetic changes. Administration of the hills was brought under the president of the Manipur State Durbar,[8] to be administered on behalf of the Raja (Hassan, 2012, pp. 296–304). It must, however, be noted that the centralized state in the valley established by the Meiteis occupied only one-tenth of the total geographical area, while the surrounding hills inhabited mainly by the Nagas and the Kukis occupied the remaining part.

---

[7] As pointed out by Hamilton, (1984, p. 119), the tea planters lobby in the valley was so strong that the civil and military elements were subordinate to the interests of the tea-planting community.

[8] The president of the Manipur State Durbar was selected by the Governor of Assam.

The colonial logic of annexation of most of the hills was essentially for protection of colonial capital invested in the valleys, because the highlanders steeply resisted penetration of the colonial capital with an alien labour force in the foothills which were the sociocultural and economic space shared by the hill societies with the people of the plains. Some of such early anti-colonial resistances were the Khasi war (1829–1833), the Jaintia rebellion (1860–1862) and the Naga-Lushai struggle (1832–1898). The rebels were to be subdued for fortification of colonial capital, labour, and revenue of the subjugated valleys.

Gradual subjugation of the hills, as pointed out elsewhere (Sarmah, 2018, pp. 166–178), was accompanied by the hitherto unknown notion of territoriality that chequered the ethnic space organized in the form of administrative districts, placing them under the control of colonial agents. The districts, with their newly intro-duced boundaries, were divided into smaller units, such as subdivi-sions, circles, and so on, enabling the administrative machinery to penetrate deep into the sphere of control of the individual chiefs. Chieftainship was, however, protected as the institution of control by making the chiefs responsible for and accountable to colonial administration. With the inclusion of the traditional power structure to the colonial system of governance, the process of subjugation was accomplished through a compromise in which the chiefs were disci-plined not to intrude into the territorial jurisdiction of others and to be responsible for tax collection and the maintenance of peace within their respective jurisdictions. Certainly, the process led to substantial erosion of traditional judicial powers and other forms of domination of the chiefs, for which they were compensated both materially and through positions of power within the emerging social relations. For instance, in the Naga Hills district, some of the chiefs were not only exempted from payment of annual house tax but also allowed to retain a share of the house tax they collected. In Lushai Hill district, the chiefs were issued lifelong leases known as '*ramrilehkha*' over land that they had possessed.

Colonial governmentality, after superimposing an alien form of administration in the hills through punitive expeditions and coercion, also had to reconstruct subjectivity of the subjugated highlanders for the hegemonic control of the colonial power structure. The colonial project was launched in collaboration with the missionaries (McCall, 2008, pp. 274–276). The ground was prepared objectively by infusing a dosage of inferiority into the hill cultural communities, categorizing them as 'Tribes', using prefixes like 'uncivilized', 'savages', 'primitive' and many other similar words (Thomas, 2016, p. 28). Such colonial constructs had certainly emanated from the teaching and preaching of the Western Enlightenment, the linear notion of modernity. The administration facilitated the process of wider and intensified influences of the gospel by helping the missionaries establish schools preceded by the Church not only to prepare the ground for smooth conversion[9] but also to significantly transform the material culture of the communities and their world view. Proselytization required making the Bible available in vernacular languages, so the translation of the Bible led to the construction of a new linguistic identity cutting across the hitherto existing primordial identities (Sarmah, 2018, pp. 166–178). Colonial governmentality in the hills, therefore, constructed a collective subjectivity of the subjugated. With the euphemism of non-interference, colonial governance, in fact, deeply penetrated at the societal level, convincingly articulating the differences reinforced by the state itself, on the one hand, and accommodating the traditional power relations, albeit with the required adjustments, on the other.

While the gradual expansion of colonial governmentality over the hills was necessary for controlling the nagging 'tribes', fortification of the valley economies also required reconstruction of a hill–valley binary, placing the colonial reproduction of the category as 'tribe', in sharp contrast to the modern, civilized and also the Hinduized valley people. The historical relations of the valleys with the surrounding hills were reformulated, first through the Inner Line Regulations of 1873. The exclusionary mechanism, legitimized as a means of protection of the cultural identities and resources in the hills, was essentially for the protection of the territory framed by the Inner Line, which

---

[9] For a comprehensive account of the spread of Christianity in the region, see the lecture on 'Colonialism and Christian Missions in North East India' delivered by David R. Syiemlieh on 1 March 2013 at the North East India Studies Programme, Jawaharlal Nehru University; Nongbri (2014).

constituted the core of the political–economic interests of the colonial state. Protection of the Inner Line encircling the tea estates also required armed forces (Patil, 1984, p. 21). Notwithstanding the fact that it reproduced sociocultural and economic divides between the people of either side, the entire geographical space beyond the Inner Line was left undefined by any 'Outer Line'. The process of cultural, political and economic exclusion of the upland societies that started with the Inner Line Regulations of 1873 continued till the Government of India Act of 1935, following the Government of India (Excluded and Partially Excluded Areas) Order, 1936.[10] The new administrative arrangement located the excluded and partially excluded areas beyond the jurisdiction of the provincial legislature by placing the former under the control of the governor in his discretion and the latter as a special responsibility. Such an exclusionary administration was rationalized by reproducing racial and cultural differences among the highlanders themselves, on the one hand, and by homogenizing them to be placed in contrast to the 'civilized' valley people, on the other.[11]

AUTONOMY FOR REPRODUCTION OF INTEGRATION

Though the historiography of the NE refutes the fuzzy and politically reproduced history of the region as a space of 'splendid isolation' (Nag, 2002, p. 17), the hierarchy of cultural differences reinforced by colonial political economy mentioned earlier is crucial for comprehending the logic of the integrationist endeavours of the nation state. The colonial

---

[10] The excluded areas of Assam covered (a) the North-East Frontier/Sadiya Balipara and Lakhimpur Tract, (b) the Naga Hills district, (c) the Lushai Hills district and (d) the North Cachar Hills subdivision of Cachar district, while the partially excluded areas included (a) the Garo Hills district, (b) the Mikir Hills (in Nowgong and Sibsagar districts) and (c) the British portion of Khasi and Jaintia Hills district (other than the Shillong municipality area and cantonment).

[11] As Robert Reid informs us, the excluded areas of Assam are different from their counterparts elsewhere in India. In addition, these areas differ markedly among themselves, but they have this one characteristic in common, that not racially, historically, culturally or linguistically have they any affinity with the people of the plains or with the peoples of India proper. It is only by an historical accident and as a natural administrative convenience that they have been tacked on to an Indian province (Reid, 1944, pp. 18–29).

state that was rooted firmly in the valleys integrated the restructured valley economies with the global colonial economy, on the one hand, and ruthless exploitation inexorably pushed the colonial subjects closer to pan-Indian nationalism, on the other. The hierarchical differences produced by colonial governmentality, however, averted the excluded and chequered cultural space from the growing political hegemony of the pan-Indian anti-colonial discourses. The nationalist movement in India neither seriously contested the exclusion inflicted upon the hill communities nor attempted to integrate the spate of political contestations to colonial governmentality often violently manifested by different cultural communities on the other side of the Inner Line.

The absence of a pan-Indian nationalist hegemony in the hills, however, provided opportunities for the colonial administration to construct cultural nationalism articulating the differences. In Naga Hills, political articulation of the differences first led to the formation of a political platform with colonial patronage involving the important village headmen, government officials and products of the missionary education. The Naga nationalist consciousness, as it was structured by colonial governance, was imbued with substantial apprehension about the future of the Nagas, even if integrated with the colonial map of India. The memorandum submitted to the Simon Commission on 10 January 1929 signed by 20 Nagas belonging to six different Naga tribes urged upon the colonial state not to include Naga Hills in the proposed Reform Scheme and to place it directly under the British government, because the Nagas had never been conquered by the Assamese or the Manipuris prior to the British annexation, they were not unified, they were educationally, as well as economically, poor and, more importantly, they were bound to be overwhelmed by the population of the plains (Chasie, 2017, pp. 46–49). Visits of the Simon Commission to the hills also provoked political activism spearheaded by different sociocultural formations such as the Khasi National Durbar, the Jaintia Durbar and several other 'tribal' organizations that grew with the patronage of colonial administration (Chaube, 1999, pp. 70–74). The highlanders, who 'were not yet suited for the elaborate legal rules laid down in the procedure codes and in several other enactments of the same class' and 'were governed in a simpler and more personal manner than those of the more civilized' (Gait, 2017, p. 385), therefore, approached the

Simon Commission politically articulating their grievances with their own imaginations of the future as distinct sociocultural categories crystallized and legitimized by the colonial governmentality. Cultural nationalist ideologies that appeared in the hills through the articulation of the differences with a deep sense of apprehension were reiterated by Robert Reid (1944), the Assam Governor during 1937–1942, in defence of the 'Crown Colony', the imperialist project proposed by Reid himself, along with others (Syiemleh, 2014, pp. 11–12).

The counterparts of the hill cultural communities in the plains legitimized as 'tribe' by colonial epistemology clearly articulated and placed their demand before the Indian Statutory Commission for political recognition as a distinct social category. The Kacharis and the Bodos forming the Assam Kachari Jubok Sammilani submitted a memorandum demanding their political recognition as a separate identity (Pathak, 2010, pp. 61–69). The chief demand made by the tribal delegates was for a separate electorate and reservation of seats in the elected bodies asserting the division between the Boros and the caste Hindus (Barpujari, 1998, p. 92), paving the way for an organized political movement.

While India was approaching Independence, the cultural communities categorized as tribes in both the hills and valleys of the region started political articulation of their primary concerns and apprehensions, with their imagination of a post-colonial future that ranged from sovereignty to autonomy. Being determined not to allow themselves to be involved in a divided and chaotic India, a section of the Naga leadership, in May 1947, not only unequivocally declared a sovereign Nagaland as their political goal but also called upon the Assamese to form an independent state without joining the Union of India and to work in cooperation with the federal Nagaland state.[12] Similarly, the Khasi Jaintia Political Association came into being in 1946 with the imagination of a federation of the Khasi areas within a 'sovereign Assam' with adequate 'cultural and political autonomy' (Chaube, 1999, p. 75). The Mizo Union demanded full autonomy for the Mizos in terms of territory

---

[12] Among many academic engagements with the Naga movement, two of the works which deserve special attention are Yonuo (1984) and Alemchiba (1970).

and culture from the Assam legislature and government immediately after its formation in 1946 (Chaltuahkhuma, 2001, pp. 80–88). The Karbi-A-Darbar, the first political party of the Karbis, was formed in 1945 to spearhead a movement for autonomy for the Karbis. Therefore, the enigma before the Indian nationalist leadership was to work out a policy for integrating the frontier taking cognizance of its strategic geopolitical importance, as well as development deficits.

A subcommittee of the Constituent Assembly, known as the North-East Frontier (Assam) Tribal and Excluded Areas Subcommittee, was constituted under the chairmanship of Gopinath Bordoloi, essentially for working out an integrationist mechanism of the frontier political space with the emerging nation state. The sub-committee constituted by the Constituent Assembly, popularly known as the Bordoloi Committee, sought to accommodate the political aspirations of the highlanders. The proposed instrumentality was the 'Autonomous District Council'. This was accepted by the Constituent Assembly and incorporated in the Constitution in the Sixth Schedule. Accordingly, the districts councils were put in place through elections in 1952 in the United Khasi-Jaintia Hills District, Garo Hills District, Mikir Hills and North Cachar Hills districts, uniting the two into an 'administrative district,' and Lushai Hills District with the Pawi-Lakhar Regional Council constituted in 1953. Though the autonomous district councils (ADCs) were constituted with limited legislative, judicial, executive and financial powers required for the protection of the cultural identities of the highlanders without altering the colonial map of Assam, the constitutional mechanism retained the 'autonomy-aspiring tribes' under the political and economic control of the political structure dominated largely by the Assamese cultural identity.

The ADCs that appeared in the guise of the 'sub-states' of the state of Assam were, however, destined to fail in their avowed objectives of cultural protection and socio–economic development of the highlanders. The basic reasons behind the failure of the integrationist structure have already been pointed out by many authoritative analyses, including officially constituted committees and commissions (Chaube, 1999, pp. 108–114). Yet, to be precise, it was attempted to 'integrate' the hill societies, which shared a distinct history different from that of the rest of the country, with a modern state system, mainly through the governor with his enormous powers to control and a frozen administrative hierarchy accountable to the state government. The district councils were given legislative powers, but paradoxically, all laws made by the district council 'shall be submitted forthwith to the Governor and, until assented to by him, shall have no effect'. Another major constraint was that the district councils had no legislative or regulatory powers on the subjects over which they could exercise their executive powers. Similarly, the districts councils were given very limited financial powers with which they could hardly plan for any development activity independent of the mercy of the state government. At the societal level, the functioning of the district councils also suffered due to frequent contradictions between their newly emerged middle-class leadership and the traditional authorities that enjoyed official blessings during the colonial era (Gassah, 2012). The district councils provided some opportunities for fulfilling political aspirations of the newly emerged middle-class leadership in the hill societies, but in turn, the political leadership hardly made sincere efforts to bring the councils nearer to the people at the grassroots through constituting village councils and courts, except in a few isolated cases. On the contrary, hegemony was sought through the expansion of the administrative staff.

Though the ADCs were initially accepted by the political leadership in the hills of Assam, except for the Nagas, growing discontent with the limited autonomy substantially provoked the newly emerged middle-class leadership to strive for more power with a renewed separatist vigour in the wake of the constitution of the States Reorganisation Commission. While the Garos, Khasis and Jaintias launched their movement for a separate state, the Mizo National Front (MNF) in the early 1960s preferred to encourage secessionism in Lushai Hills. With the objective of making Mizoram a sovereign nation, the Mizo National Front (MNF) executed its insolent plan of a coup in March 1966. The political impasse was brought to an end by the Mizo Accord signed in June 1986. The Indian state responded to the political movements in the hills of Assam by continuously redrawing the political map of Assam since the early 1960s, and the process continued till the mid-1980s.[13]

---

[13] The Parliament passed the Constitution (13th Amendment) Act, 1962, to provide for the formation of Nagaland as a separate state. Similarly, the state of

The process of political integration, initiated with the idea of autonomous districts, that culminated in the formation of the smaller states has also been accompanied by an agenda of statist developmentalism reinforcing the idea of the NE being homogenized by economic backwardness. To mark 'the beginning of a new chapter of concerted and planned endeavour for the rapid development of the Region', the North Eastern Council (NEC) was established in 1971. This was followed by the burgeoning of development agencies carrying the prefix 'North Eastern'.[14] The statist developmentalism, however, neither could substantially alter the economic scenario of the region nor could satisfy the political aspirations of the multitude of cultural identities. Notwithstanding that migration has been an integral part of the history of Tripura, the demographic transformation of the tiny state primarily caused by the partition and settlement of refugees,[15] with the resultant alienation of the land of the indigenous communities, inspired a political movement uniting the tribal communities. Formation of the Tripura Upajati Juba Samiti in 1967 provided a momentum to the movement launched mainly for restoration of tribal lands transferred to the non-tribal since 1960 and creation of an Autonomous District Council for the tribals in the state under the Sixth Schedule. While the movement assumed a violent form since the later part of 1970s with the mushrooming of various insurgent groups, the Legislative Assembly constituted the Tripura Tribal Areas Autonomous District Council (TTAADC) in 1979. The violent resistance to the autonomy provided

---

Meghalaya was carved out of Assam by the Constitution (22nd Amendment) Act, 1969, and Mizoram got statehood in 1986 after the Constitution (53rd Amendment) Act. The Mikir and North Cachar Hills districts were given the option of joining Meghalaya, but the district councils overwhelmingly decided to stay with Assam.

[14] Some of the examples are the formation of the North Eastern Handicrafts and Handlooms Development Corporation Ltd. (1997), the North Eastern Regional Agricultural Marketing Corporation Ltd. (1982), the North Eastern Development Finance Corporation Ltd. (1995), etc. For further acceleration of the pace of socio-economic development of the region, the Ministry of Development of North Eastern Region was created as a separate ministry in 2001.

[15] It had been estimated that partition-induced refugees contributed 39.19 per cent of the total population of Tripura before 24 March 1971.

by the state legislature, along with the demand for autonomy under the Sixth Schedule of the Constitution, was finally responded to by the Parliament enacting an act on 23 August 1984 for the inclusion of the TTAADC under the Sixth Schedule. The autonomous structure thus constructed covers two-thirds of the total area of the state inhabited by and one-third of its total population.

The trajectory of the political movement of the plain tribes of Assam started in 1933 with the formation of the 'Assam Backward Plains Tribal League', which later came to be known as the 'Tribal League'. While the movement politically articulated 'backwardness' to assert cultural exclusivity, it also essentially contested the sociocultural hierarchy that legitimized an inferior position to the plain tribes *vis-à-vis* the caste-Hindu Assamese. Therefore, the movement not only brought forth the question of a separate electorate for the plain tribes but also emphasized prevention of land alienation and settlement of lands to the landless tribespeople. At the time of framing the Constitution, the plain tribes were excluded from consideration of autonomy, with the assumption that they would assimilate with the larger Assamese society through the ongoing process of Sanskritization. However, their demand for protection of land amidst large-scale immigration was addressed by creating the tribal belts and blocks immediately after Independence. When their demand for a separate state was galvanized with armed struggle, a section of the militants was brought to the negotiation table to sign an accord in 2002, resulting in the creation of the Bodoland Territorial Area Districts (BTAD) to be governed by an autonomous council called the Bodoland Territorial Council (BTC), placing it under the Sixth Schedule of the Constitution.

AUTONOMY AND GOVERNANCE BEYOND THE SIXTH SCHEDULE

The movement for autonomy (self-determination) of the Nagas emanated from the nationalist consciousness crystallized by colonial governementality, and it was subsequently spearheaded by the Naga Nationalist Council, which appeared in 1946. The myriad Naga communities, homogenized as 'National', were infuriated by the move to integrate them with India through the structure of autonomy imagined by the Bordoloi Subcommittee (Yonou, 1984, pp. 185–186). The strive for self-determination of the Nagas and India's contestation pushed both sides to engage with arms in the guise of an 'insurgency-counter-insurgency' political battle, and it continued for more than decade. The impasse was partly brought to an end through negotiation, both violent and peaceful when the situation allowed (Yonou, 1984, pp. 178–197), by creating Nagaland as a distinct unit of the Indian federal structure in 1963 with the asymmetry brought about by Article 371A of the Constitution. Guarded by the Constitution, the Government of Nagaland first enacted The Nagaland Tribal, Area, Range and Village Councils Act, 1966, though it was meant for implementation only in the districts of Kohima and Mokokchung. The council for each tribe was to recommend schemes relating to welfare and community development and to assist the local authorities.

The learning from the initial experiments in the two districts prompted the state legislature to modernize governance with a three-tier institutional structure through the Nagaland Village, Area and Regional Councils Act, 1970, though it was again confined to the districts of Kohima and Mokokchung. Tuensang was to be provided with a Regional Council. Decentralization was visualized with a village council, an Area Council comprising the adjacent villages and a Regional Council at the district level. Recognizing the village as the basis of governance, the legislation provided liberty to the village councils to exercise administration of justice according to the customary law and practices, without diminishing the autonomy traditionally enjoyed by the villages. The trajectory of decentralization passed through different phases, making village councils mandatory for each recognized village with financial power, however minuscule it be, and statutorily accommodating the traditional power structure. The judicial powers enjoyed by the village councils were taken away in 1985. Nevertheless, the state legislature subsequently recognized the 'Tribal Councils', which included the multitude of sociocultural organizations, such as the Hohos, formed by different tribal communities in accordance with their respective traditions and customary practices. The limited judicial powers taken away from the village councils are relocated in such councils, as the larger statutory categories command more rigid cultural affinity than the villages.

Detaching developmentalism from the cultural domain, the state legislature conceptualized the idea of a Village Development Board (VDB) in 1978 as a statutory body to function alongside the village council. The mass campaign launched in the early 1980s made VDBs an integral part of the rural life in Nagaland. The VDB, with all permanent residents of the village as its members and controlled by a Management Committee constituted by the village council of the village, is primarily responsible for the implementation of all development activities, including the Centrally Sponsored Schemes. This romanticized developmentalist model has certainly been successful in economically uplifting rural life to some extent; however, it has proved to be a more effective instrument for reorienting the social and political life of the common Nagas with a developmentalist slant.

After its merger with the Union of India in 1949 as one of the Part C states and then becoming a Union Territory in January 1957, Manipur experienced a process of integration of the hills with the modern state system that was significantly different from the experiment with autonomy in the other hills. The political aspiration of the hill societies was sought to be fulfilled by reserving 10 seats for the hill areas in the Territorial Council constituted for the Union Territory, with 30 elected and 2 nominated members. Alongside, the Manipur (Village Authorities in Hill Areas) Act, 1956, was enacted by the Parliament without a significant shift from the colonial past, essentially to bring the traditional 'Village Authorities' closer to the modern administration. While Manipur was approaching its statehood, the Parliament enacted the 'Manipur (Hill Areas) District Councils Act, 1971', with the idea of a separate administration for the hill areas. Therefore, the imagination of autonomy for the hill district of Manipur beyond the Sixth Schedule, alongside the insertion of Article 371C in the Constitution, resulted in the formation of six autonomous districts[16] in the state.

---

[16] The autonomous districts were the Manipur North Autonomous District (Senapati ADC), the Sadar Hills Autonomous District (Sadar ADC), the Manipur

Nevertheless, the ADCs in Manipur were brought into being with a relatively smaller package of autonomy compared to the autonomous councils visualized in the Sixth Schedule. For instance, the ADCs could only make recommendations on the matters related to appointment or succession of chiefs, inheritance of property, marriage and divorce and social customs, in lieu of exercising any well-defined legislative powers. Without any judicial powers, the ADCs remained under the control of the state legislature through its administrative machinery. Experiments with autonomy through the district councils constituted in the hills of Manipur, however, have been steeply contested with the demand for inclusion of the Manipur hills in the Sixth Schedule of the Constitution. The movement for autonomy launched by the Sixth Schedule Demand Committee in the late 1970s involving all the district councils and other sociopolitical organizations, including the students, has been intensified by the creation of the TTAADC for the tribes of Tripura (Kshetri, 2006, pp. 16–25).

Integration of hill areas covered by the Sadiya Frontier Tract, the Balipara Frontier Tract and the Lakhimpur Frontier Tract, the colonial administrative categories, with the nation state system has been a long-drawn process which needs to be located beyond many obscurities. The Bordoloi Subcommittee found the vast landmass between the Inner Line and the MacMahon Line unripe for regular administration until adequate improvements were made (Rao, 1967, pp. 703–704). Not to jeopardize the aims of establishing administration and also to bring the tribes, who were well disposed, into the fold of civilization, the Committee recommended even continuation of the colonial practice of *posa*, the vestigial payments of sums which the tribes claim by way of *quid pro quo* for making peace. Therefore, the three frontier tracts were placed in the Schedule B of the Sixth Schedule of the Constitution after separating the plain areas. Consequently, franchise was denied to the people of the hill tracts by debarring their right of representation to the provincial as well as central legislatures, purportedly due to their low level of political consciousness, as shown in details elsewhere

---

East Autonomous District (Ukhrul ADC), the Tengnoupal Autonomous District (Chandel ADC), the Manipur South Autonomous District (Churachandpur ADC) and the Manipur West Autonomous District (Tamenglong ADC).

(Sarmah, 2018, pp. 166–178). However, the apprehension of 'Chinese irredentism and communist imperialism' as perceived by Sardar Patel[17] prompted rapid militarization on the south of the MacMahon Line that continued unabated through the 1950s (Guyot-Réchard, 2016, pp. 103–104) backed by a developmentalist state agenda for the people aiming essentially at establishing 'loyalty or devotion to India' (Chopra, 1991, pp. 275–279).

The ground for regular administration of the frontier tracts was prepared by promulgating the North East Frontier Area (Administration) Regulation in 1954 that re-baptized the frontier tracts as NEFA. For deeper administrative penetration, NEFA was divided into six frontier divisions,[18] placing each of them under the control of a political officer. Initially, a batch of officers were appointed for the administration of the frontier divisions, and that was followed by the creation of a distinct cadre, the Indian Frontier Administrative Service (IFAS), in 1959. The constitution of NEFA as a discrete political space with deep militarization and developmentalism followed by series of changes in its political structure finally culminated in the formation of Arunachal Pradesh in

---

[17] Sardar Patel wrote to Nehru on 11 November 1950, 'All along the Himalayas in the north and north-east, we have on our side of the frontier, a population ethnologically and culturally not different from Tibetans or Mongoloids. The undefined state of the frontier and existence on our side of a population with its affinities to Tibetans or Chinese have all elements of political trouble between China and ourselves ... There is almost an unlimited scope for infiltration'. The infiltration, as Patel was worried about, was the infiltration of the communist ideology. Therefore, he wrote, 'the Communist Party of India has found some difficulty in contacting Communists abroad, or in getting supplies of arms, literature, etc. from them... They shall now have a comparatively easy means of access to Chinese Communists and through them to other foreign Communists. Infiltration of spies, fifth columnists and Communists would now be easier' (Chopra, 1991, pp. 275–279).

[18] Balipara Frontier Division was bifurcated and renamed as Kameng Frontier Division with Bomdila as the headquarters and Subansiri Frontier Division with Ziro as the headquarters; Tirap Frontier was renamed as Tirap Frontier Division with Khonsa as the headquarters; Abor hill district was renamed as Siang Frontier Division with Along as headquarters; Mishmi hill district was renamed as Lohit Frontier Division with Tezu as headquarters; and Naga Tribal Area was renamed as Tuensang Frontier Division with Tuensang as headquarters. The last one was, however, transferred to Nagaland in 1957.

1987, rendering enormous powers to the governor, under the Article 371H of the Constitution (for details on administrative growth in Arunachal Pradesh, see Luthra, 1993).

In the plains of Assam, while the political confrontation of the Bodo separatism was initially addressed by creating the Bodoland Territorial Council (BTC) through the Bodoland Autonomous Council Act, 1993, enacted by the state legislature, political aspirations of the other plain tribes were sought to be accommodated through similar legislative mechanisms. Autonomous councils were contemplated for all the major tribal groups (Goswami, 1991, pp. 24–95) which asserted their distinct identity contesting the hegemony of the Assamese nationality. Accordingly, six different statutory satellite autonomous councils were constituted by the state legislature within a period of 10 years since 1995,[19] leading to controversies and conflicts induced by the vaguely worked out notion of territoriality of the so-called 'satellite councils' and also inclusion and exclusion of the plain tribes in the functioning of the councils. The councils named after particular tribes inevitably generated conflicts of interests among the tribes who shared the territory demarcated for such councils. Therefore, to clarify the territorial jurisdiction, amendments were made to define the 'satellite areas' to mean non-contiguous clusters of villages predominantly inhabited by an ST population. Similarly, the particular tribe names have been removed and replaced with the term 'Scheduled Tribes' to be more inclusive.

CONCLUSION

The imagination of autonomy, ranging from sovereignty to institutionalization of autonomous political space within the framework of the Indian federal structure and the connected political assertions by the cultural communities, the process understood as ethnonationalism, constituted the core of the post-colonial history of India's NE.

---

[19] The Mising Autonomous Council, The Rabha Hasong Autonomous Council and the Lalung (Tiwa) Autonomous Council in 1995, and the Deori Autonomous Council, Sonowal Kachari Autonomous Council and the Thengal Kachari Autonomous Council in 2005.

While imagination of sovereignty in the colonial frontier beyond the pan-Indian nationalist discourse was backed by the subjectivity of the ethnic communities constructed by the colonial logic, the response of the emerging nation state, more often than not, was incompatible with the ethnonationalist discourses. The integrationist model conceptualized by the Constituent Assembly in the form of ADCs was initially acceptable to most of the highland communities, though it could not satisfy the Nagas. However, the state dispensation that placed the highlanders under the hegemonic control of the Assamese political leadership, besides having other built-in structural flaws, was contested with demands for more autonomous space, which culminated in the restructuring of the colonial politico-administrative arrangement of Assam. While peace negotiations with the Nagas with the special constitutional provisions made for them temporarily resolved the political impasse, Meghalaya and Mizoram continued with the ADCs. Separatist movements of the Dimasas and the Karbis enhanced the quantum of autonomy they enjoyed without significantly altering the political arrangements with the state of Assam. Political integration of the highlanders of Manipur was sought through separate administrative arrangements to protect their cultural identities; nevertheless, their movement for autonomy is still a political reality to reckon with. Alongside, peace negotiation with the highland societies of Tripura and the Bodos in the plains of Assam resulted in the formation of two hitherto unknown autonomous administrative arrangements backed by radical amendments in the Sixth Schedule of the Constitution.

The instrument of autonomy initially designed for political integration of the highland cultural categories with the nation state, which resulted in the political rearrangement of Assam, inspired several communities categorized as plain tribes to demand autonomy under the Sixth Schedule. The movements for autonomy that gradually intensified with an avowed separatism compelled the state legislature of Assam to constitute autonomous councils for the plain tribes too. The instrument of autonomy invented by the nation state to initially counter secessionism in the hills was replicated by the state legislature to pacify separatism in the plains. The experiment with autonomy, though accompanied by statist developmentalism, has, however, failed to democratize the development process. Nevertheless, it helped in the emergence of a scrounging political class subservient to the centralized administration to reinvent and reiterate cultural protectionism. Far from being inclusive, the structure of autonomy remained largely frozen at the district level and, more importantly, denied political space to the common tribal people, especially the women, a disguised patriarchy protected by the modern institutions of development. Though land has always been the prerequisite for any development discourse in the NE, the experiment with autonomy helped the scrounging political class to accumulate community land and assert personal right over huge chunks of land through reinterpretating customary laws and taking advantage of their access to the modern administration and state patronage (Ray et al., 2017, pp. 74–79). Myriad forms of autonomy and the connected mechanism of modern administration undoubtedly satisfied the cultural aspirations of the historically excluded communities to some extent, but the process consciously or unconsciously ignored the larger question of democratization of the process of development.

REFERENCES

Alemchiba, M. (1970). *A historical account of Nagaland*. Naga Institute of Culture.

Allen, B. C. (2005). *Gazetteer of Naga hills and Manipur hills*. Mittal. [Reprinted]

Bareh, H. (1964). *Khasi democracy*. RiKhasi Press.

Barpujari, H. K. (1998). *North-east India: Problems, policies & prospects*. Spectrum.

Bhattacharjee, J. B. (1987). Dimasa state formation in Cachar. In S. Sinha (Ed.), *Tribal polities and state systems in pre-colonial Eastern and North Eastern India*. KP Bagchi & Company.

Bhattacharjee, J. B. (2010). *State and wealth: The early states in Northeast India*. DVS Publishers.

Bhattacharyya, B. (1985). *Tripura administration: The era of modernisation*. Mittal Publications.

Chaltuahkhuma. (2001). *Political history of Mizoram*. Mizoram Publication Board.

Chasie, C. (2017). *The Naga Memorandum to the Simon Commission, 1929*. Standard Printers & Publishers.

Chatterjee, I. (2013). *Forgotten friends: Monks, marriages, and memories of Northeast India*. Oxford University Press.

Chaube, S. K. (1999). *Hill politics in Northeast India*. Orient Longman Limited.

Chopra, P. N. (1991). *The collected works of Sardar Vallabhbhai Patel* (Vol. XV). Konark Publishers.

Devi, L. (1968). *Ahom-tribal relations: A political study*. Lawyer's Book Stall.

Dun, E. W. (1992). *Gazetteer of Manipur*. Manas. [Reprinted]

Gait, A. (2017). *History of Assam*. EBH Publishers.

Ganguly, J. B. (1994). The economic content of the state formation process in Medieval Tripura. In J. B. Bhattacharjee (Ed.), *Studies in the economic history of North East India* (pp. 394–414). Har-Anand Publications.

Ganguly, J. B. (2006). *An economic history of North East India: 1826 to 1947*. Akansha Publishing House.

Gassah, L. S. (2012). *Traditional institutions of Meghalaya: A case study of Doloi and his administration*. Regency Publication. [reprinted]

Goswami, P. (1991). Origin of the oil industry in Assam: A reappraisal. *Proceedings of North East India History Association*, North East India History Association, Shillong.

Guha, A. (1987). The Ahom political system: An enquiry into state formation in Medieval Assam: 1228–1800. In S. Sinha (Ed.), *Tribal polities and state systems in pre-colonial Eastern and North Eastern India* (pp. 143–172). KP Bagchi & Company.

Guha, A. (1991). *Medieval and early colonial Assam: Society, polity and economy*. KP Bagchi & Company.

Guha, A. (2006). *Planter Raj to Swaraj: Freedom struggle & electoral politics in Assam 1826–1947*. Tulika Books.

Guyot-Réchard, B. (2016). *Shadow states: India, China and the Himalayas, 1910–1962*. Cambridge University Press.

Hamilton, A. (1984). *In Abor jungle of North East India*. Mittal Publications.

Hassan, M. S. (2008). *Building legitimacy: Exploring state-society relations in Northeast India*. Oxford University Press.

Hassan, M. S. (2012). Secessionism in Northeast India: Identity wars or crisis of legitimacy? In S. Baruah (Ed.), *Ethnonationalism in India: A reader* (pp. 296–304). Oxford University Press.

Kamei, G. (2016). *A history of modern Manipur (1826–2000): Study of feudalism, colonialism and democracy*. Akansha Publishing House.

Kshetri, R. (2006). *District councils in Manipur: Formation and functioning*. Centre for Manipur Studies, Manipur University, and Akansha Publishing House.

Lalfakzuala, J. K. (2017). Encounter with the British: The legacy of autonomy in Mizo Hills. *Social Change, 47*(4), 582–597.

Ludden, D. (2019). India's spatial history in the Brahmaputra-Meghna river basin. In N. Bhattacharya & J. L. K. Pachuau (Ed.), *Landscape, culture, and belonging: Writing the history of Northeast India* (pp. 24–36). Cambridge University Press.

Luthra, P. N. (1993). *Constitutional and administrative growth of Arunachal Pradesh*. Directorate of Research, Government of Arunachal Pradesh. [Reprinted]

Mackenzie, A. (1995). *The north-east frontier of India*. Mittal Publications. [5th Reprinted in India, First published in 1884 entitled *History of the Relation of Government with the Hills Tribes of the North-East Frontier of Bengal*].

McCall, A. G. (2008). *The Lushai hills district cover*. Tribal Research Institute. [Reprinted]

Nag, S. (2002). *Contesting marginality: Ethnicity, insurgency and subnationalism in North-East India*. Manohar.

Nongbri, T. (2014). *Development, Masculinity and Christianity: Essays and verses from India's North East*. Indian Institute of Advance Studies.

Pathak, S. (2010, March 6). Tribal politics in the Assam: 1933–1947. *Economic and Political Weekly, 45*(10), 61–69.

Patil, D. K. (1984). *Sentinels of the North-east: The Assam rifles*. Patil and Patil.

Rao, B. S. (1968[1967]). *The framing of India's constitution: Select documents* (Vol. III). The Indian Institute of Public Administration.

Ray, A. K., Sarmah, B., & Chakraborty, G. (2017). *Accumulation and dispossession: Communal Landin North East India*. AAKAR Books.

Reid, R. (1944, January–February). The excluded areas of Assam. *The Geographical Journal, 103*(1/2), 18–29.

Sarmah, B. (2018). India's Northeast and the enigma of the Nation-state. *Alternatives: Global, Local, Political, 42*(3), 166–178.

Syiemlieh, D. R. (1989). *British administration in Meghalaya: Policy and pattern*. Heritage.

Syiemlieh, D. R. (2014). Introduction. In D. R. Syiemleh (Ed.), *On the edge of empire: Four British plans for North East India, 1941–47*. SAGE Publications.

Thomas, J. (2016). *Evangelising the nation: Religion and the formation of Naga political identity*. Routledge.

Yonuo, A. (1974). *The rising Nagas*. Manas Publications.

Chapter 13

Fiscal Decentralization and Development
A Study of Autonomous District Councils in Mizoram

Vanlalchhawna

INTRODUCTION

This chapter examines the broad structure and trend of the finances of autonomous district councils (ADCs) in Mizoram. The state of Mizoram has three ADCs under the provision of the Sixth Schedule of the Constitution of India. These councils are unique constitutional bodies, created to provide a self-governing structure for the tribal population living in the hilly areas of the north-eastern region. They are vested with legislative, executive and judicial powers to administer themselves according to their own traditions and customs. Since these councils have limited own revenue bases, they are highly dependent on state grants, which are far from adequate to generate rapid socio-economic development in these areas. This study assesses the district council fund with reference to own revenue receipts and grants-in-aid given by the state government and central government through the Finance Commission, Planning Commission and other agencies. Public expenditure pattern and trends are also examined. The chapter also examines the level of socio-economic development and recent administrative and fiscal decentralization initiatives undertaken by the state and central government. It argues that inadequate fiscal flows to the ADCs and poor district governance have undermined the development process in the district council–administered areas.

Fiscal decentralization refers to the allocation of expenditure functions and revenue transfers from central authority to sub-national and further to sub-state governments. Fiscal decentralization ensures the autonomy of sub-national governments, improves accountability and responsibility and promotes local development and welfare. Oates (1993) observed: 'The provision of local outputs that are differentiated according to local tastes and circumstances results in higher levels of societal welfare than centrally determined and more uniform levels of outputs across all jurisdictions'. Sub-national governments perform better at providing public goods and services according to the needs of local communities. The Indian Constitution, under the Sixth Schedule, provided for the creation of ADCs for the tribal communities living in Assam, Meghalaya, Mizoram and Tripura. One basic objective was to establish democratic self-rule among the tribal communities and to perform development works. These bodies 'have less power than the states but more than local governments' and 'represented the incorporation of the predominantly tribal population as communities into the Indian states' (Stuligross, 1999).

There are presently three ADCs in Mizoram. These were created in the early 1970s for the three ethnic communities of Lai, Mara and Chakma who live in the southern part of the state bordering Myanmar and Bangladesh. The significant feature of the autonomous councils was the recognition of the tribespeople's right over their land and other natural resources. These councils were endowed with extensive legislative, judicial, executive and financial powers. Apart from ensuring the protection of tribal culture and traditions, the institution is entrusted with undertaking development works according to the needs of the tribal community. Accordingly, they are provided with their own revenue sources. Grants-in-aid from the state government are also allocated for maintenance and development works. However, district council authorities have limited engagement over the year in development works in the absence of proper devolution of functions, functionaries and finances from the state government. These autonomous council areas continue to remain some of the most backward regions of the state.

The second section makes an attempt to understand the evolution of ADCs in Mizoram. The third section gives a brief outline of the administrative structure of autonomous councils. In the fourth section, socio-economic development in the councils has been examined. The fifth section gives an overview of the fiscal profile of the councils, as well as devolved items from the administrative department of the state under the social and economic sector. The sixth section briefly underlines fiscal issues and challenges before the three autonomous districts. The last section provides the concluding remarks of the chapter.

EVOLUTION, POWERS AND FUNCTIONS OF AUTONOMOUS DISTRICT COUNCILS IN MIZORAM

The emergence of autonomous councils could be traced back to the consolidation and extension of the colonial administration in the Lushai Hills (now Mizoram) in the early 1890s. The colonial authority, which introduced several laws and regulations to administer the hill areas of North-east (NE) India, consistently followed exclusion and isolation policies. The Codes of Criminal Procedure and Civil Codes are not applicable to these areas. The applications of the above codes are barred by District Acts of 1874 and the Frontier Tract Regulation Act 1980. The Bengal Eastern Frontier Regulation of 1873 introduced 'Inner line', through which the indigenous ethnic groups were protected against encroachment by people from the plains or outsiders. The Inner line regulated the entry of outsiders into the hill areas, their engagements in business activities and transactions in land and settlement. Further, under the Government of India Act 1935, the Lushai Hills became an excluded area. No federal or provincial legislation could be extended to the district automatically.

Independence in 1947 saw new state formations in the region. The region consisting of the Assam plains, the hill districts, the North Eastern Frontier Tract and the princely states of Manipur and Tripura were merged with India. The Constitution, which became effective in 1950, established Assam as a full state, and the hill areas were divided into autonomous districts under the Sixth Schedule of the Constitution of India. Tripura and Manipur were constituted as special administrative areas under the central government. The North-East Frontier Tract (NEFT) also became the North-East Frontier Agency (NEFA). Lushai Hills was set up as an autonomous district and the Pawi-Lakher areas as regional councils under the provision of the Sixth Schedule of the Constitution.

The status of Mizo Hills District was upgraded to Union Territory as per the North-Eastern Areas (Reorganisation) Act, 1971. In 1972, the Pawi-Lakher Regional Council was re-organized and trifurcated into three regional councils, namely, Pawi, Lakher and Chakma regional councils. These regional councils were elevated to ADCs with effect from 29 April 1972 under the Mizoram District Councils (Miscellaneous Provisions) Order, 1972. They were renamed as Lai Autonomous District Council (LADC), Mara Autonomous District Council (MADC) and Chakma Autonomous District Council (CADC). The provisions in the Sixth Schedule of the Constitution outlined the legislative, judicial, executive and financial powers of the ADCs (Actionaid, 2016; Thanhranga, 2007). These are summarized below:

Legislative powers: District councils have legislative powers over the following items: (a) allotment, occupation or use of land for the purposes of agriculture or grazing or for residential or other purposes; (b) the management of any forest that is not a reserved forest; (c) the use of any canal or water course for the purpose of agriculture; (d) the regulation of the practice of *jhum* or other forms of shifting cultivation; (e) the establishment of village or town committees or councils and their powers; (f) any other matter relating to village or town administration, including village or town police and public health and sanitation; (g) the appointment or succession of chiefs or headmen; (h) the inheritance of property; and (i) social customs. All laws made under these items shall be submitted to the governor for his assent. All laws, until and unless assented by the governor, shall have no effect (Thanhranga, 2007).

Judicial powers: The judicial powers relate to the constitution of village councils and courts for the trial of suits and cases between the parties of all who belong to Scheduled Tribes. Only the courts established by the district councils shall exercise the power of court of appeal. A regional council or district council may make rules relating to the constitution of village councils and courts and the powers to be exercised by them. Also, the procedure to be followed by village councils or courts, and the court of appeals and enforcement of the decisions and orders of councils and courts, may also be laid down by the concerned district council (Thanhranga, 2007).

Financial powers: District councils have been empowered to assess and collect land revenue and to impose taxes within their jurisdictions, such as on lands and buildings, professions, trades, callings and employments, animals, vehicles and boats and the entry of goods into a market, and tolls on passengers and goods carried in ferries and for the maintenance of schools, dispensaries or roads. District councils are also entitled to receive a share of the royalties accruing each year from licences or leases for the purpose of prospecting for, or the extraction of, minerals granted by the state government in respect of any area within an autonomous district, as agreed upon with the government. Disputes in this regard are to be referred to the governor for settlement. The estimated receipts and expenditure of ADCs, which are to be provided for from the state-consolidated fund, shall be placed before the district councils for discussion. It is then shown separately in the annual budget of the state that is laid before the state legislature for their approval, as per Article 202 of the Constitution (Thanhranga, 2007).

Executive functions: District councils have the power to establish, construct or manage primary schools, dispensaries, markets, ferries, fisheries, roads, road transport and waterways in the district. With the approval of the governor, the district councils may prescribe the language and the manner in which primary education shall be imparted in the primary schools in the district. Other functions may also be entrusted to district councils, conditionally or unconditionally, such as agriculture, animal husbandry, community projects, cooperative societies, social welfare, village planning, or any other matter to which the executive power of the state extends (Thanhranga, 2007).

ADMINISTRATIVE STRUCTURE OF AUTONOMOUS DISTRICT COUNCILS

The administrative set-up of the district councils consists of a council secretariat and an executive wing. The council secretariat consists of the chairman of the council and a secretary appointed by the chairman, and such other officials and staff as required for the functioning of the office. The district council may make rules regulating the conditions of service of officers and staff appointed to its secretariat. The executive wing undertakes all executive functions. The executive committee includes the chief executive member and other executive members who are appointed on the recommendation of the chief executive member. The executive committee is vested with the executive function of the district council. The chief executive member entrusts to each member a specific subject. The executive committee is collectively responsible for all executive functions of the district council (Actionaid, 2016; Thanhranga, 2007).

The executive secretary and other officials assist the executive committee in performing its duties. The executive secretary heads the administration of the executive department. He/she is the principal adviser of the executive members on all matters of policy and administration within his/her department. Line departments help in the formulation of policies of the council and their execution. A department is usually headed by a secretary to the executive committee of the council who acts as the administrative head of the department and principal adviser of the executive member concerning all matters of policy and administration within the department. The departmental secretariat assists the executive member in policymaking and review, drafting legislation, rules and regulations, undertaking sectoral planning and programme formulation, budgeting and controlling expenditure, according administrative and financial approval for operational programmes and plans, supervising and exercising control over the execution of policies and programmes by the executive department or field agencies, evaluating results and assisting the executive member in the discharge of his/her parliamentary responsibilities (Actionaid, 2016; Thanhranga, 2007).

Village councils constitute key governance institutions at the village level. These are grassroots democratic institutions whose members are elected by the eligible voters in the councils. A village council consists of a president, a vice-president, elected as well as nominated members and the secretary. The secretary, however, should not be an elected member of the village council. The powers of these councils include mobilizing local funds and effort for community works. A village council is allowed to distribute land for *jhumming* purposes under the provision of the Forest Act, 1955, and the Jhumming Regulation of 1954. Village councils are empowered to levy fines on individuals who refuse to undertake community works. Village councils also implement several CSSs (Centrally Sponsored Schemes) as agents of the DRDAs (District Rural Development Authority). The village council acts as a village court and is competent to try civil cases of a petty nature, involving tribal laws and customs, etc.

SOCIO-ECONOMIC DEVELOPMENT IN THE AUTONOMOUS DISTRICT COUNCILS

LADC has the largest area (1871 km²), followed by Mara (1455 km²) and Chakma (686 km²). In 2011, the population density was the highest in Chakma district at 66 people per km², followed by Mara (40) and Lai (39). Mara District had the highest literacy rate at 80 per cent, while Chakma District had a very low literacy rate of 46.36 per cent, as against the state average literacy rate of 91.33 per cent, in 2011. The gender gap in the literacy rate in Chakma District is very wide (Figure 13.1). While the male literacy rate in CADC was 60.46 per cent, the female literacy rate was found to be only 31.12 per cent, showing a gender gap of 29.34 per cent. In MADC, the gender gap was observed to be the lowest, at 5.27 per cent.

Other socio-economic indicators show dismal features. For instance, while the state's Infant Mortality Rate in 2016–2017 stood at 21 per 1,000 live births, it was as high as 29 in Lai and Chakma districts, followed by 28 in Mara District. Maternal Mortality Rate (MMR) was also very high in Mara District at 303, as compared with the state average of 104. Not only were human development indices low, but physical facilities, such as roads, health, electricity, etc., were also in poor shape. Roads lacked proper maintenance, while district hospitals, sub-centres etc. were run without proper equipment, essential

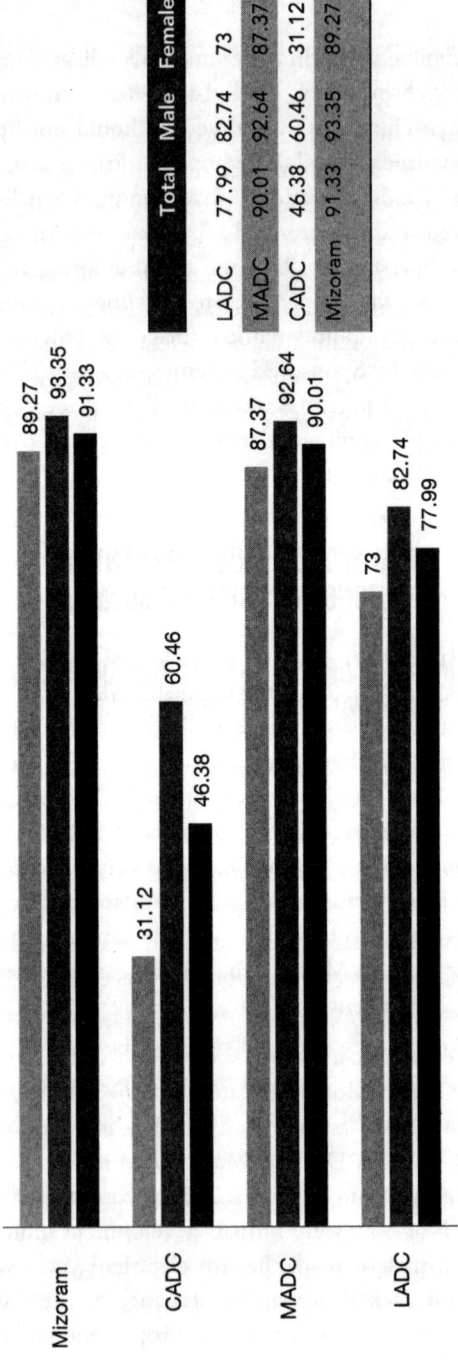

	Total	Male	Female
LADC	77.99	82.74	73
MADC	90.01	92.64	87.37
CADC	46.38	60.46	31.12
Mizoram	91.33	93.35	89.27

Figure 13.1 *Gender Gap in Literacy Rates: Mizoram, LADC, MADC and CADC*

Source: Census 2011, Mizoram.

medicines and health personnel. Electricity supply is irregular in several villages and hardly reached interior villages.

Agriculture is the main occupation of the people in the autonomous districts (Figure 13.2). Shifting cultivation has been the dominant agricultural land use system. Rice is the staple food; other important crops cultivated are vegetables and cash crops like ginger, sesame, etc. Household industries are negligible, while tertiary activities, such as administration, banking and financial institutions, trade and other services, constitute important livelihood sectors in the autonomous regions. Since the regional economy of the autonomous regions is highly backward, with little development activities, wage payments from the state and CSSs, such as Rashtriya Krishi Vikas Yojana (RKVY), Mahatma Gandhi National Rural Employment Guarantee Scheme (MGNREGS), Border Area Development Programme (BADP), etc., serve livelihood subsistence for poor people across the three districts.

BROAD OVERVIEW OF THE FISCAL PROFILE OF THE AUTONOMOUS DISTRICT COUNCILS

The Sixth Schedule provides for the constitution of a district fund for each ADC, to which shall be credited all moneys received by the council in the course of the administration of the districts, in accordance with the provision of the Constitution. The Mizoram Autonomous District Council Fund Rules, 1996 (revised in 2010), provided rules and guidelines for the management of the district fund and for the procedure to be followed in respect of money receipts and its custody, as well as any other matter connected with or ancillary to these matters. The district fund comprises all receipts realized by the district council. These include grants-in aid received from the government and taxes levied or other revenues or receipts realized under the laws, rules or regulations framed by the district councils.

The accounts of the council are stored in two parts: district fund and deposit fund. The district fund is further divided into revenue account and capital account. The revenue account consists of two heads: revenue receipts and revenue expenditure. These include all proceeds of

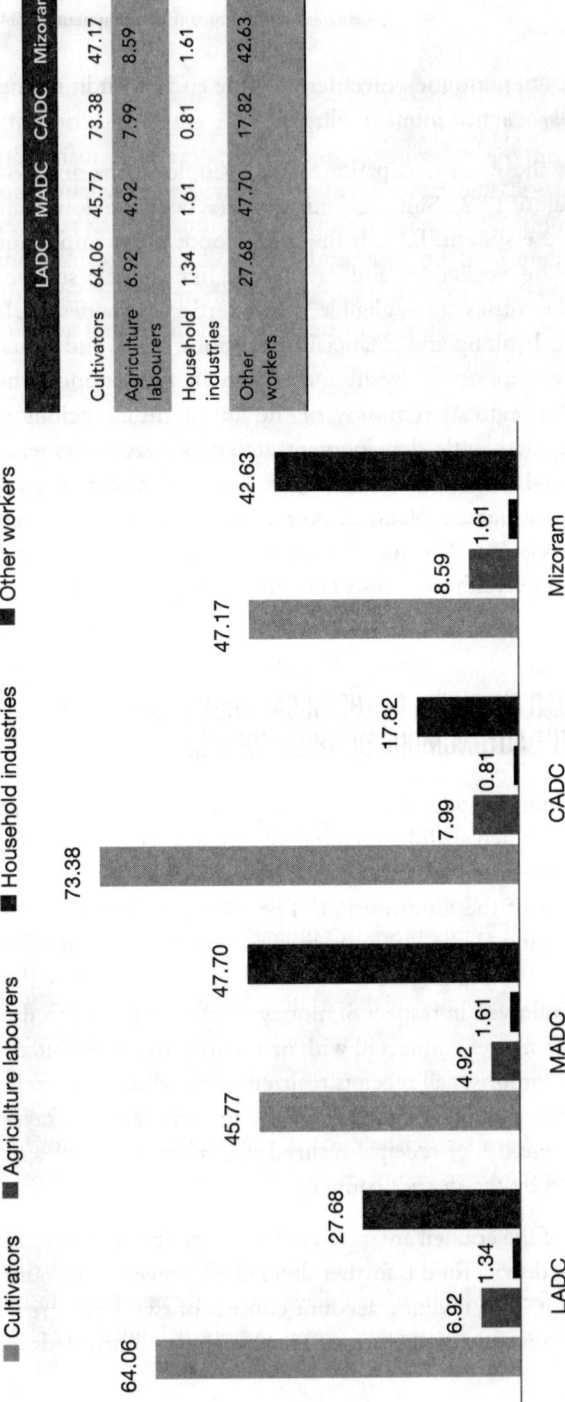

Figure 13.2 *Occupational Structure: Mizoram, LADC, MADC and CADC*

Source: Census 2011, Mizoram.

	LADC	MADC	CADC	Mizoram
Cultivators	64.06	45.77	73.38	47.17
Agriculture labourers	6.92	4.92	7.99	8.59
Household industries	1.34	1.61	0.81	1.61
Other workers	27.68	47.70	17.82	42.63

taxation and other receipts categorized as revenue and expenditure met from these receipts. The account also includes the grants and contributions received from the government, and also grants and contributions made by the council. The capital accounts deal with public debt, loans and advances. Public debt, loans and advances comprise loans received and their repayment by the council and loans and advances made and their recoveries by the council. Capital expenditure represents expenditure met from borrowed funds with the object of increasing assets or reducing recurring liabilities.

The transactions relating to the deposit funds include Contributory Provident Fund, other funds and advances. Under these accounts, either the Council incurs a liability to repay the moneys received or has a claim to recover the amount paid, together with the repayment of the deposits and the recoveries of the advances.

Revenue receipts of the district councils could further be divided into districts' own revenue receipts and revenue transfers. Since the autonomous district regions are backward and underdeveloped, they have limited sources for mobilization of resources in terms of tax and non-tax revenue. The important own revenue receipts of the councils are profession taxes, land revenue, taxes on vehicles, etc., while non-tax revenue include user charges, fees and penalty from administrative and economic and social services rendered by the district councils.

Revenue transfers consist of grants-in-aid from the state and other grants such as special grants from the Finance Commission and plan grants. Grants-in-aid from the state government constitute the most important source of revenue of the ADCs. They consist of revenue transfers for salary and non-salary purposes from the state government, transfers from central sector schemes or CSSs and others. Grants are given to the district councils for specific purposes, such as maintenance and development of primary schools, roads, water supply, sanitation and forests. These are statutory grants given to the councils under Article 275 of the Constitution of India.

Grants-in-aid from the state government consist of salary, vehicles, office expenses, remuneration of village council members, buildings, etc. Grants-in-aid for specific development schemes have also been given for the social and economic sectors, such as for rural development, sanitation, water supply, forest, art and culture, etc. Grants-in-aid have been transferred to the autonomous districts on a population basis, which is subject to revision. Grants are not released all at once but in three instalments. Central Finance Commission grants, if any, are directly transferred to the ADCs as per stipulations and norms specified by the specific commission to supplement the resources of the state government.

Fiscal Trends and Pattern in Lai Autonomous District Council

Own tax revenue receipts broadly consist of professional tax, land revenue tax and entry tax on vehicles. LADC is also collecting some non-tax revenue from economic services, such as public works, education, administrative services, etc. The fiscal trend suggests that both own revenue receipts and revenue transfers from the state government showed an upward trend between 2009–2010 and 2015–2016 (Table 13.1). Own revenue receipts, which were ₹72.32 lakh in 2009–2010, rose to ₹156.53 lakh in 2015–2016, showing a 2.16-times increase over the period. The increase came from professional tax, public works and land revenue, while revenue from social sectors like education, administrative receipts, etc. witnessed a decline during the period. Grants-in-aid from the state witnessed an increase from ₹5,519.93 lakh to ₹11,729.33 lakh during the period, representing a little more than a twofold increase.

The pattern of revenue receipts shows that transfers from the state government and other agencies contributed approximately 99 per cent of the revenue receipts of the council. The share of own revenue receipts shows a fluctuating trend over the period. The share improved from 1.39 per cent in 2009–2010 to 1.41 per cent in 2011–2012; afterwards, it shows a consistent decline, reaching 1.32 per cent in 2015–2016. Own revenue receipts have been contributed to mainly by professional tax and forest and land revenue. However, the share of professional tax shows a declining trend from 0.71 to 0.49 per cent between 2009–2010 and 2015–2016, while forest revenue increased from 0.23 per cent to 0.33

Table 13.1 Trend of Revenue Receipts in LADC (in Lakhs)

Items	2009–2010	2010–2011	2011–2012	2012–2013	2013–2014	2014–2015	2015–2016
Own revenue receipts	72.32	81.40	113.18	125.80	143.07	150.95	156.53
Taxes on income and expenditure	37.01	38.41	48.39	50.30	53.87	58.84	58.07
Land revenue	11.99	15.37	15.44	18.98	22.37	24.80	26.54
Public works	3.53	5.09	4.04	7.98	22.37	24.80	26.54
Other administrative services	0.04	0.04	0.10	0.09	0.16	0.16	0.29
Education	1.18	1.80	0.26	0.15	0.39	0.29	0.30
Other general economic services	1.29	2.29	13.74	10.70	5.63	5.00	4.16
Forest	17.07	16.83	29.60	35.93	36.58	35.56	39.34
Taxes on vehicles	0.21	1.57	1.61	1.67	1.70	1.50	1.29
Grants-in-aid from the state government	5,119.93	7,247.02	7,922.33	10,395.63	10,559.43	11,292.37	11,729.33
Total revenue receipts	5,192.25	7,328.42	8,035.51	10,521.43	10,702.50	11,443.32	11,885.86

Source: Report of the Comptroller and Auditor General (CAG) of India for the period from 2009–2010 to 2015–2016, LADC.

Table 13.2 *Pattern of Revenue Receipts in LADC (in %)*

Items	2009–2010	2010–2011	2011–2012	2012–2013	2013–2014	2014–2015	2015–2016
Own revenue receipts	1.39	1.11	1.41	1.20	1.34	1.32	1.32
Taxes on income and expenditure	0.71	0.52	0.60	0.48	0.50	0.51	0.49
Land revenue	0.23	0.21	0.19	0.18	0.21	0.22	0.22
Public works	0.07	0.07	0.05	0.08	0.21	0.22	0.22
Other administrative services	0.00	0.00	0.00	0.00	0.00	0.00	0.00
Education	0.02	0.02	0.00	0.00	0.00	0.00	0.00
Other general eco-nomic services	0.02	0.03	0.17	0.10	0.05	0.04	0.03
Forest	0.33	0.23	0.37	0.34	0.34	0.31	0.33
Taxes on vehicles	0.00	0.02	0.02	0.02	0.02	0.01	0.01
Grants-in-aid from the state government	98.61	98.89	98.59	98.80	98.66	98.68	98.68
Total revenue receipts	100.00	100.00	100.00	100.00	100.00	100.00	100.00

Source: Report of the CAG of India for the period from 2009–2010 to 2015–2016, LADC.

Table 13.3 *Trend and Pattern of Total Expenditure in LADC (in Lakhs)*

Year	Revenue Expenditure ₹	Revenue Expenditure Percentage	Capital Expenditure ₹	Capital Expenditure Percentage	Total
2009–2010	4,863.06	93.46	340.27	6.42	5,203.33
2010–2011	6,890.62	93.13	508.58	6.79	7,399.20
2011–2012	7,578.96	94.67	426.55	5.27	8,005.51
2012–2013	8,276.79	91.58	760.95	8.34	9,037.74
2013–2014	8,472.52	85.02	1,492.77	14.85	9,965.29
2014–2015	9,185.62	83.41	1,827.18	16.47	11,012.80
2015–2016	10,580.95	81.57	2,391.12	18.32	12,972.07

Source: Report of the CAG of India for the period from 2009–2010 to 2015–2016, LADC.

per cent and land revenue from 0.18 to 0.22 per cent. Contributions from social sectors were negligible (Table 13.2).

The total expenditure of LADC could be classified into capital and revenue expenditure (Table 13.3). Capital expenditure relates to expenditure for the creation of capital assets which enhance the productive capacity of the economy, while revenue expenditure indicates expenses on salary, wages and other maintenance items. In absolute terms, revenue expenditure rose from ₹4,863.06 lakh to ₹10,580.90 lakh between 2009–2010 and 2015–2016, showing a little more than a twofold increase over the period. Meanwhile, capital expenditure showed an approximately sevenfold increase, from ₹340.27 lakh to ₹2,391.12 lakh. This is a positive indication due to the fact that improved spending on the creation of capital assets promotes economic development in the district council. Relatively, the share of revenue expenditure declined, while that of capital shows a rising trend over the period of study. Revenue expenditure went down from 93.46 per cent in 2009–2010 to 81.57 per cent in 2015–2016, and capital expenditure rose from 6.42 per cent to 18.32 per cent during the same period.

Fiscal Trends and Pattern in
Mara Autonomous District Council

MADC's own tax revenue receipts come from five sources, namely, professional tax, land revenue, entry tax on vehicles, trade licence fees and stamp and registration. This shows that the council is putting itself a step ahead of the other two ADCs in terms of own revenue mobilization. The trend of own revenue receipts shows that own revenue receipts rose by 1.51 times, from ₹77.18 lakh in 2011–2012 to ₹116.85 lakh in 2014–2015 (Table 13.4). Similarly, revenue transfers from the state government indicate an increase of 1.38 times, from ₹7,381.67 lakh in 2011–2012 to ₹10,206.64 lakh in 2014–2015. The fiscal pattern indicates a high proportion of grants-in-aid from the state and a marginal contribution from internal revenue receipts. Revenue transfers constituted as much as 99 per cent of the aggregate revenue receipts of the district council. Professional tax and forest revenue are the two important sources of own revenue receipts of the district council.

Revenue expenditure improved from ₹7,560 lakh in 2011–2012 to ₹9,806 lakh in 2014–2015, showing an increase of 1.30 times. The pattern indicates that development expenditure, which had accounted for 84.23 per cent in 2011–2012, went down to 80.32 per cent in 2014–2015. In the meantime, the share of non-development expenditure had risen from 15.68 per cent to 19.68 per cent of the total revenue expenditure during the same period. The pattern has an adverse implication on the development of the district council, indicating that development expenditure such as education, rural development, agriculture, etc. had been reduced, to the disadvantage of the people.

Fiscal Trends and Pattern in
Chakma Autonomous District Council

The own tax revenue receipts of CADC comprise professional tax and land revenue only. Non-tax revenue has been collected from various fees for general and economic services. As given in the Table 13.6, own revenue receipts amounted to only ₹27 lakh in 2009–2010; this increased to ₹65 lakh in 2014–2015, indicating a 2.44-times increase

Table 13.4 *Pattern and Trend of Revenue Receipts in MADC (in Lakhs)*

Items	2011–20120		2012–2013		2013–2014		2014–2015	
	₹	%	₹	%	₹	%	₹	%
Own revenue receipts	**77.18**	1.03	**86.69**	0.94	**104.79**	1.24	**116.85**	1.13
Taxes on income and expenditure	35.02	0.47	53.33	0.58	78.99	0.93	78.72	0.76
Land revenue	2.83	0.04	6.84	0.07	3.18	0.04	7.55	0.07
Taxes on vehicles	1.09	0.01	1.19	0.01	0.00	0.00	1.24	0.01
Public works	2.43	0.03	2.48	0.03	3.77	0.04	9.14	0.09
Other administrative services	0.04	0.00	0.03	0.00	0.15	0.00	0.20	0.00
Other general economic services	0.82	0.01	1.35	0.01	2.00	0.02	3.00	0.03
Forest	34.95	0.47	21.17	0.23	16.70	0.20	17.00	0.16
Grants-in-aid from the state government	**7,381.67**	98.97	**9,106.33**	99.06	**8,374.56**	98.76	**10,206.64**	98.87
Total revenue receipts	**7,458.85**	100	**9,193.02**	100	**8,479.35**	100	**10,323.49**	100

Source: Reports of the CAG of India, 2011–2012 to 2014–2015 (MADC).

Table 13.5 *Trend and Pattern of Revenue Expenditure in MADC (in Lakhs)*

Items of Expenditure	2011–2012		2012–2013		2013–2014		2014–2015	
	₹	Percentage	₹	Percentage	₹	Percentage	₹	Percentage
Non-development expenditure	1,193	15.77	1,450	16.68	1575	17.36	1,929	19.68
District council secretariat	192	2.54	324	3.72	404	4.45	477	4.87
Administration of justice	67	0.88	64	0.73	62	0.68	81	0.83
Land and revenue	206	2.72	276	3.18	270	2.97	338	3.45
Executive member	54	0.72	84	0.96	70	0.78	79	0.81
Finance and accounts	512	6.77	500	5.75	509	5.61	616	6.28
Secretariat general services	162	2.15	203	2.33	260	2.87	337	3.44
Development expenditure	6,368	84.23	7,243	83.32	7495	82.64	7,877	80.32
Total expenditure	7,560	100.00	8,692	100.00	9070	100.00	9,806	100.00

Source: Reports of the CAG of India, 2011–2012 to 2014–2015 (MADC).

Table 13.6 *Pattern and Trend of Revenue Receipts in CADC (in Lakhs)*

Items	2009–2010		2010–2011		2011–2012		2012–2013		2013–2014		2014–2015	
	₹	Percentage	₹	Percentage	₹	Percentage	₹	Percentage	₹	Percentage	₹	Percentage
Own revenue receipts	27	0.67	28	0.68	90	1.79	61	0.86	65	1.15	65	0.93
Taxes on income and expenditure	16	0.40	20	0.49	27	0.54	29	0.41	28	0.50	30	0.43
Land revenue	7	0.17	3	0.08	7	0.14	9	0.12	9	0.16	11	0.16
Other receipts	4	0.10	5	0.12	56	1.11	23	0.33	27	0.49	24	0.34
Grants-in-aid from the state government	3,949	99.34	4,070	99.33	4,927	98.22	7,046	99.14	5,566	98.85	6,919	99.07
Total revenue receipts	3,975	100	4,098	100.	5,016	100	7,107	100	5,631	100	6,984	100

Source: Reports of the CAG of India, 2011–2012 to 2014–2015 (CADC).

over the year. Professional tax is the only reliable and consistent source of own revenue receipts. Between 2009–2010 and 2014–2015, professional tax rose from ₹15.80 lakh to ₹29.79 lakh, showing almost a twofold increase. Own revenue receipts varied between 1 and 2 per cent during the period. Absence of commitment of the council authority is partly responsible for low own revenue mobilization. As per the Chakma Autonomous District Council (Tax on Entry of Vehicles into the Autonomous District) Regulation, 2004, the council is empowered to impose tax on the entry of vehicles into the jurisdictional area of the council. However, the district council is not exercising this power. Thus, the council is unable to optimize its efforts even within the limited sphere of its tax autonomy.

In absolute terms, grants-in-aid rose from ₹3,975 lakh in 2009–2010 to ₹6,984 lakh in 2014–2015, showing a 1.75-times increase over the period. The pattern of revenue receipts showed that own revenue receipts accounted for 0.67 per cent and 1.79 per cent in 2009–2010 and 2014–2015, respectively. Professional tax hovered between 0.40 per cent and 0.54 per cent during the same period. Revenue transfers accounted for more than 99 per cent during the period.

The trend of revenue expenditure shows a consistent rise, from ₹3,494 lakh to ₹7,116 lakh, showing approximately a twofold increase over the period 2011–2012 to 2014–2015. Non-development expenditure rose from ₹655 lakh to ₹1,880 lakh, which indicates an increase of 2.87 times over the period. The increase has been mainly attributed to the expenditure on the council secretariat and land revenue. Meanwhile, development expenditure increased by 1.84 times, from ₹2,839 lakh to ₹5,236 lakh during this period.

The pattern of expenditure indicates that non-development expenditure, which accounted for 18.74 per cent, significantly increased to 26.41 per cent between 2009–2010 and 2014–2015. This was mainly attributed to the expenditure on the district council secretariat, which varied between 8.87 per cent and 12.95 per cent during this period. The district council spent between 3.20 per cent and 5.32 per cent on land revenue administration. Development expenditure over the period witnessed a decline, from 81.25 per cent in 2009–2010 to 73.58 per cent in 2014–2015.

Table 13.7 *Trend of Revenue Expenditure in CADC (in Lakhs)*

Items of Expenditure	2009–2010	2010–2011	2011–2012	2012–2013	2013–2014	2014–2015
Non-development expenditure	655	943	1,234	1,505	1,606	1,880
District council	102	104	122	184	191	180
Executive members	28	32	43	72	66	111
Administration of justice	36	44	54	54	75	70
Land revenue	112	186	230	301	298	379
District council secretariat	310	420	597	566	699	795
Pension and other retirement benefits	68	158	189	327	277	345
Development expenditure	2,839	3,353	3,376	5,335	4,059	5,236
Total expenditure	3,494	4,296	4,610	6,840	5,665	7,116

Source: Reports of the CAG of India, 2011–2012 to 2014–2015 (CADC).

Table 13.8 *Pattern of Revenue Expenditure in CADC (in %)*

Items of Expenditure	2009–2010	2010–2011	2011–2012	2012–2013	2013–2014	2014–2015
Non-development expenditure	18.74	21.96	26.76	22.00	28.35	26.42
District council	2.91	2.41	2.64	2.69	3.38	2.53
Executive members	0.79	0.75	0.94	1.06	1.16	1.56
Administration of justice	1.03	1.01	1.17	0.79	1.32	0.99
Land revenue	3.20	4.33	4.98	4.40	5.25	5.32
District council secretariat	8.87	9.77	12.95	8.27	12.35	11.17
Pension and other retirement benefits	1.94	3.68	4.09	4.78	4.89	4.85
Development expenditure	81.25	78.04	73.24	78.00	71.64	73.58
Total expenditure	100.00	100.00	100.00	100.00	100.00	100.00

Source: Reports of the CAG of India, 2011–2012 to 2014–2015 (CADC).

Revenue Transfers to ADCs Under State Finance Commission Award (2015–2020)

The First SFC recommended the devolution of share taxes (own state's taxes) and deficit grants-in-aid for the ADCs. The SFC recommended a 15 per cent share in the own tax revenue of the state. It also suggested a 5 per cent share in state excise duty. The inter se share among the ADCs, village councils and Aizawl Municipal Corporation (AMC) are worked out at 58.33, 24.17 and 17.50 per cent, respectively. The criteria and weight suggested to determine the respective share of the three district councils after devolving the aggregate share of ADCs is presented in Table 13.9.

The share of LADC in the aggregate share came to 41.97 per cent, followed by a 34.07 per cent for MADC and 23.96 per cent for CADC. Based on the estimates of the own tax revenue of the state, the share of the three ADCs has been projected in Table 13.10.

The total projected non-plan deficits of ADCs are also worked out by the SFC by calculating the absolute amount of deficit financing involved in the three autonomous councils. These are worked out on an annual basis and are highlighted in Table 13.11.

Table 13.9 *Criteria and Weight Adopted by the First State Finance Commission to Determine the Inter-se Share of Autonomous District Councils*

Sl. No.	Criteria	Weight (%)
1	Population in 2011	40
2	Area	30
3	Distance from ADC head-quarters to the state capital	10
4	Literacy	10
5	Villages electrified	10

Source: Report of the First State Finance Commission, Mizoram (2015–2020).

Table 13.10 *Projected Tax Devolution to Autonomous District Councils (in Lakhs)*

Autonomous Councils	2015–2016	2016–2017	2017–2018	2018–2019	2019–2020
Lai	1,078.15	1,240.93	1,428.25	1,643.92	1,892.12
Chakma	615.5	708.43	815.37	938.49	1,080.18
Mara	875.21	1,007.35	1,159.41	1,334.48	1,535.97
Total	2,568.86	2,956.71	3,403.03	3,916.89	4,508.27

Source: Report of the First State Finance Commission, Mizoram (2015–2020).

Table 13.11 *Projected Non-plan Deficit Grants to Autonomous District Councils (in Lakhs)*

Autonomous Councils	2015–2016	2016–2017	2017–2018	2018–2019	2019–2020
Lai	6,588.92	7,415.58	8,344.33	9,387.23	10,558
Chakma	3,437.17	3,957.98	4,558.53	5,233.23	5,961.35
Mara	6,253.3	7,319.23	8,300.03	9,324.42	10,271.85
Total	16,279.39	18,692.79	21,202.89	23,944.88	26,791.2

Source: Report of the First State Finance Commission, Mizoram (2015–2020).

Transfers Under Plan Schemes Implemented by Autonomous District Councils

Over the planning horizons, several development schemes have been operated and implemented in the ADCs. These transfers came from the state government, central sector schemes or CSSs, Ministry of Development of North Eastern Region, North Eastern Council and NITI Aayog. These are summarized in Table 13.12.

Table 13.12 *State and Central Plan Schemes in Autonomous District Councils*

Sl. No.	Particulars	Remarks
1	New Land Use Policy	This is a state-flagship anti-*jhum* rural development programme in which the beneficiaries are given alternative occupations in the horticultural–agricultural industries and the trade sector.
2	New Economic Development Policy	This is the post–Planning Commission development programme and policy initiated by the state government to address the development gap left in the aftermath of the Planning Commission. Specifically, the rural housing scheme had been implemented under the programme in the three ADCs.
3	Border Area Development Programme	This is a central sector scheme implemented by the Ministry of Home Affairs through the state governments as part of a comprehensive approach to border management. The objective of the programme is to provide for the critical infrastructural needs of people living within 15 km from the international border and promote their livelihood.
4	Backward Regions Grant Fund (BRGF)	BRGF provides financial assistance to accelerate socio-economic development of the most backward regions/districts in the country. Central funds are mainly released to states under various central sector schemes /or CSSs.
5	Rashtriya Krishi Vikas Yojana (National Agriculture Development Programme)	This is a State Plan Scheme funded by Government of India under Additional Central Assistance during Eleventh Five Year Plan. It seeks to achieve 4% annual growth in agriculture through the development of agriculture and its allied sectors.
6	NITI Aayog	Special Assistance under Central Plan Schemes sponsored by NITI Aayog for Sixth Schedule Areas during 2015–2016
7	North Eastern Council/Non-Lapsable Central Pool of Resources	Financial assistance is given for development schemes, according to state government priorities.

Source: State Planning Board, Mizoram.

Devolution of Functions Under the Social and Economic Sectors of the State

District Councils have been entrusted to execute some few plan schemes such as construction of inter-village path, water supply, sanitation and Arts & Culture programme since their formations in the early 1970s. To speed up development, the state government devolved some of its activities under different departments to the ADCs. The first attempt was made in 1986, which was followed by notifications issued in 1993 and 2011. These entrusted items are summarized in Table 13.13.

FISCAL ISSUES AND CHALLENGES

The analysis revealed several weaknesses and challenges in respect of the fiscal management of the district councils. These issues are briefly highlighted.

Large district administrative set-up: The autonomous councils are burdened with a huge administrative structure. As in 2018–2019, there were a total of more than 6,000 employees under the three ADCs out of the 9,000 sanctioned posts. Salaries and office expenditure account for a high proportion of total funds available for running the district councils. Development expenditure such as on education, health, social welfare, etc. remain highly inadequate; capital outlays on assets creation are limited. These issues need to be addressed in order to ensure fiscal sustainability of the three ADCs and to undertake more development works. It has been noted that the councils fill posts without prior sanction of the state government, and therefore the state government does not provide resources for those posts, leading to financial difficulty.

Low own revenue receipts and high fiscal dependence: The councils' own revenue receipts from tax and non-tax revenue constitute less than 2 per cent of the total revenue receipts. Despite development constraints, efforts need to be built up to improve own revenue receipts to the maximum possible. Capacity-building for the local government to function as an institution of local

Table 13.13 *Devolution of Functions/Activities by the State to the Autonomous District Councils*

Departments	Entrusted Activities/Items
Agriculture and Horticulture	Agriculture-linked roads; distribution of planting material and certified seeds, procurement of machineries, implements, water pumping machinery at 5% subsidy; land development; minor irrigation; and construction of field channels
Fisheries	Grants-in-aid to individual fish farmers for fish pond development
Public Health Engineering	Rural sanitation, spring source development, public latrines/urinals under rural sanitation schemes
Industry	Handloom and handicraft, grants-in-aid to individuals for supply of tools and implements, selection of beneficiaries for loans
Sericulture	Grants-in-aid for silkworm rearing, marketing of cocoon to state government
Animal Husbandry and Veterinary	Subsidy scheme for cattle development, piggery and animal husbandry dispensaries
Arts and Culture	Grants-in-aid for the promotion of arts and culture, district library, district museum, assistance for publication
Social Welfare	Old-age pension, assistance to voluntary organizations, pre-schools, welfare of handicapped persons, poor and destitute people
Soil Conservation	Implementation of terracing, plantation under subsidy scheme, village grassing ground
Local Administration	Urban development, construction of steps, culverts, retaining walls
Forest Department	All projects undertaken by state on forests within council areas
Transport Department	Creation of separate departments in each district; collection of road tax, goods and passenger tax, etc.

(Continued)

Table 13.13 (Continued)

Departments	Entrusted Activities/Items
Sports and Youth Services	Creation of separate departments and provision of funds by the state government
Public Works Department (PWD)	Inter-village approach road to link with the PWD roads, maintenance and improvement of satellite towns and village roads
Education	Handing over of primary and middle schools and adult education
Rural Development	Rural communications, construction of community halls, rural housing

Source: Notifications issued by the Government of Mizoram in 1986, 1993 and 2011.

governance is a crucial issue. The councils' authorities should make an effort to empower themselves financially and functionally, minimizing their dependence on the state government, and ensure people participation in the development process of the autonomous regions. Transparent and efficient local institutions need to be set up.

Inadequate entrustment and overlapping of functions: Over the years, the state government entrusted many subjects and functional items to the three ADCs. However, it has been observed that many of the entrusted items have continued to be performed by the line and administrative offices in the council areas; there is a dichotomy and overlapping in the implementation of schemes between the state government and the councils. District councils do not play a major functional role in the execution of CSSs such as MGNREGS, Indira Gandhi Awas Yojona, Backward Regions Grant Fund (BRGF), BADP, etc. An equally significant concern has been that entrustment took place without the accompanying devolution of functions, functionaries and finances, 'making the ADCs a duplication of the State Departments'. As noted by the SFC, the exercise resulted in a further increase in administrative personnel and staff.

Legislative and financial empowerment: The revised note on decentralised governance in north-eastern states by the Ministry of Panchayati Raj, 19 March 2010, recommended enlargement of the legislative powers of the three districts councils of Mizoram to bring them at par with councils in North Cachar and Karbi Anglong of Assam, as per the provision of the Sixth Schedule. The district council authorities have been demanding that direct funds be allocated to district councils from the Consolidated Fund of India. Specifically, they have been demanding to amend Paragraph 13 of the Sixth Schedules by incorporating provision for direct allocation of Plan and Non-Plan fund to the autonomous district councils by Central Government.

Amendment to the Sixth Schedule: The central government is currently proposing an amendment to Article 280 and the Sixth Schedule of the Constitution which will pave the way for the Finance Commission being mandated to recommend devolution of financial resources to the ADCs as well as the village and municipal councils in the Sixth Schedule areas. The proposed amendment also provides for the constitution of an SFC. Village councils will be empowered to prepare plans for economic development and social justice; there will be a reservation of at least one-third of the seats for women in the village and municipal councils, and at least two women nominated members in all ADCs. These amendments will have an impact on more inclusive development pathways and facilitate women's participation in decision-making at the grassroots level.

CONCLUSION

Fiscal decentralization to the autonomous councils in Mizoram brought limited development outcomes at the grassroots level. Autonomous councils could not meet their development obligations due to lack of financial autonomy, political corruption and inefficient administration. Widespread financial irregularities and leakages of fund had been observed in the three district councils of Mizoram. An innovative fiscal devolution strategy needs to be evolved with an understanding of the economic and political conditions prevailing in the region. For successful fiscal devolution to these local bodies, as observed by the First State Finance Commission Report (2015–2020), the following conditions need to be fulfilled: first, to fulfil their development obligations,

autonomous bodies must have room for flexibility through untied
resources, in order to establish priorities, devise new schemes and
allocate funds; second, there must be both opportunity and motiva-
tion to mobilize local resources through local taxes and cess and user
charges; third, the capacity of the local bodies needs to be enhanced
for them to discharge their responsibilities effectively; and finally, state
government functionaries need to recognize that local bodies must be
empowered financially and functionally to enable them to function as
institutions of self-governance, and they must respect the autonomy
of the autonomous councils.

REFERENCES

Actionaid. (2016). *Functioning of autonomous councils in sixth schedule areas of North Eastern states*. Actionaid India.
Comptroller & Auditor General of India. (2017a). *Report of the comptroller & auditor general of India for the years 2009–10 to 2015–16*. Lai Autonomous District Council.
Comptroller & Auditor General of India. (2017b). *Report of the comptroller & auditor general of India for the years 2011–12 to 2014–15*. Mara Autonomous District Council.
Comptroller & Auditor General of India. (2017c). *Report of the comptroller & auditor general of India for the years 2009–10 to 2014–15*. Chakma Autonomous District Council.
Government of Mizoram. (2015). *Report of the first state finance commission Mizoram (2015–16)*.
Oates, W. E. (1993, June). Fiscal decentralization and economic development. *National Tax Journal, 46*(2), 237–244.
Stuligross, D. (1999, October–December). Autonomous councils in Northeast India: Theory and practice. *Alternatives: Global, Local, Political, 24*(4), 497–525.
Thanhranga, H. C. (2007). *District councils in the Mizo Hills (updated)*. Lengchhawn Press.

Chapter 14

Making a Case for the Formation of Regional Councils Within Sixth Schedule Areas

Thongkholal Haokip

This chapter discusses the provisions in the Sixth Schedule of the Indian constitution for the formation of autonomous regions and regional councils in districts with multiple scheduled tribes, and stresses on the formation of such regional councils for smaller tribes within the district or territorial area. In the formation of district councils and regional councils in the erstwhile hill areas of Assam, minority groups within the Sixth Schedule districts were neglected. In recent decades, some such groups have been found to be engaged in militant activities. It is argued here that the formation of regional councils for such minority tribes within the district or territorial area can be 'a conflict management device' and a path towards peace and development in the north-eastern region.

On 23 January 2019, the Union Cabinet of India decided to increase the financial and executive powers of autonomous councils in the North East (NE) region, which are formed under the Sixth Schedule of the Constitution, by approving a constitutional amendment. Through the amendment of Article 280 and the Sixth Schedule of the Constitution,[1] it seeks to 'significantly improve the financial resources and powers of the autonomous districts councils in Assam, Meghalaya, Mizoram and Tripura, fulfilling long-standing aspirations of the tribal population in these Northeastern States'. The Union Cabinet also intends to devolve financial resources to the councils, which will end their dependency 'on grants from Central Ministries and the State governments for specific projects', and 'will substantially enhance the funds available to these local government institutions for undertaking development works in these tribal areas' (*The Hindu*, 2019).

The demand for direct funding of the district councils was long-standing, particularly that from Mizoram, as funds to autonomous councils are under the control of the state government. Indeed, it was overdue since the 73rd and 74th amendments of the Constitution in 1992, which devolved powers and functions to the panchayats and urban local bodies, respectively. The Direct Funding Demand Committee of Mizoram 'want to be re-christened as autonomous territorial councils, want powers to decide on more subjects and want all centrally-sponsored schemes to be directly sanctioned and released by concerned ministries' (*The Telegraph*, 2012). On 6 February 2019, the Constitution (One Hundred and Twenty-Fifth Amendment) Bill, 2019, was introduced in the Rajya Sabha, with the aim of 'enhancing autonomy of the existing Autonomous Councils, renaming the Councils and increasing the number of seats in the concerned Councils'. The bill was later referred to the standing committee for further examination. The bill, if passed, will rename the autonomous councils as autonomous territorial councils and increase their powers. The North Cachar Hills Autonomous Council will be renamed as Dima Hasao Autonomous Territorial Council. However, the Lai, Chakma and Mara autonomous councils in Mizoram were excluded from the renaming of the councils. There will not only be an increase in the number of seats in the councils but also a provision for the reservation of at least two seats for women.

---

[1] There were several attempts to amend the Sixth Schedule of the Constitution to enhance the provisions since 2005, during the Congress-led United Progressive Alliance administration.

The bill, through this amendment, also intends to enable the Finance Commission to review the financial position of the district councils, including the village councils and municipal councils, and 'to recommend' to the governor 'measures needed to augment the Consolidated Fund of the States to supplement resources of the Sixth Schedule Autonomous Councils, Village Councils and Municipal Councils'. This will 'provide separate funds for the Autonomous District Councils in Sixth Schedule areas which results in inadequate socio-economic infrastructure in the Autonomous District Council areas' so as to supplement resources. However, this again falls short of the 'direct funding' that is being demanded. The amendment bill also provides for the establishment of 'Village Councils for a village or a group of villages in the rural areas and the Municipal Councils for an urban area or an agglomeration of such urban areas of the district'.

One of the interesting features of this amendment bill is the nomination of a specific number of not only women but also members of 'unrepresented tribes' in the council by the governor. Currently, there is no such provision to ensure the nomination of unrepresented tribes as members of the autonomous district councils (ADCs). It is purely at the governor's discretion whom to nominate. At a time when there are plans to increase the powers of and number of members in the councils, the Government of Meghalaya has not only opted out of the provision for elected village and municipal councils and reservation of one-third seats for women in this proposed amendment for the time being, but it is also attempting to remove the word 'unrepresented tribes' from the proposed amendment to the Sixth Schedule. This was decided on 26 September 2019 by a subcommittee constituted by the state government to recommend to the standing committee of Parliament (*The Hindu*, 2019, September 28). Leaders of the five 'unrepresented tribes' in Meghalaya, namely Hajong, Koch, Rabha, Bodo and Mann, express their concern over the development. They feel: 'It is sad the minority tribes have run into tribal majoritarianism. We have virtually been made non-indigenous and unwanted in our own homeland'. Apart from these five 'unrepresented tribes', there are several other smaller unrepresented tribes, such as the Biate, Hmar, Synteng, Mikir, Naga and Kuki tribes.

The proposed amendment to the Sixth Schedule is long due, but it is still short of the expectations of minority tribes in such districts or territorial areas. They are not only the most neglected in policy, but even the institutions that were created to serve their interests are denied to them.

This chapter is divided into four parts. The second part briefly discusses the genesis of the Sixth Schedule and the demand for autonomous councils in other parts of India, including Manipur and Tripura. The third part looks into the history of how smaller groups within the then–Lushai Hills district of Assam demanded smaller councils for the Pawis and Lakhers. The fourth part deals with the politics of recognition in the north-eastern region and examines whether the creation of regional councils can accommodate ethnic diversity.

GOVERNING NORTH-EAST INDIA: ORIGIN OF AUTONOMOUS COUNCILS

In NE India, the so-called indigenous or 'non-state people' had been governed differently since the advent of the British colonial rule in Assam province.[2] When the British were about to leave, a secret plan for a crown colony was conceived for the hill areas of NE India, and for the tribal areas of Burma, by the colonial officers who were at one point of time posted in the North East Frontier.[3] Such proposed scheme was not realized, perhaps due to the haste in which the British had to leave India. However, the statement of the Cabinet Mission on 16 May 1946 reflected the need for special attention to be given to the excluded tribal areas by the Constituent Assembly of India.

---

[2] The term 'non-state people' is widely used today to denote upland people in NE India and Southeast Asia who had different forms of governance other than the 'state system'. For details on this, see Scott (2009).

[3] Such plans were "'A Note on the Future of the Present Excluded, Partially Excluded and Tribal Areas of Assam', written by Robert N Reid; 'A Note on the Future of the Hill Tribes of Assam and the Adjoining Hills in a Self-governing India' by James P Mills; 'The Future Government of the Assam Tribal Peoples' by Andrew G. Clow; and 'Some Notes on a Policy for the Hill Tribes of Assam' by Philip Adams. These plans are compiled together by Syiemlieh (2014).

Constituent Assembly and Autonomous Councils

An advisory sub-committee on North-East Frontier Tribal Areas and Assam Excluded and Partially Excluded Areas was set up by the Constituent Assembly of India under the chairmanship of Gopinath Bordoloi 'for the purpose of enquiring into the tribal situation in Assam' (Constituent Assembly Of India Debates, 1949) and preparing schemes for the administration of the North-eastern tribal areas. After an extensive tour to different hill districts of the then–composite state of Assam, the sub-committee submitted its report to the Constituent Assembly, and it was placed for debate on 6 September 1949. While 'the Sub-committee thought that the best way to satisfy these people is to give them a certain measure of self-government so that they may develop themselves according to their own genius and culture',[4] those who opposed the sub-committee's view 'want to assimilate the tribal people' into the mainstream.

Rev. J. J. M. Nichols Roy, a member of the sub-committee, stated: 'The village councils in the autonomous districts and the District Councils will enable the hills people to rule themselves in their own way and to develop themselves according to their own methods'. During the debate, Gopinath Bordoloi stressed on how

> some of these areas were war zones. During the war, the then rulers and officers developed in the minds of these tribal people a sense of separation and isolation and gave them assurances that at the end of the war they will be independent States managing their affairs in their own way. They were led to believe that the entire hill areas would he constituted into a province and put under some irresponsible Governor.

Supporting the sub-committee's view, Dr B. R. Ambedkar, Chairman of the Drafting Committee of the Constitution, stated: 'I agree that we have been creating Regional and District Councils to some extent on the lines which were adopted by the United States for the purpose of the Red Indians'.

---

[4] Constituent Assembly Debate, Vol. IX, No. 26, dated 6 September 1949, p. 1023.

The assimilationists were filled with the overriding concerns of 'irredentism', 'secessionism' and the tribespeople not learning Indian culture. Lakshminarayan Sahu from Orissa expressed these views:

> The regional councils we propose to set up for them, will, in my view, neither benefit these people nor us; for these people have got an organisation for each tribe, which is like our panchayat. They hold their Panchayat in every village. Their customs differ from village to village. The regional councils set up there would make uniform laws and these are likely to cause any number of difficulties among the various villages. In view of this, I would say that the powers vested in us, the Centre and the States should be kept intact. For a moment let us consider the likely consequences if we delegated these powers to these councils. The result would be that these people would develop on their own lines without in any way being connected with you.

To ward off the fear of assimilationists, Ambedkar explained: 'However, what I was saying was that the Regional Councils have been given certain autonomy for certain purposes and at the same time they have been bound together in the life of the province and in the life of the country as a whole'. Despite such concerns, the recommendations of the Bordoloi Sub-Committee was accepted by the Constituent Assembly with slight amendments. Thus, 'Provisions as to the Administration of Tribal Areas' were made in Articles 244(2) and 275(1) under the Sixth Schedule of the Constitution. In a nutshell, 'The scheme was conceived with a view to building up autonomous administrations in these areas so that the tribal people may continue to follow their traditional way of life with such changes as they themselves may like to introduce' (Agnihotri, 1994, p. 83).

The formation of ADCs in the NE under the Sixth Schedule of the Constitution is considered to be a milestone in providing tribal autonomy in India. It provides for the tribespeople of Assam, Meghalaya, Mizoram and Tripura to be 'administered as autonomous groups' through 'self-governing institutions of their own'. Tillin (2006, p. 56) considers 'the varieties of special status' in some of the NE states as 'the closest India comes to de jure asymmetrical federalism'. Looking into the wide array of provisions for autonomy under the Sixth Schedule, Hidayatulla, former Chief Justice of India, described it as a 'Constitution within a Constitution'. Article 244(2) of the Constitution provides that the Sixth Schedule shall apply to the administration of the tribal areas in Assam and the states carved out of it, along with the tribal areas of Tripura. In other words, such areas would be governed not by other relevant provisions of the Constitution which apply to the other constituent states of the Union of India but by the provisions contained in the Sixth Schedule.[5] A cursory glance at the Sixth Schedule reveals that it provides limited powers, barely enough for the tribespeople to govern themselves in the traditional mode. The schedule limits itself to the day-to-day life in the village and an overriding concern since the colonial period, of the exploitation by moneylenders and traders. L. S. Gassah (2013, p. 4) said that the Constitution makers, while recognizing 'the necessity of a separate political and administrative structure for the hill Tribal Areas of the erstwhile province of Assam', were guided by three major considerations while enacting the Sixth Schedule:

(i) the necessity to maintain the distinct customs and socio-economic and political culture of the tribal people of the region and to ensure autonomy of the tribal people and to present their identities;

(ii) the necessity to prevent their economic and social exploitation by the more advanced neighbouring people of the plains;

(iii) to allow the tribal people to develop and administer themselves according to their own genius.

Aspiring 'Autonomous Councils'

Within the NE, there were demands from Manipur since 1978 and from Tripura in the 1980s to extend the provisions of the Sixth Schedule to the tribal areas of both the states. In Manipur and Tripura, district councils came into being after the Parliament of India passed the Manipur (Hill Areas) District Councils Act, 1971, and the Tripura Tribal Areas Autonomous District Council Act in 1979. However,

---

[5] *Edwingson v. State of Assam, A.I.R. 1966 S.C. 12.*

the provisions of the Sixth Schedule were not given to Manipur and Tripura. Due to persistent demands, the Tripura Tribal Areas Autonomous District Council was brought under the Sixth Schedule on 1 April 1985. In Manipur, the demand for the Sixth Schedule intensified in the late 1980s when all the six district councils were suspended by tribal bodies in 1987. However, the demands by the hill tribespeople of Manipur were ignored. In protest against such apathy towards the tribespeople, elections to the ADCs were not held for 20 years, from 1991 till 2009. During this time, the central government sent three reminders to the Manipur government for the inclusion of the hills in the Sixth Schedule of the Constitution (*Imphal Free Press*, 2015).[6] The Manipur government insisted on the extension of the provisions of the Sixth Schedule to the Constitution of India with 'local amendments and adjustments'.

There is a demand for autonomous councils even outside NE, mainly from the former excluded and partially excluded areas during the British rule. Indeed, since the beginning in the late 1980s, 'autonomous councils have been used as an institutional device to accommodate cultural pluralism outside of Assam' (Sonntag, 1999, p. 423). Despite such growing demands for autonomous councils outside Assam, in reality, the ADCs are far from achieving full autonomy, particularly in the hills of Manipur (see Haokip, 2017; Suan, 2007). The functioning of the autonomous councils is far from satisfactory, mainly laden with undue and inordinate interference from the state governments and financial irregularities. The functioning of ADCs is out of the scope of discussion of this chapter, but it also needs attention. More research and timely necessary rectification is very much needed.

As of today, the Sixth Schedule, pertaining to the 'Provisions as to the Administration of Tribal Areas in the States of Assam, Meghalaya, Tripura and Mizoram', in paragraph 20, specifies three districts of Assam, three districts of Meghalaya, one district of Tripura and three districts of Mizoram as 'Tribal Areas', being territories administered by autonomous councils and ADCs. As noted by Singh (2007, p. 154),

---

[6] For details on demand for the Sixth Schedule in Manipur, see Kom (2010).

'The para omits any mention of regional councils, reference to which recurs in the Sixth Schedule, commencing with para 1'.

REGIONAL COUNCILS IN RETROSPECT

When the Bordoloi Sub-Committee visited the then–Lushai Hills on 18 April 1947 and 19 April 1947, different organizations' representatives and individuals appearing before the subcommittee submitted various memoranda that reflected the views of their communities. Most of the Mizo (Lushai) representatives demanded a 'Home Rule', where 'the internal affairs of the Lushai Hills should be in the hands of the Mizo people' (Zahluna, 2010, p. 1237). In Southern Lushai Hills, the Lakher chiefs submitted a memorandum several times to the Bordoloi Sub-Committee for the creation of a regional council for the Lakher people. Until the Constitution was adopted and India became a republic on 26 January 1949, identity politics was played by the dominant Mizo leaders and the Pawi and Lakher leaders.

The Mizo leaders, who were mainly Lushais, were spearheading a Mizo movement under the banner of the Mizo Union, with Lushai (Duhlain) as the common language of this generic identity. The initial politics of the Mizo Union was rejecting the imposed colonial identity—Kuki and Chin—and uniting all clans and tribes of such groups of people as 'Mizo', meaning people from the hills. However, the Pawis and Lakhers saw this as attempts at assimilation and imposition of an identity by a dominant group. They were reluctant to be a part of it, even though they recognized them as 'brothers' with a linguistic and cultural affinity. When the demand for a separate council for the Southern Lushai Hills came up, the leaders of the Mizo Union and United Mizo Freedom Organisation attempted to persuade the leaders Z. Hengmang and Vako 'not to proceed with their demand for the sake of Mizo integrity'. However, they 'were firm in their determination, not to retreat but to achieve their political goal' (Doungel, 2005). To articulate their demand, the two leaders went to Lunglei for the possibility of the formation of a political party. Consultations were held with other leaders of the Pawis and Lakhers, and thereafter, a circular was issued to all villages of the Pawi–Lakher region urging villages to send three representatives each for an assembly to be held on 25 October 1949 at Lawngtlai. During this meeting, a political party called the Pawi-Lakher Tribal Union (PLTU) was formed, in which Z. Hengmang was elected as the president. The PLTU vigorously pursued its demand for the creation of a regional council for the Pawis and the Lakhers. Z. Hengmang and Vako were also said to have taken advantage of the visit of Nari Rustumji, an Indian Civil Service (ICS) officer and Advisor to the Governor of Assam, to Lushai Hills in 1949. The duo 'submitted a memorandum to him asking for a Regional Council and said that if their demand was not fulfilled, they would abstain from all meetings of Advisory Council' (Doungel, 2005).

Consequent upon such demands, the subcommittee recommended a provision for the creation of a regional council.[7] The subcommittee reiterated that the regional council should be created for the smaller tribes other than the major ones in an autonomous district, if the tribes so desired. The provision was recommended because there were a number of tribes with a distinct culture and civilization of their own (Prasad & Agarwal, 1991). The Sixth Schedule, under sub-paragraph (2) of paragraph 1, provided that 'If there are different Scheduled Tribes in an autonomous district, the Governor may, by public notification, divide the area or areas inhabited by them into autonomous regions', and, under sub-paragraph (2) of paragraph 2, provided that '[t]here shall be a separate Regional Council for each area constituted an autonomous region'. Accordingly, the Government of Assam enacted the Assam (Constitution of District Councils) Rules, 1951, and the Pawi-Lakher (Constitution of the Regional Council) Rules, 1952, for the conduct of business of these councils. The first election to the Pawi-Lakher Regional Council (PLRC) was held in January 1953.

The PLRC was established to meet the political demands of the Pawis (Lai) and the Lakhers (Mara), who occupied the southern fringe of the Lushai Hills. The Pawis and Lakhers are culturally and linguistically related, and they were known as Shendoo by the British. With the upgradation of the Lushai Hills to the union territory of

---

[7] R. T. Zachono, a prominent Mara politician of Mizoram, cited in R. Hmingthanzuala (2002, p. 85).

Mizoram, the Mizo District Council was abolished. The PLRC was upgraded to a district council. Since then, no regional council has ever been created under the Sixth Schedule of the Constitution of India.

THE POLITICS OF RECOGNITION: REGIONAL COUNCIL AS ACCOMMODATING DIVERSITY

Since the early days of Indian independence, the north-eastern region has been unsettled by different political problems, of which many persist even today, albeit in smaller measures. The aspirations of major tribes for autonomy were accommodated with the creation of new states out of Assam. When the state of Nagaland was formed in 1963, the Naga tribes' 'minority status changed to majority' in the new state. With this, 'the need for protection may be regarded as having largely disappeared, the concerned state being deemed capable of looking after the interests of the resident ST communities'. Hence, it is largely viewed 'that the autonomous councils have outlived their utility' (Singh, 2007, p. 161), and thus they were abolished. The non-Nagas in the state, that is, the Kacharis, Garos and Kukis, became the new minority tribespeople. Similarly, other hill districts of Assam gained statehood, such as Meghalaya in 1972 and Mizoram and Arunachal Pradesh in 1987. In Meghalaya, despite the attainment of statehood, the three district councils continued, while in Arunachal Pradesh the Fifth Schedule was adopted and the *panchayati* system of local governance is followed. In Mizoram, the Mizo Hills District Council was abolished, and the PLRC was not only upgraded to a district council but also trifurcated into three councils for the Lais, Maras and Chakmas after Mizo Hills became a union territory. Since then, no such regional council has been formed under the Sixth Schedule. Even the basis on which the regional council was formulated seems to be largely forgotten, despite that smaller minority groups within such new states and the existing autonomous councils can adequately be accommodated through relevant provisions.

It is a fact that smaller or microscopic minority groups were largely ignored within the north-eastern states. The aspiration for smaller provisions of autonomy, such as regional councils and district councils, was even opposed by the larger groups. In his oft-quoted lines, Charles Taylor (1994, p. 25) said:

> ...identity is partly shaped by recognition or its absence, often by the misrecognition of others, and so a person or group of people can suffer real damage, real distortion, if the people or society around them mirror back to them a confining or demeaning or contemptible picture of themselves. Non-recognition or misrecognition can inflict harm, can be a form of oppression, imprisoning someone in a false, distorted, and reduced mode of being. (Taylor, 1994, p. 40)

In Canada, the aboriginals 'demand for native self-government'. In NE India, the demand for some measure of autonomy is a 'politics of recognition' in the form of granting a certain form of self-rule.

Currently, the only known group demanding a regional council is the Kuki National Assembly of Karbi Anglong district of Assam. Various Kuki militants operating in the Kuki areas of Karbi Anglong are demanding political autonomy and endorsing the demand for a Kuki Regional Council.[8] In Dima Hasao district of Assam, there is a current negotiation to accommodate the Hmar militants' demand for a regional council for Hmars within the North Cachar Autonomous District Council. In the state of Mizoram, the Brus, Paites and Hmars are demanding some form of political autonomy within the state. Currently, the Mizoram government is holding negotiations with the Hmar militant group HPC(D) [Hmar People's Convention (Democratic)]. The creation of such autonomous regions will be the solution for the nagging political demands for autonomy of minority groups within the state.

THE CASE FOR REGIONAL COUNCILS

In NE India, minority ethnic groups are not only aplenty but the languages of many of them are also listed in *UNESCO Atlas of the World's Languages in Danger*. Some of these groups are not only interspersed in

---

[8] For details of the demand for Kuki Regional Council in Karbi Anglong, Assam, see Touthang (2013).

different districts within states but also present in multiple states of the region. To illustrate the precarious nature of their existence, the case of Komrems in Manipur and Biates in Meghalaya and Assam are discussed.

Komrem is the nomenclature of a community 'consisting of the six kindred ethnic groups constitutionally categorized as Aimol, Kom, Kharam, Chiru, Purum and Koireng', who are 'a third lived reality that goes beyond the colonial binary constructs strengthened and propagated by ethno-exclusivist ideologies and armed groups' in the state of Manipur (Akhup, 2012, pp. 6, 8). According to the 2011 Census of India, the population of these tribes were: Aimol—3,643, Kom—15,467, Kharam—1,000, Chiru—5,487, Purum—503 and Koireng—1,056, with a total population of 27,156 persons. There were attempts by leaders of these small tribes to bring them together under the banner Komrem Union, NE India. However, the association was not much successful, as dissenters within soon emerged, reducing the union to a paper tiger. The kindred Komrem tribes are scattered all over the state of Manipur but mainly settled in the districts of Churachandpur, Kangpokpi, Tengnoupal, Senapati and Chandel, and even in the valley districts of Bishenpur and Thoubaland Kakching. Their small population coupled with their inability to come together under one platform, and worst, their resistance as it may appear, to join either of the bigger groups—the Kuki or Naga, has made them more vulnerable and invisible. Akhup (2012, p. 9) laments:

> It is an issue of grave concern that the status of "invisibility" of culturally indigenous tribes who are numerically fewer in number, are often "notionally non-existent" within the realm of the consciousness of both state and dominant ethnic groups. A democratic system that facilitates, provides and promote a responsive public space for a respectful articulation of voices of the "invisibles" within the public sphere is imperative.

The Biates also share a similar lived experience as a minority group like the Komrems. In Meghalaya, they mainly live in East Jaintia Hills and are included in the list of Any Kuki Tribes, which numbered 14,275 in the 2011 census, in which they constitute the majority among these tribes. In Assam, they are mainly concentrated in the North Cachar Hills and again are included in the list of Any Kuki

Tribes, which recorded a population of 33,399 persons in 2011. As per the Assam government task force on tribes, their population is around 3,000. The Joshua Project estimated the Biate population in NE India to be around 16,000 (Joshua Project, 2020). In 2017, the Meghalaya government attempted to delete certain STs from the existing list of STs in the state as part of an effort to regulate alienation of indigenous land. This led to an agitation of the indigenous minorities living in the state. The unobtrusiveness of the Biate tribe in the state, along with that of some other tribes, might be the cause of such a move by the government of Meghalaya (Haokip, 2014, pp. 309–310). They are unable to exert their identity openly due to the fear of being tormented and subdued and even having their properties (both movable and immovable) seized by the majority community. Indeed, such incidents have occurred a couple of times in the recent past (Haokip, 2013, p. 90).

As per the lived experiences of these two microscopic minority groups, besides being linguistically endangered, they continually face sociopolitical exclusion, as they are not able to exert their presence as a distinct ethnic group out of several compulsions. Apart from their low population, their dispersion, not only among different districts but also beyond state boundaries, has made them even more invisible. Taking a cue from the formation of the Chakma Autonomous District Council in Mizoram, which is based not on a compact territorial district but on the ethnic population of the Chakmas in the state, regional councils can be formulated for microscopic minorities in NE India.

REGIONAL COUNCILS THAT NEED TO BE FORMED

As found from the Lai Autonomous District Council, minority tribes in this district council area, namely, Bawm, Pang, Tlanglau, Mara, Bru and Chakma, are not appointed at all in the nominated posts of the member of the district council (Doungel, 2018, p. 55). This clearly shows the flaw in the current system, in which unrepresented groups can still be unrepresented in the nominated posts of the district/territorial Council. One way to ensure a smaller and minimal form of self-governance of such groups of people is to form regional councils for them and ensure a representation in the district council from such regional councils.

In 2010, the Government of Assam renamed the conflict-ridden North Cachar Hills as Dima Hasao district, an ethnicized name after the Dimasa tribe. This provoked other smaller ethnic groups in the district to join hands in protest at a time when the memories of the three ethnic conflicts that were fought by smaller tribes against the Dimasas were still fresh—the conflicts of Dimasa–Hmar (2003), Dimasa–Karbi (2005) and Dimasa–Zeme Naga (2009). Considering the diversity of the district and keeping the ethnic equation in mind, regional councils for the Nagas, Hmars and Kukis can be formed for these hills. In Karbi Anglong District, the Government of Assam is holding a dialogue with several armed groups of the Kukis for a regional council.

Despite being outside the purview of the Sixth Schedule, Manipur is in dire need of regional councils, due to the presence of numerous small ethnic groups in the state. For instance, as indicated earlier, the Koms need a regional council along the lines of the Chakma Autonomous District Council, which is not based on a compact geographical area but on ethnicity. In Mizoram, groups such as Hmar, Paite and Bru (Reang) are demanding some forms of autonomy within the state. The Brus and Hmars had taken to arms for such demands but currently are in negotiations with the state government. Similarly, in Nagaland, the non-Naga indigenous tribes, such as the Kacharis, Garos, Kukis and Karbis, can be brought under the Sixth Schedule for their self-governance.

CONCLUSION

When the Sixth Schedule was first enacted as a framework of governance for the tribal areas in the NE, it was primarily concerned with indigenous people's control over land and forest and acted as a mechanism to protect such resources from outsiders. Coupled with this was the recognition of the indigenous people's social practices and customary laws. It was the minimal form of self-governance in 'protecting the customary lives of the tribes'. Nevertheless, many of the provisions under the Sixth Schedule 'had remained only on paper' (*The Indian Express*, 2018). In recent years, the tribespeople have been demanding not only greater control over their simple, customary life but also enhancement in their autonomy and higher empowerment.

In NE India, there are several smaller ethnic groups that are often not taken into account due to their inherently limited political clout. In the case of Meghalaya, the only existing representative mechanism of smaller ethnic groups in the District Councils are sought to be removed. Sadly, the major tribes who were once fighting for some form of autonomy are now unwilling to grant even minuscule power to smaller tribes for their self-governance.

The need for formation of regional councils for microscopic groups in the NE region is urgent and requires immediate attention. These councils can provide an institutional platform and a means of countering the fear of losing identity in the midst of aggressive constructivist identities much prevalent in the region. The granting of regional councils need not necessarily stem from a strong agitational demand or even an armed movement. It has to be established as per the need of minority groups existing in the former districts of Assam. As much as the major tribes needed a protective mechanism of self-rule in the composite Assam, microscopic minority groups need much more to continue existing and maintain their culture and identity.

REFERENCES

Agnihotri, S. K. (1994). District councils under sixth schedule. *Journal of the Indian Law Institute, 36*(1), 80–89.

Akhup, A. (2012). The lived reality of Koms (Komrem) in Manipur: An emerging political perspective. *Journal of North East India Studies, 2*(2), 1–12.

Constituent Assembly of India Debates. (1949, September 6). *Proceedings* (Vol. IX). http://cadindia.clpr.org.in/constitution_assembly_debates/volume/9/1949-09-06.

Doungel, J. (2005). The uniqueness of the Erstwhile Pawi-Lakher regional council. *Journal of North-East India Council for Social-Science Research, 29*(2), 28–35.

Doungel, J. (2018). Discretionary powers of the governor with special reference to the sixth schedule area of Mizoram: A study during the tenure of Mr. A.R. Kohli. *Mizoram University Journal of Humanities & Social Sciences, IV*(2), 47–60.

Gassah, L. S. (2013). The sixth schedule and the 73rd amendment: An analysis. In M. NaranKarna, L. S. Gassah, & C. J. Thomas (Eds.), *Power to people in Meghalaya* (pp. 3–12). Regency Publications.

Ghai, Y. (2000). Ethnicity and autonomy: A framework for analysis. In Y. Ghai (Ed.), *Autonomy and ethnicity: Negotiating competing claims in multi-ethnic states* (pp. 1–28). Cambridge University Press.

Hannum, H., & Lillich, R. B. (1980). The concept of autonomy in international law. *American Journal of International Law, 74*(4), 858–889.

Haokip, T. (2013). The Kuki tribes of Meghalaya: A study of their socio-political problems. In S. Ranjan Padhi (Ed.), *Current tribal situation: Strategies for planning, welfare and sustainable development* (pp. 85–93). Mangalam Publications.

Haokip, T. (2014). Inter-ethnic relations in Meghalaya. *Asian Ethnicity, 15*(3), 302–316.

Haokip, T. (2017). Dereliction of duties or the politics of 'political quadrangle'? The governor, hill areas committee and upsurge in the hills of Manipur. *Indian Journal of Public Administration, 63*(3), 456–474.

Hmingthanzuala, R. (2002). *Regional council in Mizoram: A case study of Pawi-Lakher regional council (1952–1972)*. PhD Dissertation, North-Eastern Hill University.

Imphal Free Press. (2015, June 30). Centre ready to implement 6th schedule in hill areas of Manipur, awaits chief secretary's reply. https://www.ifp.co.in/page/items/27291/centre-ready-to-implement-6th-schedule-in-hill-areas-of-manipur-awaits-chief-secretarys-reply.

Joshua Project. (2020) *Biate in India*. https://joshuaproject.net/people_groups/19742/IN

Kom, C. S. (2010). Identity and governance: Demand for sixth schedule in Manipur. *The Indian Journal of Political Science, 71*(1), 313–322.

Prasad, R. N., & Agarwal, A. K. (1991). *Political and economic development of Mizoram*. Mittal Publication.

Scott, J. C. (2009). *The art of not being governed: An Anarchist history of upland Southeast Asia*. Yale University Press.

Singh, B. (2007). The sixth schedule: Its concept and praxis. *Indian Journal of Public Administration, 53*(2), 151–169.

Sonntag, S. K. (1999). Autonomous councils in India: Contesting the liberal nation-state. *Alternatives, 24*, 415–434.

Suan, H. K. K. (2007). Salvaging autonomy in India's northeast: Beyond the sixth schedule way. *Eastern Quarterly, 4*, 5–16.

Syiemlieh, D. R. (2014). *On the edge of empire four British plans for North East India, 1941–1947*. SAGE Publications.

Taylor, C. (1994). The politics of recognition. In A. Gutmann (Ed.), *Multiculturalism: Examining the politics of recognition* (pp. 25–73). Princeton University Press.

The Hindu. (2019, January 23). Cabinet decides to strengthen Northeast autonomous councils. https://www.thehindu.com/news/national/cabinet-decides-to-strengthen-northeast-autonomous-councils/article26071900.ece.

The Hindu. (2019, September 28). Meghalaya minor tribes fear exclusion from Sixth Schedule. https://www.thehindu.com/news/national/other-states/meghalaya-minor-tribes-fear-exclusion-from-sixth-schedule/article29543948.ece.

The Indian Express. (2018, December 29). Will bring Bill to strengthen autonomous councils in Northeast: KirenRijiju. https://indianexpress.com/article/india/rijiju-will-bring-bill-to-strengthen-autonomous-councils-in-northeast-5514415/.

The Telegraph. (2012, September 20). Mizoram councils seek direct funds—Delhi hints at rejection of demand. https://www.telegraphindia.com/states/northeast/mizoram-councils-seek-direct-funds-delhi-hints-at-rejection-of-demand/cid/383071.

Tillin, L. (2006). United in diversity? Asymmetry in Indian federalism. *Publius: The Journal of Federalism, 37*(1), 45–67.

Touthang, T. (2013). The state of Kuki people in the hills of Assam. In T. Haokip (Ed.), *The Kukis of Northeast India: Politics and culture* (pp. 25–45). Bookwell.

Zahluna, J. (2010). Constituent assembly and the sixth schedule: With special reference to Mizoram. *The Indian Journal of Political Science, 71*(4), 1235–1242.

SECTION VII

Challenges

Chapter 15

Unique Challenges to Social Sector Development in North-east India
An Insider's Perspective

Patricia Mukhim

This chapter seeks to veer away from economics and focus on the term 'social development'. But before that, one has to deconstruct the word 'social development', which has far-reaching connotations. Social development, simply put, means all-round or holistic development of a society. It refers to the development of its constituents or the people that make up the society. It takes into account access to education and health, which helps in the development of human resources that bring knowledge and wisdom back to the society for its betterment. Social development also means having in place mechanisms for addressing ills, including those of economic development that brings in its wake problems like displacements on account of power projects in north-eastern states and environmental degradation, with adverse impacts on the life and livelihoods of people dependent on such natural resources. Displaced and affected people have no effective voice, or their voices are subsumed in the larger debate of development. At least, this has been the case in North-east (NE) India.

SOCIAL DEVELOPMENT

Social development includes peoples' opportunities for self-actualization in terms of what defines development, be that health, education, employment opportunities, connectivity, access to markets or a well-maintained garbage collection system that does not pollute or kill rivers and hills. It is the kind of development that does not leave behind a trail of death and destruction through extractive mining processes and deforestation, which destroy the natural environment of the people and deprive them of the right to clean air, water and biodiversity.

Social development means that people are at the centre of development interventions. It should not result in stirring up dystopia, resentment and social disharmony between members of a society where one group, with access to public goods, climbs the social ladder at the cost of many that are left behind because they are not educated enough and do not have the same opportunities as the 'developed' section of the same society. In India's NE, it has been observed that funds for infrastructural development are cornered by a tribal political and bureaucratic elite, while the large majority in the society do not have the wherewithal to meet their basic needs. This has created a schism in society and a distrust of the political, bureaucratic and business elite, who are seen as creaming off funds that are intended for the development of an entire society. In fact, in many cases, development has further impoverished people who, at one time, had access to non-timber forest products (NTFPs) that included medicinal herbs, foods like mushrooms and vegetables, etc., which are no longer available to them because the forests they relied on for NTFPs have been cleared for mining purposes. That mining is carried out unscientifically, using archaic methods that have led to acid mine drainage (AMD) into rivers and erstwhile fertile farmlands and turned them toxic, has divided societies like never before. It has created malcontents. People feel alienated from the development processes that have been pushed into their respective areas, in which they have no hand in planning and participating.

For decades, the central government in Delhi has doled out money for development projects in the NE without seeking accountability from the power holders about how the funds have been deployed.

Delhi's lack of imagination was seen in how the erstwhile Planning Commission would craft schemes that were totally unsuited to the hilly and largely underdeveloped north-eastern states without taking into consideration that development in far-flung areas requires a different kind of approach and an understanding of the terrain, people, ecology, etc. Hence, several road projects, for instance, have remained incomplete even after several decades, and no one is held accountable for time and cost overruns. Social development actually entails helping people to develop themselves at their own pace and understanding, and with their participation. This makes people stakeholders in the development process. This has not happened due to reasons of poor governance, bad politics and the loss of social harmony in village communities divided by political loyalties.

Drug addiction has become a menace in some states of the NE. There are a number of young people taking to drugs, whereas the institutions to deal with this new and destructive phenomenon are so few and inadequate.[1] The problem of drug addiction has spread even to those states that once did not have to deal with the drug scene. This might be the biggest challenge to social development in the north-eastern states, since the bulk of the youth population is afflicted by this menace. It would be prudent for institutions engaged in the all-round development of the region to invest in qualitative and quantitative research to explore the extent of this problem, particularly in Nagaland, Mizoram, Manipur, Assam, Arunachal Pradesh and now Meghalaya, which has suddenly become the centre of drug trade, where every second day police are making a big haul of drugs from peddlers coming from the other north-eastern states and using Meghalaya as a selling and transit point.

OUTLINING A ROAD MAP

A road map outlines the strategic planning and programmes of action to achieve defined goals. We talk of Sustainable Development Goals (SDGs) within a particular time frame, but these must be translated in

---

[1] It is instructive to note here that the Church, which has become very influential in states like Mizoram and Nagaland, has failed to address this menace.

a language that ordinary citizens in villages are able to understand, so that they are 'participants' in development rather than mere recipients of development without any stakeholdership in the entire exercise. Indeed, the problem of development in the NE, or for that matter in India, is that people are not at the centre of the planning process. For decades, we have used the top-down approach which has left people out of the decision-making process. It is only when international NGOs, such as the International Fund for Agricultural Development (IFAD), involve people that people actually take part in the management of natural resources and understand that they too have a voice and that their voices should be included in the development paradigm.

In bringing about social development, we need both formal and informal institutions. In the tribal areas, particularly, the informal, traditional institutions are respected, and people work with these institutions when called to. Formal institutions, which are government-led, are usually not easily accessible and hierarchical in nature. Informal traditional institutions, despite their many faults and a very gender-unequal composition, are still institutions that can build social cohesion. Social cohesion builds social capital without which no development, whether physical, social or intellectual, can be attained.

However, informal institutions have not been given the kind of importance that they should get. Nor have they reinvented themselves to become more inclusive and gender-sensitive, considering that women make up half the world. Also, informal traditional institutions that hitherto were completely non-political have now developed a vested interest in politics, because they are now being gradually appropriated by political actors, mainly the local Members of the Legislative Assembly (MLAs) who try to use them while implementing development schemes in their local area. When politics enters these institutions, the community becomes fragmented by people's political leanings.

Speaking about social, there is bridging capital and bonding capital. Today, the bonding is between members of the same social class. Tribal communities were egalitarian when they started off, at a time when most resources, including land, forests and water catchments and water resources, were community-owned. Today, subversive forces within the community, aided and abetted by those heading traditional institutions, have succeeded in turning common property resources (CPR) such as catchment areas and forests, including community land, into privately owned property. Hence, bridging capital, which actually connects communities, has all but broken. These community bridges have to be rediscovered and rebuilt if we are to address the development needs of the north-eastern states.

India's NE was, until a few years ago, known as a region of conflicts. The conflicts have subsided, but as yet, informal social links to integrate into the society those who have given up arms have not been created. The erstwhile militants continue to live in camps and still operate as armed overground cadres. These conflicts have left deep hurts and pains among different tribal communities, especially those that have lost their family members to insurgency. The healing process should have been set in motion, but we have not been able to develop institutions for peace and reconciliation. Attempts to build such an institution in Nagaland were thwarted by the militant outfit, which discredited the institution that crumbled under the weight of contradictions.

The region has, in so many years, given birth to pressure groups of all kinds that try and interface with the government of the day but with little success, since they too are rived by inherent contradictions and vested interests. Civil society that is critical to the growth and sustenance of democracy has not emerged or evolved to cope with the growing power of the state. As a result, the state has become more oppressive and mercenary.

Social development also means better access to institutions that promote human development and, essentially, healthcare, so that people live longer and lead more productive lives. This has not happened. Health and education in the eight states of the NE are still not accessible to many (as shown in previous chapters), and literacy alone does not translate to better citizenship and engagement with the state or result in better gender equality. Mizoram is one state that is equal to Kerala in literacy, but its womenfolk suffer gender discrimination of a high order. A woman who is divorced has absolutely no rights and is not entitled to any property. She is virtually out in the cold. This is true of Nagaland too, where women have traditionally never owned land.

Land is linked to the identity of the tribe, and a woman who marries outside the tribe, if she owned property, would add to the land of the tribe to which her husband belongs. All these cultural practices actually disempower women greatly and leave them with no decision-making role in the family or outside it.

For overall social development, it is important that formal institutions created for the speedy development of the NE be audited to see where they have failed us. The North Eastern Council (NEC), which was conceived to be a regional planning and development body, failed to implement inter-state communication projects, thereby leaving many states disconnected by road, train or plane. The inability of the NEC to meet the demands of various states led the central government headed by A. B. Vajpayee to send a study team to the region. This led to the creation of the Ministry of Development of North Eastern Region (DoNER)' in 2000. But the ministry, with an office in Delhi, has not been able to bridge the emotional gap with the people of the region. On the contrary, it has created more dystopia. Other institutions created to meet the healthcare needs of the people of the region, such as the North East Indira Gandhi Regional Institute for Health and Medical Sciences (NEIGRIHMS) in Shillong, have not had visionary leaders. Most officials have been posted from outside the region and have taken this as an experimental posting with no commitment to the people of the region. The central universities too need to be audited to see if they have met the educational needs and whether these institutions have created a critical mass of questioning citizens. To my mind, these institutions have largely become self-serving monoliths.

GENDER CONCERNS IN THE NORTH-EASTERN STATES

There is an assumption in this country that North-east (NE) India is some kind of Shangri-La where women enjoy more rights than their counterparts in the rest of the country. This is a fallacy that must be corrected. The gender lenses, when applied here, will show that women suffer from lack of access to healthcare. Better literacy rate for women does not necessarily translate into a greater gender parity in other walks of life. The assumptions gain currency especially when people hear of the Khasi matrilineal society of Meghalaya. It is important for insiders to dispel the myths that surround all such discourses about the status of women here. Many an inquisitive journalist has visited Meghalaya to try and figure out the gender dynamics in a Khasi matrilineal society. It is easy to assume that women of Meghalaya are much empowered because of the existence of a matrilineal society. This is an incorrect presentation of women in Meghalaya's matrilineal society. The truth is that children take the name of the mother's clan and the youngest daughter inherits the ancestral property. Her husband moves in with her ancestral house to stay with her. Her unmarried brothers and sisters are part of the family. It is a kind of a joint family system with a provision of matrilineal descendants. However, the matrilineal society of Meghalaya has many problems. For example, there is a very high level of teenage pregnancy (53% in Meghalaya). (However, what is surprising is that Mizoram, with a high literacy rate, has a teenage pregnancy rate of 61%.) Further, in Meghalaya, the Infant Mortality Rate is high (39 deaths per 1,000 live births). According to nutritionists, this is mainly due to poor health of the mother (under-nutrition and anaemia) and the lack of access to institutional delivery. Only 51 per cent of women in Meghalaya give birth under some kind of medical care.

The high Maternal Mortality Rate in Meghalaya is because of the poor health and nutrition conditions of women, apart from low access to healthcare and a low level of institutional delivery. As per the NFHS-4 survey, more than half (52%) of the women in Meghalaya are anaemic. The high prevalence of anaemia in women is despite the pattern of consumption of food that contains a lot of meat and lentils—rich sources of protein. This contradiction suggests that women are either deprived of high-protein food or discriminated against. The situation is that amidst increasing poverty and deprivations, women are the worst affected.

Another disturbing fact is the rise in the incidence of physical and sexual violence against women. There is a high level of divorce and abandonment of women in the matrilineal society of Meghalaya that is often presented in a rosy manner to the outsider. Children are brought up by the mother on her own. It is often suggested that such (divorced) women should seek maintenance and compensation from their husbands. However, the issue is the fact that it becomes difficult to either get relief or to get the court order regarding maintenance complied with if the male is unemployed or employed in the informal sector. Consequently, there is a growing number of such households wherein a woman has to earn not only to run the household but also to bring up her children. Many of the children from such families soon become child labourers to support their mothers.

Coming to politics, the north-eastern states have a poor record of gender equality and equity. Nagaland has not had a single woman MLA since the state was created in 1963. There have never been more than four women members in the legislative assembly of Meghalaya at any point of time ever since the formation of the state. Assam has, at present, 8 women MLAs out of 126 members, Tripura has 3 out of 60, Arunachal Pradesh 3 out of 60, Manipur 1 out of 60 and Mizoram nil. Yet, women have always outnumbered men while voting. Why has this happened? This question has been asked by many people. It is expected that women conform to certain social norms. A woman in politics is given different labels. This restricts women's entry into politics. The male-centric traditional institutions of the tribal societies of NE reinforce this phenomenon by not allowing women to contest elections in these institutions and thereby deny their entry into politics, as these institutions are, in a way, a gateway to the legislative assembly and the Parliament. Many of the male politicians enter into the assembly and the Parliament through their political initiation in traditional institutions like autonomous district councils (ADCs) and village councils.

The Government of India introduced the 125th Constitutional Amendment Act, 2019, to reserve one-third of seats for women in the ADCs of the Sixth Schedule areas, with a view to providing reserved representation to women and broadening the scope of activities of the ADCs. The erstwhile exemption from the reservation of 33 per cent seats for women was given to the ADCs on the assumption that traditional institutions of the tribal societies take care of the interests of women and, hence, their formal representation in ADCs and other such bodies was not required. However, prejudices against women are so entrenched even in the tribal societies of the NE that when 33 per cent seats in urban local bodies of Nagaland were reserved for women, there were violent protests by male members of the community. In the violence, one woman lost her life. Women were simply not allowed to contest elections. The protagonists of the *status quo* stated that this was against the practices of customary law of the Naga society that has been given constitutional protection under Article 371(A). In other words, this provision is tantamount to ensuring status quo. There are similar provisions for other states of the NE and other tribal societies. Customary practices keep women out of politics. As long as these practices are constitutionally protected, entry of women from such societies into politics is a difficult proposition. This is the reason why in the NE only a few women, that too with political lineage, have succeeded in politics. No doubt, the evils of a dowry system, female foeticide and bride-burning are absent from the NE society, but women's political deprivation is acute and entrenched. A moot question is whether the traditional institutions, including customary laws and practices, should be allowed to exist at the cost of denial of political and economic rights to women of NE India.

In Meghalaya, the number of female-headed households, on account of divorce and abandonment, has been increasing. Since children live with their mothers in a matrilineal society, the burden on women is unimaginable. With growing poverty, many of these women slip further below the poverty line. Tourism is becoming a livelihood-generating sector, but here too, there are such less opportunities for women, and the fear is that women could unwittingly become involved in commercial sex, as happens in Thailand, if the checks and balances are not in place.

(*This chapter has been written as a participant observer, and therefore, apart from statistics being culled from the latest NHFS-4, many of the points presented here are observations of a journalist.*)

About the Editors and Contributors

EDITORS

Ashok Pankaj is Professor and former Director at the Council for Social Development, New Delhi. He specializes in law and political economy of development. His edited books include: *Right to Work and Rural India: Working of the Mahatma Gandhi National Rural Employment Guarantee Scheme (MGNREGS)* (SAGE Publications, 2012); *Subalternity, Exclusion and Social Change in India* (2014); and *Dalits, Subalternity and Social Change in India* (2018). He has contributed numerous articles and reviews to journals such as *South Asia Research, Contribution to Indian Sociology, Journal of Asian and African Studies, Economic and Political Weekly, International Studies, Journal of Commonwealth and Comparative Politics, Social Scientist, Contemporary South Asia* and *Poverty in Focus*, among others.

Atul Sarma is currently Visiting Professor at the Institute for Studies in Industrial Development, New Delhi, and Chairman, OKD Institute for Social Change and Development, Guwahati. Formerly, he was Visiting Professor at the Institute for Human Development, New Delhi, Vice Chancellor, Rajiv Gandhi University, Itanagar, Member, Thirteenth Finance Commission, ICSSR National Fellow, and a Post-doctoral Fellow at MIT, Cambridge, USA. He was the Head, Delhi Centre, and Professor of Economics at the Indian Statistical Institute. He served as an independent Director in the Board of Directors of SAIL and as a Consultant to several international agencies such as ADB, FAO, ESCAP, IDRC and UNIDO. He was a Member of the Technology Development Board as also of Assam and Manipur State Planning Boards. He was President, Indian Econometric Society. His research interests include development economics, public finance and policy, macroeconomics and trade and development.

Besides contributing over 100 articles to various Indian and international journals and editing volumes in the areas of public finance and policy, trade, development economics, etc., he has published, singly or jointly, several books, including *Exploring Indo-ASEAN Economic Partnership in Globalizing World*. His latest books are *Integrating the Third Tier in the Indian Federal System: Two Decades of Rural Local Governance* (2018) and *Mainstreaming the Northeast in India's Look and Act East Policy* (Edited) (2018); *String of Thoughts on North East India: An Economist's Perspectives* (2018); and *Demonetisation: Claims and Reality* (Edited) (2019).

Antora Borah is a Research Associate in the Council for Social Development, New Delhi. She is currently pursuing her PhD on inter-community relations at the foothill border of Assam and Nagaland from the Department of Sociology, University of Delhi. She has contributed a number of articles on the North-east and authored a book, *Assam-Nagaland Border Conflict in Foothills of Golaghat District: A Case Study* (2013).

CONTRIBUTORS

Suli Yohana Ayemi is a doctoral research scholar at the Department of Geography, Gauhati University, Guwahati, where she received her MSc in Geography with a specialization in Social Geography in 2017. She is a recipient of Professor HP Das Memorial Award of the North-East India Geographical Society (NEIGS) for Best Post-graduate in Geography in 2017.

Joydeep Baruah is an Associate Professor at OKD Institute of Social Change and Development, Guwahati. His interests include political economy of development, in general, and poverty and inequality, in particular. He has been the principal coordinator and lead author of *Assam Human Development Report 2014.*

Rajshree Bedamatta is Associate Professor of Economics at the Department of Humanities and Social Sciences, Indian Institute of

Technology, Guwahati. She teaches Development Economics and researches on issues pertaining to food and nutrition security, with a focus on the eastern and north-eastern regions of India.

Kalyan Das is a professor at OKD Institute of Social Change and Development, Guwahati. He received his PhD from Jawaharlal Nehru University, New Delhi. His research interests are industry, environment, labour market and livelihood issues. He has worked on a number of research projects on North-east India.

Surajit Deb is Associate Professor at Aryabhatta College, University of Delhi. He did his PhD in Economics in 2003 from the Department of Economics, Delhi School of Economics, University of Delhi, in the area of Macroeconomic Implications of Agricultural Price Movements and Time Series Econometrics. He has published extensively in academic journals, participated in international conferences and completed commissioned research projects for international organizations (IFPRI, SANEI). His important contributions include a chapter on Social Development Index in the Social Development Reports of 2012, 2014, 2016 and 2018. He has acted as a member of the working group on terms of trade between agricultural and non-agricultural sectors during 2012–2015 for the Ministry of Agriculture, Government of India. His current research interests include multi-dimensional indices of human and social development, analysis on inclusive growth, disability prevalence and its implications, gender inequality issues, ageing impacts and India–China comparisons.

Jayashree Doley, after completing her master's degree in Azim Premji University, is pursuing a PhD in Education from the Department of Education, University of Delhi. Her current research interests include education–society linkages in Assam.

Nirmali Goswami is an Assistant Professor of Sociology at Tezpur University, Assam. After completing her Master of Arts in Sociology from Banaras Hindu University, Varanasi, she pursued a PhD from the Indian Institute of Technology, Kanpur. She has published a book, *Legitimising Standard Languages: Perspectives from a School in Banaras,* with

SAGE Publications. She completed a University Grants Commission (UGC)–funded research project on the language of education at schools in the context of multilingual traditions of Assam. Her current research interests include urban spaces and the gendered dimension of school choice in India.

Thongkholal Haokip is an Assistant Professor at the Centre for the Study of Law and Governance, Jawaharlal Nehru University, New Delhi, India. He was formerly with the Department of Political Science, Presidency University, Kolkata, India. He has authored *India's Look East Policy and the Northeast* (2015), edited *The Kukis of Northeast India: Politics and Culture* (2013) and co-edited *The Anglo-Kuki War, 1917–1919: A Frontier Uprising Against Imperialism During the First World War* (2019). Dr Haokip is the Editor of the *Journal of North East India Studies* and Executive Editor of *Asian Ethnicity*.

Jumi Kalita is currently pursuing PhD from the Department of Economics, Rajiv Gandhi University, Itanagar, Arunachal Pradesh.

Bimal Kumar Kar is a Professor and former Head of the Department of Geography, Gauhati University, Guwahati, Assam. His fields of research interest include population, social and urban geography and development studies. He has to his credit around 80 research articles published in national and international journals and edited books, and a few books on human geography, including gender issues in North-east India. He has also edited a number of books relating to regional and human geography. Besides Commonwealth Geographical Bureau, he is associated with many professional bodies of geographers and allied disciplines in the country. Presently, Professor Kar is the General Secretary of NEIGS, Vice-President of the Institute of Indian Geographers (IIG) and Executive Committee member of the Indian National Cartographic Association (INCA). He also served as the Editor of *North Eastern Geographer*, a research journal published by NEIGS for about a decade.

Saket Kushwaha, currently the Vice Chancellor of Rajiv Gandhi University, Itanagar, specializes in resource management and sustainable agriculture development. After his higher studies from Banaras Hindu University (BHU), Varanasi, he joined Abubakar Tafawa Balewa University (ATBU), Bauchi, Nigeria, in 1993. In 2006, he joined BHU, as Professor of Agriculture Economics and became the Vice Chancellor of Lalit Narayan Mithila University, Darbhanga, serving for the period of 2014–2017. He has more than 100 publications in national and international journals. He has supervised 24 PhD students and authored 17 books or book chapters.

Joseph K. Lalfakzuala received his PhD degree from the Centre for Political Studies, Jawaharlal Nehru University, New Delhi. From 2015 to 2019, he was a faculty at Omeo Kumar Das Institute of Social Change and Development, Guwahati, where he taught and pursued his research. He is currently a teacher of Political Science at Govt. T. Romana College, Aizawl.

Geling Modi has done her graduation from Jawaharlal Nehru College, Pasighat, Arunachal Pradesh, post-graduation from Banaras Hindu University, Varanasi, Uttar Pradesh, and MPhil from Rajiv Gandhi University, Itanagar, Arunachal Pradesh. She is currently pursuing PhD in Economics at Rajiv Gandhi University, Itanagar, Arunachal Pradesh.

Patricia Mukhim is an Indian social activist, writer, journalist and the founder–editor of the *Shillong Times* known for her social activism and her writings on mining in Meghalaya and the Khasi people of the state. A recipient of honours such as Chameli Devi Jain award, ONE India award, Federation of Indian Chambers of Commerce and Industry FLO award, Upendra Nath Brahma Soldier of Humanity award, Siva Prasad Barooah National award and North East Excellence award, she was honoured by the Government of India, in 2000, with the fourth highest Indian civilian award of Padma Shri.

Sushanta Kumar Nayak is Professor of Economics in Rajiv Gandhi University, Itanagar, Arunachal Pradesh. He has more than 20 publications in national journals and chapters in edited volumes. He has contributed to the first Human Development Report of Arunachal Pradesh, 2005, and Arunachal Pradesh Development Report. He was a non-official member of the 70th Round of National Sample Survey, Ministry of Statistics, Government of India. He was the principal author and coordinator of the study 'State Finance of Arunachal Pradesh', done for the 14th and 15th Finance Commissions.

Mahsina Rahman completed her PhD in Economics from the Department of Humanities and Social Sciences, Indian Institute of Technology, Guwahati. Her research is focused on the functioning of food-based welfare programmes in rural Assam.

Bhupen Sarmah is Professor at the OKD Institute of Social Change and Development, Guwahati, and his areas of research are political economy, ethnicity and governance, specifically in the context of India's North East. Two of his important contributions are *Rejuvenating Panchayati Raj: Ideology, Indian State and Lessons from Periphery* and *History of Judiciary in Assam: Law, Law Courts and Lawyers*. In addition, he has contributed a large number of papers to different academic journals.

Chandan Kumar Sharma is a Professor of Sociology at Tezpur University, Tezpur. After completing graduation from Cotton College, Guwahati, he did his MA, MPhil and PhD from Delhi School of Economics. His research areas include development, environment, urbanization, migration, social movement and identity politics, with special reference to North-east India, and he has published widely in various journals and edited volumes. He has been a visiting fellow to several universities in India and abroad. Currently, he is the Editor of *Explorations*, the e–journal of the Indian Sociological Society.

Vanlalchhawna is a Professor in the Department of Economics, Mizoram University. His research interests include Economics of Education, Public Economics, International Trade and Environmental Economics. He was a member of the State Planning Board and Public Expenditure Review Committee under the State Government of Mizoram during 2014–2017. He is currently a Finance Officer of Mizoram University.

Index